French theories on text and discourse

Beihefte zur Zeitschrift
für romanische Philologie

Herausgegeben von
Éva Buchi, Claudia Polzin-Haumann, Elton Prifti
und Wolfgang Schweickard

Volume 473

French theories on text and discourse

Edited by
Driss Ablali and Guy Achard-Bayle

DE GRUYTER

Published with the support of the Centre de Recherche sur les Médiations (CREM UR 3476) Université de Lorraine (crem.univ-lorraine.fr).

ISBN 978-3-11-162729-8
e-ISBN (PDF) 978-3-11-079443-4
e-ISBN (EPUB) 978-3-11-079449-6
ISSN 0084-5396

Library of Congress Control Number: 2022945735

Bibliographic information published by the Deutsche Nationalbibliothek
The Deutsche Nationalbibliothek lists this publication in the Deutsche Nationalbibliografie; detailed bibliographic data are available on the internet at http://dnb.dnb.de.

© 2024 Walter de Gruyter GmbH, Berlin/Boston
This volume is text- and page-identical with the hardback published in 2023.
Typesetting: Integra Software Services Pvt. Ltd.

www.degruyter.com

Contents

Driss Ablali/Guy Achard-Bayle
Introduction
Language/speech vs. text/discourse: A "family resemblance"? —— 1

Part 1: Text-discourse links

Jean-Michel Adam
Chapter 1
Micro-level, meso-level and macro-level of textual structuring and complexity —— 21

Michel Charolles
Chapter 2
"Framing adverbials" as markers of discourse organization —— 57

Guy Achard-Bayle
Chapter 3
Text, discourse, cognition —— 77

Catherine Kerbrat-Orecchioni
Chapter 4
From discourse analysis to analysis of discourses —— 95

Alain Rabatel
Chapter 5
Enunciator position, positioning and posture —— 107

Part 2: Text epistemologies

François Rastier
Chapter 6
Dissipative units —— 133

Driss Ablali
Chapter 7
Corpus semantics, the unfinished project of Greimas' *Structural semantics* —— 153

Bernard Combettes
Chapter 8
Suggestions for a diachronic text linguistics —— 169

Lita Lundquist
Chapter 9
40 years of text linguistics and its didactic application in teaching French as a foreign language —— 185

Part 3: Epistemologies of discourse – and beyond

Patrick Charaudeau
Chapter 10
A socio-communicational model of discourse (between communication situation and individuation strategies) —— 207

Dominique Maingueneau
Chapter 11
Discourse, discourse analysis, and discourse genres —— 231

Ruth Amossy
Chapter 12
Integrating argumentation in discourse analysis? Problems and challenges —— 245

André Petitjean
Chapter 13
Linguistics and literature: Style in question —— 269

Index nominum —— 279

Index rerum —— 283

Driss Ablali/Guy Achard-Bayle
Introduction
Language/speech vs. text/discourse: A "family resemblance"?

To begin with, we would like to recall the history of two duos which have endured in French linguistics for almost a century. In reality, these duos involve dichotomies: the first – language/speech – dominated theoretical and epistemological debates during the first half of the last century; the second – text/discourse – emerged only in the mid-1960s, and since then has been regarded as complementary.

Although Saussure's *Cours de linguistique générale*[1] made a categorical choice by opting for language over speech, the *Écrits de linguistique Générale*,[2] by this same Swiss linguist, reversed the order. Some further philological information is necessary in order to clarify this remark. Everyone is aware of the famous phrase that figures on the last page of the *CGL* (1959, 232): "The true and unique object of linguistics is language studied in and for itself";[3] in fact, as Bouquet (1999) repeats, it turns out that this phrase never appeared in Saussure's manuscripts, for one of Saussure's originalities is that his name is claimed equally by both elements of the first duo and therefore by supporters of the second also! The 'return'[4] (Bouquet 1999) to Saussure has taken place in the name of speech, and therefore of discourse.

Like all returns – to Wittgenstein, Vygotsky, Bakhtin, Volochinov, or Benveniste –, the return to Saussure has not been accomplished in an atmosphere of euphoria. The extraordinary history of the publication of Saussure's texts on general linguistics continues to divide linguists. The gap is increasing between those who consider that major differences exist between the Saussure of the *CGL* and the Saussure who wrote the manuscripts (Bouquet 1999; Adam 2001; 2010; Utaker 2002; Rastier 2015) and those who think that the fundamental theses of the second work

---
1 (*CLG* 1916; transl. *Course in general linguistics*, *CGL* 1959).
2 (*ÉLG* 2002; transl. *Writings in general linguistics*, *WGL* 2012).
3 "La linguistique a pour unique et véritable objet la langue envisagée en elle-même et pour elle-même." (The original French versions of the translated quotations are given in foot notes.)
4 "Retour". (All subsequent translations from other works are by Rosemary Rodwell, the translator of this chapter, unless stated otherwise.)

Driss Ablali/Guy Achard-Bayle, Université de Lorraine, CREM

https://doi.org/10.1515/9783110794434-001

(the *WGL*) were already present in the critical editions (1968–1974) of the *CGL* published by Engler (Arrivé 1986; Normand 2000; Trabant 2005; Sofia 2012; 2018).

Once posited, the distinction becomes intriguing. Let us begin with this observation: the text/discourse duo appears nowhere in the *CGL*, where the word "discourse" occurs only four times, and then in its grammatical sense of "part of discourse". In the *WGL*, "discourse", which 'in Saussure and Benveniste maintains a relative ambiguity' (Adam 1999, 29),[5] appears in plain language, but in different places within his manuscripts, where it is liable to assume a variety of conceptual constructions: might "discourse", in these contexts, be interchangeable with "speech", "discursive order", or "discursive language", as often happens in other of Saussure's citations? By way of example, here is one taken from *Course 1* (1907), where the substitution appears striking:

> For a form to penetrate language, it is necessary 1. for someone to have improvised it and 2. improvised it during the course of speech, of discourse; and the same applies to all who have come across it subsequently. (Depecker 2009, 125)[6]

For as Arrivé (1986, 53) rightly says, 'in [Saussure], there is a tendency to give different names to similar, or even identical concepts'.[7] And this is confirmed by Depecker (2012, 4):

> In many places, the *Course in general linguistics* proves to be problematic. The layout is substantially altered, the argumentation often abrupt, and the terminology apt to change. For example, replacements to the published *Course* can be seen, in students' handwriting, where 'acoustic substance' is replaced by 'phonic substance', 'acoustic figure' by 'material sign', 'expression' by 'linguistic complexus', and so on. The number of irregularities and glosses for which the *Course*'s editors are responsible is breathtaking.[8]

The famous note on discourse initially poses a crucial epistemological question, regarding the modalities of enunciation and exposition of scientific texts, and

---

5 "['Discours'] garde chez Saussure et chez Benveniste une relative ambiguïté."
6 "Pour qu'une forme pénètre dans la langue, il faut que 1° quelqu'un l'ait improvisée et 2° improvisé à l'occasion de la parole, du discours, et il en est de même pour tous ceux qui sont tombés ensuite dessus."
7 "[C]hez [Saussure], on observe la propension à donner des noms différents à des concepts voisins, voire identiques."
8 "À bien des endroits, le *Cours de linguistique générale* s'avère problématique. L'ordonnancement en est profondément modifié, l'argumentation souvent abrupte, la terminologie fluctuante. Ainsi, on voit remplacés, des manuscrits d'étudiants, au *Cours* publié, 'substance acoustique' par 'substance phonique', 'figure acoustique' par 'signe matériel', 'locution' par 'complexus linguistique', etc. L'accumulation des déformations et gloses dues aux rédacteurs du *Cours* est impressionnante."

this question must be taken into account in order to be precise about the boundaries and links between concepts. A solid conceptual framework is required in order to envisage "discourse" as a discourse-level mode of organization that can be transformed into a concept (Ablali 2016). What, then, is "discourse" for Saussure? To what is it opposed? To "phrase", "text", "language", or "speech"? How is it structured into a whole that deploys structures of an order that is different from that of the sign or syntactic unit? And under what conditions is it dealt with in the analysis? By separating it from the social conditions governing its production, in favor of an immanentist approach? Or rather by opening it up to the community as the necessary means of connecting language with society? These are complex questions, and can only be answered with confidence once the whole of Saussure's corpus has been closely examined, because a concept does not necessarily correspond with naming – and naming does not mean that the concept has been defined.

Let us summarize, therefore, in the wake of Turpin (1995), who reminds us that "discourse", as an effective manifestation, cannot, for Saussure, go beyond the limits of the syntactic unit. Fortunately, Saussure is sometimes very explicit about this:

> This continuous <opposition> between members of the group, which ensures the choice of a constituent at the moment of the discourse [. . .] at the moment when the syntactic construction is produced, the group of associations intervenes. (*CLG*, ed. Engler 1968, vol. 1., 2020 II C, cited by Turpin 1995, 262)[9]

This conception of discourse as limited to the syntactic construction is far from being a foundation for a linguistics of text and discourse; and Turpin (1995, 261) adds this categorical conclusion:

> This is perhaps why, from *Course* III onwards, Saussure was to abandon the term of discourse in this sense, replacing it with phrase structure: the word perhaps had too much of a tendency to slip towards the notion of speech.[10]

As a result, in the well-known 'Note on discourse',[11] as in other fragments of Saussure's manuscripts, we are a long way from the conception of discourse devel-

---

9 "Cette <opposition> continuelle entre les membres du groupe, qui assure le choix d'un élément au moment du discours [. . .] au moment où le syntagme se produit, le groupe d'associations intervient."
10 "C'est peut-être pourquoi Saussure abandonnera en ce sens le terme de discours à partir du *Cours* III, le remplaçant par syntagmatique: le mot avait en effet peut-être trop tendance à glisser vers la notion de parole."
11 The 'Note on discourse' ("Note sur le discours") is a paragraph by Saussure which figures in his manuscripts. It was published by Starobinski (1971, 14) and states (extract from *ÉGL*): "Le

oped by the specialists of French discourse analysis who, since Pêcheux, as we shall later see, have defined discourse as the crucial point at which linguistic, situational, social, and political threads intersect – what Robin (1979, 70) calls, in relation to the language vs. speech opposition, 'a setting-aside of what is outside the text'.[12]

But although Saussure was a true pioneer of a discourse and discursivity theory, it is essential to answer the following questions, which are no more than posed here: what does the category of "discourse" become in the work of those who are currently returning to Saussure's manuscripts? And on what empirical basis do these theoreticians of text and discourse rely, in order to support the notion that the objective of Saussure's conception of discourse is to introduce conceptual tools with a view to apprehending and analyzing all discursive representation of meaning as it is inscribed in the linguistic material? More precisely, is Saussure now a linguist who theorizes the discursive as a way of apprehending language by drawing upon structures of another order than the sign? What we are trying to pinpoint with these questions concerns the "common fund", both heuristic and epistemological, on which these theories of discourse and text – in all their variety of usage – rest; the purpose of this is to consider the notes in question, in the diversity of their discursive approach, with a discursive depth that goes beyond the syntactic construction. A "beyond" which another successor of Saussure has attacked, not by introducing "discourse" into the fold of the language/speech duo, but by making the "text" the fast track for accessing language.

This successor is none other than Hjelmslev, the founder of glossematics. But why refer to him here? The answer is clear: it is because Hjelmslev's innovative contribution, which was to have a strong impact on French semiotics, was causing linguistics to emerge from sign conversion and thus to break with the tradition of its time, which was much more preoccupied with sign analysis than with the text. Analysis should therefore begin not with signs but with the relationships they have with a scale, in a superior dimension, which Hjelmslev considers as "text". Evidence of this can be found in these few extracts from *Prolegomena*, as well as

---

discours consiste, fût-ce rudimentairement, et par des voies que nous ignorons, à affirmer un lien entre deux des concepts qui se présentent revêtus préalablement de la forme linguistique, pendant que la langue ne fait préalablement que réaliser des concepts isolés qui attendent d'être mis en rapport entre eux pour qu'il y ait signification de pensée." (*ÉLG* 2002, p. 275). ('Discourse consists, albeit in a rudimentary way and by means of which we are unaware, in affirming a link between two of the concepts that present themselves, clothed beforehand in linguistic form, while language produces only isolated concepts beforehand, which wait to be interconnected for there to be meaningful thought.')

12 "[U]ne mise à l'écart du hors-texte".

elsewhere. This work was written in Danish in 1943, only three decades after Saussure's death: "Linguistic theory starts from the text as its datum and attempts to show the way to a self-consistent and exhaustive description of it through an analysis." (Hjelmslev 1943, transl. 1969, 21).

The text is therefore what is "given", given to be seen and given to be analyzed, and whether it is written or oral is of no importance. Elsewhere, Hjelmslev (1973, 107) also says this: 'The object of the analysis is, of course, a text – whether it exists graphically manifested in the form of a written message or acoustically manifested in the form of a oral message.'[13]

Once the theory's objective has been defined, what Hjelmslev understood by text – a delicate and multiform concept – remains to be established. Thus, in the semio-linguistic field, the concept of text can be "correlated" with more technical terms which are not, however, without their ambiguities. It is often taken to be a synonym of discourse or utterance, and even extended to non-linguistic semiotics: for example, a film sequence, an opera, or a dance may be considered either as text, discourse, or utterance. The ambiguity of the term in question increases and the notion becomes more complex when it is also found in Barthes, Benveniste, Todorov, Riffaterre, Bakhtin, Halliday, Kristeva, Van Dijk, Maingueneau, Adam, and Greimas, to name but a few. Various perspectives are therefore offered to describe text and textuality, the problem at the heart of disciplines whose focus is on the discursive functioning of language; and this is not exclusive to the language sciences, as has clearly been shown by research in cognitive psychology (Bruner) and in hermeneutics (Ricœur, Szondi).

Posing the problem of the text where Hjelmslev is concerned therefore means touching on one of the cornerstones of his theory. But, unless we are mistaken, Hjelmslev gives no specific definition of this; his definition then has to be sought in his written work, in chapters which make no claim to approach the question of the text as such. Nevertheless, in entry thirty-nine of the *Summary*, the following definition may be read: "A TEXT (...) is the Syntagmatic of a Denotative Semiotic whose Chains are Manifested by all Purports." (Hjelmslev 1975, 14).

The concept of text thus exists independently of the fact that it uses natural language as its "plan of expression". The genetic viewpoint is not the decisive one. A text is liable to be "manifested by all purports".

At this point, a crucial difference emerges between Hjelmslev and, for example, Jakobson. Whereas the latter favors oral expression, Hjelmslev, on the other hand, thinks that the nature of the substance is not relevant. The text in

---

[13] "L'objet de l'analyse est, bien entendu, un texte, que celui-ci se manifeste graphiquement sous la forme d'un message écrit ou phoniquement sous la forme d'un message oral."

glossematics is therefore only a transitory means of access, used for the manifestation of language, as seen below. For let us remember that language, according to Hjelmslev, can be subdivided into two levels: "text" vs. "system", which may be equated with the opposition "syntactic unit" vs. "paradigm". To "Saussurize" Hjelmslev, the text is word and the system is language. On this point, Hjelmslev (1943, transl. 1969, 96) remains faithful to the premises of the *CGL* in affirming the primacy of system over text, although the latter remains the only means possible of "knowing" language: "linguistic theory prescribes a textual analysis, which leads us to recognize a linguistic form behind the 'substance' immediately accessible to observation by the senses, and behind the text a language (system)."

The "text" is therefore defined in relation to the language that is allowed to emerge from it, and solely in relation to language. Hjelmslev does not focus his attention on textuality, and still less on interpretation: for him, the text is none other than a manifestation of language. As a result of this, we draw the conclusion that no relationship can exist between Hjelmslev's conception of the text and the conception of theories of texts and discourse that exists in France. Hjelmslev is not the precursor of textual theories since, for him, the text is not the intended object of theory; it is merely a starting point for the analysis that leads to the system of language.

In order to advance towards the mid-1960s, we believe it is useful here to recall the mutual indifference that existed between language research and textual and discursive research. From both an epistemological and methodological perspective, it is the question of observables that enables us to understand this indifference. The reticence of grammarians to tackle the text object – whose difficulties appeared to be of direct interest to syntax and morphology – is explained by the vogue for artificial examples to the detriment of confirmed data. For the linguist – with the exception of Guillaume to whom we shall return later – the sentence was often the unbreachable limit for describing language rules. Where textual research was concerned, this was blatantly obvious: the place accorded to textual phenomena in order to explain questions of grammar was very small, not to say non-existent. It was research focused more on enunciative, poetic and stylistic perspectives, as in Jakobson, which occupied the textual center stage. However, this explanation, given for purely illustrative purposes, should be further enlarged upon.

To end with, we propose to go back more than forty years, to the 1970s, in order to find an exception to the rule going by the name of "text grammar". The project's originality is evident at first glance, in that it conceives of textuality on the basis of grammatical models. This originality is to be found in the epistemological area of TGG (transformational and generative grammar)[14] and, according to Ihwe (1973, 54), its purpose is 'to destroy and replace traditional literary science'[15] – which follows the 'hermeneutic method of interpretation known as *Geisteswissenschaft*'[16] – by a literary theory based on the results of generative grammar research.

From this perspective, textual production is conceived according to the model of sentence production to establish links of inter-phrasal dependence that are not strictly linear, but nevertheless necessary; Van Dijk (1972, 182–183) describes it thus: 'we shall require our theory to be productive, which means (formally) generating an infinite series of texts from a finite set of rules and lexical constituents.'[17]

The problem then arises of the boundary between sentence grammar and text grammar or, in other words, of the place occupied by sentence grammar within text grammar. . . In fact, with hindsight it would be proper to acknowledge the true value of text grammar's contribution to the description of grammatical rules. Indeed, the text grammar project[18] was a purely textual one, established without grammar proper being extended to the text. For example, it reveals nothing about the actantial structure of adjectives, irregular plural nouns, or even the contexts conditioning the use of a definite article – and it is this that distinguishes it from the semantic and textual models of the 1980s, to which we shall subsequently return, citing some examples from Guillaume mentioned by Martin. Neither does it specify how to describe relationships between the components of the sentence

---

14 Charolles (1976, 134) clearly states in the following passage: 'The project for a text grammar (GT) has its origins in a problem with a fundamentally Chomskyan frame of reference. Briefly, it might be said that, at least to begin with, the need to construct a grammar that goes beyond the structure of the sentence appeared when: a) certain shortcomings in transformational and generative grammar (TGG) were revealed; b) it was seen to be possible to transfer the founding empirical rationale of TGG to the level of the text.' ("Le projet d'une Grammaire de Texte (GT) trouve ses origines dans une problématique à référence fondamentalement chomskyenne. D'une manière schématique on peut dire, qu'au départ au moins, la nécessité de construire une grammaire qui dépasse le cadre de la phrase est apparue quand: a) se sont révélées certaines insuffisances de la grammaire générative et transformationnelle (GGT); b) on s'est aperçu qu'il était possible de transférer au niveau textuel les attendus empiriques fondateurs de la GGT.")
15 "[R]uiner et remplacer la science littéraire traditionnelle".
16 "[M]éthode d'interprétation herméneutique, *Geisteswissenschaft*".
17 "[N]ous demanderons à notre théorie d'être productive, c'est-à-dire d'engendrer (formellement) un ensemble infini de textes à partir d'un ensemble fini de règles et d'éléments lexicaux."
18 On this point, Adam's article on textual linguistics in France is enlightening, particularly as regards the relationship between text grammar and discourse analysis (Adam 2010).

and the structure that encompasses them in the text. It then becomes evident that the said text grammar is not a grammar governing the forms of language expression in texts.

Also in the 1970s, but following a progression which might be said to be the reverse, Martin (1975)[19] published a volume in English entitled *Theories of language and methods in syntax*; at the same time, this work was the first in a collection, *Recherches linguistiques*, then being set up under the umbrella of the *Centre d'analyse syntaxique* (CAS) at the University of Metz, and which has continued ever since.[20]

The title drew great inspiration from American linguistics, at that time the dominant model, and carries a surtitle of no less importance: *The French contribution to modern linguistics*. This made the book's intention abundantly clear, namely to make Anglophone linguists acquainted with the existence and variety of another linguistics than the dominant one.

However, this did not exclude the two being interlinked. From this perspective, Martin's project was similar to that of Van Dijk, since the work of the former set out to assess how "the American models of distributional and generative linguists" had been adapted (1975, 7).

But the relationships between linguistic models and the book's objective went beyond this: at the outset, Martin (1975, 13) recalled how France had experienced "the decisive influence of Prague school functionalism" prior to that of the American models; and then, that a number of, one might say, "specifically" French models preceded the American models – notably those of Tesnière and Guillaume. However, although this latter "enjoys considerable prestige among many linguists in France",[21] it has to be acknowledged that the two linguists chosen by Martin were little known "abroad" (Martin 1975, 30). It was therefore necessary to make them known, which meant making people aware that they may have preceded if not inspired the Chomsky model that dominated the decade between 1960 and 1970.

---

19 On the very prolific career of the author, who was director of research at the CNRS, professor at the Sorbonne, and who is now a member of the Académie des Inscriptions et Belles-Lettres at the Institut de France, see: https://www.aibl.fr/membres/academiciens-depuis-1663/article/martin-robert [last consultation: 12.06.2021] and Duval (2011).
20 Under the name of *Études linguistiques et textuelles*, publication of the CREM (*Centre de recherche sur les médiations*): https://crem.univ-lorraine.fr/edition-publications/collections/etudes-linguistiques-et-textuelles [last consultation: 12.06.2021].
21 And "in Canada", Martin later adds (1975, 30).

Now Martin did this without any hint of chauvinism since he began by analyzing the influences of two major foreign models, namely functionalism and structuralism, from their source and in their European and American variants; and he admitted that, although Tesnière and Guillaume received no international recognition, it was because both of them "worked [. . .] in isolation, not seeking to place themselves within this or that stream of more general thought" (Martin 1975, 23), and that the former "remained well apart from the main linguistic trends of his day" (ibid.).

This does not prevent us today from acknowledging the astonishing richness of their work, which might be described as trail-blazing, even though they were little-known. For example, Tesnière's hierarchical model of connections in the *Éléments de syntaxe structurale* (1959), with its tree representations, is surprisingly innovative; in fact, Martin does not fail to compare it with the later model of *immediate constituent* analysis (1959, 28–29).

The same was true of Guillaume who, as early as the first half of the twentieth century, and thus well before the substantial development of semantics as we now know it, proposed a model for "analysis of meaning" (Martin 1975, 31). There is no question of developing this model here, but we shall content ourselves with recalling and highlighting two of its original features:

(1) If the "signifié" is one in language ("potential signifié" = *signifié de puissance*), it can produce "an infinite variety of 'effects' in speech" ("actual signifié" = *signifiés d'effet*): for example, the present in French can take the form of a general present (*la Lune tourne autour de la Terre* 'the moon moves around the earth') or a specific or instantaneous present (*l'éclair jaillit* 'the lightning flashes').

(2) But these "effects", however numerous they may be, do not constitute "compartmentalized" categories (Martin 1975, 33); the movement from one to the other, from one "extreme" to the other, is "imperceptible" (ibid.), as in these examples of the present which take place in the "interval" between the general or universal and the specific or instantaneous: *il aime les voyages, il est malin, il est malade. . .* 'he likes travelling, he's crafty, he's ill. . .'

Meaning, therefore – and this is its "kinetic nature" or aspect –, is a "movement of thought" which is ordered around a temporal axis, and whose use or "effects" correspond to so many moments of "uptake" on this axis, as in the following examples of definite determiners: *la maison de campagne se fait de plus en plus chère* 'country houses are becoming increasingly expensive', *la maison de campagne que je viens d'acheter* 'the country house that I have just bought'.

We have considered it important to provide these few reminders, from Saussure to Guillaume, and from Hjelmslev to Tesnière, because, over and above their historic value, not only are they epistemologically topical but they enable us to put our own work into perspective, after positioning it in the wake of authors whose endeavors to "defend and illustrate", adapt or confront, we were keen to reconsider. These reminders then enabled us to expound on the intention and content of our own work.

Among the multiple schools, trends and influences, but also the periods – notably since the 1980s, with the development of semantics and pragmatics – linguistics has become, or has diversified into "language sciences". It could be alleged that the character of the present-day French linguistic landscape is distinctive, among other things, for the way in which it links the epistemology of two fields or domains, namely that of text and that of discourse. We shall not repeat here what formed the subject of the symposium we organized in Metz in 2015, the proceedings of which are contained in a substantial volume (cf. Ablali/Achard-Bayle/ Reboul-Touré/Temmar 2018). We are more concerned to reconsider this link (or this dichotomy, when seen in reverse) by presenting the texts themselves and, through them, the authors who have enabled us to create this body of work, which will consist of three parts: the first is specifically devoted to the text-discourse connection, and the following two to the epistemologies of text and discourse, if indeed it is possible to maintain the text-discourse dichotomy after all the contributions have been read.

Text-discourse links

Jean-Michel Adam opens the debate since, in the panorama of textual-discursive theories and models, he is conspicuous for his desire to bring together the two notions and to show their complementarity in the linguistic analysis of units known as "texts". This leads him, on the one hand, to distinguish the various stages of analysis which correspond to levels of composition; and, on the other, to highlight the meso- and macro-textual stages. For example, at the midway stage, between sentence and text, Jean-Michel Adam discerns two other levels, the period and the sequence. From the meso stage to the macro stage, he demonstrates the role played by the paragraph, among other subdivisions or groupings, thereby giving the impression that the text is made up of signifying sub-units. Finally, Jean-Michel Adam links the textual and the discursive by taking discourse genres into account, since these have an influence on the different stages of textualization.

The work of **Michel Charolles** is also situated at the point where text and discourse meet, where there are tools in operation that guarantee cohesion and coherence, in continuous association. Among these tools are connectors, anaphora, and "framing adverbials". Michel Charolles has particularly devoted himself to the latter: these are introducers of sentences whose scope can go beyond the simple sentence; the space thus determined constitutes a "discursive frame", where the truth value of the clause or clauses is governed by this introducer, and brought together in this space; in other words, their "veridicity", or the supposed truth of what is said, is or must be calculated within this space and only in this space, which can be closed by another introducer. In the second part, Michel Charolles shows that these introducers, which are factors of cohesion and coherence, do not function solely in scientific or technical text genres, but also in narrative ones.

Guy Achard-Bayle, in his contribution, sets out to analyse the three notions of text, discourse and cognition, comparing them by means of text-discourse and text-cognition pairings. This dual comparison thus takes the text as common denominator. But in taking up this textual position, two difficulties arise: that of maintaining a strict separation between text and discourse at the present time; and that of reconciling a (textual) linguistics of structures – even if they are macrostructures – and a (cognitive) linguistics of representations of the world. In relation to this second comparison, an analysis of the dual role of the conjunction "if" in narrative and literary texts enables the two models, textual and cognitive, to be reconciled. Where the first comparison – not to say opposition – is concerned, Guy Achard-Bayle refers to the work of Jean-Michel Adam who brings together text and discourse in a theory and method of "textual analysis of discourses".

The following two contributions subsume the text-discourse dichotomy more than they highlight the boundaries and specific nature of models and schools of texts and discourses.

Catherine Kerbrat-Orecchioni, for example, examines oral conversations as forms of discourse whose analysis implies diverse methodologies, originating from sometimes remote traditions and including ancient or recent disciplines such as philology, stylistics and rhetoric, theories of argumentation, semiotics and textual linguistics, utterance theories, various pragmatic trends, and interactionist approaches. She uses two typological criteria to analyze the documented discourses: the written-oral opposition and their degree of interactivity. To end with, she approaches another epistemological question, which touches not only upon interactionist theories but textual and discursive theories in general: for her, "the recent explosion of research into discourse", oriented towards mathematical, semiotic, interactionist or political science linguistics, is related, willingly or not, to the discourse(s) analysis field.

Alain Rabatel makes a connection between the notion of *enunciator*, borrowed from Ducrot (1984), and that of *enunciative positions*: he intends by this to account for the fact that, when the first enunciator refers to the objects of their discourse, they position themselves in relation to these objects – in other words, in linguistic terms, they make their view of them known. Alain Rabatel then considers the fact that discourses are generally dialogical, and that, therefore, these *positions* apply to both the first and second enunciators equally, since the latter are present in the discourse of the former. On the basis of this, Alain Rabatel distinguishes two levels of *commitment*: one in which the enunciator takes responsibility for the discourse and one where the second enunciators, who are present in the discourse of the first, serve as instances of *validation*; in other words they take responsibility for the commitment. This distinction has repercussions on the *positioning strategies* which operate through *reduplication* if the points of view converge (*autodialogism*), and through *splitting* if they diverge (*heterodialogism*).

Epistemologies of text

Dealing with the interpretation of textual complexity, **François Rastier** contrasts two paradigms which dominate the tradition: the logical-grammatical paradigm of the sign and the rhetorical-hermeneutic paradigm of the text. He evokes this contrast in order to challenge the weaknesses of sign theory when it attacks textuality, and to establish postulates for a new heuristics with which to think of semantic forms and their dynamics. From there he shows that the text in its complexity is governed as much by the norms of discourse and genre as by the *a priori conjectural character* of interpretation, which is at work in both text and intertext. François Rastier prefers form and content over units, transformations and enunciative and interpretative transpositions over rules, and the inference of probability over deduction: the purpose of these choices is to avoid reducing the meaning of a text to a series of clauses. In contrast to the ontological presuppositions of the logical-grammatical paradigm, the author demonstrates that meaning results both from intertextual scanning and from the semantic forms linked to expressive forms.

Driss Ablali approaches the text from the viewpoint of a semiotician. He examines the project developed by Greimas in *Structural semantics* (French edition published 1966, English edition 1984), in order to distinguish it from the rest of

Greimas' work. This distinction is essential for gaining an understanding of epistemological and heuristic issues in the work of the founder of French semiotics of the Paris School. Although in his other works, ranging from *Du sens* in 1970 (*On meaning*, 1987) to *Sémiotique des passions* in 1991 (*Semiotics of passions*, 1993), Greimas opted for an immanentist analysis of texts – cut off from the world, the subject, and the reference –, the founding gesture of *Structural semantics*, from the epistemological and empirical perspectives, rests on three descriptive categories, namely text, genre and corpus, which open the way not to a semiotics of the text or of discourse, but of a corpus-based semantics. Driss Ablali then goes on to deal with the holistic conception of meaning as established in *Structural semantics* using the text-corpus combination. Finally, he shows that, contrary to what is still believed, there is in this work a reflection on discourse genre, which is essential to the description of narrative.

Bernard Combettes considers textual linguistics from another point of view, which is diachronic. His objective is to examine how it can "constitute a specific discipline" when, on the one hand, it studies the development of notions which relate to discursive coherence and, on the other, the changes that can affect the linguistic facts which ensure this coherence. Insofar as the first part of the objective is concerned, it was necessary to avoid applying notions and frameworks of analysis used in synchronic studies relating to contemporary texts. Furthermore, in the same way linguistic systems are considered to evolve, so there is a similar need to consider the development of phenomena concerning textuality, along with textual competence and, more generally, the linguistic consciousness of speakers. This being the case, the difficulty of the enterprise is for the linguist to access this skill and this consciousness where past eras are concerned.

Lita Lundquist recalls her dual career, as a researcher in textual linguistics and as a teacher of French as a foreign language; this career led her from a structural approach to the text in the 1970s to a "dynamic reading model", or reading as "navigation" in the 2000s. As for her recent activities, Lita Lundquist has been working on objects and following a method that combines linguistics with the language-learning potential of texts: "contrastive textual linguistics" enables her to compare academic texts in Danish and French, and also to analyze – and to show Danish students who have reached an advanced level in French as a foreign language – how and to what extent the two languages differ, whether in theme-rheme organization or in the choice of anaphora (nouns vs. pronouns). Finally, these comparative studies enable her to acquire a cognitive perspective: the way of "creating text" in two languages leads to the way "of thinking" in two cultures.

Epistemologies of discourse – and beyond

Patrick Charaudeau questions the theoretical and empirical bases of a *discipline of discourse*, through the relationship between the speech act and its exteriority: indeed, if what is internal escapes verbalization, the implications of this exteriority are necessary for it to be understood and interpreted. One of these implications concerns the links between the objectives of the analysis and the methodological instrumentation proclaimed by the theory. The various directions taken by discourse analysis are subsequently evoked, and examples discussed which explore discursive markers and modes of organizing discourse; questions are also posed in relation to argumentative rhetoric, language rituals, and systems of ideas. The connection between the speech act and its environment forms the substance of the second part; three points are put forward, or three *locations*: the conditions of production, interpretation, and construction of the text. To end with, emphasis is placed on the interpretation of observables and the meaning that the discourse analyst, as the analyzing subject, gives to the results of their analyses. It is mainly the practice of interpreting the data from the analysis and their theorization that are described by the author.

Dominique Maingueneau questions the notion of *discourse* both in its particularities and its vagueness: it can be thought of as outside communication ("discourse structures our beliefs") and on the other hand as referring to genres ("the discourses around publicity"). Having distinguished discourse from text (such-and-such a *text* relates to political discourse), discourse from sentence (the former being a *discourse-level* matter), and discourse from language (according to the language/speech distinction), Dominique Maingueneau examines the diversity of discourses but also the four *modes* on which the *genericity* of these latter are based: mode 1 concerns limited genres (weather forecasts); mode 2, genres which "have room for manoeuvre" (television news); mode 3, where the genre forces the speaker to invent an original scenography (advertisements); and finally, mode 4, in which the *author* "takes part in categorizing their own verbal production by deciding on its name" (essays, thoughts). Finally, Dominique Maingueneau looks at a *regime* which develops in its own *space*: this is the internet which, among other things, foregrounds aphorizing utterances.

Ruth Amossy questions the links that exist between argumentation theories and models of discourse analysis. For the purpose of reframing theories and methodologies, she invites us to rethink the need for "French-style" discourse analysis to fully integrate argumentation as a constituent element of discourse, this integration being fundamental to distinguish it from CDA – *Critical Discourse Analysis*. By comparing the two trends, Ruth Amossy aims to specify the nature of the relationships between theories of argumentation inspired by Aristotle and reassessed by Perelman, and the trends in discourse analysis. In the wake of Heinich, and taking account of the current importance of argumentative data for the study of discourse, Ruth Amossy follows close upon the heels of Patrick Charaudeau, choosing to examine a web post on the wearing of the *burqa* in France, and thereby posing the question of the analyst's political or ethical commitment when confronted with the analysis of social discourse or with societal issues.

To end with, and by way of opening up the debate towards intertexts and interdiscourses, **André Petitjean** questions the notion of *style* and, through this, the links that exist between literature and linguistics, particularly since the 1960s. The first part of his contribution provides a history of stylistic studies which, from the 1940s to 1950s, defined *style* as an expressive and aesthetic marker, and therefore through its intentional markers, which confined it to the literary field. André Petitjean then examines the "textualist" period of the 1960s to 1970s, which were particularly noted for linguistic theories such as intertextuality or dialogism. Finally, he proposes a linguistic "overhaul" of literary stylistics, in which it would be up to the specialists of literature to reconstruct the context of literary works in their intertextual and interdiscursive dimensions; while linguists would be responsible for developing models to take account of the fact that *style* can assume different forms of conceptualization, according to the status – collective or individual – that is accorded to it and on which the nature of observables depends.

This collective work does not claim to be exhaustive; its aim is rather to take a unifying look at the different "French-style" theories regarding texts and discourses. While offering an account of current research in this very diverse field it cannot, of course, be all-inclusive, but it is nevertheless possible to give it meaning. And since this collection of essays will not be the last word on these subjects, it will inevitably stimulate new research, and the exploration of other aspects of the discipline.

References

Ablali, Driss, *Que faire, que penser des "manuscrits saussuriens" dans les théories du discours et du texte en France aujourd'hui ?*, in: Cruz, Marcio Alexandre/Piovezani, Carlos/Testenoire, Pierre-Yves (edd.), *Le discours et le texte. Saussure en héritage*, Louvain-la-Neuve, Academia/L'Harmattan, 2016, 133–158.

Ablali, Driss/Achard-Bayle, Guy/Reboul-Touré, Sandrine/Temmar, Malika (edd), *Texte et discours en confrontation dans l'espace européen*, Berne, Peter Lang, 2018.

Adam, Jean-Michel, *Linguistique textuelle. Des genres de discours aux textes*, Paris, Nathan, 1999.

Adam, Jean-Michel, *Discours et interdisciplinarité. Benveniste lecteur de Saussure*, Cahiers Ferdinand de Saussure 54 (2001), 201–218.

Adam, Jean-Michel, *L'émergence de la linguistique textuelle en France (1975–2010). Parcours bibliographique en 100 titres*, Verbum 32 (2010), 237–261, https://www.unil.ch/files/live/sites/fra/files/shared/CONSCILA_Verbum.pdf. [last consultation: 14.05.2021]

Arrivé, Michel, *Linguistique et psychanalyse*, Paris, Méridiens-Klincksieck, 1986.

Bouquet, Simon, *La linguistique générale de Ferdinand de Saussure. Textes et retour aux textes*, texto ! Textes & cultures (1999), http://www.revue-texto.net/index.php?id=1717. [last consultation: 14.05.2021]

Charolles, Michel, *Grammaire de texte – Théorie du discours – Narrativité*, Pratiques 11–12 (1976), 133–154, DOI: https://doi.org/10.3406/prati.1976.969.

Depecker, Loïc, *Comprendre Saussure d'après les manuscrits*, Paris, Armand Colin, 2009.

Depecker, Loïc, *Les manuscrits de Saussure. Une révolution philologique*, Langages 185 (2012), 3–6, DOI: https://doi.org/10.3917/lang.185.0003.

Ducrot, Oswald, *Le dire et le dit*, Paris, Éditions de Minuit, 1984.

Duval, Frédéric, *La logique du sens. Autour des propositions de Robert Martin*, Metz, Université Paul-Verlaine, 2011.

Greimas, Algirdas Julien, *Sémantique structurale. Recherche de méthode*, Paris, Larousse, 1966; *Structural semantics. An attempt at a method*, transl. McDowell, Daniele/Schleifer, Ronald/Velie, Alan, Lincoln, University of Nebraska Press, 1984.

Greimas, Algirdas Julien, *Du sens. Essais sémiotiques*, vol. 1, Paris, Seuil, 1970; *On meaning. Selected writings in semiotic theory*, transl. Perron, Paul/Collins, Frank, Minneapolis, University of Minnesota Press, 1987.

Greimas, Algirdas Julien/Fontanille, Jacques, *Sémiotique des passions. Des états de choses aux états d'âme*, Paris, Seuil, 1991; *The semiotics of passions. From states of affairs to states of feeling*, transl. Perron, Paul/Collins, Frank, Minneapolis, University of Minnesota Press, 1993.

Hjelmslev, Louis, *Omkring sprogteoriens grundlæggelse*, København, Ejnar Munksgaard, 1943; *Prolegomena to a theory of language*, transl. Whitfield, Francis J., Madison, University of Wisconsin Press, ²1969.

Hjelmslev, Louis, *Essais linguistiques II*, København, Nordisk Sprog- og Kulturforlag, 1973.

Hjelmslev, Louis, *Résumé of a theory of language*, København, Nordisk Sprog- og Kulturforlag, 1975.

Ihwe, Jens, *Aspects empiriques et aspects théoriques d'un modèle de littéralité basé sur un modèle de la communication verbale*, in: Avalle D'Arco, Silvio/Bouazis, Charles/Brandt, Per Aage/Ihwe, Jens/Madsen, Peter/Van Dijk, Teun A. (edd.), *Essais de la théorie du texte*, Paris, Galilée, 1973, 54–77.

Martin, Robert, *The French contribution to modern linguistics. Theories of language and methods in syntax*, Paris/Metz, Klincksieck/Université de Metz, Centre d'analyse syntaxique, 1975.

Normand, Claudine, *Saussure*, Paris, Les Belles Lettres, 2000.

Rastier, François, *Saussure au futur*, Paris, Les Belles Lettres, 2015.

Robin, Régine, *Le hors-texte dans le discours politique*, Cahiers Recherches et Théories 19 (1979), 23–32.

Saussure, Ferdinand de, *Cours de linguistique générale*, edd. Bally, Charles/Sechehaye, Albert/Riedlinger, Albert, Lausanne/Paris, Payot & Cie, 1916; *Course in general linguistics*, transl. Baskin, Wade, New York, The Philosophical Library, 1959; *Course in general*

linguistics, transl. Baskin, Wade, edd. Meisel, Perry/Saussy, Haun, New York, Columbia University Press, 2011.
Saussure, Ferdinand de, *Cours de linguistique générale*, ed. Engler, Rudolf, 2 vol., Wiesbaden, Otto Harrassowitz, 1968–1974.
Saussure, Ferdinand de, *Écrits de linguistique générale*, edd. Bouquet, Simon/Engler, Rudolf/Weil, Antoinette, Paris, Gallimard, 2002; *Writings in general linguistics*, transl. Sanders, Carol/Pires, Matthew, Oxford, Oxford University Press, ²2012.
Sofia, Estanislao, *Quelques problèmes philologiques posés par l'œuvre de Ferdinand de Saussure*, Langages 185 (2012), 35–50, DOI: https://doi.org/10.3917/lang.185.0035.
Sofia, Estanislao, *Aux prises avec les prises de notes sur les prises de notes sur les prises de notes. Retour à la genèse du "Cours de linguistique générale" de Saussure*, Langages 209 (2018), 59–75, DOI: https://doi.org/10.3917/lang.209.0059.
Starobinski, Jean, *Les mots sous les mots. Les anagrammes de Ferdinand de Saussure*, Paris, Gallimard, 1971.
Tesnière, Lucien, *Éléments de syntaxe structurale*, Paris, Klincksieck, 1959.
Trabant, Jürgen, *Faut-il défendre Saussure contre ses amateurs? Notes item sur l'étymologie saussurienne*, Langages 159 (2005), 111–124, DOI: https://doi.org/10.3406/lgge.2005.2655.
Turpin, Béatrice, *Discours, langue et parole dans les cours et les notes de linguistique générale de F. de Saussure*, Cahiers Ferdinand de Saussure 49 (1995), 251–266, https://halshs.archives-ouvertes.fr/halshs-02357777. [last consultation: 13.03.2020]
Utaker, Arild, *La philosophie du langage. Une archéologie saussurienne*, Paris, Presses universitaires de France, 2002.
Van Dijk, Teun A., *Aspects d'une théorie générative du texte poétique*, in: Greimas, Algirdas Julien, et al. (edd.), *Essais de sémiotique poétique*, Paris, Larousse, 1972, 180–206.

Part 1: **Text-discourse links**

Jean-Michel Adam
Chapter 1
Micro-level, meso-level and macro-level of textual structuring and complexity

Abstract: Jean-Michel Adam is a specialist in text linguistics and the originator of what he calls the *textual analysis of discourse*. Here he summarizes the overall framework of his theory of textual complexity. He distinguishes the units and analysis levels or scales of *sentence* and *group of sentences* (micro-textual level), *paragraphs* and *sequences* (meso-textual level), *peritext, groups of paragraphs, parts* and *text plans* (macro-textual level). Each higher level or scale of complexity is not in itself more complex; they are completely different in the task they perform, embedded into each other and interacting in multiple ways. This theory of textual complexity is illustrated step by step through analysis of a political poster of the French Resistance (1940) together with its historical English translation.

Keywords: macro-, meso-, micro-textual levels, paragraphs, sequences, text plans, translation

1 A certain conception of text linguistics

The considerable body of work on anaphors, connectors, and other phenomena, catalogued by Stati under the *trans-phrasal* (1990) and by Berrendonner under *macro-syntax* (1990; 2002), extends the morpho-syntax and grammar of a given language through an inter-phrasal linguistics. However, linguists who study these questions only rarely link them to the text as a unit of meaning and communication, or to compositional sub-units, classes of texts, or discursive genres. Inter-phrasal and periodic grammars, focused on basic discursive units, do not attempt to develop a theory of the text. This is the task that *text linguistics* (subsequently referred to as TL) has set itself,[1] following the founding work of Coseriu (2001; 2007), Weinrich

---
[1] The theory presented here has been developed in several works on the subject (Adam 1990; 2015; 2017; 2018; 2019).

Jean-Michel Adam, Université de Lausanne

https://doi.org/10.1515/9783110794434-002

(1964), and the second Prague Circle (the work of Mathesius 1929 [1969], Firbas 1964, and Daneš 1978).[2]

The purpose of TL is to describe and theorize, on the one hand, *segmentation operations*, which define different units of rank and length and, on the other hand, the different effects of continuity created by the range of these units' *linking operations*. These two complementary operations cause segments of texts to emerge, and it is not sufficient to demarcate only sentence units (Le Goffic 2011), periodic units (Groupe de Fribourg 2012; Prandi 2013), basic textual units (Gardes Tamine 2004) or basic discursive units that are both syntactic and prosodic (Simon/Degand 2011; Degand/Martin/Simon 2014). Indeed, this says nothing about the way in which these sentential or periodic units are integrated, at a higher level, into segments presenting a certain semantic homogeneity and textual macro-organization.

The problem to be solved is well summed up by Halliday/Hasan: "A text [...] is not just a string of sentences" (1976, 293). Harris, in a seminal paper, had already put it differently: "Language does not occur in stray words or sentences, but in connected discourse [...] The successive sentences of a connected discourse [...] offer fertile soil for the methods of descriptive linguistics, since these methods study the relative distribution of elements within a connected stretch of speech" (1952, 3). And, a little further on: "And there may be successive sections of the text, each of which contains its own equivalence classes different from those of other sections. These may be paragraph-like or chapter-like sub-texts within the main text" (1952, 13–14).

It is with the theorization of these "connected stretches of speech" or "sections" that Teun A. Van Dijk is concerned when he speaks of *ordered n-tuples of sentences*: "The difference with sentential grammars, however, is that derivations do not terminate as simple or complex sentences, but as ordered n-tuples of sentences (n 1), that is as SEQUENCES" (1973, 19).

In other words, and temporarily leaving aside the graphic concept of sentence to focus on the concept of clauses (c) assembled in periods (P), these latter are not directly related to the text as a whole. Diagram 1 shows the transition from the *micro-textual level* of clauses assembled in periods (P) to the *macro-textual level* (T) limited by the initial and final boundaries or borders of the peritext (< >), by introducing the *trans-periodic intermediary level* of segments or *sequences* (S):

---

[2] Disseminated in the UK by Halliday (1967–1968), and in France by Slakta (1975), Adam (1977), and Combettes (1977; 1983).

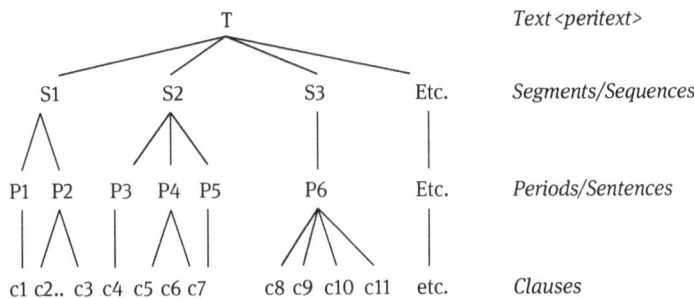

Diagram 1: Levels of textualization.

This distinction of the three levels of textualization is especially present in Anglo-Saxon research on the paragraph – particularly in a paper where Van Dijk cuts up the eleven "orthographic paragraphs" from an article in *Newsweek* into thirteen "episodes" or "semantic paragraphs". He situates these notions of *paragraph* and *episode* "at a 'meso-level' in between the unit of a clause or sentence on the one hand, and the unit of a text, discourse, or conversation as a whole" (1981, 177). These distinctions extend those established by Longacre in *Discourse, Paragraph and Sentence Structure* (1968), where he was already making a clear differentiation between these three levels of structuring and complexity. He speaks elsewhere of a *paragraph level* situated between the *micro-segmentation* and the *macro-segmentation of the texts* (Longacre 1992). Spillner (1979, 192–193), reprised by Albaladejo Mayordomo/García Berrio (1983, 163), considers the description of paragraph structure as a bridge between the *textual structure* and the *sentence structures*. For Ohori/Takahashi/Yamada/Yanagiya, the paragraph is an "intermediate level" (1986, 18) "between micro- and macro-structures" (1986, 25), a position adopted by Allison/Gemma/Heuser/Moretti/Tevel/Yamboliev (2013), and by Algee-Hewitt/Heuser/Moretti, who make the paragraph a "mid-level structure" occupying "a uniquely central position in the economy of texts" (2015, 22). I have devoted two books to the meso-textual level of analysis: one on the paragraph (Adam 2018) and the other on the theory of sequences (Adam 2017).

As to the *textual macro-level*, it is made up of the peritextual borders and subdivisions of a text written in paragraphs, chapters, sections or parts, which give the impression of a textual unit formed of signifying sub-units, of variable length and semiological nature (certain parts or modules of a text may be iconic).

These three levels of utterance-structuring form a complex and dynamic architecture from meaning to production and to reception-interpretation: one does not pass from the micro-level to the meso-level, then to the textual macro-level and discursive macro-level according to an ascending order of backlooping of structural units: "Between sentences, there are no structural relations, and this is where the study of cohesion becomes important" (Halliday/Hasan 1976, 146). An example will allow these different theoretical points to be illustrated and the complexity of the bottom-up and top-down articulation of these structural stages to be outlined. I have chosen a famous bi-lingual poster of the French Resistance, which appeared on the walls of London and was secretly distributed throughout France from the summer of 1940.[3] I have transcribed the French and English text below in order to facilitate analysis and access to quotations, and have considered the minimal units as clauses, numbered from c1 to c18.

T1   **[c1] A TOUS LES FRANÇAIS**

[c2] *La France a perdu une bataille !*

[c3] *Mais la France n'a pas perdu la guerre !*

§1 [c4] Des gouvernants de rencontre ont pu capituler, cédant à la panique, oubliant l'honneur, livrant le pays à la servitude. [c5] Cependant, rien n'est perdu !

§2 [c6] Rien n'est perdu, [c7] parce que cette guerre est une guerre mondiale. [c8] Dans l'univers libre, des forces immenses n'ont pas encore donné. [c9] Un jour, ces forces écraseront l'ennemi. [c10] Il faut que la France, ce jour-là, soit présente à la victoire. [c11] Alors, elle retrouvera sa liberté et sa grandeur. [c12] Tel est mon but, mon seul but !

§3 [c13] Voilà pourquoi je convie tous les Français, où qu'ils se trouvent, à s'unir à moi dans l'action, dans le sacrifice et dans l'espérance.

[c14] Notre patrie est en péril de mort.

[c15] Luttons tous pour la sauver !

[c16] VIVE LA FRANCE !

[c17]   [*signature manuscrite*]

GÉNÉRAL DE GAULLE

[c18] QUARTIER-GÉNÉRAL,

4, CARLTON GARDENS,

LONDON, S.W.1

---

3 One of the original posters can be seen at the Musée de l'Armée (Paris) and online under the following link: https://www.musee-armee.fr/uploads/tx_mdaobjects/06-502492-recadre.jpg [last consultation: 23.08.2022].

T2   **[c1] TO ALL FRENCHMEN**

[c2] *France has lost a battle!*

[c3] *But France has not lost the war!*

§1 [c4] A makeshift Government may have capitulated, giving way to panic, forgetting honour, delivering their country into slavery. [c5] Yet nothing is lost!

§2 [c6] Nothing is lost, [c7] because this war is a world war. [c8] In the free universe immense forces have not yet been brought into play. [c9] Some day these forces will crush the enemy. [c10] On that day France must be present at the Victory. [c11] She will then regain her liberty and her greatness.

§3 [c12] That is my goal, my only goal!

§4 [c13] That is why I ask all Frenchmen, wherever they may be, to unite with me in action, in sacrifice and in hope.

§5 [c14] Our Country is in danger of death. [c15] Let us fight to save it!

[c16] LONG LIVE FRANCE!

[c17]   *[handwritten signature]*

GÉNÉRAL DE GAULLE

[c18]   QUARTIER-GÉNÉRAL,

4, CARLTON GARDENS,

LONDON, S.W.1

2 Inter-clauses, periods and sentences: a micro-textual structuring level

Le Goffic (2011, 22) argues that the textual level is too 'labile' to assert the importance and even the necessity of a lower level that is 'stabilizing, likely to provide [. . .] regular, consistent, and objective support'.[4] In his view, this is the role of the 'organizing concept of the *sentence*'; since the 'solid reference point of the

---

4 "[S]tabilisateur, susceptible de fournir [. . .] un appui régulier, consistant, objectif." (All subsequent translations from other works are by Rosemary Rodwell, the translator of this article, unless stated otherwise.)

sentence' offers 'a stable marker, a prop', he makes it 'the key point of the text's construction'. Based on this supporting prop, each sequence of syntactic processing is integrated 'in a global process of construction of the text, during which the autonomy of each constituent unit is reassessed' (2011, 11).[5] Similarly, Riegel (2006, 53) defines the text purely as an 'organized set of sentences'. He proposes to complete the 'tools of a good sentence grammar' by simply taking account of the 'strictly textual conditionings of sentences when they are put into a sequence' (2006, 53).[6] The problem is that these strictly textual conditionings resulting from putting sentences into sequences, and reassessing the autonomy of sentences, cannot be described and theorized by simply adding to the tools of sentence grammar. This has been confirmed by other linguists, working in very different theoretical contexts.

Culioli is categorical: 'The written text forces us, in an exemplary way, to understand that we cannot go from the sentence (outside prosody, out of context, outside any situation) to the utterance, through a process of extension. This represents a theoretical breakdown whose consequences are unavoidable' (1984, 10).[7] For Soutet: 'In the particular case of the text, the relation of the whole to the part does not involve the same type of predictability as that which exists between each of the sub-phrasal units and their immediate constituents' (2005, 325).[8] Indeed, the syntactic solidarities between language units have only a very limited range. As soon as one passes the threshold of the syntactic construction and the core of the sentence to enter the domains of the inter-phrasal/periodic and the trans-phrasal/periodic, other junction systems appear, based on junction markers whose scope is more or less distant and whose 'conventional function [is] to indicate to the addressee that such and such a unit must be understood as maintaining a particular relationship with such and such another' (Charolles 1993, 311).[9]

---

[5] "[C]oncept organisateur de *phrase* [. . .] solidité du repère de la phrase [. . .] un point stable, un point d'appui [. . .] le point clé de la construction du texte [. . .] dans un processus global de construction du texte, au cours duquel l'autonomie de chaque unité constituante est réévaluée."
[6] "[O]utils d'une bonne grammaire phrastique [. . .] conditionnements proprement textuels des phrases lorsqu'elles sont mises en séquence".
[7] "Le texte écrit nous force, de façon exemplaire, à comprendre que l'on ne peut pas passer de la phrase (hors prosodie, hors contexte, hors situation) à l'énoncé, par une procédure d'extension. Il s'agit en fait d'une rupture théorique, aux conséquences incontournables."
[8] "Dans le cas particulier du texte, le rapport du tout à la partie ne relève pas du même type de prévisibilité que celui qui existe entre chacune des unités subphrastiques et leurs constituants immédiats."
[9] "[Leur] fonction conventionnelle [est] de signaler au destinataire que telle ou telle unité doit être comprise comme entretenant telle relation avec telle ou telle autre."

Going beyond the border of the sentence's core to approach the natural products of linguistic interaction represented by texts does not mean that a simple trans-phrasal extension of the limits of linguistics is being embarked on. As Prandi states, it involves moving 'from the sentence dimension, governed by grammar, to a textual dimension, governed by the coherence of concepts supported by appropriate cohesive means' (2007, 75).[10] This Italian linguist criticizes the grammatical tradition which doggedly favors 'form over content, rules over options, the sentence dimension over the textual dimension' (2007, 75).[11] It is these 'specialized cohesive resources' (2007, 81)[12] available to the speaker which interest me.

Reichler-Béguelin/Berrendonner (Groupe de Fribourg 2012, 12), who recognize the stability of syntactic and prosodic islands, propose to 'end the *sentence* category':

> In order to segment discourse, it might be possible to base the action on the sole property of syntactic autonomy; but the grammatical monads thus obtained (or *clauses*) will not all be sentences. On the other hand, it might also be analyzed according to the prosodic closure markers scattered within it; but what will be singled out by this means are tonal paragraphs (= *periods*) and still not sentences.[13]

Phrasal segments, the graphic equivalents of simple clauses or periods, often show discrepancies between syntax and punctuation, comparable to the discrepancies between syntax and prosody in oral production (Simon/Degand 2011, 53): a) rection-punctuation congruence (a clause = a graphic sentence, or period = a graphic sentence); b) a single period for several graphic sentences; c) a single graphic sentence for several periods. This stage of the clause, period, and graphic sentence is the first structuring factor of written micro-textual units.[14] We move from this first stage of structuring to the *inter-phrasal/periodic texture* by applying

---

10 "[D]e la dimension phrastique, régie par la grammaire, à une dimension textuelle, régie par la cohérence des concepts supportée par des moyens cohésifs appropriés".
11 "[L]es formes par rapport aux contenus, les règles par rapport aux options, la dimension phrastique par rapport à la dimension textuelle".
12 "[R]essources cohésives spécialisées".
13 "[D]issoudre la catégorie *phrase* : pour segmenter le discours, on peut éventuellement se fonder sur la seule propriété d'autonomie syntaxique ; mais les monades grammaticales qu'on obtiendra ainsi (ou *clauses*) ne seront pas toutes des phrases. On peut aussi, d'un autre côté, l'analyser d'après les marques de clôture prosodiques dont il est parsemé ; mais ce qu'on isolera par ce moyen, ce sont des paragraphes tonaux (= *périodes*) et toujours pas des phrases."
14 The present study refers mainly to the written word; iconotexts and oral and digital textualities require different expositions and complementary concepts.

substantial linking procedures which ensure the connectedness and cohesion of linguistic groupings between units of textualization.

I therefore distinguish between two micro-textual levels of structuring:

- An *intra-phrasal/periodic level* articulating morpho-syntax (clauses and periods) and punctuation (segmentation in graphic sentences).
- An *inter-phrasal level* (linking graphically separated units) *and inter-periodic level* in which the connecting up of utterances goes through six phases which I describe without putting them in numerical or alphabetical order because it is not an ordered system:
  - S. Semantic connectivity and cohesion (anaphora, thematic progression, isotopies)
  - C. Connectivity supported by junction markers (organizers and connectives)
  - M. Linkings operated by signifying materiality (graphic, phonic, parallelisms)
  - I. Linkings based on what is implicit (the unsaid)
  - E. Enunciative cohesion and transitions
  - A. Links between discourse acts

The fact of being able to resort to these different linking procedures, which are active at both the intra-periodic stage (from the complex sentence to the period) and the inter-periodic stage, explains the diversity of the judgments made about connectivity and the cohesion of texts or portions of texts. When several of these procedures jointly guarantee the linking of a series of utterances, the impression of connectivity and cohesion is very strong. In the opposite case, this impression and therefore the *textuality effect* gradually become weaker. Other factors may then intervene and take over: the genre of discourse, the meso-textual structuring, and the macro-textual organization.

2.1 Semantic connectivity and cohesion (S)

At the inter-phrasal/periodic level, semantic structuring may be examined from four angles.

S1. *Anaphora and chains of reference* are one of the areas most studied by linguists. These questions can be illustrated by means of our example. Referential continuity is ensured in T1 and T2 by the repetition of the lexeme "France" (c2, c3, c10 & c16) and of "Tous les Français/All Frenchmen" (c1 & c13). A lexical variation (co-referential lexeme) appears in c4 with the singulative definite lexeme *le* *pays* and in c14 with the appropriation of the nation: "notre patrie". The English translation makes the contrast in more binary fashion between "their country" (the France of those in power who have just accepted defeat) and "our country" (the France of the resistance). The way in which the referent moves throughout the text thus becomes apparent. On the other hand, the referent's integral stability is guaranteed by the pronominal anaphors and the possessive determiners which link c10 ("la France/France") to c11 ("*elle, sa* liberté, *sa* grandeur/*she, her* liberty, *her* greatness") or "la France/country" (c14) to "elle/it" (c15), or "tous les Français/all Frenchmen" to "ils/they" (c13).

The demonstrative repetition of "*la* guerre/*the* war" (c3) by "*cette* guerre"/"*this* war" (c7) is, on the other hand, a modification of the referent which is reinforced by a reformulation of the type [this N1 is an N2 [N + Adjective]]: "*cette guerre est une guerre mondiale*". This reformulation is at the heart of the argument. The same demonstrative repetition of "des forces/forces" (c8) by "*ces* forces/*these* forces" (c9) or of "un jour/some day" (c9) by "*Ce* jour-*là*/On *that* day" (c10) accompanies the transformation which leads from the lost "bataille/battle" (c2) to the "guerre/war" (c3, c7) that has been won ("victoire/victory" c10), based on a dissociation of the notions of "bataille" and "guerre".

Two other forms of repetition here ensure semantic groupings and textual organization. Placed at the head of the sentence, "Tel" (end of paragraph §2) and "Voilà" (beginning of §3) in the French text, summarize the preceding content. In the translation, the intra-textual cross-reference (which I shall return to later) is highlighted by a repeated "that" at the beginning of §3 and §4. These two *anaphoric encapsulations* (Conte 1999) ensure that c10 and c11 are packaged together by "Tel/That$_1$," and the whole of §2 by "Voila/That$_2$." It is thus possible to see how the unity of the text is based on returns-repetitions, and its progression on transformations of the reference, that is to say a schematization which involves modification of the discursive memory (Reichler-Béguelin 1988): the transition from *bataille* to *guerre* and then to *guerre mondiale* modifies, by reformulating it, the dominant schematization of the referent and therefore of the military and political context.

S2. *Thematic/rhematic progressions.* I will not emphasize types of thematic progressions (Adam 2019, 75–80), but will simply single out the structure of the c2-MAIS-c3 linking, based on repetitions of the same *theme* (*France*) and the same *verbal transition* (verb *perdre/lost*), together with the opposition between the two *rhemes* (*bataille/battle* vs. *guerre/war*) supported by the negation (*a perdu/has lost* vs. *n'a pas perdu/has not lost*).

S3. The concepts of *isotopy, cotopy, polyisotopy,* and *heterotopy* (Adam 2019, 115–122) were too general in Greimas' first definition: 'The existence of discourse – rather than of a series of independent sentences – can only be affirmed if it is possible to presuppose an isotopy that is common to all the sentences of which it is formed, and which is recognizable thanks to a body of linguistic categories [present] throughout its development' (1976, 28).[15] If we refocus this definition on all the vocabulary items of a text (whatever its length), we can see that semantic cohesion is ensured, in our example, by an isotopy of combat: *bataille/battle* (c2), *guerre/war* (c3, c6), *écraseront/crush* (c9), *ennemi/enemy* (c9), *luttons/fight* (c15), *capituler/capitulated* (c4) and *Victoire/Victory* (c10). A lexeme like "forces" (c8, c9) thus, co-textually, becomes an allusion to the armed forces. The whole text is dramatized by the creation of an allegory of France, which ends with the "péril de mort/danger of death" (c14) for soldiers engaged in the battle on behalf of an anthropomorphized nation.

The local particularity of figures such as the metaphor and hypallage, and the more global specificity of the allegory and of texts like parables and fables, demands an interpretative decoding of the heterotopical utterances and polyisotopy that are substantially developed in them.

S4. *Collocations of vocabulary items* (Adam 2019, 122–127). The text adopted as an example enables us to see how lexical collocations in language are reactivated or reinvented in the argumentative framework of the text: "gouvernants de rencontre/makeshift Government" (c4) allows Marshal Pétain's decision[16] to be condemned without naming him; the syntactic unit "guerre mondiale/world war" (c7) is at the center of the argument; "univers libre/free universe" (c8) is contrasted with "servitude/slavery" (c4) and the conventional formula "Vive la France/Long live France" (c16) expresses the allegorization of the nation. The stereotypical exclamatory utterance is in a sense reactivated to take on a dramatic co(n)textual meaning (life vs. death).

2.2 Connection sustained by markers of connectivity (C)

I have proposed to distinguish several types of "connectives" (Adam 1990, 141–252; Adam 2019, 140–160): *textual organizers* (C1), *connectives* proper (C2), and *discursive markers* (C3).

---

[15] "L'existence du discours – et non d'une suite de phrases indépendantes – ne peut être affirmée que si l'on peut postuler à la totalité des phrases qui le constituent une isotopie commune, reconnaissable grâce à un faisceau de catégories linguistiques tout au long de son développement."
[16] For a comparative analysis of Marshal Pétain's speech of June 17, 1940, and of General de Gaulle's on June 18, I refer the reader to chapter 7 of Adam (2019, 251–268), and Herman (2008). I analyze the poster in chapter 4 of Adam (2013, 83–95).

C1. *Textual organizers* make groupings of graphic sentences and periods visible. They facilitate the reading-comprehension of texts, but they do not have the argumentative and enunciative function of connectives. *Spatial organizers* segment portions of text corresponding to parts of the referent (which are active in description and in travel, walking, and mountain-climbing guides). *Temporal organizers*, such as *Un jour/Some day* (c9) and *Alors/then* (c11), at the head of a sentence, open and punctuate the moments or episodes of a narration (predictive in this case). To these two major primary classes of textual organizers should be added (Adam 2019, 143–146) *enumerative organizers* (additives and linear integration), *change of topic markers*, and *illustration and exemplification markers*.

C2. *Connectives* are very numerous in text T1 and its translation. It is the argumentative connective *Mais/But* (c3) that forms the pivot of the refutation of the French government's position (the indented line emphasizes this opposition). The particularity of the concessive connective *Cependant/Yet* (c5) is to express the hiatus between two opposing points of view about the same situation: after the catastrophic outcome of the Battle for France, should capitulation (*tout est perdu*) or resistance (*Rien n'est perdu*) be the order of the day? This hiatus is reinforced by the strong punctuation of the full stop before the connective. The explanatory connective *Parce que/Because* (c7) opens the justification section, while *Voilà pourquoi/That is why* (c13) is there to close the explanation and introduce the Appeal itself, which is based on and legitimized by the explanation.

C3. *Discursive markers* in the written text. Among the macro-textual junction factors which cannot be illustrated in our corpus (but are visible at many points in the writing of the present article), textual cohesion markers such as: "we shall see later/hereafter/below", "see above/earlier page x/chapter y", etc. reveal intra-textual relations at variable distances. In addition to this anaphoric role, these markers have an enunciative value (to summon the writer and reader to a point *here* in the text) as well as a meta-enunciative value (Lefebvre 2014), insofar as they reveal aspects of the enunciative activity in progress: the choice not to say *here*, but *elsewhere* in the text (local intra-textual cross-reference), in the text considered as a whole (global intra-textual cross-reference: *dans le présent ouvrage/ dans cet article*) or as it is said in the text of someone else (intertextual cross-reference: *see X, X 2011, Cf. X*). On this point, as for many connectives, the strict textual conjunction intersects with enunciation and meta-discursive reflexivity.

2.3 Linkings operated by signifying materiality (M)

Repetitions of groups of graphemes and groups of phonemes (*isographic and isophonic linkings* M1) form kinds of isotopies at the level of expression, and are named "isoplasmies" by the Groupe μ (1970, 34–36). With *morpho-syntactic parallelisms* (M2) and *rhythmic structuring* (M3), these signifier linkings are important factors in textual organization, and are particularly present in slogans, proverbs, songs and poetry, puns, slips of the tongue, and witticisms, but also in written press titles and advertising, as well as oratory in general.

M1. *Isographic and isophonic linkings.* The untranslatable initial saturation of T1 by the nasal vowel /ã/, converging upon the consonants /r/ (fRANce / fRANçais / RENcontre / livRANt / gRANdeur) or /d/ (DANs / céDANt / cepenDANt) is impressive and, in particular, it provides the basis for most of the two other forms of linking. The grapho-phonic link between "l'espéRANCE" (c13) and "la FRANCE" is certainly not due to chance and this, too, carries the whole meaning of this appeal.

M2. Constructed on the principle of *morpho-syntactic parallelism* (Ruwet 1975), the sentences-paragraphs c2 and c3 repeat the theme in its entirety (*La France/ France*), and then take up the verbal transition (*perdre*) by modally opposing the statement of fact (*a perdu/has lost*) and its negation (*n'a pas perdu/has not lost*), ending up with the opposition, in rhematic position, of the lexemes *bataille/ battle* and *guerre/war*. Supported by the paragraph, the centered typographical arrangement, and the choice of italic characters, this parallelism is at the heart of the refuting argument emphasized by the argumentative connective *Mais/But*.

Moreover, the repetition of the phrase "*tous les Français/all Frenchmen*" at the beginning and end of the text highlights the transition from the address without a subject in enunciation c1: "À *tous les Français*/To *all Frenchmen*" to the actual appeal in c13: "je convie *tous les Français*/I ask *all Frenchmen*". The repetition links up two utterances that are distant from one another.

M3. *Rhythmic structuring.* There are two occasions on which parallelisms develop into ternary expansions to the right, closing a long periodic sentence:

c4	Des gouvernants de rencontre ont pu capituler,	1. cédant à la panique, 2. oubliant l'honneur, 3. livrant le pays à la servitude.
c4	A makeshift Government may have capitulated,	1. giving way to panic, 2. forgetting honour, 3. delivering their country into slavery.

In c4, the detached construction at the end of the periodic sentence is tripled, thus making the accusation of the French government's capitulation weightier. The paragraph in which the appeal is formulated is based on the same ternary expansion to the right. The last sentence, introduced by the textual organizer closing a series, namely *et/and*, is thus highlighted in relation to the two others and refers to the predictive futures of c9–c11:

§3 c13   Voilà pourquoi je convie tous les Français, où qu'ils se trouvent,
                               à s'unir à moi   1. dans l'action,
                                                 2. dans le sacrifice
                                                 3. ET dans l'espérance.
§4 c13   That is why I ask all Frenchmen, wherever they may be,
                               to unite with me   1. in action,
                                                  2. in sacrifice
                                                  3. AND in hope.

2.4 Linkings based on the inferred reestablishment of implicit information (i)

There is no text that "says it all" – in relation to this, Umberto Eco even speaks of the text as a 'lazy machine' (1985, 29)[17] – and the inferred reestablishment of implicit information is an essential element both for understanding and producing a text (Coirier/Gaonac'h/Passerault 1996, 104). The enunciator is supposed to be able to foresee the missing information that his/her reader will be capable of reestablishing. Several forms of the unsaid have to be envisaged: *ellipses* (i1), *presuppositions* (i2), *implied* (i3) and *intertextual* data (i4), which all participate in the creation of meaning by filling in blanks and silences. Our example contains only an ellipse (i1) which has already been mentioned earlier: c1 ["*je m'adresse/I speak to*] à tous les Français/all Frenchmen" or "[*ce message s'adresse/this message is for*] à tous les Français/all Frenchmen." On the other hand, where a retrievable ellipse is possible and would, for example, reconnect c2 and c3 in a periodic sentence – "*La France a perdu une bataille, mais* [ellipse of the subject and the verb] *pas la guerre*", the text opts, on the contrary, for the repetition and creation of a graphically marked parallelism.

The first utterance "*La France a perdu une bataille !/France has lost a battle!*" (c2) is presented as the acknowledgment of a state of affairs, a schematization

---

17 "[M]achine paresseuse".

and a state of discursive memory[18] which refers to the Battle for France and the fact that the French army has just been crushed by the mechanical power of the German army. This utterance is not called into question by the following one. Saying that "La France n'a pas perdu la guerre !"/"France has not lost the war!" (c3) is made possible through a dissociation of ideas and recognition of the fact that a war does not come down to a single battle. In other words, it is presuppositions about the concept of *war* which make possible the assertion of c3 and the non-contradiction of c2 and c3. In fact, this concatenation is argumentatively an enthymeme or incomplete syllogism: c2 posits a major premise accepted by all and c3 sets out the conclusion of the reasoning without expressing the necessary minor, but supposedly acknowledged, premise in language and therefore in the discursive memory: *une bataille perdue ne signifie pas pour autant la fin d'une guerre*. The following section of text condemns an error of reasoning: the non-p negation of c3 implies that some people – the "gouvernants de rencontre" of c4 – have deduced from c2 a p conclusion of the type *la guerre est perdue* and have therefore been able to take the decision to "capitulate". In this sense, the negation here is clearly a refutation of the French government's view of the situation. The purpose of the repeated negation "Rien n'est perdu !"/'Nothing is lost!" is to reverse the conclusions that have led Pétain to order a stop to the fighting. The implicit utterance implied by the negation [p *tout est perdu/all is lost*] is presented as a false analysis of the political and military situation. The purpose of the following paragraph, explaining why non-p is likely despite present appearances, is to reverse the state of the national discursive memory created by Marshal Pétain's June 17 speech.

The implied (i3) conveyed by certain utterances are interesting and form part of the text's meaning. The phrase "gouvernants de rencontre"/"makeshift Government" is very demeaning because it implies that the President of the Republic's appointment of Marshal Pétain to the head of the French government is *makeshift* and not lawful. The choice of the verb "capitular"/'capitulate' does not quite match the situation. On June 17 Pétain asked the French to "cesser le combat" ("C'est le cœur serré que je vous demande de *cesser le combat*"/'It is with a heavy heart that I ask you to *stop fighting*') and he initiated negotiations with a view to signing an armistice on June 22 with Germany and on June 24 with Italy. The term chosen by de Gaulle is stronger because it implies unconditional capitulation.

---

18 I refer the reader to what Berrendonner (Groupe de Fribourg 2012, 22–25) has to say about these concepts.

Let us return to the *Alors/then* which concludes the catenation of clauses c9 to c11: "(c9) *Un jour, ces forces écraseront l'ennemi/Some day these forces will crush the enemy.* (c10) *Il faut que la France, ce jour-là, soit présente à la victoire/On that day France must be present at the Victory.* (c11) ALORS, *elle retrouvera sa liberté et sa grandeur/She will then regain her liberty and her greatness.*" This *ALORS/ THEN* is not so much a temporal organizer as an argumentative connector underpinned by the deontic modality *Il faut que/must be*, which opens c10. This strong grammatical determinant implies a conditional periodic sentence of the type: *SI la France n'est pas présente à la victoire. ALORS, elle ne retrouvera ni sa liberté ni sa grandeur.* 'IF France is not present at the victory. THEN, she will regain neither her liberty nor her greatness.' It is indeed because of this necessity and with the underlying implication *SI/IF non-p ALORS/THEN non-q* that de Gaulle argues in favor of p and q, that is of resisting and continuing to fight.

The more one continues to analyze the poster, the more obvious it appears that a text cannot be read in isolation, but that it is part of an intertextual chain (i4) of speeches given by the same locutor or by others. In this case, we need to take account of the intertexts of radio speeches broadcast by Marshal Pétain on June 17, 1940 and General de Gaulle on June 18. The poster is a summary of this latter text and a response to Pétain's address. An utterance such as "oubliant l'honneur/forgetting honour" (c4) answers this paragraph by Pétain: "Je me suis adressé cette nuit à l'adversaire pour lui demander s'il est prêt à rechercher avec moi, entre soldats, après la lutte *et dans l'honneur*, les moyens de mettre un terme aux hostilités./I addressed the enemy last night to ask whether he was prepared to seek with me, between soldiers, after the struggle *and with honor*, the means to put an end to the hostilities." Similarly, the words at the end of the poster appear to echo Pétain's words: "Que *tous les Français* se groupent autour du gouvernement que je préside pendant ces dures épreuves et fassent taire leur angoisse pour n'obéir qu'à leur foi dans le destin de la patrie"/May *all Frenchmen* rally around the government I have presided over during these great hardships and conceal their anguish, to obey only their faith in the country's destiny." The repetition of the phrase "tous les Français" forms the basis of a counter-proposition for rallying forces. Likewise, de Gaulle opposes "l'action/action" (c13), "la lutte/ fight" (c15) and "l'espérance/hope" (c13) to Pétain's passive "foi dans le destin de la patrie/faith in the country's destiny".

The intertextuality that is internal to General de Gaulle's speech (intratextuality) enables us to read certain utterances on the poster as summaries of the argumentation developed in the June 18 1940 Appeal. To take just a few examples, c7 retains only the third sentence of this ternary period of the June 18 Appeal: "Cette guerre n'est pas limitée au territoire malheureux de notre pays. Cette guerre n'est pas tranchée par la Bataille de France. *Cette guerre est une guerre mondiale/*

This war is not limited to the unfortunate territory of our country. The outcome of the struggle has not been decided by the Battle of France. *This war is a world war.*" In the same way, c8 and c9 summarize the following passage: "Toutes les fautes, tous les retards, toutes les souffrances, n'empêchent pas qu'il y a, dans *l'univers*, tous les moyens nécessaires pour écraser un jour nos ennemis. Foudroyés aujourd'hui par la *force* mécanique, nous pourrons vaincre dans l'avenir par une *force* mécanique supérieure. Le destin du monde est là./Mistakes have been made, there have been delays and untold suffering, but the fact remains that there still exists in the world everything we need to crush our enemies some day. Today we are crushed by the sheer weight of mechanized force hurled against us, but we can still look to a future in which even greater mechanized force will bring us victory. The destiny of the world is at stake." The repeated phrase in c5 and c6 is spelled out at greater length: "Croyez-moi, moi qui vous parle en connaissance de cause et vous dis que *rien n'est perdu* pour la France. Les mêmes moyens qui nous ont vaincus peuvent faire venir un jour la victoire/Speaking in full knowledge of the facts, I ask you to believe me when I say that the cause of France is not lost. The very factors that brought about our defeat may one day lead us to victory." Finally, the heart of the Appeal (c13) summarizes this long periodic sentence: "Moi, Général de Gaulle, actuellement à Londres, j'invite les officiers et les soldats français qui se trouvent en territoire britannique ou qui viendraient à s'y trouver, avec leurs armes ou sans leurs armes, j'invite les ingénieurs et les ouvriers spécialistes des industries d'armement qui se trouvent en territoire britannique ou qui viendraient à s'y trouver, à se mettre en rapport avec moi/I General de Gaulle, now in London, call on all French officers and men who are at present on British soil, or may be in the future, with or without their arms; I call on all engineers and skilled workmen from the armaments factories who are at present on British soil, or may be in the future, to get in touch with me."[19]

2.5 Enunciative cohesion and transitions (E)

Three broad categories of enunciative facts ensure the unity of portions of texts and transitions between sections that are more or less enunciatively heterogeneous: the *acceptance* or *assignment of utterances* resulting in confrontations of *points of view* (E1), variations in *enunciation levels* (E2) and *meta-enunciative* returns of the saying over the said (E3).

---

[19] All translations from de Gaulle's speech by Alison Browning, BBC Radio, https://www.nhd.org/sites/default/files/Resistance%20Rising%20-%20Lesson%20Plan.pdf [last consultation: 05.07.2022].

The question of the *acceptance* (or not) of utterances by the speaker or the various enunciators that are produced in and by the discourse is an essential point in the functioning of language in discourse. The transition from *direct discourse* and the use of *quotation marks* – to indicate the fact that the utterances emanate from different speakers – to *free indirect discourse*, via transitions from *indirect discourse* and *narrative discourse* in between, are the best example of enunciative heterogeneity that is more or less marked.

Equally characteristic is a negation like that in c5, which closes a paragraph, implying that the speaker is not accepting the implicit conclusion that might be drawn from c4 (*Des gouvernants de rencontre ont pu capituler, cédant à la panique, oubliant l'honneur, livrant le pays à la servitude/A makeshift government may have capitulated, giving way to panic, forgetting honour, delivering their country into slavery*). While marking c4 as a concession (*Cependant/Yet*), the enunciator signing the poster fully accepts c5 – this is the entire meaning of the exclamation *rien n'est perdu !/Nothing is lost!*

According to Benveniste, enunciators, through their very enunciation:

> [...] appropriate the formal apparatus of language and enunciate their position as speaker by means of specific cues [...] But immediately, as soon as they declare themselves to be the speaker and assume the language, they set the *other* in opposition to themselves, whatever degree of presence they attribute to this other. All enunciation, explicit or implicit, is an address, and presupposes an addressee. (1974, 82)[20]

The pronominal traces (personal pronouns and possessive determiners) mark out portions of texts and an enunciative configuration. JE/I and MOI/ME only emerge in c13, triggered by the determiner MON/MY, repeated in c12, and this signifies a progression of the text leading to the emergence of a general subject, namely de Gaulle – resulting from his oral discursive action of June 18, 1940, resurrected and set in writing by the poster. The exclamatory utterances in c2, c3, c5, and c12, which were present before the explicit affirmation of this enunciative position, already bore traces of acceptance and therefore of the presence of an enunciative subject whose status changes from the enunciation of the Appeal onwards – making him an opponent of the government and a founder of the French Resistance, calling upon citizens to resist and soldiers to desert.

It is noteworthy that the text of this poster includes no second-person pronoun. The address is in the third person (*les Français/all Frenchmen, ils/they*), so the

---

20 "[S]'approprie l'appareil formel de la langue et il énonce sa position de locuteur par des indices spécifiques [...]. Mais immédiatement, dès qu'il se déclare locuteur et assume la langue, il implante l'*autre* en face de lui, quel que soit le degré de présence qu'il attribue à cet autre. Toute énonciation est, explicite ou implicite, une allocution, elle postule un allocutaire."

addressee is maintained at a distance and is not part of a co-locution. Despite the imperative (hyperthetic modality), the "nous" which emerges in c14 and c15 appears not so much to unite an I/ME and a YOU as an I/ME and THEY. This very formal distancing contrasts with the enunciative stage of an implied enunciation and a discursive representation linked to the parameters of the enunciative situation: the *here* (in exile in London) and the *now* (opened by June 18, 1940). The writing and subsequent diffusion of this political poster, which became a banner of the Resistance, certainly disassociated locators of the reference points of enunciation and reading, but the presents, perfects, futures, and imperatives are all tenses characteristic of implied and actual enunciation. The predictive futures in c9 and c11, with their use of the categoric future rather than the conditional, which would have introduced a feeling of distance, are traces of a strong assertion predicting the transformation of the present state of the world. This implies total enunciative commitment, prolonged by the imperative of c15 and the archaic use of the subjunctive in c16 (without *que* and in an independent clause).

Weinrich was one of the first to examine the textual role of verbal tenses (1964). In the perspective of what he was already describing as text linguistics, his theoretical thinking was not restricted to the framework of lexical (temporal morpheme linked to a lexeme) and sentential manifestations of temporal-verb forms. Emphasizing, with Vetters, that 'a satisfactory description of the use of verbal tenses cannot be limited to a single level of analysis, whether sentential or textual, but must integrate these two levels' (1993, 8),[21] it is nevertheless noteworthy that research in this area continues to be limited, as far as text is concerned, to series of two sentences (rarely more). Weinrich was interested in textual effects linked to series of identical sentences (series of past historic or present tenses, etc.) and in transitions between close tenses (past historic + imperfect, different from present + future, for example) or between tenses involving different sub-systems (present or future in between past historic + imperfect, or past historic in between present + perfect). I will qualify his position, not by saying that homogeneous transitions "guarantee a text's consistency, its textuality" (1973, 204), but that "heterogeneous transitions play a very small part, or even none at all, in textuality" (1973, 205).[22] Defining textuality as a tension between continuity and discontinuity, I would say that the enunciative variations marked by specifiers of persons and by verbal forms are a very important element in the textual dynamic of meaning.

---

[21] "[U]ne description satisfaisante de l'emploi des temps verbaux ne peut pas se limiter à un seul niveau d'analyse, qu'il soit phrastique ou textuel, mais doit intégrer ces deux niveaux."
[22] "[L]es transitions homogènes garantissent la consistance d'un texte, sa textualité." vs "les transitions hétérogènes ne participent guère à la textualité, ou même pas du tout."

Diagram 2 enables us to summarize the opposing points of view on which the argument is based, by articulating connection (C) and enunciation (E):

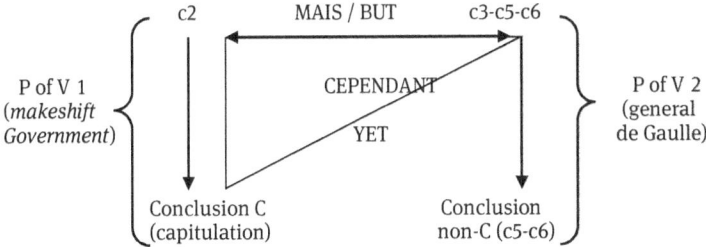

Diagram 2: Opposing points of view.

Finally, we should mention the fact that meta-discursive returns (E3) of enunciation upon itself can have the benefit of correcting a previous utterance. A sort of adjustment after the event – which is very frequent in the flow of oral speech – intervenes during the course of enunciation in the repetition of c12, "Tel est mon but, *mon seul but* !/That is my goal, *my only goal!*" The exclamation demands the addition of the adjective.

2.6 Links between discourse acts (A)

A text is not a simple series of discourse acts which possess a certain illocutionary value (from assertion to interpellation, from injunction to warning), but a series of more or less linked discourse acts forming sequences of acts. The principle of these sequences was considered by Viehweger very early on: 'Concrete analyses show that the illocutionary acts that constitute a text form illocutionary hierarchies with a dominant illocutive act backed up by subsidiary illocutionary acts [. . .]' (1990, 49).[23] Viehweger very rightly criticizes text grammars for not understanding the activating structure of discourse and he insists on the fact that identifiable discourse acts are 'linked to one another in order to realize complex objectives' (1990, 48),[24] thus forming "illocutionary structures" which he quite correctly notes 'are in a systematic relationship with global structures of texts (for example, structures

---

[23] "Les analyses concrètes montrent que les actes illocutoires qui constituent un texte forment des hiérarchies illocutoires avec un acte illocutif dominant étayé par des actes illocutoires subsidiaires. . ."
[24] "[Les actes de langage sont] rattachés les uns aux autres pour réaliser des objectifs complexes."

of argumentative, descriptive, narrative texts, etc.)' (1990, 48).[25] Vanderveken, too, stressed this textual structuring of discourse acts: 'A true discourse is much more than simply a completed sequence of illocutionary acts. It has its own particular structure and conditions for success and these cannot be reduced to those of the isolated illocutionary acts which form part of it' (1992, 64).[26] He even speaks of *complex interventions*, which are very close to Viehweger's *structures of texts* and to my own (proto)types of basal sequences: 'descriptions, argumentations, explanations, justifications, and questionings' (Vanderveken 1992, 58). He considers them as discourse acts 'whose nature is more complex than that of the auxiliary elementary illocutionary acts that make them up' (1992, 58).[27]

The text of the political poster is a good example of this activating dimension of textuality. It is presented as a sequence of discourse acts, but the location of this succession of identifiable acts as such gives no indication as to their links and therefore of the textuality and dynamic of this argumentative text.

In fact, the assertions at the beginning (c2 to c5) are encompassed within a movement of concession followed by a refutation: c2 > c3 and c4 > c5. The fact that the strongest argument follows the connectives *cependant/yet* and *mais/but* and is a negation, implies, as we saw earlier when dealing with negation, an assertion that can be imputed to a point of view (P of V1) which is different from the enunciator's viewpoint (P of V2). These two acts of concession are caught in an enveloping macro-act of refutation.

This initial movement of refutation is then substantiated by an explanation which starts from c6 (*rien n'est perdu/nothing is lost*) and the connective *parce que/because*. This explanatory movement includes the following series of utterances and micro-acts: Acts of assertion c6, c7 and c8; Assertive-predictive act c9; Act of assertion c10; Assertive-predictive act c11; Act of assertion c12. The close of this explanatory movement is indicated by *C'est pourquoi/That is why* (c13).

Affirmation of the subject's position in the enunciation only occurs in c12 where the purpose of the socio-discursive interaction engaged in is clarified: it is, namely, to act in such a way that France's liberty and greatness will be restored

---

25 "[Les] structures illocutoires [. . .] se trouvent dans un rapport systématique avec des structures globales de textes (par exemple structures de textes argumentatifs, descriptifs, narratifs, etc.)" (1990: 48)
26 "Un véritable discours est bien plus qu'une simple séquence finie d'actes illocutoires. Il a une structure et des conditions de succès qui lui sont propres et qui sont irréductibles à celles des actes illocutoires isolés qui en font partie."
27 "[D]es descriptions, des argumentations, des explications, des justifications et des questionnements [. . .] dont la nature est plus complexe que celle des actes illocutoires élémentaires auxiliaires qui les composent."

(c11). The initial refutation, once backed up by this explanation, makes it possible to accomplish the directive act c13, in the form of a performative (first person, present, and lexicalization of the act): "Je convie. . ./I ask. . .". The verb *convier* is, in French, a specific directive act: 'It is asking someone to go somewhere or to be present at something [. . .]; furthermore, when inviting someone, one generally presupposes [. . .] that what the addressee is being invited to do is good for him' (Vanderveken 1988, 183).[28] Of course, what is being promised here is not a peaceful invitation, but a dangerous military engagement ("*dans l'action, dans le sacrifice et dans l'espérance/in action, in sacrifice and in hope*"). Unlike an order, this directive act remains open to *deliberation* by the recipient: it is the latter who has to decide whether or not he wishes to respond to the invitation addressed to him. The enunciator restricts himself to offering the addressee the choice of what he thinks is good for him and for the nation. The whole discursive genre of this poster – a deliberately political discourse – resides in this directive act. The attenuation of the directive by the invitation moderates the discursive action of the call for dissidence, disobedience, and even desertion. Coming from a high-ranking official, this is a particularly radical act.

So we have a global argumentative structure of three macro-acts among which *the explanation* (II) plays the role of an argumentative shoring up of *the refutation* (I), while justifying and making possible *the Appeal-invitation* (III). The text closes with an expressive act (c16) which follows two utterances (the assertive c14 and the directive c15) with the first person plural marking the union of the enunciator and the addressee. We can thus see how, in a text, one-off discourse acts only assume meaning through their insertion into hierarchical structures with greater levels of complexity. It is precisely at this point that it becomes necessary to pass from micro-textual organization (sentences/periods) to meso-textual and macro-textual structuring.

3 Meso-textual and macro-textual levels

3.1 The meso-textual structuring level

Awareness of the written text as an independent act and no longer as a transcription of oral expression has encouraged the emergence of a linguistic study of *textual punctuation* and of the 'visi-legibility' (Moirand 1978) of subdivisions marked by

---

[28] "C'est prier quelqu'un de se rendre quelque part ou d'assister à quelque chose [. . .] ; de plus, en invitant, on présuppose généralement [. . .] que ce à quoi l'on convie l'allocutaire est bon pour lui."

'indentations in writing' (Peytard 1982).²⁹ In accordance with the concept of 'textual image', which has since been developed by Franck Neveu (2000, 2 [on-line]),³⁰ we can distinguish two types of phenomena in textual punctuation:

- *Modulation phenomena*, envisaged by Neveu (2000), are 'typographical additions' such as italics, bold characters, underlining, quotation marks, and different graphic emphasis processes such as 'punctuating signs of affectivity'.³¹ These phenomena, linked to the enunciative requirements of the written text, have been very well described by Véronique Dahlet in *Ponctuation et énonciation* (2003). In the 1940 political poster, utterances such as c1 and c16 simultaneously use capitals, bold characters, and centering; paragraphs c2 and c3 use italics, centered text and an exclamation mark – a form of punctuation with dramatic effect.
- *Segmentation phenomena (graphic boundaries)*:

    > [. . .] engaged in mechanisms for grading locality zones and forming intra-phrasal or transphrasal graphic boundaries: punctuation for detaching and closing syntactic segments, ways of inserting textual sequences into enveloping structures, titles, types of plans – numeric, alphanumeric, etc. –, numbering and volumetric structure of paragraphs, managing indented lines and spaces, etc. (Neveu 2000, 2 [on-line])³²

In speaking of "sequence punctuation", Dahlet describes these *segmentation phenomena* as 'means of marking out, grouping/ungrouping, and grading contents' (2003, 52).³³ This idea was already present in Laufer's work; for him, "Typographical enhancement visually articulates the depth of text levels" (1986, 76).³⁴ This is valid both at the meso-textual level of paragraphs and typographical sentences which make up the text and at the macro-textual level of sections, parts, chapters and peritextual boundaries.

I therefore believe it is useful to distinguish between *meso-textual segmentation phenomena* (the indented line and the paragraph) and *macro-textual segmentation phenomena* (titles, subtitles and intertitles, numeric and alphanumeric

---

29 "[V]i-lisibilité" (Moirand 1978); "entailles scripturales" (Peytard 1982).
30 "[I]mage textuelle" (Neveu 2000).
31 "[S]ignes ponctuants de l'affectivité" (Neveu 2000).
32 "[E]ngagés dans les mécanismes de hiérarchisation des zones de localité et qui forment des frontières graphiques intraphrastiques ou transphrastiques : ponctuation de détachement et de clôture des segments syntaxiques, modes d'insertion des séquences textuelles dans les structures englobantes, titres, types de plans – numériques, alphanumériques, etc. –, numérotation et structure volumétrique des paragraphes, gestion des alinéas et des espaces, etc."
33 "Ponctuation de séquence", "moyens de baliser, regrouper/dégrouper et hiérarchiser les contenus".
34 "La mise en valeur typographique articule visuellement la profondeur des niveaux textuels."

levels, inserted spaces, etc.). At the meso-textual level, the *simple indented line* demarcates the graphic boundary of the paragraph by virtue of being set back and having a space at the end of the line (hollow line). At the macro-textual level, the *marked indented line* with a space of one or several lines between *paragraphs* enables boundaries of groups of paragraphs, and therefore the parts of a text plan, to be marked out.

Starting a new line in order to begin a fresh paragraph serves to highlight a clause or a period forming a graphic sentence, or to group a set of sentences/periods which have close links. This enables the direct discourse to be disconnected (or not) from its narrative or argumentative co-text, for example; a narrative to be separated from the dialogal or argumentative or explanatory co-text in which it is inserted; a descriptive block of text to be detached; a description to be broken up into sections or a narrative into episodes, and so on.

Psycholinguists and linguists make the *paragraph* not only a unit of text segmentation, but also an index of the writer's *metadiscursive* activity, the trace of an "explicit effort to organize the enunciation with the particular aim of facilitating the task of interpretation" (Charolles 1988, 9).[35] Much empirical and experimental research has shown that segmentation into paragraphs facilitates and programs reading because, through notches or indentations between paragraphs and between sections grouping sets of paragraphs, it gives instructions for the temporary maintenance of information in the working memory and the linking of this textual information by stages or processing loops. Le Ny has summarized this in a formula repeated many times: "Now stop incorporating the information I communicate to you with what has preceded it, and open a new sub-structure" (1985, 133).[36] Paragraphs thus facilitate access to the topic organization of the text (Albaladejo Mayordomo/García Berrio 1983, 167). The progressive packaging of meaning is made necessary by the limits of the buffer memory and working memory. Memory space needs to be freed up in order to process new information.

In fact, the meso-textual structuring stage includes two units which are very easily combined: *segments* at the level of graphic segmentation and *groupings of sentences/periods in macro-propositions* (henceforth referred to as MP) at the semantic level.

---

[35] "[T]ravail explicite d'organisation de l'énonciation visant en particulier à faciliter la tâche de l'interprétation".
[36] "Maintenant cessez d'agréger l'information que je vous transmets à ce qui a précédé, et ouvrez une nouvelle sous-structure."

```
                        MESO-TEXTUAL LEVEL
         ┌──────────────────────────────────────────┐
              GRAPHICALLY        ⇔      SEMANTICALLY
               SEGMENTS                 SENTENCES/PERIODS GROUPINGS
                                        INTO MACRO-PROPOSITIONS (MP)
                /      \                    /            \
           VERSE      SENTENCES      SUBSUMED        PROTOTYPED SEQUENCES
                     (TYPO)GRAPHICS  UNDER A MP       OF RELATED MP
             │          │                            /     |      \
             │          │                     Narration  Dialogue  Explanation
             │          │                     Description  Argumentation
          STANZAS    PARAGRAPH
```

Diagram 3: Meso-textual level.

As units of meaning, the *segments* marked by new lines are made up of an indeterminate number of linked *clauses* within graphic sentences and periods. The new line confers upon the paragraph (or the stanza in the case of texts in verse) a *connectedness* and *semantic cohesion* that are subsumable by at least one MP. MPs correspond to sequences of processing during which groupings of clauses, sentences and periods end up constructing units of meaning of a higher level of complexity. These groupings form either free MPs or MPs linked to several other MPs (an *argument*-MP to a *conclusion*-MP in an argumentative sequence, a *node*-MP to a *dénouement*-MP, and a *final situation*-MP to an *initial situation*-MP in a narrative sequence,[37] a *question*-MP to a *response*-MP in a dialogal sequence (or exchange) sequence, and a *why?*-MP to a *because*-MP in an explanatory sequence).

Longacre's typology of paragraphs (1980) gives an idea of types of MP and the elementary links that can unite them: *Coordinate & Alternative paragraphs*; *Temporal paragraphs*; *Antithetical & Contrast paragraphs*; *Paragraphs that encode logical relations*; *Embellishment paragraphs*; and *Interaction paragraphs*, to which might also be added: *Hortatory paragraphs, Procedural paragraphs*, and *Explanatory paragraphs*. Arabyan (1994 ; 2012) and Gardes Tamine/Pellizza (1998) opted for a simplified typology, distinguishing *thematic paragraphs*, which

---

37 In his *Apostille au nom de la rose* 'Reflections on the name of the rose', Umberto Eco alludes to this concept of *macro-proposition*: "In narrative, the breath is not confined to sentences, but to broader macro-propositions, to scansions of events." (1985, 50).

relate to distinct objects of discourse; *enunciative paragraphs*, which highlight a change of speaker, a new discourse act (question, exclamation, response, etc.), or a commentary on a description or an action; and *generic paragraphs*, which involve strong typological characterization, in the form of argumentative, narrative, or descriptive segments. These paragraphs, incorrectly described as "generic", are close to what I consider to be *sequences*: descriptive sequences, narrative sequences (a narratized version of Longacre's simple *temporal paragraphs*), argumentative sequences, explanatory sequences, or dialogal sequences (corresponding to Longacre's *interaction paragraphs*). We should not confuse the dual organization of discourse by *discursive genres*, on the one hand, and by 'the rules, running across genres, which govern a narrative, a dialogue, an argumentation, an explanation...' on the other (Maingueneau 2014, 19).[38] At a pre-generic meso-textual level, which therefore runs across genres, sequences are transphrasal periodic organizations articulating and grading groups of utterances into several linked MPs.

Like discourse genres, sequential meso-structurings have to be mastered in the same way as learning a language. When we learn the language of a social group, we are simultaneously learning the discursive genre systems in which this language is produced and which constrain it; but we also learn to distinguish what Swales (1990) considers to be *pre-generic* forms. My book on the theory of sequences (Adam 2017) theorizes five of these preformatted ways of articulating series of sentences/periods in packages of linked MPs. Although in this preformatted *sequential packaging* each MP is made up of an indeterminate number of clauses, each type of sequence contains a specific number of basic MPs that have strong links with one another; they are even arranged in order, except in the case of the descriptive sequence, which is less hierarchized and has a less restrictive order than that of the four other types of sequences. Each of these MPs can form a paragraph or the linked MPs can be grouped within a single paragraph.

In my example and its translation, the particular feature of clause c1 is that it covers the whole of the text of the poster. It functions macro-textually as a title (its scope covers the entire text) and as the cue to a generic epistolary form (an open letter disseminated by means of a poster). It is not part of a sequential meso-textual composition, and its typography, very different from the rest of the text, confirms this separate status.

On the other hand, the paragraph effect produced by the new lines setting c2 and c3 apart from one another is somewhat reduced by the italic characters, the

---

[38] "[L]es règles, transversales aux genres, qui gouvernent un récit, un dialogue, une argumentation, une explication".

centering, the connective, the two exclamation marks, and the morpho-syntactic parallelism which unite c2 and c3.

Although the translation respects this modulation and segmentation of the initial clauses, this is not so when it comes to c14 and c15, although they follow the same model of creating fresh lines and centering the two paragraphs (without the italics). The absence of the strong parallelism seen in c2 and c3 no doubt explains the translators' decision to group these two clauses into a single paragraph (§5) with a single unit of meaning (reinforced by the anaphor), rather than two utterances of equal force as in the French text. The link between cause (c14) and consequence (c15) is strengthened by the unity formed by the paragraph.

Conversely, clause c12 is detached from paragraph §2 to become a paragraph in its own right (§3) in the translation. Consequently, the strongly modulated exclamatory clause no longer forms the simple conclusion to paragraph 2: it is highlighted and thereby forms a parallel with c13 (§4 of the translation), a parallelism which is absent from T1. The direct consequence of this parallelism is to weaken the force of c13, which is graphically emphasized in T1 by being made one of the five central paragraphs in the body of the open letter.

At this sequential level, the argumentative structure formed by c2-MAIS-c3 does not develop as an argumentative sequence. On the other hand, the three paragraphs of T1 grouping c4 and c5 (§1), c6 to c12 (§2), and c13 (§3) are consistent with an explanatory sequential movement. With clauses c4 and c5, a *problematic situation* is set out and forms the MP which triggers the explanatory movement ($MP^{ex}0$): how to declare that "nothing is lost" when the French army has just been crushed? The assertion is repeated in c6, at the beginning of the second paragraph, and the implicit demand for justification – *pourquoi ?/why?* ($MP^{ex}1$) – is answered by the *"parce que/because"* that opens c7. The explanation is set out at length from c7 to c12 ($MP^{ex}2$). The paragraph beginning with "*Voilà pourquoi/ That is why*" very explicitly introduces the definitive closure of the explanation ($MP^{ex}3$). As we have just seen, the translation (T2) obscures this sequential structure whereas T1 makes it visible and legible.

3.2 The macro-textual structuring level

The impression of overall unity of a verbal whole, generating a *textuality effect*, results from the *semantic cohesion* that a title is able to impart and from the *interactional coherence of a discursive macro-action* summarized by the moral maxim of a fable or tale; and, in the case of the political poster taken as example, the fact that it is globally described as "the June 1940 Appeal" or "General de Gaulle's Appeal".

Every text appears as a combination of the linear (connectedness oriented by the written word constrained by language) and of two non-linear modes of constructing meaning: the perception of a wholeness of meaning which creates the text's unity (*configurational structuring*) and the perception of recurrent and co-occurring networks of vocabulary items (*reticular structuring*). Legallois very rightly notes that 'The reticular organization of the text is in perfect harmony with the etymology of the word *text*. It is indeed a *fabric* of entangled sentences, a *weft*, a *texture*, an entire construction and conception of a complex object that is revealed by analysis of the lexical repetition in discourse' (2006, 70).[39] As we have seen, the identification of repetitions or collocations of vocabulary items is an important cohesive factor. Co-occurrences are a determining element of textuality. Going from the lexicon (in language) to the vocabulary that is specific to a text (its structuring in vocabulary items) demands a view and methods that are free of linearity, like the automatic processing of textual data (Viprey 2006a; 2006b).

This dual inter-phrasal (micro-textual) and trans-phrasal (meso-textual) interweaving produces a 'network of determinations' (Weinrich 1973, 174)[40] which turn any text into an organized system of "interdependent relationships". The reticular distribution of temporal-verb forms all along the surface of the text was described by Weinrich very early on: 'Temporal forms first come to us – and come back to us – through texts. That is where, together with other signs, and also with other times, they form a complex of determinations, a network of textual values [. . .]' (1973, 13).[41] As we saw earlier, temporal-verb forms are linked in levels of enunciation whose catenations (continuity and disconnections) go well beyond the sentential boundaries within which certain linguistic descriptions confine them, instead of recording groupings of local sub-sets.

In the segmentation of a text-plan, a title and intertitles are markers of the configurational structuring which summarizes, generally through nominal utterances, the *thematic cohesion* of an entire text or of its parts and sub-parts, which themselves go to make up so many units of meaning. A text-plan makes macro-textual segments more or less visible and legible and these, between the title and the

---

39 "L'organisation réticulaire du texte est en parfaite congruence avec l'étymologie du mot *texte*. C'est bien un *tissu* de phrases enchevêtrées, une *trame*, une *texture*, toute une construction et une conception d'un objet complexe que met en évidence l'analyse de la répétition lexicale dans les discours."
40 "Réseau de determinations".
41 "Les formes temporelles viennent d'abord à nous – et nous reviennent – à travers des textes. C'est là qu'elles dessinent, avec d'autres signes, et aussi avec d'autres temps, un complexe de déterminations, un réseau de valeurs textuelles. . ."

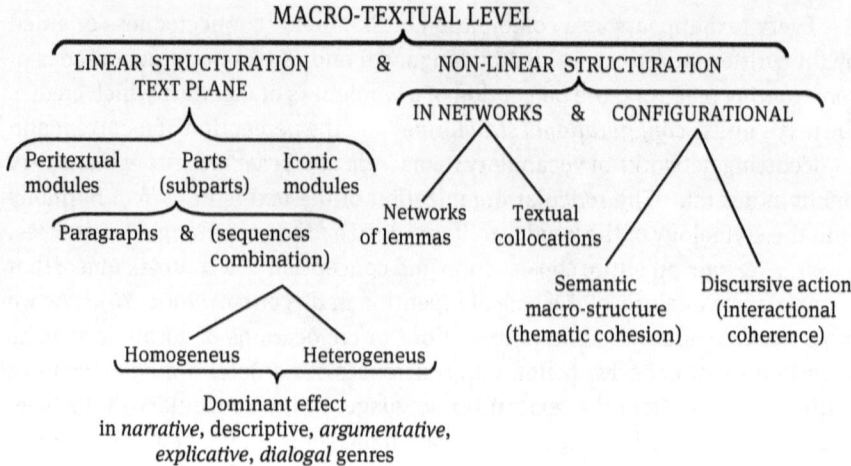

Diagram 4: Macro-textual level.

final full stop, organize the meaning in *paragraphs*, *groups of paragraphs*, *parts*, *sub-parts*, and *chapters*. This visi-legibility is the result of cooperation between the white macro-punctuation (new lines, intercalated spaces, page breaks) and black macro-punctuation (intertitles, decimal or alphabetic numbering, bullet points or dashes at the beginning of lines). The degree of visi-legibility of text-plans depends on the number of peritextual utterances and the (typo)graphical segmentation. The minimal peritext of a text-plan is the presence of a *title* but it is also possible to add a *subtitle*, an *introductory paragraph*, a *summary*, a *dedication* and an *epigraph*, a *preface* and a *postface*, *intertitles*, *numbering of sections* or *place (order number) of a text in a collection*, and *illustrations* (together with their captions), to which *notes* may be added. Internal peritextual utterances mark the boundaries of the sub-parts to create so many sub-units of meaning. This is the case with editions of journals and collective works, magazines and the written press, manuals and encyclopedias, and collections of articles, tales, short stories, anecdotes, funny stories, or poems. *Summaries* and *tables of contents* generally encapsulate these text-plans.[42]

It is important to include in the concept of *text-plan* not only the verbal peritextual modules or components, but also the iconic peritextual components

---

[42] I refer the reader here to Genette's (1987) work on the *peritext*, to Dionne's (2008) history of the division into chapters in romantic prose, or to footnote references and types of notes in Lefebvre (2011).

(vignette, photos, graphics, illustrations and captions to illustrations, tailpieces, and floral borders). These graphic modules are particularly important in pluri-semiotic iconotexts like cooking recipes, written press articles, advertisements, posters and the like, but also in encyclopedias and schoolbooks, illustrated books or ones including a writer and an artist.

By way of example, the preformatted plan of display advertisements published in the press or on city posters may link *three verbal modules*: an *eye-catching slogan*, a *basic slogan and/or brand* and a *write-up*, to which must be added – for certain products such as tobacco and alcohol – a legal warning; *two iconic modules*: an *eye-catching image* (photographed or drawn) creating a referential context or world and an *image of the product* that is strongly referential and denotative; and finally *two mixed modules*: a *logo* and *brand name* in which the verbal is very strongly iconized. These modules form a repertoire of optional and complementary parts that each publicity iconotext makes use of in an original way.

Being dependent on the languages, genres and intertextual models circulating in a given social sphere, text-plans are subject to tension between, on the one hand, the type of non-repeatable enunciative event that characterizes any unique text and, on the other hand, the more or less strong preformatting by *discursive genres* and *pre-generic sequences*. This means that "top-down" factors, which form part of the stores of knowledge about subjects, can generate text-plans that are more or less close to a preformatted pattern. In this case, both production and interpretation start from this preliminary global information in order to organize textual information in graded segments. The work of interpretation is then facilitated by the recognition, in local details, of traces of this organization stored in the inter-discursive memory. These schematic textual patterns are applied in the case of a specific text and adjusted, or even modified, in the light of each new application.

Genres influence the distribution of the narration, dialogue, description, argumentation, and explanation: a fairy tale usually has as much narration as dialogue, but very little description and an optional moral in the form of an argumentation; a theater play is largely dominated by dialogue with very little description; a *narrative exemplum* is, unsurprisingly, inserted in an argumentation; an etiological tale is inserted in an explanatory endeavor with the word *why?*; in an anecdote or funny story, the sudden fall in the narrative usually takes the form of a pun; and so on.[43]

---

[43] I make a study of these various cases in *Genres de récits. Narrativité et généricité des textes* (Adam 2011).

To return to our example of the Liberation poster, the particular feature of posters is that they are iconotexts, combining text (verbal) and image (iconic) in variable quantities. This poster is distinctive in that it does not include a great deal of iconography (just two tricolor flags and the frame, which is also tricolored). It is the verbal element that dominates, together with the page layout, to the extent that this text creates an image by virtue of the way in which the utterances are arranged on the page-poster and by the different sizes and shapes of the typographical characters used: large capitals, small italics, and Roman characters of the same size, a handwritten signature and small capitals for the signatory's address. The poster was created in two versions: three successive print runs with British-style tricolor framing – blue on the outside, red on the inside and with the English translation T2 in the left-hand corner. The second type of poster, from September 1944, did not include this translation and its French frame was red on the outside and blue on the inside.

The comparison of the translation with the French text is illuminating. Although the number of utterances does not change (the translation is very faithful), the typography is different, as we have seen, and this is particularly the case at the end of the text. The visual segmentation of the French poster consists of three substantially differentiated rows of typography, which gives a text-plan in the form of an embedded structure: [A1 [B1 [3§] B2] A2] leading to three levels of reading: A1 & A1 in very large characters, then B1 & B2, then three central paragraphs in smaller characters.

- A1 (c1) & A2 (c16) = Large capitals, centered, in bold characters.
- B = Two lines justified in the center: B1 (c2–c3) in italic characters, B2 (c14–c15) in Roman characters. This creates a textual structure with an echo: c14 and c15 reflect c2 and c3, thus creating a minimal text that can be read quickly.
- Three paragraphs justified to the left, in smaller Roman characters which demand more attentive reading of the framed text.

The translation repeats A1 and A2 (capitals, bold characters, and centered) and B1 (italics, centered), but it modifies B2, which is included after the paragraphs justified to the left (five paragraphs instead of three, in smaller characters).

This typographical arrangement, including the signature (c17) and the London address (c18) form a text-plan that is very close to epistolary genres, where the plan is based on the rhetorical model of the *disposition* (with the exordium and peroration framing the argumentative body of the letter). However, this structure is not so much linear as embedded, with two rows of legibility of a text-frame and a framed text:

TEXT-PLAN OF THE POSTER

	OPENING <A1>	CLOSURE
	Term of address (c1)	Signature & address (c17-18)
Row 1 of	EXORDIUM <B1>	PERORATION <B2 & A2>
legibility	Italics (c2-3)	(c14-15 & c16)
	ARGUMENTATIVE BODY OF THE LETTER	
Row 2 of	Refutation <<< Explanation >>> Appeal	
legibility	§1 (c4-5) §2 (c6 à c12) §3 (c13)	

Diagram 5: Text-plan.

The translations change the way the peroration is highlighted by including c14 and c15 in the body of the letter, to form the concluding paragraph, and by appearing to limit the peroration to c16. Clauses c14 and c15 therefore no longer echo c2 and c3, destroying the reading of the embedded textual structure, which thus becomes more linear: c2 and c3 become an introductory paragraph to the text formed of five paragraphs and framed by clauses c1 and c16 in very large, bold characters.

4 Concluding remarks

> From the 1960s – that is to say at the same time as discourse analysis – a new discipline developed, namely text linguistics, which, aiming to uncover regularities beyond the sentence, provided discourse analysts with valuable tools for understanding how texts are structured. (Maingueneau 2014, 12)[44]

Everything that involves inter-phrasals/periodics and trans-phrasals/periodics, and all that contributes to the dynamic of meaning within a unit of communication-interaction with a beginning and end, is the subject of text linguistics. Discursivity, on the other hand, resides in the uniting of a text or some of its utterances to an inter-discourse and to genres of discourse. Indeed, no text is totally closed upon itself, unlike the impression given by the promotion of structural closure methodology. Like it or not, any *textual effect* is accompanied by an *effect of genericity* and is thus part of an uninterrupted chain of discourse. For a text to

---

44 "À partir des années 1960 – c'est-à-dire en même temps que l'analyse du discours –, s'est développée une nouvelle discipline, la linguistique textuelle, qui, visant à dégager des régularités au-delà de la phrase, fournissait aux analystes du discours des instruments précieux pour appréhender la structuration des textes."

acquire meaning, it has to be projected against "the background of a pre-existing discursive pattern" (Stierle 1977, 427),[45] as well as being identifiable (possibly deviantly) by reference to the *system of discursive genres* of a social group and of a given period.

At the point of articulating the textual and discursive, *discourse genres* play a decisive role, and they influence the distribution of components in the three stages of textualization. These top-down determinations combine with bottom-up determinations.

Following Maingueneau in this respect, I advocate both a strong distinction and an explicit complementarity between the fields of text linguistics and discourse analysis. The purpose of text linguistics is not to theorize and describe genres of discourse; this task is the responsibility of discourse analysis and it plays a highly important role in textual analyses, which have to take account of the influence of discourse genres on the shaping of a text and on the singular use of language made in that text. The task of text linguistics is therefore to provide discourse analysis – and literary stylistics, the theory of argumentation, and all disciplines dealing with texts – with the textual theory that they need.

References

Adam, Jean-Michel, *Ordre du texte, ordre du discours*, Pratiques 13 (1977), 103–111, DOI: https://doi.org/10.3406/prati.1977.987.

Adam, Jean-Michel, *Éléments de linguistique textuelle. Théorie et pratique de l'analyse textuelle*, Bruxelles, Mardaga, 1990.

Adam, Jean-Michel, *Genres de récits. Narrativité et généricité des textes*, Louvain-la-Neuve, Academia/L'Harmattan, 2011.

Adam, Jean-Michel, *Problèmes du texte. Leçons d'Aarhus*, Pré-Publications 200, Aarhus, Fransk Institut for Æstetik og Kommunikation/Aarhus Universitet, 2013, https://docplayer.fr/8410133-Problemes-du-texte-la-linguistique-textuelle-et-la-traduction.html. [last consultation: 10.04.2020]

Adam, Jean-Michel (ed.), *Faire texte. Frontières textuelles et opérations de textualisation*, Besançon, Presses universitaires de Franche-Comté, 2015.

Adam, Jean-Michel, *Les textes. Types et prototypes*, Paris, Armand Colin, ⁴2017.

Adam, Jean-Michel, *Le paragraphe. Entre phrases et texte*, Paris, Armand Colin, 2018.

Adam, Jean-Michel, *La linguistique textuelle. Introduction à l'analyse textuelle des discours*, Paris, Armand Colin, ⁴2019.

Albaladejo Mayordomo, Tomás/García Berrio, Antonio, *Estructura composicional. Macroestructuras*, Estudios de Lingüística 1, Universidad de Alicante (1983), 127–180.

---

[45] "[L]'arrière-plan d'un schème discursif préexistant".

Algee-Hewitt, Marc/Heuser, Ryan/Moretti, Franco, *On paragraphs. Scale, themes, and narrative form*, Pamphlets of the Stanford Literary Lab 10 (2015), 1–22, https://litlab.stanford.edu/LiteraryLabPamphlet10.pdf. [last consultation: 10.04.2020]
Allison, Sarah/Gemma, Marissa/Heuser, Ryan/Moretti, Franco/Tevel, Amir/Yamboliev, Irena, *Style at the scale of the sentence*, Pamphlets of the Stanford Literary Lab 5 (2013), 1–29, https://litlab.stanford.edu/LiteraryLabPamphlet5.pdf. [last consultation: 10.06.2022]
Arabyan, Marc, *Le paragraphe narratif*, Paris, L'Harmattan, 1994.
Arabyan, Marc, *Des lettres de l'alphabet à l'image du texte. Recherches sur l'énonciation écrite*, Limoges, Lambert-Lucas, 2012.
Benveniste, Émile, *Problèmes de linguistique générale*, vol. 2, Paris, Gallimard, 1974.
Berrendonner, Alain, *Pour une macro-syntaxe*, Travaux de linguistique 21 (1990), 25–36.
Berrendonner, Alain, *Les deux syntaxes*, Verbum 24 (2002), 23–35.
Charolles, Michel, *Les plans d'organisation textuelle. Périodes, chaînes, portées et séquences*, Pratiques 57 (1988), 3–13, DOI: https://doi.org/10.3406/prati.1988.1468.
Charolles, Michel, *Les plans d'organisation du discours et leurs interactions*, in: Moirand, Sophie/Ali Bouacha, Abdelmadjid/Beacco, Jean-Claude/Collinot, André (edd.), *Parcours linguistiques de discours spécialisés. Actes du colloque en Sorbonne (Paris, septembre 1992)*, Berne, Peter Lang, 1993, 301–314.
Coirier, Pierre/Gaonac'h, Daniel/Passerault, Jean-Michel (edd.), *Psycholinguistique textuelle. Une approche cognitive de la compréhension et de la production des textes*, Paris, Armand Colin, 1996.
Combettes, Bernard, *Ordre des éléments de la phrase et linguistique du texte*, Pratiques 13 (1977), 91–101, DOI: https://doi.org/10.3406/prati.1977.986.
Combettes, Bernard, *Pour une grammaire textuelle. La progression thématique*, Bruxelles/Paris, De Boeck/Duculot, 1983.
Conte, Maria-Elisabeth, *Anaphoric encapsulation*, in: Conte, Maria-Elisabeth, *Condizione di coerenza*, Alessandria, Edizioni dell'Orso, 1999, 107–114.
Coseriu, Eugenio, *L'homme et son langage*, Louvain/Paris, Peeters, 2001.
Coseriu, Eugenio, *Lingüística del texto. Introducción a la hermenéutica del sentido*, ed. Loureda Lamas, Óscar, Madrid, Arco/Libros, 2007.
Culioli, Antoine, *Préface*, in: Grésillon, Almuth/Lebrave, Jean-Louis/Atlani, Françoise/Danon-Boileau, Laurent/Simonin, Jenny (edd.), *La langue au ras du texte*, Villeneuve-d'Ascq, Presses universitaires de Lille, 1984, 9–12.
Dahlet, Véronique, *Ponctuation et énonciation*, Guyane, Ibis rouge, 2003.
Daneš, František, *De la structure sémantique et thématique du message*, Linguistique et sémiologie 5, Presses universitaires de Lyon (1978), 177–200.
Degand, Liesbeth/Martin, Laurence J./Simon, Anne-Catherine, *Unités discursives de base et leur périphérie gauche dans LOCAS-F, un corpus oral multigenre annoté*, in: Neveu, Franck/Blumenthal, Peter/Hriba, Linda/Gerstenberg, Annette/Meinschaefer, Judith/Prévost, Sophie (edd.), *Actes du 4ᵉ Congrès Mondial de Linguistique Française, Berlin, 19–23 juillet 2014*, SHS Web of Conferences 8, Paris, Institut de linguistique française, 2014, DOI: https://doi.org/10.1051/shsconf/20140801211.
Dionne, Ugo, *La voie aux chapitres. Poétique de la disposition romanesque*, Paris, Seuil, 2008.
Eco, Umberto, *Lector in fabula*, Milan, Bompiani, 1979; *Lector in fabula*, trad. Bouzaher, Myriam, Paris, Grasset, 1985.
Eco, Umberto, *Reflections on the name of the rose*, London, Secker & Warburg, ²1985.

Firbas, Jan, *On defining the theme in functional sentence analysis*, Travaux linguistiques de Prague, vol. 1 (1964), 267–280.

Gardes Tamine, Joëlle, *Pour une grammaire de l'écrit*, Paris, Belin, 2004.

Gardes Tamine, Joëlle/Pellizza, Marie-Antoinette, *La construction du texte. De la grammaire au style*, Paris, Armand Colin, 1998.

Genette, Gérard, *Seuils*, Paris, Seuil, 1987.

Givón, Talmy (ed.), *Topic continuity in discourse. A quantitative cross-language study*, Amsterdam/Philadelphia, John Benjamins, 1983.

Givón, Talmy, *L'approche fonctionnelle de la grammaire*, Verbum 20 (1998), 257–288.

Greimas, Algirdas Julien, *Maupassant. La sémiotique du texte: exercices pratiques*, Paris, Seuil, 1976.

Groupe de Fribourg, *Grammaire de la période*, Berne, Peter Lang, 2012.

Groupe µ, *Rhétorique générale*, Paris, Larousse, 1970.

Halliday, Michael Alexander Kirkwood, *Notes on transitivity and theme in English*, Journal of linguistics 3 (1967), 199–244 and Journal of linguistics 4 (1968), 179–215.

Halliday, Michael Alexander Kirkwood/Hasan, Ruqaiya, *Cohesion in English*, London/New York, Longman, 1976.

Harris, Zellig Sabbetai, *Discourse analysis*, Language 28 (1952), 1–30.

Herman, Thierry, *Au fil des discours. La rhétorique de Charles de Gaulle 1940–1945*, Limoges, Lambert-Lucas, 2008.

Laufer, Roger, *L'énonciation typographique. Hier et demain*, Communication et langages 68 (1986), 68–85, DOI: https://doi.org/10.3406/colan.1986.1762.

Lefebvre, Julie, *L'appel-renvoi de note comme observatoire de l'interpénétration des ponctuations blanche et noire*, Langue française 172 (2011), 69–82, DOI: https://doi.org/10.3917/lf.172.0069.

Lefebvre, Julie, *"Nous le verrons plus bas", "voir ci-dessus", "je ne reviens pas ici". Retour sur les propriétés de la langue écrite*, in: Neveu, Franck/Blumenthal, Peter/Hriba, Linda/Gerstenberg, Annette/Meinschaefer, Judith/Prévost, Sophie (edd.), *Actes du 4ᵉ Congrès Mondial de Linguistique Française, Berlin, 19–23 juillet 2014*, SHS Web of Conferences 8, Paris, Institut de linguistique française, 2014, DOI: https://doi.org/10.1051/shsconf/20140801264.

Legallois, Dominique, *Des phrases entre elles à l'unité réticulaire du texte*, Langages 163 (2006), 56–70, DOI: https://doi.org/10.3917/lang.163.0056.

Le Goffic, Pierre, *Phrase et intégration textuelle*, Langue française 170 (2011), 11–28, DOI: https://doi.org/10.3917/lf.170.0011.

Le Ny, Jean-François, *Texte, structure mentale, paragraphe*, in: Laufer, Roger (ed.), *La notion de paragraphe*, Paris, CNRS Éditions, 1985, 129–136.

Longacre, Robert E., *Discourse, paragraph and sentence structure in selected Philippine languages*, vol. 2: *Sentence structure*, Santa Ana, Summer Institute of Linguistics, 1968.

Longacre, Robert E., *An apparatus for the identification of paragraph types*, Notes on Linguistics 15 (1980), 5–23.

Longacre, Robert E., *The discourse strategy of an appeals letter*, in: Mann, William C./Thompson, Sandra A., *Discourse description. Diverse linguistic analyses of a fund-raising text*, Amsterdam, John Benjamins, 1992, 109–130.

Maingueneau, Dominique, *Discours et analyse du discours. Une introduction*, Paris, Armand Colin, 2014.

Mathesius, Vilém, *Les thèses de 1929*, Change 3 (^{2}1969), 21–49.

Moirand, Sophie, *Les textes aussi sont des images*, Le Français dans le monde 137 (1978); reproduced in Moirand, Sophie, *Situations d'écrit. Compréhension, production en langue étrangère*, Paris, CLE International, 1979, 74–91.
Neveu, Franck, *De la syntaxe à l'image textuelle. Ponctuation et niveaux d'analyse linguistique*, La Licorne 52 (2000), 201–215, https://licorne.edel.univ-poitiers.fr/index.php?id=5688. [last consultation: 01.08.2014]
Ohori, Toshio/Takahashi, Etsuko/Yamada, Aki/Yanagiya, Keiko, *Discourse and paragraph. Visions and revisions*, The Geibun-Kenkyu. Journal of arts and letters 48 (1986), 15–28.
Peytard, Jean, *Instances et entailles du texte littéraire*, in: Peytard, Jean (ed.), *Littérature et classe de langue. Français langue étrangère*, Paris, Hatier/Credif, 1982, 139–155.
Prandi, Michele, *Les fondements méthodologiques d'une grammaire descriptive de l'italien*, Langages 167 (2007), 70–84, DOI: https://doi.org/10.3917/lang.167.0070.
Prandi, Michele, *L'analisi del periodo*, Roma, Carocci, 2013.
Reichler-Béguelin, Marie-José, *Anaphore, cataphore et mémoire discursive*, Pratiques 57 (1988), 15–43, DOI: https://doi.org/10.3406/prati.1988.1470.
Riegel, Martin, *Cohérence textuelle et grammaire phrastique*, in: Calas, Frédéric (ed.), *Cohérence et discours*, Paris, Presses de l'université Paris-Sorbonne, 2006, 53–64.
Ruwet, Nicolas, *Parallélismes et déviations en poésie*, in: Kristeva, Julia/Milner, Jean-Claude/Ruwet, Nicolas (edd.), *Langue, discours, société. Pour Émile Benveniste*, Paris, Seuil, 1975, 307–351.
Simon, Anne-Catherine/Degand, Liesbeth, *L'analyse en unités discursives de base. Pourquoi et comment?*, Langue française 170 (2011), 45–59, DOI: https://doi.org/10.3917/lf.170.0045.
Slakta, Denis, *L'ordre du texte*, Études de linguistique appliquée 19 (1975), 30–42.
Soutet, Olivier, *Linguistique*, Paris, Presses universitaires de France, ^{4}2005.
Spillner, Bernd, *Lingüística y literatura*, Madrid, Gredos, 1979.
Stati, Sorin, *Le transphrastique*, Paris, Presses universitaires de France, 1990.
Stierle, Karlheinz, *Identité du discours et transgression lyrique*, Poétique 32 (1977), 422–441.
Swales, John M., *Genre analysis. English in academic and research settings*, Cambridge, Cambridge University Press, 1990.
Vanderveken, Daniel, *Les actes de discours*, Bruxelles, Mardaga, 1988.
Vanderveken, Daniel, *La théorie des actes de discours et l'analyse de la conversation*, Cahiers de linguistique française 13 (1992), 9–61.
Van Dijk, Teun A., *Text grammar and text logic*, in: Petöfi, János S./Rieser, Hannes (edd.), *Studies in text grammar*, Dordrecht/Boston, Reidel, 1973, 17–78.
Van Dijk, Teun A., *Episodes as units of discourse analysis*, in: Tannen, Deborah (ed.), *Analyzing discourse. Text and talk*, Washington, Georgetown University Press, 1981, 177–195.
Vetters, Carl (ed.), *Le temps. De la phrase au texte*, Villeneuve-d'Ascq, Presses universitaires de Lille, 1993.
Viehweger, Dieter, *Savoir illocutoire et interprétation des textes*, in: Charolles, Michel/Fischer, Sophie/Jayez, Jacques (edd.), *Le discours. Représentations et interprétations*, Nancy, Presses universitaires de Nancy, 1990, 41–51.
Viprey, Jean-Marie, *Quelle place pour les sciences des textes dans l'analyse de discours?*, Semen 21 (2006), 167–182, DOI: https://doi.org/10.4000/semen.1995 (= 2006a).
Viprey, Jean-Marie, *Structure non-séquentielle des textes*, Langages 163 (2006), 71–85, DOI: https://doi.org/10.3917/lang.163.0071 (= 2006b).
Weinrich, Harald, *Tempus*, Stuttgart, Kohlhammer, 1964; *Le Temps*, transl. Lacoste, Michèle, Paris, Seuil, 1973.

Michel Charolles
Chapter 2
"Framing adverbials" as markers of discourse organization

Abstract: This paper is situated at the crossroads of text and discourse, where tools guarantee cohesion and coherence, in continuous association. Among these tools are connectors, anaphora, and "framing adverbials": the latter are introducers of sentences whose scope can go beyond the simple sentence; the space thus determined constitutes a "discursive frame", where the truth value of the clause or clauses is governed by this introducer and brought together in this space. In the second part, we show that these introducers, which are factors of cohesion and coherence, do not function solely in scientific or technical text genres, but also in narrative ones.

Keywords: cohesion/coherence, relevance, discourse markers, connectives, anaphora, framing adverbials

Introduction

The understanding of any message is based on a general principle of coherence or relevance (Grice 1975; Sperber/Wilson 1986) which means that listeners or readers can expect the utterances they are hearing/reading to develop a consistent theme whose intelligibility, if it escapes them, can be reconstructed. This principle holds true for all complex verbal productions, from compound words of the type *homme-sandwich* (*sandwich man*),[1] which, in order to be understood requires the meaning to be pieced together, to discourse itself. It is not even specific to

---

[1] To designate people carrying two advertising panels in public spaces, one in front of them and the other behind.

Note: This text first appeared in a book of tributes to Maria-Elizabeth Conte: Charolles, Michel, *Les cadres de discours comme marques d'organisation des discours*, in: Venier, Federica (ed.), *Tra pragmatica e linguistica testuale. Ricordando Maria-Elisabeth Conte*, Alessandria, Edizioni dell'Orso, 2009, 401–420.

Michel Charolles, Université Paris III, LATTICE

language: it is valid for all non-natural behaviors involving successive actions (Charolles 1983).

The application of this principle is conditioned by material factors. In order for it to be applied, the assembled units (actions or verbal productions) have to be produced in a continuous fashion and the participating actors or witnesses must have cues leading them to think that these productions belong to a same "action plan". When these conditions are fulfilled, application of the coherence principle affects the understanding of the verbal or non-verbal actions in question. These effects lie in the fact that the addressees or witnesses will assign, to each of the actions successively accomplished, a plausible intention that seems compatible with the recognized "overall purpose", knowing that this inferred purpose can be revised along the way (Charolles 1995; 2006a). Once it is accepted that verbal or non-verbal actions belong to a "coherent program", understanding the way they may be linked does not exhaust their potential for signification – but it forms the basis for subsequent further interpretations. This is particularly noticeable with pieces of discourse where all kinds of more or less expert extra-linguistic knowledge can lead recipients to think that they convey other significations than those which may be assigned by simply observing the forms of expression they contain and the way these are composed.

Of course, the processes implied in understanding discourse are determined, in the first instance, by the expressions and constructions which go to make them up. At this level, the contribution of linguistic and psycholinguistic analyses is invaluable. But this contribution is no less crucial for recording the activation of scholarly interpretation; a point which will not, however, be addressed in what follows. It is at a relatively basic level of understanding that the different systems of linguistic solidarity contribute in the first instance to the cohesion, and therefore the coherence of verbal productions, from the word right up to the text (cf. Conte/Petöfi/Sözer 1989). Words are the most cohesive linguistic units insofar as they blend complex semantic-conceptual components in an impenetrable form, as may be seen above with *homme-sandwich*. The sentence, as a predicative unit, enables already sophisticated micro-situations to be expressed in a compact structural format. This system offers wide-ranging integration possibilities, notably through the different forms of subordination. These possibilities range from the most integrative structures, such as complement clauses, to the least integrative, such as dislocated constructions and paratactic adverbials which are increasingly free; indeed, some of them end up floating between their host sentence and the one preceding it. Since this system of structural integration is limited, languages offer a whole range of relational lexical markers that allow semantic and pragmatic links between successive clauses or their components to be indicated. These markers give rise to:

- *Rhetorical assemblages* which, when they are indicated, are expressed by connectives
- *Referential assemblages* indicated notably by *anaphoric* forms[2]
- *Circumstantial assemblages* which are induced, as we shall see, by *framing* adverbials

These assemblages develop in parallel, permanently interacting, and guiding readers step by step to construct a coherent interpretation of the text.

In the first section of this chapter, I shall show how certain adverbials, when they are used at the beginning of a sentence, are likely to play a role in organizing the discourse, because they may not only integrate in their scope the content of their host sentence but also that of one or several following sentences (cf. Charolles 1997; Charolles/Prévost 2003; Prévost 2003; Charolles/Péry-Woodley 2005; Vigier/Terran 2005). In the second part, I shall attempt to show that this mode of organization, illustrated by extracts from scientific and technical texts, is also well attested in narrative fictions, namely in two extracts from *Madame Bovary*.[3]

1 Function of framing adverbials

Some prepositional phrases (PPs) can index several sentences following the sentence wherein they are pre-posed.[4] This is the case in the following extract, where the scope of the spatial PP *in France* extends as far as the end of the paragraph:

> (1) '"Strokes", or "cerebral vascular accidents" (CVAs) have a very heavy cost for public health. *In France*, where 140,000 new cases are declared each year, they are the third cause of death and the prime cause of handicap. It has been established that 25% to 30% of patients having suffered a stroke die quickly. And, although a quarter of survivors recover without apparent after-effects, others suffer from handicaps of different nature and amplitude, depending on the extent of the damage and which area of the brain has been affected (paralysis, learning deficit, memory loss, behavioral and motor disturbances).' [Extracts from secondary works are translated by RR, unless indicated otherwise].

---

2 Cf. Conte (1990; 1991).
3 All subsequent translations from other works are by Rosemary Rodwell, the translator of this chapter, unless stated otherwise.
4 The ability of an adverbial to index several sentences is a remarkable phenomenon which grammars generally ignore, because it goes beyond the boundaries of the sentence.

If we compare (1) with (1') where the PP *in France* is inserted in a post-verbal position:

> (1') "Strokes", or "cerebral vascular accidents" (CVAs) have a very heavy cost for public health. 140,000 new cases are declared *in France* each year, where they are the third cause of death and the prime cause of handicap. It has been established that 25% to 30% of patients having suffered a stroke die quickly. And, although a quarter of survivors recover without apparent after-effects, others suffer from handicaps of different nature and amplitude, depending on the extent of the damage and which area of the brain has been affected (paralysis, learning deficit, memory loss, behavioral and motor disturbances).[5]

We see that in (1'), the spatial complement and the temporal complement accompanying it (*each year*) are linked to the predication, even though they are not governed by the verb.[6] This forced link tends to limit their influence to the single sentence in which they appear: for this reason I am inclined to consider that the data mentioned after *it has been established that* concerns all the countries for which statistics on CVAs are available, and not just France, as is the case in the original version.

In the following extract, the detached PPs (in italics) at the beginning of the sentence function as in (1), but they are used in a serial manner, which is very common in expositive texts. These PPs are opposed in the first series (*in many mollusks* versus *in insects*) which is wholly opposed to the following one (*in birds, reptiles and fish* versus *in mammals*), with a transitional sentence (in normal typeface) between the two groups:

---

[5] (1) "Les attaques cérébrales, ou 'accidents vasculaires cérébraux' (AVC) ont un coût très lourd en matière de santé publique. *En France,* où 140 000 nouveaux cas sont déclarés chaque année, elles constituent la troisième cause de mortalité et la première cause de handicap. Il est établi que 25 % à 30 % des patients ayant subi une attaque cérébrale décèdent rapidement. Et, si un quart des survivants récupère sans séquelles apparentes, les autres souffrent de handicaps dont la nature et l'ampleur différent selon l'étendue et la localisation de la région cérébrale affectée (paralysie, déficits d'apprentissage, pertes de mémoire, troubles comportementaux et moteurs)." vs (1') "Les attaques cérébrales, ou 'accidents vasculaires cérébraux' (AVC) ont un coût très lourd en matière de santé publique. 140 000 nouveaux cas sont déclarés *en France* chaque année où elles constituent la troisième cause de mortalité et la première cause de handicap. Il est établi que 25 % à 30 % des patients ayant subi une attaque cérébrale décèdent rapidement. Et, si un quart des survivants récupère sans séquelles apparentes, les autres souffrent de handicaps dont la nature et l'ampleur différent selon l'étendue et la localisation de la région cérébrale affectée (paralysie, déficits d'apprentissage, pertes de mémoire, troubles comportementaux et moteurs)."
[6] Cf. Charolles (2003) and Lacheret-Dujour/François (2005).

(2) Is it possible to restrict an organism's circadian oscillator (its 'internal clock') to highly determined structures? Yes, but the structure in question differs according to the zoological group. Clock neurons. *In many mollusks*, the oscillator has been located at the level of a restricted group of nerve cells situated behind the retina, while, *in insects*, several circadian rhythms are placed under the control of a small group of neurons called "lateral neurons." The biological clock in superior organisms is to be found in specific areas of the central nervous system. *In birds, reptiles, and fish*, it is the epiphysis (or pineal gland), a small gland at the top of the brain which, *in these animals*, captures light – the famous 'third eye'. *In mammals*, the situation appears in fact to be more complex. Certainly, the pineal gland preserves the ability to synthesize melatonin (a hormone, one of whose well-known functions is to regulate seasonal changes in reproductive activity) in a cyclical fashion, specifically at night, but it is not itself a clock. It indeed depends on other structures to generate oscillations. The central clock is located in a tiny region at the base of the brain, namely the suprachiasmatic nucleus (SCN), a compact group of several thousand neurons found in the front part of the hypothalamus. The SCN produces several neuropeptides in a circadian manner and sends oscillating signals to the pineal gland. (La Recherche)[7]

The manner of organizing information adopted in (2) can be schematized as follows:

---

[7] (2) "Est-il possible de circonscrire l'oscillateur circadien d'un organisme (son 'horloge interne') à des structures bien déterminées ? Oui, mais la structure en question diffère selon les groupes zoologiques. Neurones horlogers. *Chez de nombreux mollusques*, l'oscillateur a été localisé au niveau d'un groupe restreint de cellules nerveuses situées à l'arrière de la rétine, tandis que, *chez les insectes*, plusieurs rythmes circadiens sont placés sous le contrôle d'un petit groupe de neurones appelés 'neurones latéraux'. L'horloge biologique des organismes supérieurs se trouve, elle, dans des régions spécifiques du système nerveux central. *Chez les oiseaux, les reptiles et les poissons*, elle est constituée par l'épiphyse (ou glande pinéale), petite glande située au sommet du cerveau qui, *chez ces animaux*, est un capteur de lumière – le fameux 'troisième œil'. *Chez les mammifères*, la situation apparaît, de fait, plus complexe. Certes, la glande pinéale conserve la capacité de synthétiser de façon cyclique, en l'occurrence la nuit, la mélatonine (hormone dont l'un des quelques rôles connus consiste en la régulation des 5 changements saisonniers de l'activité reproductrice), mais elle ne constitue pas en elle-même une horloge. Elle dépend, en effet, d'autres structures pour générer des oscillations. L'horloge centrale est localisée dans une petite région située à la base du cerveau, le noyau suprachiasmatique (NSC), groupe compact de quelques milliers de neurones qui se trouve dans la partie antérieure de l'hypothalamus. Le NSC produit plusieurs neuropeptides de manière circadienne et envoie des signaux oscillants à la glande pinéale." (La Recherche)

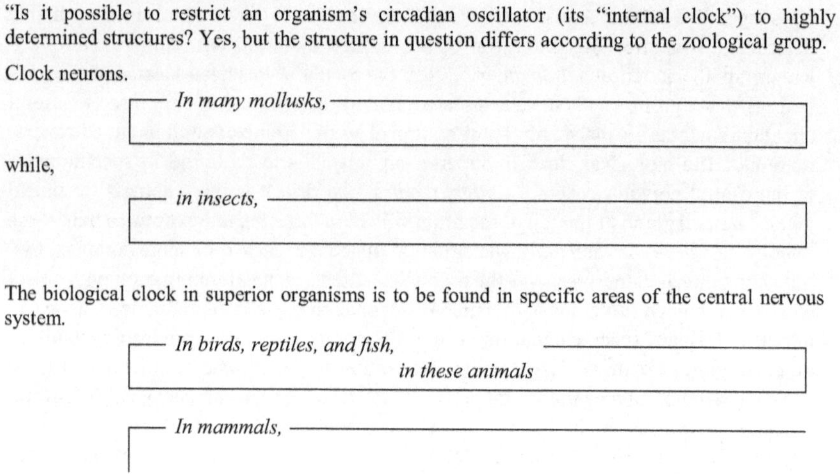

"Is it possible to restrict an organism's circadian oscillator (its "internal clock") to highly determined structures? Yes, but the structure in question differs according to the zoological group. Clock neurons.

⎡— In many mollusks, ─────────────────────────⎤

while,

⎡— in insects, ───────────────────────────⎤

The biological clock in superior organisms is to be found in specific areas of the central nervous system.

⎡— In birds, reptiles, and fish, ─────────────────⎤
⎣   in these animals   ⎦

⎡— In mammals, ─────────────────────────────⎤

Figure 1: Framing Structure of (2).

In (2), as in (1), PPs detached in pre-verbal position open location frames which tend, by default, to extend their scope to the upcoming clauses and to index the situations they denote. This extension is only interrupted by the occurrence of one or several cues, indicating that the information being dealt with no longer falls under the scope of the criteria specified by the introductory adverbial. This is especially the case when a new adverbial of location appears, and ends the influence of the preceding one. This is what happens in (2), where the opening of the frame initiated by *in insects* results in the closing of the one initiated by *in many mollusks*. The same process is reproduced, a few lines further on, by *in mammals*, which closes the frame introduced by *in birds, reptiles, and fish*.

The framing potential of pre-posed PPs can be exploited to a greater or lesser extent. This also appears in (2), where the first three frames contain only their host sentence, unlike the last frame whose scope extends as far as the end of the extract. In texts, the use of pre-posed adverbials for organizing information is usually limited to rather small segments and it often involves adverbials of the same semantic type.

Spatial and temporal scenic adverbials are excellent framers, but they very soon took on a more abstract meaning, as in (2), where the preposition *in* does not refer to a specific place in a three-dimensional space. Similarly, praxeological adverbials (Vigier 2004; 2005), referring to domains sometimes called "notional" (of the type *by right, legally*) are somewhat abstract localizers. One might consider the evidential or epistemic PPs in *according to/for X* (Schrepfer-André 2005; 2006) in the same way, assigning contents to enunciators and localizing them as they do, also in an abstract manner. The pre-posed hypotheticals in *if* likewise evoke a possible situation which serves as point of reference for the "localization" of one or several other situations shown to result from it (Charolles/Pachoud 2001). In fact, all constituents denoting an aspect of situations can be used for organizational purposes as long as one manages to detach them from the predication, which excludes the pre-posed PP arguments of the verb (cf. *From his trip to Paris(,) Paul has not remembered very much*). Potentially contrasting adverbials are much more able to play a role in the structuring of the discourse than those which do not lend themselves to contrasts. This factor explains why evaluative adverbs like *unfortunately* or *fortunately*, which frequently appear at the beginning of a sentence, are poor framers and remain modal adjuncts. Not only are these adverbs predicative (in the sense that they make a judgment about the situation denoted by the clause they prefix, which is not the case with locative adverbs), but it is difficult to imagine contexts in which a writer might be led to share the information s/he wishes to report, according to whether or not it is of a beneficial character. The fact that evidential PPs (*According to X, . . .*) often appear in isolation, without being opposed to others, does not call this observation into question insofar as the simple use of *according to X* in a text leads us to infer that the segments of discourse processed up to that point are retrospectively imputed to an enunciator different from X.[8]

In extracts like (1) and (2), the writer takes advantage of the content of the situations s/he is reporting in order to underline one or other of their accompanying circumstances, and in this way dividing what s/he has to say about them into lists. One might speak of location, like Culioli (1982), of referential, like Desclés (1994), of universe of discourse, like Martin (1983), or of "space builders", like Fauconnier (1984), Fauconnier/Sweetser (1996), or Huumo (1996; 1999). But the idea is always very much the same, and it goes along, more or less, with the concept which sees this way of using "circumstances" as resulting from a strategic approach (Enkvist 1987; Virtanen 1992; Ho-Dac 2007) that is highly attentional and therefore more or less confined to the written word.

The fact that detached adverbials in a pre-verbal position have an organizing potential can be related to the frequently defended idea that these constituents function as discourse topics. However, this analysis is not self-evident because it is difficult to accept that propositional contents indexed by a framing adverbial can be "about" the adverbial in question. On the other hand, it should be emphasized that these expressions are predestined, because of the place they occupy, to reflect information activated in the preceding discourse. This is exactly what

---

8 Cf. Charolles (1997) and Charolles/Pachoud (2002).

can be observed in (2), where the localization PPs are begun in the preceding sentence with *according to the zoological group* (non-evidential) which signals the review of species that follows.

The connectives indicating discourse relations between situations denoted by clauses gathered together in a frame do not in principle fall within the scope of the framing adverbial.[9] For instance, the relation of contrast indicated in (2), by *while*, articulates the information grouped in the preceding and subsequent frames. In the same way, the sentence:

> The biological clock of superior organisms is to be found in specific areas of the central nervous system.

is not included in the frame opened by *in insects*: it plays a transitional role between the two prior frames opened up and the two others which appear after it. The noun phrase (NP) *biological clock* reflects the "title" (*clock neurons*), the adnominal complement *superior organisms* refers to the initial sentence, and the use of a tonic pronoun (*elle*) in French (*l'horloge se trouve, elle...*) indicates a contrast between the two types of living creatures mentioned beforehand and those dealt with subsequently. The writer could have taken advantage of this allusion to use a construction such as:

> (2') *In superior organisms*, the biological clock is to be found in specific areas of the central nervous system.

with a detached PP at the start of the sentence, which would have changed how the beginning of the extract was organized:

```
              ┌─── In many mollusks, ─────────────────────────────────┐
              │                                                        │
while,        │   ─── in insects, ─────────────────────────────────    │
              │                                                        │
              └─── In superior organisms, ───────────────────────────  
```

Figure 2': Framing Structure of (2').

The fact that, in the passage from (2) reproduced below, the writer felt the need to specify *in animals* is also interesting to note:

> In birds, reptiles, and fish, it is the epiphysis (or pineal gland), a small gland at the top of the brain which, *in these animals*, captures light – the famous "third eye".

---

9 Cf. Charolles (2005) and Charolles/Vigier (2005).

The detached anaphoric PP at the head of the relative clause cannot extend its scope beyond that clause, but as it refers resumptively to the same species as those alluded to by the PP at the head of the main clause, this means that closure of the two frames coincides. In order to understand what made the writer specify that the content of the relative clause indeed applied to these species, it is enough to simply remove this indicator. Without the phrase *in these animals*, it would be understood that the epiphysis captures light in all living beings, and not only, as is the case, in birds, reptiles, and fish. This phenomenon is due to the fact that the explanatory relative clauses are parenthetical ones: the writer is introducing general information on the referents already mentioned. This information escapes the semantic scope of the introductory PPs,[10] which means there was effectively no other solution available to the writer than the one retained in the original version, which consists in quite simply resetting the current frame at the head of the relative clause.

Concerning connectives, it would seem quite legitimate to consider that, when they appear before a framing PP, as is the case with *while* in (2), they mark a discourse relationship not only between the facts indicated by the utterances gathered within the frames, but also between themselves. If we look at what happens in (2) after the PP *in mammals*, we are tempted to think that the PP includes in its scope not only the sentence it introduces (*the situation appears in fact to be more complex*), which is trivial,[11] but also the whole of the remainder in which connectives abound (*certainly*, *indeed*). Instead of closing the current frame, these connectives invite us to continue it: the PP's host sentence denotes a fact which is then elaborated, with new developments on what happens in mammals. If we refer to the informational level, where the locational PPs are used to organize the text, nothing prevents us including the whole of the remainder of paragraph (2) under the presentational construction highlighted by the PP *in mammals*. The data and reasoning set out in this part of the text certainly relate to this species, and it is this that counts in the end.

2 The role of framing adverbials in narrative texts

The manner of organizing textual information that we have just examined is mainly encountered in books or articles of a scientific and technical nature. But, in narrative prose, it is also common to find sequences structured by PPs, par-

---

[10] On the parallel difference between semantic and framing scope, and between ideational and textual scope, cf. Charolles/Vigier (2005) and Le Draoulec/Péry-Woodley (2005).
[11] One wonders whether *in fact* is not also a connective.

ticularly spatial and temporal ones (cf. Sarda 2005). The following extract from *Madame Bovary* offers a good example of this type of usage:

> (3) *From that moment* her existence was but one tissue of lies, in which she enveloped her love in veils, as if to hide it.
>
> It was a want, a mania, a pleasure carried to such an extent that if she said she had the day before walked on the right side of a road, one might know she had taken the left.
>
> *One morning, when she had gone,* as usual, rather lightly clothed, it suddenly began to snow, and as Charles was watching the weather from the window, he caught sight of Monsieur Bournisien in the chaise of Monsieur Tuvache, who was driving him to Rouen. Then he went down to give the priest a thick shawl that he was to hand over to Emma as soon as he reached the "Croix-Rouge." Hardly had he arrived at the inn than Monsieur Bournisien asked for the wife of the Yonville doctor. The landlady replied that she very rarely came to her establishment. So *that evening,* when he recognised Madame Bovary in the "Hirondelle," the cure told her his dilemma, without, however, appearing to attach much importance to it, for he began praising a preacher who was doing wonders at the Cathedral, and whom all the ladies were rushing to hear.
>
> Still, if he did not ask for any explanation, others, later on, might prove less discreet. So she thought well to get down each time at the "Croix-Rouge," so that the good folk of her village who saw her on the stairs should suspect nothing.
>
> *One day,* however, Monsieur Lheureux met her coming out of the Hotel de Bourgogne on Leon's arm; and she was frightened, thinking he would gossip. He was not such a fool. But *three days after* he came to her room, shut the door, and said, "I must have some money."
>
> She declared she could not give him any. Lheureux burst into lamentations and reminded her of all the kindnesses he had shown her [. . .]
>
> He came back *the following week* and boasted of having, after much trouble, at last discovered a certain Langlois, who, for a long time, had had an eye on the property, but without mentioning his price..."
>
> [The Project Gutenberg eBook of Madame Bovary, by Gustave Flaubert, Part III, Chap. 5, translated from the French by Eleanor Marx Aveling, released February 26, 2006].[12]

---

12 (3) "*À partir de ce moment*, son existence ne fut plus qu'un assemblage de mensonges, où elle enveloppait son amour comme dans des voiles, pour le cacher.
C'était un besoin, une manie, un plaisir, au point que, si elle disait avoir passé, hier par le côté droit d'une rue, il fallait croire qu'elle avait pris par le côté gauche.
Un matin qu'elle venait de partir, selon sa coutume, assez légèrement vêtue, il tomba de la neige tout à coup ; et comme Charles regardait le temps à la fenêtre, il aperçut M. Bournisien dans le boc du sieur Tuvache qui le conduisait à Rouen. Alors il descendit confier à l'ecclésiastique un gros châle pour qu'il le remît à Madame, sitôt qu'il arriverait à la Croix-Rouge. À peine fut-il à l'auberge que Bournisien demanda où était la femme du médecin d'Yonville. L'hôtelière répondit qu'elle fréquentait fort peu son établissement. Aussi, *le soir*, en reconnaissant madame Bovary

The organization of this passage may be represented as follows:

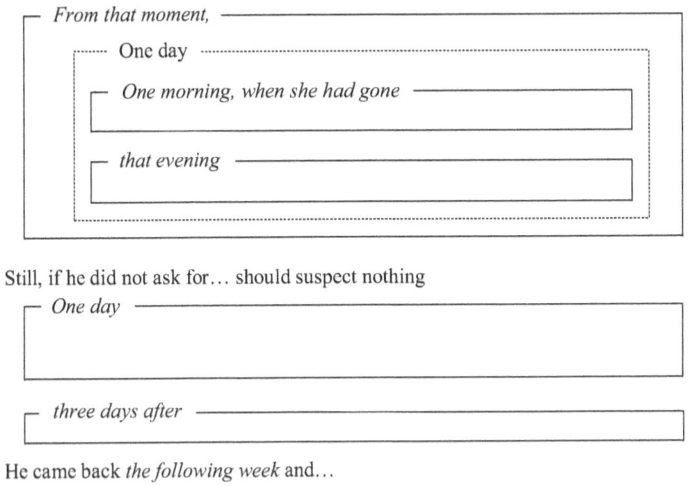

```
┌─ From that moment, ─────────────────────────
│   ┌──── One day ····························
│   │   ┌─ One morning, when she had gone ──
│   │   │
│   │   └────────────────────────────────────
│   │   ┌─ that evening ────────────────────
│   │   │
│   │   └────────────────────────────────────
└───┴───┴────────────────────────────────────
```

Still, if he did not ask for... should suspect nothing
```
┌─ One day ──────────────────────────────────
│
└────────────────────────────────────────────

┌─ three days after ─────────────────────────
│
└────────────────────────────────────────────
```
He came back *the following week* and...

Figure 3: Framing Structure of (3).

In this extract, the initial temporal presentational construction (*from that moment*) makes the link with what precedes it (cf. the anaphoric demonstrative NP). The change in Emma's behavior, alluded to in the first sentence, is specified by the relative clause and then developed in the following paragraph. It is therefore part of the initial frame, despite the separate paragraph. This transition determines the new background state (cf. the succession of stative processes in the imperfect) in which the character moves during the time interval opened by *from that moment*.

---

dans l'Hirondelle, le curé lui conta son embarras, sans paraître, du reste y attacher de l'importance ; car il entama l'éloge d'un prédicateur qui pour lors faisait merveille à la cathédrale, et que toutes les dames couraient entendre.

N'importe s'il n'avait point demandé d'explications, d'autres plus tard pourraient se montrer moins discrets. Aussi jugea-t-elle utile de descendre chaque fois à la Croix-Rouge, de sorte que les bonnes gens de son village qui la voyaient dans l'escalier ne se doutaient de rien.

Un jour pourtant, M. Lheureux la rencontra qui sortait de l'hôtel de Bourgogne au bras de Léon ; et elle eut peur, s'imaginant qu'il bavarderait. Il n'était pas si bête.

Mais *trois jours après*, il entra dans sa chambre, ferma la porte et dit :
– J'aurais besoin d'argent.

Elle déclara ne pouvoir lui en donner. Lheureux se répandit en gémissements, et rappela toutes les complaisances qu'il avait eues [. . .].

Il revint *la semaine suivante*, et se vanta d'avoir, après force démarches, fini par découvrir un certain Langlois qui, depuis longtemps, guignait la propriété sans faire connaître son prix. . ."

The indefinite temporal NP *one morning, when she had gone*, which appears at the head of the following paragraph, selects a specific morning against this background interval, and this specific morning serves as a frame for the series of perfective processes that follow. The clauses grouped within this temporal frame maintain a narrative relationship, and this includes the clause starting with the adverbial group *hardly had he arrived*, which is not framing since the sentential NP is integrated syntactically (cf. *than*). The chronology progresses, with the intervention of other characters, but the particular structuring pattern adopted leads us to understand that the situations depicted are taking place during the morning in question.[13] This intuition is confirmed by the associative definite NP *that evening*, which closes the frame introduced by *one morning* and opens a new one. The two frames are referentially linked and the perfective processes which follow one upon another up to the end of the paragraph are included in the evening's events. The subsequent *one day* introduces a new temporal frame whose scope extends throughout the paragraph it initiates, and the same is true for *three days after*, which comes at the beginning of the following paragraph. The two final frames are linked anaphorically by the adverb *after*; but the way in which the frame introduced by the second *one day* is linked to those introduced by *one morning* and *that evening*, and to *from that moment*, is not self-evident.

In order to understand how the frames can combine in Figure 3, we need to return to the following paragraph, which has not yet been mentioned:

> (3a) Still, if he did not ask for any explanation, others, later on, might prove less discreet. So she thought well to get down each time at the "Croix-Rouge," so that the good folk of her village who saw her on the stairs should suspect nothing.[14]

The first sentence, in free indirect speech, alludes to Emma's thoughts. This change in enunciative register is very noticeable, especially as it is accompanied by a new paragraph. Although it may appear insignificant, this arrangement is important: without the paragraph, we would have understood that it was during the evening when she returned with the Abbé Bournisien that Emma thought she should be more prudent. The fact that Flaubert did not adopt this form of presentation is quite understandable when we read on. The lesson Emma has learned from her day in

---

13 For a discussion of this subtle point cf. Terran (2002) and Vigier/Terran (2005); Le Draoulec/Péry-Woodley (2003; 2005); and Charolles/Le Draoulec/Péry-Woodley/Sarda (2005).

14 (3a) "N'importe s'il n'avait point demandé d'explications, d'autres plus tard pourraient se montrer moins discrets. Aussi jugea-t-elle utile de descendre chaque fois à la Croix rouge, de sorte que les bonnes gens de son village qui la voyaient dans l'escalier ne se doutaient de rien."

Rouen leads straight on to the repeated implementation (*each time*) of the strategy she has adopted and to the situations that have regularly resulted from it (cf. the processes in the imperfect); these situations cannot be included in the frame introduced by the last ongoing temporal adverbial, namely the NP *that evening*. Although it is difficult to precisely reconstruct its effects on on-line understanding, we might conjecture that:
- the paragraph before the transition to free indirect speech alerts the reader to the possible closure of the last ongoing time frame;
- this hypothesis is first confirmed by the use (in a non-framing position) of the adverb *later*, a reference that is calculated in relation to the preceding day (one morning + that evening);
- hence the retrospective inference that the two frames introduced by *one morning* and *that evening* are included in the same implicit *one day* (as indicated in Figure 3).

Consequently, calculating the reference to the second *one day* no longer poses a problem. The reader can choose a particular (non-specified) day out of all the days during which Emma had adopted the habit of staying *each time* at the "Croix-Rouge". These days are unconnected to the one required for interpreting the preceding *one day*, and this disconnection results from the fact that the paragraph reproduced in (3a) is not included in the frame introduced by *from that moment*. If this were so, we would have to have *another day*, which is not the case and so confirms the proposed analysis.

In the following extract from *Madame Bovary*, Flaubert also uses the framing potential of temporal adverbials (underlined):

(4) People wondered at his despondency. He never went out, saw no one, refused even to visit his patients. Then they said "he shut himself up to drink."

Sometimes however, some curious person climbed on to the garden hedge, and saw with amazement this long-bearded, shabbily clothed, wild man, who wept aloud as he walked up and down.

In the evening in summer he took his little girl with him and led her to the cemetery. They came back at nightfall, when the only light left in the Place was that in Binet's window.

The voluptuousness of his grief was, however, incomplete, for he had no one near him to share it, and he paid visits to Madame Lefrançois to be able to speak of her. But the landlady only listened with half an ear, having troubles like himself. For Lheureux had at last established the "Favorites du Commerce," and Hivert, who enjoyed a great reputation for doing errands, insisted on a rise of wages, and was threatening to go over "to the opposition shop."

One day when he had gone to the market at Argueil to sell his horse – his last resource – he met Rodolphe.

[The Project Gutenberg Ebook of Madame Bovary by Gustave Flaubert, Part III, Chap. 11, translated from the French by Eleanor Marx-Aveling, released February 26, 2006].[15]

Establishment of the frames introduced by the NPs and temporal adverbs is set out in the following diagram:

People wondered at his despondency. He never went out, saw no one, refused even to visit his patients. Then they said "he shut himself up to drink".

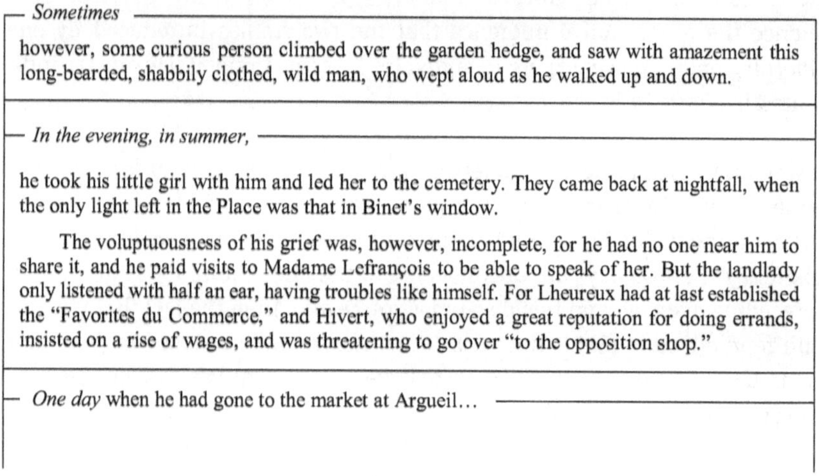

⸺ *Sometimes* ⸺

however, some curious person climbed over the garden hedge, and saw with amazement this long-bearded, shabbily clothed, wild man, who wept aloud as he walked up and down.

⸺ *In the evening, in summer,* ⸺

he took his little girl with him and led her to the cemetery. They came back at nightfall, when the only light left in the Place was that in Binet's window.

The voluptuousness of his grief was, however, incomplete, for he had no one near him to share it, and he paid visits to Madame Lefrançois to be able to speak of her. But the landlady only listened with half an ear, having troubles like himself. For Lheureux had at last established the "Favorites du Commerce," and Hivert, who enjoyed a great reputation for doing errands, insisted on a rise of wages, and was threatening to go over "to the opposition shop."

⸺ *One day* when he had gone to the market at Argueil... ⸺

Figure 4: Framing structure of (4).

---

15 (4) "On s'étonna de son découragement. Il ne sortait plus, ne recevait personne, refusait même d'aller voir ses malades. Alors on prétendit qu'il s'enfermait pour boire.

Quelquefois pourtant, un curieux se haussait par-dessus la haie du jardin, et apercevait avec ébahissement cet homme à barbe longue, couvert d'habits sordides, farouche, et qui pleurait tout haut en marchant.

Le soir, dans l'été, il prenait avec lui sa petite fille et la conduisait au cimetière. Ils s'en revenaient à la nuit close, quand il n'y avait plus d'éclairée sur la place que la lucarne de Binet.

Cependant, la volupté de sa douleur était incomplète, car il n'avait autour de lui personne qui la partageât ; et il faisait des visites à la mère Lefrançois afin de pouvoir parler d'elle. Mais l'aubergiste ne l'écoutait que d'une oreille, ayant comme lui des chagrins, car M. Lheureux venait enfin d'établir les Favorites du Commerce, et Hivert, qui jouissait d'une grande réputation pour les commissions, exigeait un surcroît d'appointements et menaçait de s'engager 'à la Concurrence'.

Un jour qu'il était allé au marché d'Argueil pour y vendre son cheval, dernière ressource, – il rencontra Rodolphe."

The frame introduced by *sometimes* continues the previous paragraph. *Sometimes* refers to an indeterminate set of situations (namely, occasions that were repeated) during the course of which *some curious person climbed...* (cf. the succession of verbs in the imperfect). The question here is over what time span did the occasions alluded to by *sometimes* take place.

We might initially be tempted to think that these occasions refer to the (unlimited) interval of time corresponding to *he never went out, saw no one, refused even to visit his patients*, the reason being that these background states might be thought to cover a sufficiently long period to provide *sometimes* with the implied occasions it needs. However, there are several reasons to oppose such an analysis. The sentences in the imperfect are semantically subordinated to *people wondered at his despondency*. They are only there to justify this assertion (in fact, the word *for* might have been added). If we also take into account *then they said "he shut himself up to drink"*, the rhetorical structure of the paragraph appears as follows:

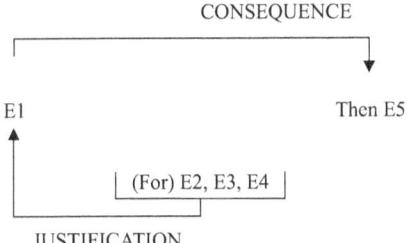

People wondered at his despondency (E1). He never went out (E2), saw no one (E3), refused even to visit his patients (E4). Then they said "he shut himself up to drink" (E5).

It is no longer possible, after E5, to link *sometimes* to the background states E2, E3 and E4, since they are subordinated to E1. E5 marks a forward movement in time and we are led to suppose that *sometimes* selects an indefinite number of time intervals over the period following the one during which it was claimed that Charles was locking himself up to drink – in other words, after the villagers had stopped being preoccupied with Charles' state.

Consequently, there is no difficulty in explaining the *however* (*pourtant* in French) which follows *sometimes*. *However* indicates a relationship of contrast with this new state. The fact that *some curious person climbed over the garden hedge* is presented as paradoxical given the situation of general indifference. Instead of *Sometimes however*, we might have had *However sometimes*: this observation reveals that *however* does not come under the scope of *sometimes* and is therefore not part of the frame. *But sometimes* would also have been possible, except that, unlike *however*, the word *but* would have led us to think that those who were curious went away "reassured" ("no, he wasn't drinking, he was weeping"). *However* focuses on the unexpected nature of the situation; it does not force us to go beyond the contrast, as would be the case with *but*.

The temporal frame opened by *In the evening, in summer,* is not understood as falling under the scope of the frame introduced by *sometimes*. The fact that the situations indicated by *in the evening, in summer,* return Charles to the foreground and have nothing more to do with the curiosity of those around, is a referential indicator inviting closure of the frame introduced by *sometimes*. The new paragraph also plays a part: without the paragraph, we would probably understand, at least initially, that *sometimes. . . in the evening in summer, Charles. . .* In the third paragraph of the original version, since the imperfect tense of the verbs denotes habitual actions, we might well infer that he did not take his daughter to the cemetery every evening. . . and thus be tempted to put a *sometimes* before *in the evening in summer*. This possibility cannot be excluded, but if this is the case, the *sometimes* would apply to a series of occasions out of all the evenings in summer rather than to the period indicated by the *sometimes* at the head of the preceding paragraph.

The expression introducing the second temporal frame involves two temporal NPs: *in the evening* and *in summer*. The NP *summer* describes a longer interval than *evening*. The two NPs do not have the same value: *summer* is interpreted deictically, as referring to the summer following Emma's death (*that summer*) and *evening* as pertaining associatively (partitively) to each evening of the summer days mentioned. This is why we are inclined to read it as habitual action, a tendency already indicated with regard to the imperfect tenses; and this reading is perfectly compatible, as we have seen, with a non-universal interpretation (cf. the possibility of adding *sometimes*). The order in which the two NPs are presented is not insignificant. *In the evening, in summer* emphasizes evening activity, which means that the frame introduced tends to be closed by *one day when he had gone. . .* at the beginning of the fifth paragraph.[16] The reverse order (*in summer, in the evening*) would have been possible, but this would have left it open to (even demanded) an interpretation in which the market day subsequently referred to took place during this season:

---

16 On the temporal NPs in *un jour* (*one day*), cf. Charolles (2006b; 2007).

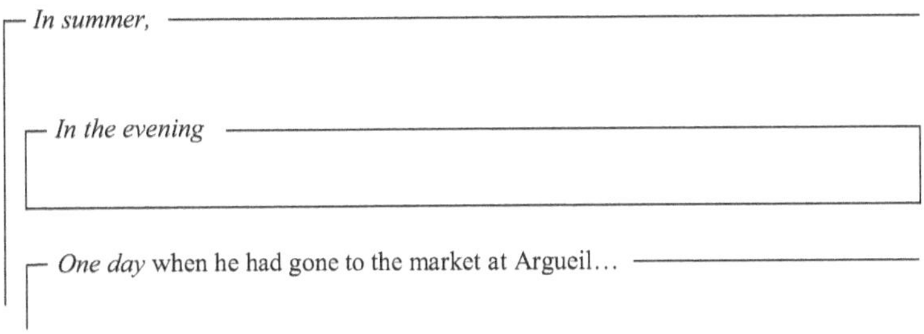

```
┌─ In summer, ──────────────────────────────────────────
│
│  ┌─ In the evening ──────────────────────────────┐
│  │                                                │
│  │                                                │
│  └                                                ┘
│
│  ┌─ One day when he had gone to the market at Argueil… ────
│  │
```

Figure 5: Modified framing structure of Figure 4.

The remainder of the text clearly indicates that the meeting with Rodolphe on market day took place during the summer:

> The next day Charles went to sit down on the seat in the arbour. Rays of light were straying through the trellis, the vine leaves threw their shadows on the sand, the jasmines perfumed the air, the heavens were blue, Spanish flies buzzed round the lilies in bloom, and Charles was suffocating like a youth beneath the vague love influences that filled his aching art.[17]

However, this observation is not in contradiction with the idea that the preferred reading of *in summer, in the evening* favors an interpretation matching the one illustrated in Figure 4. Indeed, readers' understanding, on a first reading, may well go along the lines I have indicated and subsequently rectified. But, of course, readers may not be sensitive to this kind of detail, especially as iteration blurs the calculation of time intervals.

In any case, the frame introduced by *in the evening* covers both the paragraph at the head of which it figures and the one following it. It includes in its scope the connective *however* (*cependant* in French at the head of the ensuing paragraph) as it does those which follow (*for, and, but, for*), in addition to those which might be restored in order to clarify the discourse relationships between utterances. From this point of view, the situation is very different from what is happening with the *sometimes however* (*pourtant*) where *however*, as we have noted, cannot be included in the temporal frame opened by *sometimes*. In this place, *however* (*pourtant*) makes a link with what preceded it: every time some curious person looked into Charles' garden, he saw that Charles was weeping. The connective applies to each of the occasions. It is the same with the *however* (*cependant*) at the beginning of the fourth paragraph, which has both a temporal and contras-

---

[17] "Le lendemain, Charles alla s'asseoir sur le banc, dans la tonnelle. Des jours passaient par le treillis ; les feuilles de vigne dessinaient leurs ombres sur le sable, le jasmin embaumait, le ciel était bleu, des cantharides bourdonnaient autour des lis en fleur, et Charles suffoquait comme un adolescent sous les vagues effluves amoureux qui gonflaient son cœur chagrin."

tive value, except that the contrast implies a situation – namely the grief Charles felt when visiting the cemetery with his daughter – together with the incomplete voluptuousness he drew from it. The link is made with an already-framed situation, which is not the case with *sometimes however* (*pourtant*). The same is true for the connectives which appear in the remainder of the fourth paragraph. These connectives establish discourse relationships between events that form part of the repeated episodes in which Charles visits his wife's grave with his daughter before going to speak with Madame Lefrançois.

3 Conclusion

The elements of analysis presented in this study show that framing adverbials play an important role in the organization of texts. They contribute to discourse cohesion, in the same way as the connectives and anaphora with which they permanently interact, as has just been highlighted when studying the second extract from *Madame Bovary*. Framing adverbials function as markers
- of segmentation: within texts, they define homogeneous blocks of information fulfilling the semantic criteria (spatial, temporal, enunciative, etc.) specified by the adverbial;
- of integration: once they are in place, they tend by default to include the incoming information. They establish descending relationships of scope, which globally differentiates them from anaphora and connectives that signal backward links.

References

Charolles, Michel, *Coherence as a principle in the interpretation of discourse*, Text. Interdisciplinary journal for the study of discourse 3 (1983), 71–99.

Charolles, Michel, *Cohésion, cohérence et pertinence du discours*, Travaux de linguistique 29 (1995), 125–151.

Charolles, Michel, *L'encadrement du discours. Univers, champs, domaines et espaces*, Cahier de recherche linguistique 6 (1997), 1–73, https://hal.archives-ouvertes.fr/hal-00665849/document. [last consultation: 13.06.2021]

Charolles, Michel, *De la topicalité des adverbiaux détachés en tête de phrase*, Travaux de linguistique 47 (2003), 11–51.

Charolles, Michel, *Framing adverbials and their role in discourse cohesion from connexion to forward labelling*, in: Aurnague, Michel/Bras, Myriame/Le Draoulec, Anne/Vieu, Laure (edd.), *Proceedings of the Symposium on the exploration and modelling of meaning*

(SEM-05 Biarritz, 2005), Toulouse, Université de Toulouse-le-Mirail (ERSS, Équipe de Recherche en Syntaxe et Sémantique), 2005, 13–30.

Charolles, Michel, *Cohérence, pertinence et intégration conceptuelle*, in: Lane, Philippe (ed.), *Des discours aux textes. Modèles et analyses*, Rouen, Presses universitaires de Rouen et du Havre, 2006, 39–74 (= 2006a).

Charolles, Michel, *La référence des compléments en un jour*, in: Riegel, Martin/Schnedecker, Catherine/Swiggers, Pierre/Tamba, Irène, *Aux carrefours du sens. Hommages offerts à Georges Kleiber pour son 60ᵉ anniversaire*, Leuven, Peeters, 2006, 53–69 (= 2006b).

Charolles, Michel, Un jour *(one day) in narratives*, in: Korzen, Iorn/Lundquist, Lita (edd.), *Comparing anaphors. Between sentences, texts and languages. Proceedings of the international symposium held at the Copenhagen Business School, September 1st-3rd 2005*, Copenhagen, Samfundslitteratur Press, 2007, 11–26.

Charolles, Michel/Le Draoulec, Anne/Péry-Woodley, Marie-Paule/Sarda, Laure, *Temporal and spatial dimensions of discourse organization*, Journal of French language studies 15 (2005), 115–130.

Charolles, Michel/Pachoud, Bernard, *"Si la Lorpailleur est folle. . ." et si le plus fou n'était pas celle que l'on croit?*, in: Roulet, Eddy/Burger, Marcel (edd.), *Les modèles du discours au défi d'un "dialogue romanesque". L'incipit du roman de R. Pinget "Le Libera"*, Nancy, Presses universitaires de Nancy, 2002, 307–350.

Charolles, Michel/Péry-Woodley, Marie-Paule (edd.), *Les adverbiaux cadratifs*, Langue française 148 (2005).

Charolles, Michel/Prévost, Sophie (edd.), *Adverbiaux et topiques*, Travaux de linguistique 47 (2003).

Charolles, Michel/Vigier, Denis, *Les adverbiaux en position préverbale. Portée cadrative et organisation des discours*, Langue française 148 (2005), 9–30, DOI: https://doi.org/10.3406/lfr.2005.6604.

Conte, Maria-Elisabeth, *Anaphore, prédication, empathie*, in: Charolles, Michel/Fisher, Sophie/Jayez, Jacques, *Le discours. Représentations et interprétations*, Nancy, Presses universitaires de Nancy, 1990, 215–225.

Conte, Maria-Elisabeth, *Anaphores dans la dynamique textuelle*, Cahiers de praxématique 16 (1991), 11–33, DOI: https://doi.org/10.4000/praxematique.3145.

Culioli, Antoine, *Rôle des représentations métalinguistiques en syntaxe*, 1982, communication à la session plénière du XIIIᵉ Congrès international des linguistes, Tokyo, 1982; repris dans: *Pour une linguistique de l'énonciation. Formalisation et opérations de repérage*, vol. 2, Paris, Ophrys, 1999, 95–114.

Desclés, Jean-Pierre, *Quelques concepts relatifs au temps et à l'aspect pour l'analyse des textes*, Studia kognitywne. Semantika kategorii aspektu i czasu 1 (1994), 57–88.

Enkvist, Nils E., *Text strategies: single, dual, multiple*, in: Steele, Ross/Threadgold, Terry (edd.), *Language topics. Essays in honour of Michael Halliday*, vol. 2, Amsterdam, Benjamins, 1987, 203–211.

Fauconnier, Gilles, *Espaces mentaux*, Paris, Les Éditions de Minuit, 1984.

Fauconnier, Gilles/Sweetser, Eve (edd.), *Spaces, worlds, and grammar*, Chicago, University of Chicago Press, 1996.

Grice, Herbert Paul, *Logic and conversation*, in: Cole, Peter/Morgan, Jerry L. (edd.), *Syntax and semantics*, vol. 3: *Speech acts*, New York, Academic Press, 1975, 41–58.

Ho-Dac, Lydia-Mai, *La position initiale dans l'organisation du discours. Une exploration en corpus*, thèse de doctorat, Toulouse, Université Toulouse-II-Le Mirail, 2007.

Huumo, Tuomas, *A scoping hierarchy of locatives*, Cognitive linguistics 7 (1996), 265–299.
Huumo, Tuomas, *Space as time. Temporalization and other special functions of locational-setting adverbials*, Linguistics 37 (1999), 389–430.
Lacheret-Dujour, Anne/François, Jacques, *Circonstance et prédication verbale en français parlé. Contraintes sémantico-pragmatiques et filtrage prosodique*, Syntaxe et sémantique 6 (2005), 35–56, DOI: https://doi.org/10.3917/ss.006.0035.
Le Draoulec, Anne/Péry-Woodley, Marie-Paule, *Time travel in text. Temporal framing in narratives and non-narratives*, in: Lagerwerk, Luuk/Spooren, Wilbert/Degand, Liesbeth (edd.), *Determination of information and tenor in texts. Multidisciplinary approaches to discourse*, Amsterdam/Münster, Stichting Neerlandistiek/Nodus Publikationen, 2003, 267–275.
Le Draoulec, Anne/Péry-Woodley, Marie-Paule, *Encadrement temporel et relations de discours*, Langue française 148 (2005), 45–60, DOI: https://doi.org/10.3917/lf.148.0045.
Martin, Robert, *Pour une logique du sens*, Paris, Presses universitaires de France, 1983.
Prévost, Sophie, *Les compléments spatiaux. Du topique au focus en passant par les cadres*, Travaux de linguistique 47 (2003), 51–77, DOI: https://doi.org/10.3917/tl.047.0051.
Sarda, Laure, *Fonctionnement des cadres spatiaux dans les résumés de films*, Langue française 148 (2005), 61–79, DOI: https://doi.org/10.3917/lf.148.0061.
Schrepfer-André, Géraldine, *Les "selon X" énonciatifs. Portée phrastique et textuelle et indices de clôture*, Verbum 27 (2005), 215–229.
Schrepfer-André, Géraldine, *La portée phrastique et textuelle des expressions introductrices de cadres énonciatifs. Les syntagmes prépositionnels en "selon X"*, thèse de doctorat, Paris, Université Paris 3, 2006.
Sperber, Dan/Wilson, Deirdre, *Relevance. Communication and cognition*, Oxford, Blackwell, 1986.
Terran, Élise, *Le cadrage temporel en français*, thèse de doctorat, Paris, Université Paris 3, 2002.
Vigier, Denis, *Les groupes prépositionnels en "en N". De la phrase au discours*, thèse de doctorat, Paris, Université Paris 3, 2004.
Vigier, Denis, *Les adverbiaux praxéologiques détachés en tête de phrase et leur portée. Études sur corpus*, Verbum 27 (2005), 293–312.
Vigier, Denis/Terran, Élise (edd.), *Les adverbiaux cadratifs et l'organisation des textes*, Verbum 27 (2005).
Virtanen, Tuija, *Discourse functions of adverbial placement in English. Clause-initial adverbs of time and place in narratives and procedural place descriptions*, Abo, Abo Akademi University Press, 1992.

Guy Achard-Bayle
Chapter 3
Text, discourse, cognition

Abstract: The purpose of this chapter is to question the three notions of text, discourse and cognition, together with the complementary or contrasting theoretical models which illustrate and support them. These three subjects will not therefore be analyzed consecutively, but in parallel. Based on the direction of my current work in text and cognitive linguistics, I shall approach them in two stages: text vs. discourse and text vs. cognition. This dual strategy, with the text as common denominator, implies, therefore, that although I take account of discourse as the contextual, situational, and generic framework in which the text appears, my focus is on the text as an object of analysis. In this I am following the "Prague" tradition, which is structural or macro-syntactic as well as functional. It also implies that this conception of the text enables neo-Prague theories to be reconciled with those being developed today in cognitive linguistics, centered on a range of mental, semantic, pragmatic, and semiotic skills, activities or processes and often grouped under the umbrella term of *representation*, involving mental spaces, projections, blending, and emergence of meaning. Finally, I show how the conceptual and predicative *dual integration* procedure enables the complementarity of the two models – mental-cognitive and macrosyntactic-textual – to be illustrated.

Keywords: text, discourse, cognition, blending/blend, dual integration (syntactic and conceptual)

Introduction

My intention in this chapter is not to approach the three subjects of the title one by one but, based on the direction of my current work in text and cognitive linguistics (henceforth referred to as "TL" and "CL"), to compare them in two stages: text versus discourse and text versus cognition. This dual strategy, with the text as common denominator, therefore implies that although I take discourse into account, I am more interested in the text, while being well aware of the difficulty that now exists in maintaining a separation between text and discourse (henceforth referred to as "T-D"): this will be one of the main points dealt with here.

Guy Achard-Bayle, Université de Lorraine, CREM

My position now being within the framework of epistemology, which I began to define in 2006 for the publication of *Textes-Contextes* in the journal Pratiques,[1] and having subsequently organized two TL events,[2] I can firmly state that TL is alive and well, at least in Europe: certainly in Central Europe,[3] where it originated, but in Western Europe too.

I will later return to this geographical approach to the discipline; for the present, and in relation to the T-D comparison, I will recall that one of the highlights of the study day I organized in May 2010 was precisely this T-D distinction, defended by Adam among others, and questioned by Maingueneau.[4]

But beyond this, and therefore more generally, it is possible to observe that with the spread or extension of discursive linguistics, it is usually TL which now has to justify its survival; in other words, the position of someone like Adam, which consists in maintaining the entity of the *text* as a subject, or indeed a disciplinary field, is not self-evident, or is becoming less so.

My initial focus will be on justifying this maintenance of textual specificity. I will then give an account of the lines of research I am conducting, which attempt to combine text and cognition.

But before that, I would like to return to my positions and clarify my propositions.

Pro/positions

I have said that my inclination is toward the text; to be more specific, I would say that I share Adam's position, which is to keep the text – as a metalinguistic entity – distinct from discourse. I have recently developed these positions-propositions in Achard-Bayle (2014), and I will return to them in the following section. But it is also possible to see from my 2012 book what my other positions are, accord-

---

[1] Pratiques 129–130; online presentation: https://www.persee.fr/doc/prati_0338-2389_2006_num_129_1_2091 [last consultation: 15.06.2022].
[2] In May 2010 at the ENS-Ulm (Paris) for *Conscila* and in October 2012 at the University of Lorraine (Nancy) for the network *Théories et concepts du Cercle linguistique de Prague au seuil du XXIe siècle*, both of them involving the legacy of the Prague Linguistic Circle. The proceedings of these events were published in Verbum 32 (Achard-Bayle 2010) and 35 (Achard-Bayle/Chabrolle-Cerretini 2013).
[3] See Verbum 32:2 and Verbum 35:1–2.
[4] For Adam, see Adam (2010) (in the proceedings cited note 2, Verbum 32:2); for Maingueneau, see Maingueneau (2006).

ing to my sources, particularly those of Martin (1983),[5] Fauconnier (1984), and Charolles (1977); this point too will be dealt with later. But I can already say that these various influences, which mean that I find myself at a crossroads between text linguistics, natural logic and cognitive linguistics, enable me to retain key notions (cohesion, coherence, world views, beliefs, mental spaces, frames. . .), which, in their turn, enable me to unite two of the notions I have indicated above and which form the orientation of my research, namely text and cognition.[6]

The question I shall ask is therefore the following: "How can continuity or convergence between these two epistemological frames be envisaged?" knowing that the difficulty of the undertaking stems from the remoteness of the models in their historical roots and geographical developments – functionalist and (Mittel-) European on the one hand, cognitivist and American (Californian) on the other; but it also derives from the fact that, from this perspective, the T-D distinction tends to become much less marked. This allows me to echo the question I asked in Achard-Bayle (2014): 'Do *text* and *discourse* comprehend one another?'[7] It is a question I shall repeat and reformulate to make it the subject of my first section, which will question T-D continuity.

1 Text-Discourse (T-D)

In *Les grandes théories de la linguistique*, Paveau/Sarfati (2003) devote their penultimate chapter to *discursive linguistics*, which, following the exact order of presentation chosen by the authors, includes *text linguistics* followed by *discourse analysis*. This chapter, with its title and two sections, is a good illustration of the problem I would like to develop in this first part: does *discursive* include *text*? But if we follow the authors' logic of inclusion closely, it turns out also to include *discourse*; in other words, *text* and *discourse* combine to create the *discursive*.

I can and must therefore rephrase the problem, and this means it is both the T-D articulation and inclusion of the *text* in the *discursive* that I will be questioning here.

---

[5] Martin (1983) took note of the work done by the Prague Linguistic Circle.
[6] I owe a particular debt to Charolles, who is one of the first French linguists, or simply one of the first linguists, to have worked at the crossroads of text and cognition (see Achard-Bayle 2015; 2016).
[7] "Texte et discours se comprennent-ils ?" All subsequent translations from other works are by Rosemary Rodwell, the translator of this chapter, unless stated otherwise.

1.1 The discursive background of the text

If we take Adam's famous equation (1989), *text = discourse – context* as our reference point; in other words, if we consider, with him, that the *text* is a *decontextualized discourse*, we have to admit from the start that discourse is certainly the discursive background to TL. In his later work (particularly in the 2000s), Adam abandoned this formulation, which, in a certain way, means that the text is deprived, or dispossessed, of its actuality; I will later explain why I say "in a *certain* way".

Meanwhile, I return to the term *actuality* and, therefore, to the supposed T-D inclusion: *actuality* or *actualization* is a key concept in Prague linguistics and in Czech linguistics more generally[8] which, although they founded TL, or were subsequently founded upon it, can, despite this, not be called discursive. They are essentially (fundamentally) *functionalist*; and it is through *function* that they introduce into language[9] what will become the *natural* conveyor of Martin's logical semantics (Martin 1983, 206),[10] namely 'communicative dynamics'.[11]

In order to progress in our questioning of convergence *versus* divergence in T-D, we should clarify this model somewhat. Martin's *natural* semantics shifts between two poles or, to be more precise, follows a logic that leads us from one to the other (including in the way the chapters are arranged); Martin therefore knows, at the time he is writing in the early 1980s, that his model is completely unprecedented, though not exempt from tensions insofar as his project or his demand (cf. the very title of his work, *Pour une logique du sens* 'For a logic of meaning') is to bring together two domains, namely semantics and pragmatics, which until then had appeared to be opposed to one another; and yet, between a logical semantics focused on predication and clause (or the sentence), and a pragmatics focused on the utterance, and therefore enunciation, interaction and context – in other

---

8 See Daneš (2010) for the Prague Linguistic Circle, or else Cusimano (2011) for Brno. Pešek, who represents a third Czech center at the University of South Bohemia, notes that what he calls "'textual linguistic discourse' [is] characteristic of the Czech countries in the last decades of the twentieth century" (Pešek 2010, 264; "le 'discours linguistique textuel' [est] propre aux pays tchèques dans les dernières décennies du XXe siècle").
9 Subsequently, and before the emergence of the "second Prague School" with its renewed focus on the text, Skalička (1948) argued for a linguistics of "parole" (sic; cf. Pešek 2010, 266).
10 In opposition to formal logical semantics: Martin, in his *Introduction* (1983, 13), thus speaks of "the poverty of a logic that is strictly limited to the true/false opposition" ("l'indigence d'une logique strictement limitée à l'opposition du vrai et du faux").
11 "[L]a dynamique communicative".

words *discourse* as we now understand it – Martin in fact introduces a textual factor or level, which will make the connection between them.

I shall now look at Martin's demonstration in its chronology and in the text. At the beginning of his book, Martin explains the "division" at the basis of his model:

> One of the divisions in the [i.e., my] theory is the separation made, as clearly as possible, between *semantics* and *pragmatics*. One reflects *meaning*, while the other reflects *interpretations*. Meaning is attached to the *sentence*, the locus of conditions of truth; and interpretations to the *utterance*, the locus of truth and falsehood. (Martin 1983, 14; the author's italics)[12]

These domains influence three *components* in their turn:
- 'The *sentential component*, the locus of conditions of truth, where the *acceptability* and *meaning* of sentences as such are determined, as are the *truth relations* uniting them;
- The *discursive component*, where the sentence is inserted in the text's *cohesion*;

---

12 "Un des clivages de [ma] théorie est dans le départ qui est fait, aussi nettement que possible, entre *sémantique* et *pragmatique*. L'une rend compte du sens, l'autre des *interprétations*. Le sens s'attache à la *phrase*, lieu des conditions de vérité ; les interprétations à *l'énoncé*, lieu du vrai et du faux." (All translations from secondary and literary works are by Rosemary Rodwell, the translator of this chapter.)

We find the same form of dichotomy-convergence in Adam (1989, 190–191): 'Text linguistics and pragmatics must therefore define a limited field of research, within the vaster area of discourse which other disciplines (history, sociology, psycho-sociology, psychoanalysis, etc.) are probably more able to describe.' ("Linguistique et pragmatique textuelles doivent donc définir un champ de recherche limité, à l'intérieur du domaine plus vaste du discours que d'autres disciplines (histoire, sociologie, psycho-sociologie, psychanalyse, etc.) sont probablement plus à même de décrire.") Adam's "text pragmatics" therefore tends to be distinguished from lesser- or non-linguistic pragmatics; for Martin, the dichotomy, whatever the complementarity of meaning ("textual") and interpretation (or "situational meaning") is more contrasted (Martin 1983, 15): 'It is impossible to deal with such dissimilar realities in the same place [. . .] Semantic relations are foreseeable relations, that is to say calculable; it is not the same for pragmatic relations, which depend on discursive situations as variable as the situations themselves. Pragmatics, understood as the locus of "situational meaning," is difficult to "integrate." It is opposed to semantics, of which it is not a part.' ("Impossible de traiter en un même lieu des réalités aussi dissemblables [. . .] Les relations sémantiques sont des relations prévisibles, c'est-à-dire calculables ; il n'en est pas ainsi des relations pragmatiques, dépendantes des situations discursives, aussi variables que les situations elles-mêmes. Comprise comme le lieu du 'sens situationnel', la pragmatique peut difficilement être 'intégrée'. Elle s'oppose à la sémantique ; elle n'en est pas une partie.") That said, did we not find the same mistrust on the part of Adam (1989, 187): "Is 'discourse' a linguistic subject?" ("Le 'discours' est-il un objet linguistique ?")

- The *pragmatic component*, the locus of truth and falsehood, where the sentence that has become an utterance *is interpreted* in the enunciative situation.' (Martin 1983, 204; the author's italics again)[13]

What also appears unprecedented in Martin's thinking is that, even though his theory still involves two distinct poles or domains, it enables two models of analysis, semantic and pragmatic, to be brought together, before text and discourse are assimilated or joined – in other words, what we are considering in this section to be the *discursive background*:

> The discursive component, as the place of 'communicative dynamics' (Prague School) and of 'textual function' (M.A.K. Halliday), calculates the sentence's adequacy for its context. In this sense it belongs to semantics. Textual cohesion is based on criteria such as isotopy, anaphora, and common presuppositions, which function *inside the text itself*, independently of any situational variation. (Martin 1983, 206; the author's italics again)[14]

This assimilation of T-D by Martin at the same *component* level enables me to return to the question of *actuality*, and to explain how, "in a certain way", as I said, this actuality is never, even at a strictly textual level, completely decontextualized.

---

13 "– [L]a *composante phrastique*, lieu des conditions de vérité, où se déterminent l'*acceptabilité* et le *sens* des phrases en tant que telles, ainsi que les *relations de vérité* qui les unissent ;
– la *composante discursive*, où la phrase s'insère dans la *cohésion* du texte ;
– la *composante pragmatique*, lieu du vrai et du faux, où la phrase devenue énoncé, *s'interprète* dans la situation énonciative."

14 "Lieu de la 'dynamique communicative' (École de Prague), de la 'fonction textuelle' (M.A.K. Halliday), la composante discursive calcule donc l'adéquation de la phrase à son contexte. En ce sens elle appartient à la sémantique. La cohésion textuelle se fonde sur des critères comme ceux d'isotopie, d'anaphore, de communauté présupositionnelle, dont la fonction s'exerce *à l'intérieur même du texte*, indépendamment de toute variation situationnelle."

I am adding the remainder of Martin's text (1983, 206) as a note so as not to interrupt the thread of my own argument: 'There is nothing similar for the pragmatic component, whose function is precisely to complete the semantic calculation of data that are not exclusively linguistic. Its role is interpretative, with the aim of taking account of everything in the enunciative situation that contributes to the development of *signification*: codes other than linguistic ones (gestures, facial expressions, etc.); situational knowledge and, more generally, world knowledge; intentions concealed by the discourse; implicit...' ("Rien de tel pour la composante pragmatique dont le propre justement est de compléter le calcul sémantique de données qui ne sont pas exclusivement linguistiques. Interprétative, elle vise à tenir compte de tout ce qui, dans la situation énonciative, contribue à élaborer la *signification* : codes autres que linguistiques (gestes, mimiques...) ; connaissances situationnelles et, plus largement, connaissances d'univers ; intentions que le discours recèle ; implicite...")

What I meant by this was that *actuality* is, epistemologically speaking, a notion that varies according to need: from a theoretical point of view, it is the basis of the notion of linguistic production which brings sentence and utterance together; from the viewpoint of the history of ideas, although it is now linked to context(s), it was first, chronologically speaking, decontextualized, in the pragmatic sense in which Martin views and defines the context as the "enunciative situation".

To summarize, it is possible, by means of the text, to reconcile de-contextualization with actualization:
– Martin shows for example how, 'among the criteria of cohesion, the *theme* [can] illustrate the discursive component', insofar as it is a "given" (Martin 1983, 207–208; his italics),[15] and that it introduces a presupposition which can be calculated out of context (situational); the same factor works for interrogative clauses, even though, out of the multiple presuppositions associated with an utterance, some of them can refer to (or must be determined with reference to) the *here and now* of the enunciation, as in: "Pierre joined Sophie *this morning*" (Martin 1983, 210). Here, we are in the Prague tradition of "identification of known information", to which this author claimed allegiance (see above, note 14, the quotation by Martin 1983, 206), and which has been illustrated by Daneš (2010) too.
– As for Adam, he upholds (2011, 30) "text linguistics in discourse analysis", the first belonging to "bottom-up" operations (i.e. from the word to the text) which concern segmentation and binding (discontinuity vs. continuity) at the level of sentence linking; and the second to "top-down influences [from the context in the widest sense to effective linguistic production] which interactive situations in social places, languages and genres impose on utterances" (Adam 2011, 30); this therefore extends or diffuses the Prague legacy.[16]
– But he does it, in these same years of the 2000s, by insisting on the phase that I will call *textic* and he calls "the hermeneutic moment of understanding":

I would say that the hermeneutic moment of understanding a text as form-meaning does not occur without account being taken of its texticity: the effect of a text (texticity)[17] only takes place if a reader has the impression of a cohesive and coherent unit between co-textual

---

15 "[P]armi les critères de cohésion, le *thème* [peut] illustrer la composante discursive."
16 See also his article (2010), which appears next to that of Daneš (2010).
17 A link can be made with the *texture* of Halliday/Hasan (1976) and then Brown/Yule (1983); links that I make in Achard-Bayle (2015; 2016).

utterances (in Adam 2005, I speak of centripetal forces in relation to this). The first contextualization is therefore that of the text as a co-textual unit of utterances. (Adam 2006, 23)[18]

– Finally, I would like to point out that this "hermeneutic turning point" made by Adam in the 2000s enabled him to become fully involved in the discursive field of genericity – a notion already mentioned by him in previous work, in 1989 for example when commenting on Bakhtin:

From the moment there is a *text*, which is to say when a subject recognizes that a series of utterances forms a unit of communication, there is an *effect of genericity*, meaning that this series of utterances is registered in a class of discourse. (Adam 2011, 20; the author's italics)[19]

– He thus affirms the dual necessity of *linguistic observation of discourse-level regularities* while at the same time *asking himself what genres of discourse are* (I am slightly rephrasing his 1989 text, but one can clearly see the continuity in his work up to 2011); in other words, he is linking two forms (metalinguistic) or two conceptions of the text:

THE TEXT as abstract object [...] of a general theory of unit organization (what we will call **texture** for micro-linguistic events and **structure** for macro-linguistic events [vs.] **TEXTS as concrete, material, empirical objects.** (Adam 1999, 40; the author's emphasis)[20]

1.2 Partial conclusions

Although the limits of T-D are now tending to disappear, at least in TL, and so long as the particular focus of the latter is thought to be on "co-textual grammar",[21] this is at the expense of a certain number of what we might call adjustments:

---

18 "Je dirai que le moment herméneutique de la compréhension d'un texte comme forme-sens ne va pas sans une prise en compte de sa texticité : il n'y a effet de texte (texticité) que si un lecteur éprouve un sentiment d'une unité cohésive et cohérente entre des énoncés co-textuels (je parle à ce propos de forces centripètes dans Adam 2005). La première contextualisation est donc celle du texte comme unité co-textuelle d'énoncés."
19 "Dès qu'il y a texte, c'est-à-dire reconnaissance par un sujet du fait qu'une suite d'énoncés forme une unité de communication, il y a effet de généricité, c'est-à-dire inscription de cette suite d'énoncés dans une classe de discours."
20 "LE TEXTE comme objet abstrait [...] d'une théorie générale des agencements d'unités (ce qu'on appellera la texture pour désigner les faits microlinguistiques et la structure pour les faits macrolinguistiques) [vs] LES TEXTES comme objets concrets, matériels, empiriques."
21 In the Prague tradition: this, as Martin (1983) says, Combettes (1983) shows, and Adam repeats by applying progression-cohesion processes to types of textual sequences, focuses on what Adam (2006, 32) was to call "relations of co-textual interdependence which make a text into a network of co-determinations".

- Introducing and taking account of a sentence dynamism that is both informative and communicative ("second Prague School" following Pešek 2010);
- Redistributing fields, subjects, and practices between semantics and pragmatics, the distinguishing criteria being the notion of regularity (Martin, among others);
- Rearticulating T-D inclusion (in other words "opening" the text to discourse, in accordance with Adam's view), with account being taken of genericity, and moving from the singular to the plural of discourse which, in TL, has the effect of making the notion of discursivity less important:

> To talk of discourse is to open up the text, on the one hand to a situation of enunciation-interaction that is always singular and, on the other, to the interdiscursivity in which each text is confined – particularly that of genres. I prefer to replace **analysis of discourse/discourse analysis**, which is a general theory of discursivity, by **analysis of DISCOURSES**, which is attentive to the diversity of human discursive practices. **DISCOURSE GENRES** provide the means to think about this diversity... (Adam 1999, 40; the author's emphasis)[22]

2 Text-Cognition (T-C)

I will not now expound on my position in cognitive linguistics (CL), having done so in detail in Achard-Bayle (2015), to which the reader may refer. I shall therefore limit myself to stating or recalling that CL has a long tradition (which Marie-Anne Paveau and I attempted to trace in 2012), and that, still today, various strands often have very close ties, existing alongside or in opposition to one another.

There is thus a school known as "Californian", whose centers are, or have been in recent times, Berkeley and San Diego: the names and work of Lakoff,

---

[22] "Parler de discours, c'est ouvrir le texte, d'une part, sur une situation d'énonciation-interaction toujours singulière, d'autre part, sur l'interdiscursivité dans laquelle chaque texte est pris – en particulier celle des genres. À **l'analyse de/du discours**, qui est une théorie générale de la discursivité, nous préférerons substituer une **analyse DES discours** attentive à la diversité des pratiques discursives humaines. **LES GENRES DE DISCOURS** sont le moyen de penser cette diversité..."

I have dealt elsewhere (Achard-Bayle 2018) with the comparative study of the notion of text following this "co-textual" tradition and hermeneutics and, more generally, Ricœur's philosophy of language, the latter having written conclusively on the T-D articulation-distinction, notably in his 1986 book. This marginalization on the one hand, and the delay, on the other, can here be justified in two ways: Ricœur does not cite "co-textualist" or indeed functionalist linguistic works, but rather the semantics-pragmatics of Benveniste, Searle, Austin; Adam embraced hermeneutics relatively recently (2000s).

Langacker, Fauconnier, and Sweetser are associated with these. But this school naturally extends beyond the area of California, if we consider the joint work of Fauconnier and Turner, or Sweetser and Dancygier, which emanated from these two centers. Within this same "time space", we might also mention the work of Fillmore, whose *case grammar* has now become a branch of CL (see Fillmore 1975; Östman/Fried 2004; see also Charolles 2013).

What I will say here is that one of the theoretical concepts that has become most widespread on a global scale (I will simply give the example of the Iberian Peninsula)[23] but is equally the most debated in CL worldwide, is that of *blend*, as a process of creation or *emergence* of meaning; it is a concept from which I personally have benefited (Achard-Bayle 2012, and below for my analyses of *If*). This notion of *blend*, which is part of the seminal work of Lakoff/Johnson (1980) on *conceptual metaphors* (from which their *conceptual metaphor theory*, CMT, derives) and Fauconnier's work on *mental spaces*, was developed by Fauconnier/Turner (2002) in particular.[24]

These notions have given rise to a range of commentaries and numerous applications to languages and cultures (in South-East Asia, for example), as well as extended analyses. Thus Gibbs (2011) assesses the CMT of Lakoff/Johnson; and Brandt/Brandt (2005) study the strict semantic-logical or referential conception of Fauconnier and Turner's *blend* theory. Indeed, for our Danish authors, who defend a pragmatic, psychological (*intersubjective*) and semiotic approach, the metaphoric sense of the canonical utterance *This surgeon is a butcher* does not come from the projection between spaces of features belonging to the referents and therefore from the blend of features projected into the two spaces thus related, so much as from the communicative situation in which the blend takes *effect*, and therefore *makes an effect*; for example, in a hospital where a patient is speaking of the surgeon who has performed an unsatisfactory operation, leaving her with large scars: if she talks of him in this way, it is because he has left her in this condition.

Utterances such as these therefore truly involve *representation*, as much if not more than referentiation and characterization, leading our two authors to propose their *semiotic approach to metaphor* as a semiotic alternative to CMT and blend theory.

---

[23] Several large-scale CL conferences took place at the turn of the twentieth century, notably in Braga and Logroño. See the *Annual Review of Cognitive Linguistics* edited by Mendoza Ibáñez of La Rioja University; and in volume 3 of this journal, the articles by Achard-Bayle (2005) and Brandt/Brandt (2005; of which more below).
[24] For a recent review of these theories, see Fortis/Col (2018).

Following this brief geo-historical reminder of contemporary trends in CL, and to return to my theme, which consists of comparing text, discourse and cognition, I shall now examine how CL can be part of the lineage of TL research, in accordance with the Prague and neo-Prague traditions previously referred to.

2.1 TL-CL articulations

If we take the notions of *functional syntax, communicative dynamics* or *informational content* favored by the Prague school, we can see a relationship taking shape between TL and CL via the "world-grammar" link espoused by Fauconnier/Sweetser in particular, in their introductory text on the subject (Sweetser/Fauconnier 1996).

The lineage involved is in fact based on an older tradition: thus, when Combettes (1983, 7–9) sets out the antecedents to Prague TL, he goes back to the nineteenth and early twentieth centuries, to the work of Humboldt, Weil, and Bühler, who stressed both referential function and word order as marks of subjectivity or of *world vision*. This is why Humboldt's *Weltanschauung*, reprised by Bühler, can be related to Fauconnier/Sweetser's *world views* (1996, 3).

However, I do not directly assimilate these schools and models. I am content to acknowledge a more distant relationship because, although CL recognizes the presence and importance of *world views* in language, its interest lies in their *linguistic reflections of cognitive connections* (Fauconnier/Sweetser 1996, 7). This means that language does not reflect *objective phenomena*, but that *linguistic reflections* are mental phenomena[25] – among which a choice position appears to be occupied by the *principle of access* from one referent (*source*) to another (*target*), by means of re-identification: hence the major importance accorded to the metaphor in CL (since Lakoff/Johnson 1980).

To continue the search for links, we might note that Fauconnier, who is one of the leading authors of CL, devoted his early work in France, in the 1980s, to *espaces mentaux* (*mental spaces*); and these are unquestionably parallel to and contemporary with Martin's *univers de croyances* (*universes of belief*) and *images d'univers*.

Fauconnier's semantics, which is logical and modal but also mentalist and subjectivist, has considerably influenced his later work with Turner, which made *mental spaces* the foundation of their *conceptual integration theory* (CIT). Accord-

---

[25] See further: "Linguistic structure does reflect precisely the aspects of human cognition." (Fauconnier/Sweetser 1996, 7)

ing to this, semantic features, projected onto one or several other conceptualized spaces, will blend to create a brand-new innovative space of signification, in other words another form of conceptualization.

However, although it is mentalist and therefore subjectivist,[26] this model is nevertheless profoundly contextualist and therefore externalist,[27] in that it places great importance on the *frames* of conceptualization.

To close this section and proceed to the link with T-C, I would finally say that if Fauconnier and Sweetser (1996, 26) quote Charolles, Charolles, for his part, based the definition of his model of *cadres discursifs* (*discursive frames*, 1997) on Martin (1983) and Fauconnier (1984); then, having studied *integration* in this model, from its textual or macro-syntactic aspect,[28] he has spoken more recently of CIT (2006)[29] – in the same way as he now speaks (2013) of *projection*:[30] this juxtaposition, indeed this convergence of models will form the main theme of the following and last section.

2.2 Dual integration

I began to work on "dual integration" for my 2012 book, and what I understand by it is the following. First of all, in the tradition of Charolles, I consider two forms or manners of integration: one of them is formal, involving the syntactic and semantic attachment of an argument to a predicate – a link that can be more or less close, or strong; the other is mental, in the tradition of Fauconnier and Turner's CIT, mentioned above. But what I would like to show and enlarge upon here is that these two forms are also two sides, or two phases, of a process of conceptualization-representation, which cannot always be separated.

My 2012 book focuses on *if*, which I take to be both "operator" and "projector": what I mean here is that *if* serves both (i) to open a predication, a frame of *verid-*

---

26 We have seen that Fauconnier/Sweetser (1996) emphasize *world views*.
27 *Versus* internalist: cf. Achard-Bayle/Paveau (2012).
28 In other words: integration (or lack of it) with the predicate.
29 'The Conceptual Integration Theory of Gilles Fauconnier and Mark Turner [...] opens up [...] interesting possibilities for analyzing interpretation processes in general, and, in particular, for studying the processes involved in establishing textual coherence.' (2006, 46: "La Théorie de l'Intégration Conceptuelle de Gilles Fauconnier et Mark Turner [...] ouvre [...] des perspectives intéressantes pour l'analyse des processus d'interprétation en général, et, en particulier, pour l'étude des opérations intervenant dans l'établissement de la cohérence textuelle.")
30 *Mapping* in CL. On CL and particularly CIT (in CL), see Fauconnier/Turner (2002) and Fauconnier (2005).

iction, to set a condition, and to announce a correlation (it is obviously already difficult to disassociate the formal and logical-semantic levels in a macro-syntactic *and* conceptual type of analysis); and (ii) to project ourselves (i.e. to become integrated) into a non-actual space.[31]

It is more difficult to show why the two operations are inseparable; in other words, why macro-syntactic processing and conceptual processing go together. In my 2012 book, I touch on the question thanks in particular to the example of an attested utterance in which a *percontative if* (in other words an indirect interrogative, which is therefore intra-predicative) answers a hypothetical (extra-predicative) *if*:

> Si tu le touches, il te demande pendant un kilomètre de temps si tu le touches vraiment. . . (B.-M. Koltès, *La Nuit juste avant les forêts*).[32]
>
> If you touch him, he asks you during a kilometer of time if you are really touching him. . .

The utterance is indeed remarkable for its somewhat paradoxical structure: it is both echoic, and therefore binary, but also ternary when we consider the core predication surrounded by its two subordinate clauses. The tour de force, one might say, is to ensure that through the echo *effect*, the two subordinate clauses manage, if not to merge with one another, at least to give the impression that they are substituting for one another; and so in some way they are equivalent, even though their relation to the syntactic and semantic core is extra-predicative for one and intra-predicative for the other.

We also see here, to remind us of Brandt and Brandt's semiotic approach referred to above, the extent to which *effect* is involved, and that the said linguistic tour de force is also, at the communicational level – in other words as a stage *performance* – a dramatic "coup", from an *intersubjective* point of view.

The linking of the two *ifs* is nothing new: it was envisaged by Moignet (1974; 1981) and then by Martin (1983), and for both of them *if* suspends, in its own way (hypothesis, question), the truth-value of the proposition.

---

31 On the semantics of *if* in terms of factuality-counterfactuality-probability-unreality, see Athanasiadou/Dirven (1997) and Werth (1997).
32 Video with English subtitles: https://www.cinematheque.fr/henri/film/136529-la-nuit-juste-avant-les-forets-hugo-becker-2017/ [last consultation: 06.07.2022].

Nevertheless, what the above example from Koltès further suggests to me, even though it may not be new, is that the succession of *ifs* not only creates an echo effect, surprising or startling, but seems to reveal a movement, or even a boost toward integration which is not merely syntactic (predicative), in other words formal: the integration is also conceptual, in the sense that it is more attached to one of the subjects or to the actant subjects of the dialogue, via the predicates; the subject or subjects thus claim for themselves – they literally "integrate" – the initial potentiality.

In terms of integration, therefore, non-actual predication and conceptualization seem no longer to belong – at least here – to modes or levels of operation and thus of distinct interpretation.

The following example, which appears to follow the reverse process, only reinforces this impression of "split" reading and interpretation:

> Pourtant, avant, parce que c'est grave ce que je vais vous dire, grave pour moi, et pour vous aussi, selon qu'on sera d'accord ou pas, je veux savoir si vous avez confiance en moi. Je veux dire: si vous croyez que, vous demandant quelque chose, je vous le demande parce que c'est juste, et pour le bien de tous ? (Giono, *Colline*).

> First, however, because what I am about to tell you is serious, serious for me and for you too, depending on whether we agree or not, I want to know if you trust me. What I mean is: if you believe that, in asking you something, I am asking you because it is right, and for the good of all?

If I say that in this example there is a reverse process, it is because Giono's text involves a detailed explanation; in other words, because the integrated *if* needs to be justified, it will be – it has to be – detached from the predication which, unsurprisingly, is dominated here by verbs of *propositional attitude*: verbs of speech or intention, of knowledge, of telling, and of telling what to do.

The reasoning could be repeated and extended using other examples, which are distinctive in featuring isolated *ifs* (or propositions introduced by an *if*, or *If P* which are non-correlative, at least in the way they are presented):

> Cette architecture [baroque] a l'inconvénient d'être en désaccord avec le climat. Si l'on pouvait du moins, pendant les hivers de Bohême, mettre ces palais italiens en serre chaude avec les palmiers ? (Chateaubriand, *Mémoires d'Outre-tombe*, Prague Visit, 1833).

> This [baroque] architecture has the disadvantage of being out of tune with the climate. If one might at least, during the Bohemian winters, put these Italian palaces in a hothouse with the palm trees?

In a similar way, the English-language authors mentioned above link together *Wish, Hypotheticality*, and *Counterfactuality* (Athanasiadou/Dirven 1997, 84), *Conditionality* and *Inversion* (Werth 1997, 251).[33]

Where our example is concerned, Chateaubriand can be paraphrased in two ways, amply demonstrating that his interrogative *if* proposition is both a complement clause in its form and hypothetical in its meaning:

> **If** one might, during the Bohemian winters, [put] these Italian palaces in a hothouse with the palm trees?
>
> = [Even though it might be **unachievable**] Could one not, during the Bohemian winters, put these Italian palaces in a hothouse with the palm trees?
>
> = [I suggest the possibility **that**] one might, during the Bohemian winters, put these Italian palaces in a hothouse with the palm trees."

In other words, and here we return to the commentary of the extract from Koltès, the description of the suggested possibility, although it does not fuse the two possible forms of integration with the predicate (intra-extra-predicative), at least links them together or causes them to coincide: thinking and saying in the conditional, thinking and saying the conditional.

3 In conclusion...

I will first return to the example of Giono. As I have said, the extract includes a remarkable number of predicates *of attitude* which reflect the knowledge, beliefs, and doubts of the interlocutors or actants represented in and by the interlocution; in Koltès, the explicative dimension of the utterance is not as pronounced, but what these (attested) examples have in common – the purpose that each is working to achieve – is the restoration of a form of mental calculation that we, on our part, follow and share in, both as readers/listeners and as analysts of texts.[34]

It is therefore evident that, in linguistics (at the TL-CL intersection), it is difficult to separate mental operations from symbolic or semiotic forms, on the one

---

[33] Werth cites a series of examples of inversion, which go from interrogation to exclamation, and from condition (without *If*: *Should you see Ben, tell him...*) to negation (*Seldom had I seen such a beautiful view*), of which he says: "We can, I believe, isolate a communicative property they all share. Rather than simply depicting a situation, they all take some situation and hold it up for inspection."
[34] This dual position was developed by Brandt/Brandt (2005) in the form (mentioned above) of *intersubjectivity*.

hand; while on the other, and to go further still, the said forms are just as logical, i.e. rational, as they are discursive: my examples, or the enunciations I have chosen as examples, link fiction and diction (Koltès) as well as diction and fiction (Giono), or otherwise form a single whole (Chateaubriand).

References

Achard-Bayle, Guy, *The "literary mind" and changes. Conceptual and referential (dis)continuity in the construction of identities*, Annual review of cognitive linguistics 3 (2005), 41–55.

Achard-Bayle, Guy (ed.). *Textes/discours et co(n)textes. Entretiens avec Jean-Michel Adam, Bernard Combettes, Dominique Maingueneau, Sophie Moirand*, Pratiques 129–130 (2006), 20–49, DOI: https://doi.org/10.3406/prati.2006.2094. [last consultation: 06.07.2022]

Achard-Bayle, Guy (ed.), *Linguistique textuelle. États de lieux*, Verbum 32 (2010), Metz/Nancy, Presses universitaires de Nancy.

Achard-Bayle, Guy, *"Si quelque chat faisait du bruit..." Des textes (aux discours) hybrides. Essais de linguistique textuelle et cognitive*, Metz/Nancy, Éditions de l'Université de Lorraine, 2012.

Achard-Bayle, Guy, *"Texte" et "discours" se comprennent-ils?*, in: Monte, Michèle/Philippe, Gilles (edd.), *Genres et textes. Détermination, évolutions, confrontations. Hommage à Jean-Michel Adam*, Lyon, Presses universitaires de Lyon, 2014, 23–38, DOI: https://doi.org/10.4000/books.pul.3024.

Achard-Bayle, Guy, *Interfaces texte-cognition*, in: Rabatel, Alain/Ferrara-Léturgie, Alice/Léturgie, Arnaud, *La sémantique et ses interfaces. Actes du colloque 2013 de l'Association des Sciences du Langage*, Limoges, Lambert-Lucas, 2015, 49–68.

Achard-Bayle, Guy, *Les référents évolutifs, objets et objets du discours*, in: Sarda, Laure/Vigier, Denis/Combettes, Bernard (edd.), *Connexion et indexation. Ces liens qui tissent le texte*, Lyon, ENS Éditions, 2016, 83–97.

Achard-Bayle, Guy, *Texte-discours, sur fond d'action, dans les "Essais d'herméneutique II" de Ricœur*, in: Ablali, Driss/Achard-Bayle, Guy/Reboul-Touré, Sandrine/Temmar, Malika (edd.), *Textes et discours en confrontation dans l'espace européen*, Berne, Peter Lang, 2018, 151–167.

Achard-Bayle, Guy/Chabrolle-Cerretini, Anne-Marie (edd.), *Perspective fonctionnelle de la phrase. Du Cercle linguistique de Prague à la linguistique textuelle*, Verbum 35 (2013).

Achard-Bayle, Guy/Paveau, Marie-Anne, *Réel et cognition. Contribution à une histoire de la linguistique cognitive*, Histoire épistémologie langage 34:1 (2012), 97–114, DOI: https://doi.org/10.3406/hel.2012.3238.

Adam, Jean-Michel, *Pour une pragmatique linguistique et textuelle*, in: Reichler, Claude (ed.), *L'interprétation des textes*, Paris, Éditions de Minuit, 1989, 183–222.

Adam, Jean-Michel, *Linguistique textuelle. Des genres de discours aux textes*, Paris, Nathan, 1999.

Adam, Jean-Michel, *La Linguistique textuelle. Introduction à l'analyse textuelle des discours*, Paris, Armand Colin, 2005.

Adam, Jean-Michel, *Textes/discours et co(n)textes*, Pratiques 129–130 (2006), 21–34.

Adam, Jean-Michel, *L'émergence de la linguistique textuelle en France (1975–2010). Parcours bibliographique en 100 titres*, Verbum 32 (2010), 237–261, https://www.unil.ch/files/live/sites/fra/files/shared/CONSCILA_Verbum.pdf. [last consultation: 09.06.2022]

Adam, Jean-Michel, *La linguistique textuelle. Introduction à l'analyse textuelle des discours*, Paris, Armand Colin, 2011.

Athanasiadou, Angeliki/Dirven, René, *Conditionality, hypotheticality, counterfactuality*, in: Athanasiadou, Angeliki/Dirven, René (edd.), *On conditionals again*, Amsterdam, John Benjamins, 1997, 61–96.

Bakhtin, Mikhaïl, *Esthétique de la création verbale*, Paris, Gallimard, 1984.

Brandt, Line/Brandt, Per Aage, *Making sense of a blend. A cognitive-semiotic approach to metaphor*, Annual review of cognitive linguistics 3 (2005), 216–249.

Brown, Gillian/Yule, George (edd.), *Discourse analysis*, Cambridge, Cambridge University Press, 1983.

Charolles, Michel, *L'encadrement du discours. Univers, champs, domaines et espaces*, Cahier de recherche linguistique 6 (1997), 1–73, https://hal.archives-ouvertes.fr/hal-00665849/document. [last consultation: 10.06.2022]

Charolles, Michel, *Cohérence, pertinence et intégration conceptuelle*, in: Lane, Philippe (ed.), *Des discours aux textes. Modèles et analyses*, Rouen, Presses universitaires de Rouen et du Havre, 2006, 39–74.

Charolles, Michel, *Du noyau prédicatif au discours. Une affaire d'assemblages*, Paper given at the study day *Frontières du discours*, Université de Tours, May 23, 2013.

Combettes, Bernard, *Pour une grammaire textuelle. La progression thématique*, Bruxelles/Paris, De Boeck/Duculot, 1983.

Cusimano, Christophe (ed.), *Actualisation et virtualisation*, Études romanes de Brno 32:2 (2011).

Daneš, František, *À propos de l'identification de l'information connue (contextuellement liée) dans le texte*, Verbum 32 (2010), 283–308.

Fauconnier, Gilles, *Espaces mentaux*, Paris, Les Éditions de Minuit, 1984.

Fauconnier, Gilles, *Cognitive linguistics*, in: Nadel, Lynn (ed.), *Encyclopædia of cognitive sciences*, Chichester /Hoboken, John Wiley, 2005, https://www.academia.edu/9394494/Encyclopedia_of_Cognitive_Science [last consultation: 06.07.2022]

Fauconnier, Gilles/Sweetser, Eve (edd.), *Spaces, worlds, and grammar*, Chicago, University of Chicago Press, 1996.

Fauconnier, Gilles/Turner, Mark, *The way we think. Conceptual blending and the mind's hidden complexities*, New York, Basic Books, 2002.

Fillmore, Charles J., *Quelques problèmes posés à la grammaire casuelle*, Langages 38 (1975), 65–80, DOI: https://doi.org/10.3406/lgge.1975.2284.

Fortis, Jean-Michel/Col, Gilles, *Espaces mentaux et intégration conceptuelle. Retour sur la constitution de théories sœurs*, Cognitextes 18 (2018), DOI: https://doi.org/10.4000/cognitextes.1111.

Gibbs, Raymond, *Evaluating conceptual metaphor theory*, Discourse processes 48 (2011), 529–562.

Halliday, Michael Alexander Kirkwood/Hasan, Ruqaiya, *Cohesion in English*, London/New York, Longman, 1976.

Lakoff, George/Johnson, Mark, *Metaphors we live by*, Chicago, University of Chicago Press, 1980.

Maingueneau, Dominique, *Textes/discours et co(n)textes*, Pratiques 129–130 (2006), 40–42.

Martin, Robert, *Pour une logique du sens*, Paris, Presses universitaires de France, 1983.
Moignet, Gérard, *Études de psycho-systématique française*, Paris, Klincksieck, 1974.
Moignet, Gérard, *Systématique de la langue française*, Paris, Klincksieck, 1981.
Östman, Jan-Ola/Fried, Mirjam, *Historical and intellectual background of construction grammar*, in: Fried, Mirjam/Östman, Jan-Ola (edd.), *Construction grammar in a cross-language perspective*, Amsterdam, John Benjamins, 2004, 1–10.
Paveau, Marie-Anne/Sarfati, Georges-Élia, *Les grandes théories de la linguistique. De la grammaire comparée à la pragmatique*, Paris, Armand Colin, 2003.
Pešek, Ondřej, *La linguistique textuelle tchèque au seuil du XXIe siècle. La genèse d'une discipline et la tradition pragoise*, Verbum 32 (2010), 263–282.
Ricœur, Paul, *Du texte à l'action. Essais d'herméneutique II*, Paris, Seuil, 1986.
Skalička, Vladimir, *The need of a linguistics of "la parole"*, Recueil linguistique de Bratislava 1 (1948), 21–38.
Sweetser, Eve/Fauconnier, Gilles, *Cognitive links and domains. Basic aspects of mental space theory*, in: Fauconnier, Gilles/Sweetser, Eve (edd.), *Spaces, worlds, and grammar*, Chicago, University of Chicago Press, 1996, 1–28.
Werth, Paul, *Conditionality as cognitive distance*, in: Athanasiadou, Angeliki/Dirven, René (edd.), *On conditionals again*, Amsterdam, John Benjamins, 1997, 243–271.

Catherine Kerbrat-Orecchioni
Chapter 4
From discourse analysis to analysis of discourses

Abstract: This paper examines oral conversations as forms of discourse whose analysis implies diverse methodologies. We use two typological criteria to analyse the documented discourses: the written-oral opposition and their degree of interactivity. To end with, we approach another epistemological question, which touches not only upon interactionist theories but textual and discursive theories in general: "the recent explosion of research into discourse", oriented towards mathematical, semiotic, interactionist or political science linguistics, is related, willingly or not, to the discourse(s) analysis field.

Keywords: description, interaction, interpretation, oral, pragmatics, prosody

1 Preliminaries

Rather than starting from a priori considerations regarding the difference between discourse analysis, textual analysis, and conversation analysis, I intend to start from the subjects themselves to which these different disciplines are supposed to be committed.

Unlike "language" (an abstract system), "discourse" is a concrete object, produced from essentially linguistic natural materials and forming a more or less complete and independent unit. This implies that it is on a higher scale than the sentence (or its oral equivalent): discourse analysis emerged in tandem with the realization that there were rules and principles of discourse-level coherence (anaphoric mechanisms, isotopies, text grammars, etc.).

In the same way as "texts" (more so written ones), "conversations" (more so oral ones) may be considered as forms of discourse. As such, they relate to "discourse analysis" seen in its broad sense, and include the knowledge contributed by both old and more recent disciplines such as philology, stylistics and rhetoric, argumentation theories, semiotics and text linguistics, enunciation theories, and the various trends in pragmatics, as well as interactionist approaches with conversation analysis stricto sensu at their center.

Catherine Kerbrat-Orecchioni, Université Lumière Lyon 2, ICAR

https://doi.org/10.1515/9783110794434-005

Different forms of discourse show common features which are linked to their linguistic essence, but they also have all kinds of specific attributes which mean that a variety of methodologies need to be used. The enormous quantity of discourses evident in a given society can be typologized on the basis of many levels of criteria. I shall begin by looking at two dimensions that might be considered as superordinate to all the others, given that their methodological implications are truly decisive: these are the written versus the oral character of the discourse subject to analysis, and its degree of interactivity.

2 Two fundamental distinctions for a typology of discourses

2.1 Oral versus written discourse

Language has the particularity of having two forms, oral and written, between which there is no continuum: either the material used is of a phonic nature, or it is graphic. In this sense, we cannot speak of discourses being "intermediary" between oral and written, even though it is true that:
- Some types of written discourses (such as *chats*) possess certain features of the oral, and vice versa (it can be said that someone speaks "like a book");
- Communication can draw upon written and oral material simultaneously: mixed interactions ("oralographic") are frequent, particularly in the teaching context, but also in certain situations encountered in daily life;
- The two systems are mutually convertible: a written text can be spoken just as an oral discourse can be written, although these "transubstantiation" processes necessarily involve more or less substantial changes to the original message (it is not only its materiality that is affected).

The main characteristic of oral communication is that it is "multimodal", that is to say *plurisemiotic* (simultaneous use of linguistic, voco-prosodic, and mimo-gestural units) and *multichannel*: it uses both auditory and visual channels (and possibly tactile ones), whereas writing is exclusively visual – and, incidentally, on this note, the well-attested custom of certain semioticians appears strange when, describing an advertising poster for example, they oppose "visual" material (in reality "iconic") to "linguistic" material, whereas the latter is of an equally visual nature (even though it relates to an auditory reality whose influence on the way the message is received remains rather problematic).

It nevertheless remains true that these different types of units function in synergy, but it seems difficult to describe any sample of oral discourse without taking account of the "totext" (Cosnier 1987); and it is possible to cite a large number of phenomena that are not configured in the same way at all in the two types of discourse, starting with grammatical units (we know that the breakdown into "sentences" is only relevant to the written form – we know it, but we often forget it: for example, some analysts unhesitatingly state, with no mincing of words, that in the 2007 Royal-Sarkozy debate that we will study below, Royal's sentences were distinctly longer than those of Sarkozy. . .). We should also mention the *repairs* which are very characteristic of oral communication.[1] These can only be constructed by successive amendments: discourse is developed step by step and possibly by retracing one's steps, which obviously leaves its mark on the product itself; whereas writing offers the possibility of erasing what has been crossed out and replacing the rough draft with a corrected version. In oral discourse, it is the rough draft that is delivered to others, and where "the worksite of speech development" (Barbéris 1999, 3) is exposed in public. Another example, relating to a completely different level of discourse functioning, is the notion of *ethos*. This can certainly be applied to writing, as some discourse analysts (such as Amossy and Maingueneau) have rightly shown; but it is only fully effective when applied to oral communication, when the body is truly, both concretely and physically, engaged in the discursive activity.[2] To be convinced of this, it is sufficient to compare the previously-mentioned debate with the various transcriptions made of it: we find in them a very distant echo of the two protagonists' "voices". However faithful they may be, these written artefacts inevitably produce a considerable leveling of the *éthè*.

2.2 "Monologal" discourse vs. "discourse-in-interaction"

It is often heard said that all discourses have an "interactive" dimension, insofar as they generally incorporate other enunciative voices. But in monologal discourses (however "dialogic" and "polyphonic" they may be) the incorporation is achieved under the leadership of the same locutor-writer, which changes everything. This person certainly constructs their discourse according to what they imagine about the addressee – but this has little relationship to situations where two (or more)

---

[1] Especially prototypical, that is to say improvised oral communication – the *fresh talk* that Goffman contrasts with "memorization" and "reading aloud" (1987, 171).
[2] See, for example, de Chanay/Kerbrat-Orecchioni (2007).

interlocutors are present, who *co-construct* a sort of "text" that is cobbled together on line, constantly interrupting one another, adapting their joint behavior on an ad hoc basis and, throughout the interaction, *negotiating* the various aspects of the way it works (how it opens and closes, the alternating opportunities to speak, the themes dealt with, the signs manipulated, the interpretations made, the opinions expressed, the identities displayed, the "places" and roles claimed, and so on).[3]

This axis covers the preceding one to a large extent – but only to an extent, because these days there are forms of interactive writing and, conversely, certain forms of oral communication that are only slightly interactive. This second axis is in fact gradual: we must accept the existence of *degrees of interactivity*, the maximum degree being represented by informal conversations but also by certain types of exchange of an institutional nature, such as political debates. To take once more the case of the Royal-Sarkozy debate, a close examination reveals that a not-inconsiderable portion of the semiotic material produced throughout the exchange served, among other things (because most units are multifunctional), to co-construct the discourse. Among these are the nominal forms of address, whose use is remarkably asymmetrical in this debate: Sarkozy produces 137 of them ("Madame"/"Madame Royal") compared with only 9 on Royal's side. But what interests us here is the fact that the great majority of these forms are sacrificed in the transcription made by the newspaper *Libération*, where only 38 appear in Sarkozy's text. This is because one of the main functions of these forms of address relates to the management of real time during the course of the interaction: they serve first and foremost to enable people to take, or resume, their turn to speak. They are therefore much more useful in situ, when the interaction is ongoing, than they are in later written reconstructions, where "they are now presented only as signs (a few of these are therefore preserved) but not as tools (it is therefore not necessary to have all of them)", as de Chanay (2010, 266) has effectively shown.

2.3 Other distinctions

In each of the vast groups circumscribed by the two main axes previously referred to, all kinds of relevant distinctions can and must be introduced, but there is no question of repeating the list here.[4] I would simply mention the importance of

---

[3] For the different types of conversation negotiations, see Kerbrat-Orecchioni (2005, chap. 2).
[4] See, among other things, issue 153 (2004) of the journal Langages with a contribution by Kerbrat-Orecchioni/Traverso on "Les types d'interactions et genre de l'oral" ('Types of interactions and genres of oral communication'; all subsequent translations from other works are by Rosemary Rodwell, the translator of this chapter, unless stated otherwise.)

"genre" constraints, with their respective "communication contracts" (to reprise a valuable concept introduced by Charaudeau);[5] or the contrast between "institutional" vs. "non-institutional" discourses, a contrast on which Maingueneau rightly insists, and which concerns both written and oral discourses. In relation to this, I would like to clarify a point that is often misunderstood by "discursologists" who are unfamiliar with conversation analysis per se (i.e. ethnomethodologically-inspired conversation analysis): despite the official designation, this trend, far from dealing exclusively with what are commonly called "conversations" (friendly and informal), also focuses on exchanges taking place in an institutional context (academic or hospital environments, company workplaces, courts, businesses, services, etc.). These different forms of talk-in-interaction have enough shared features for a common procedure to be applied.

3 Methodological remarks

3.1 That discourse analysis is part of linguistics

The diversity of discursive language productions prompts us to speak of analysis of *discourses* rather than analysis of *discourse*, and to accept a corresponding diversity of the methods used to describe them. We are indebted to conversation analysts for having established a new analytical approach and for inventing descriptive tools that are both original and perfectly suited to the specific nature of talk-in-interaction – namely its collective and gradual development through the alternation of speaking opportunities, whose workings were meticulously dissected by the supporters of this trend (cf. Sacks/Schegloff/Jefferson 1974). It is also due to them that we became aware of the need to take account of the smallest "details" of discursive materiality (applied to dialogal and multimodal material, this attitude is reminiscent of that of philologists and stylisticians, who painstakingly describe the particularities of a written corpus "as the text unfolds").

"Hard-line" conversationalists, however, sometimes have a tendency to focus only on certain types of details and to neglect others, which belong to different levels of operating and have been described in other theoretical contexts. These are rejected on grounds of the supposed incompatibility of conversation analysis' "analytic mentality" with other types of approaches.[6] My own advice is to

---

[5] "Contrats de communication". For an overall summary of the concept, see the article on "communication contract" in Charaudeau/Maingueneau (2002).
[6] On this incompatibility, see for example Gülich/Mondada (2001, 196).

adopt an "eclectic" approach (Kerbrat-Orecchioni 2005), insofar as there is not only compatibility between certain notions of diverse provenance but even a need to connect them (for example, "conditional dependency" refers to a theory of speech acts, reflected also by the notion of "preferential linking", which has everything to gain from appealing to the theory of face-work...). I will do no more than insist here on the fact that conversations, in the same way as other forms of discourse, are linguistic productions and, therefore, cannot be described without permanent recourse to the various tools developed in all sectors of the language sciences. In other words, to make useful analyses of conversations it is first of all necessary to be a good linguist, and not make do with simply examining the way in which repairs and successive opportunities to speak are co-handled, but also to look at all sorts of phenomena which can only be described thanks to the contributions of more "traditional" linguistics (conversation analysis was not built upon a tabula rasa).

An example of this is the way the anaphora functions (intervening between two different turns to speak in the first case and within the same turn in the second), with two illustrations (borrowed once again from presidential debates) of the uses to which this mechanism may give rise on the part of skillful debaters.

(1) François Mitterrand (FM)-Jacques Chirac (JC) debate, 1988 presidential elections
JC: permettez-moi juste de vous dire que ce soir/ (.) je ne suis pas/ le Premier ministre\ (.) et vous n'êtes pas/ le président de la République\ (.) nous sommes\ (.) deux candidats/ (.) à égalité/ (.) et qui se soumettent au jugement des Français (.) le seul qui compte\ (.) vous me permettrez donc de vous appeler monsieur Mitterrand\

FM: **mais vous avez tout à fait raison/ monsieur le Premier ministre**

JC: just allow me to say that this evening\ (.) I am not/ the Prime Minister\ (.) and you are not/ the president of the Republic\ (.) we are (.) two candidates (.) on equal terms\ (.) submitting to the judgment of the French people/ (.) which is all that counts\ (.) allow me therefore to call you Monsieur Mitterrand\

FM: **but you are entirely right Prime Minister**

With regard to this very celebrated output by Mitterrand, Trognon and Larrue (1994, 76) speak of "denial" and an enunciation with the appearance of a "paradox". This is probably true. But a closer look reveals that the answer lends itself to two interpretations, depending on the "significance" attributed to "you are entirely right": it is an anaphoric expression, but what exactly is its antecedent? What does the agreement really "concern"?

– The most natural interpretation is to consider that the judgment contained in Mitterrand's reply concerns the whole of Chirac's previous argument, especially its crux stating that "we are two candidates on equal terms". According to this interpretation, there is a contradiction between the content of Mitter-

rand's utterance and the form of address accompanying it: it is a quip, giving rise to laughter. But at the same time, Mitterrand is covering his back: he can claim to be innocent of this discursive scandal of the contradiction by taking refuge behind the second interpretation.
– Indeed, "you are entirely right" can also be interpreted as concerning only the end of the preceding speech ("allow me therefore to call you Monsieur Mitterrand"): do what you like, where I'm concerned I'll continue to call you what I like. . . . Although the first interpretation of the reply is the more likely, hence the laughter it arouses, the second is also possible. Since Chirac has made the error of leaving the logical culmination of his reasoning implicit ("allow me therefore to call you Monsieur Mitterrand [*and please do call me Monsieur Chirac*]"), Mitterrand loses no time in exploiting this fatal error of forgetfulness to his own advantage – together with the vagueness which generally affects the impact of signs of agreement.

(2) Ségolène Royal (SR)-Nicolas Sarkozy (NS) debate, 2007 presidential elections

NS: eh bien, je veux en finir avec **ces discours creux**\ (.) **pas le vôtre/ je ne veux pas être désagréable**/(.) ces promesses incantatoires\ (.) cette grande braderie au moment de l'élection (.) on rase gratis / on promet tout\ (.)

NS: well, I'd like to end **all this empty talk**\ (.) **not yours/ I don't want to be unpleasant**/ (.) these hackneyed promises\ (.) this big sell at election time\ (.) we bore [people] stiff for nothing/ we promise everything\ (.)

Here, the ambiguity of the anaphoric expression "not yours" is based on a contradiction, partly between what is suggested by semantic coherence (since Sarkozy states he does not want to be unpleasant to Royal, it seems right to interpret "not yours" as "your talk is not empty"); and partly what is imposed by syntax ("not yours" can only refer to the complete syntactic unit "this empty talk", which implies "your talk is empty"). Just like Mitterrand (concealing under a rhetoric of tolerance his stubborn desire to evoke his interlocutor's inferior status), Sarkozy here kills two birds with one stone: he displays a courteous (or at least "not unpleasant") attitude through the precaution he takes with this aside, while at the same time insidiously suggesting that his adversary's discourse is well and truly "empty". He thus manages to create a favorable image of himself and an unfavorable one of his rival, both at the same time.

We might obviously ask whether this "dual language" is, in each of these cases, conscious and deliberate. What is certain is that it produces certain particular effects on the listeners and, whatever may be the case, the analyst has a duty to take account of it since this duplicity is fully registered in the text of the interaction; and this takes us back to the thorny question of interpretation.

3.2 Interpretation of discourse and position of the analyst

Whatever certain defenders of a radical "constructionism" (or "emergentism") may think, all discourses are manufactured from preexisting material, namely language, with its phonetic and prosodic, grammatical, and lexical units – if the meaning of words is more or less vague and therefore negotiable, they nevertheless possess a conventional core with a certain robustness. Negotiations are, in the end, carried out "on the margin", running the risk of being concealed by the fact that it is precisely these margins, and not the invisible base on which they are anchored, that are made "salient" through the strategic uses to which they may give rise, and which discourse analysis turns to its advantage. Here, we might again take the example of the famous so-called "healthy anger" sequence in the Royal-Sarkozy debate; a sequence that has been analyzed elsewhere[7] and so I shall simply recall the principle. This passage of the debate is especially interesting, because we are directly witnessing the conflictual construction of two partly-divergent lexical micro-systems, centered round the word "anger" ("colère"), whose meaning is obviously more or less the same for both debaters (we cannot make language say just anything). But Royal is operating within the notion of a disassociation between "healthy" anger ("colère saine") and other forms of anger, thus introducing the more specific concept of "healthy anger", of which she offers a definition ('healthy anger is what emerges from a feeling of revolt when faced with suffering').[8] For her, it is a notion laden with positive axiological value, diametrically opposed to the notion of "agitation": 'no, I'm not getting worked up, I am angry (.) *it's not the same thing*, don't be contemptuous Monsieur Sarkozy'[9] – contempt consisting in this instance of reducing a generous and considered emotion to a vulgar, uncontrolled fit of rage. This is indeed what Sarkozy attempts to do throughout the sequence: he puts anger *in the same category* as agitation, successively using "getting worked up", "getting agitated", "flying off the handle", "losing [her] temper", and "losing [her] cool": for him, all these expressions are synonymous and equally laden in this context of negative connotation. According to Sarkozy, therefore, Royal is agitated (she shows herself to be in a state of non-calm, one might say), whereas 'in order to be president of the Republic one must be calm'.[10]

---

[7] See de Chanay/Giaufret/Kerbrat-Orecchioni (2011).
[8] "Il y a des colères qui sont parfaitement saines, parce qu'elles correspondent à la souffrance des gens..."
[9] "Je ne perds pas mes nerfs, je suis en colère. Pas de mépris, M. Sarkozy..."
[10] "Pour être président de la République, il faut être calme..." https://www.vie-publique.fr/discours/166574-debat-televise-entre-mme-segolene-royal-depute-ps-et-m-nicolas-sarkoz [last consultation: 09.08.2022].

Thus, it is nothing less than Ségolène Royal's "presidentiability" that is at stake in this debate, and it is what explains the length (more than eight minutes) of this highly charged lexical negotiation from an argumentative point of view.

But finally, is Ségolène Royal "angry" or "agitated"? A detailed analysis of her behavior in this sequence – both verbal and non-verbal – encourages us to consider that the answer is no, she has not "flown off the handle". Contrary to this opinion, however, many commentators of the episode, both laypeople and political discourse experts, have spoken and still speak of the "moment when Ségolène Royal got worked up", and have no hesitation in espousing Sarkozy's interpretation, whatever their political leanings may be. In fact, it is permissible to think that analysts should not be scornful of these "erroneous" interpretations (since they are not isolated) and that the interactional text, together with certain contextual data, must surely to a certain extent be responsible for these constructions of meaning. In this instance, it could be alleged that there are various factors favoring this interpretation. There is first of all the fact that by dint of drumming out "don't get agitated", Sarkozy ended up convincing the mass of spectators-listeners that Royal was indeed agitated (this at least is what registered in people's memories). There is also the fact that the – doubtless legitimate – distinction Royal attempts to establish between two emotions that are close to one another is probably too subtle for such a context (this is not a philosophical debate on France Culture radio channel): ordinary language does accept that "being angry" and "being agitated" are in some way synonymous; Sarkozy's position thus complies more with common sense than does Royal's – it is more in accordance, too, with the stereotypical view of anger (implying a degree of violence and leading to behavior that is somewhat uncontrolled). Finally, there is the excessive length of the sequence: Royal is unrelenting, repeating ad nauseam "I'm not getting worked up, I am angry". And it was obvious why she refused to let it go: it was because her presidential ethos was at stake. But by insisting in this way she risked arousing the exasperation of the public – they wished to move on to something else and see an end to this digression which gave the impression of taking place at the expense of more important problems. It was as if this rather phony and theatrical spectacle in which Royal played the passionate and offended activist was a sort of camouflage. It would seem that by allowing herself to be drawn in to this over-long psychological-ethical digression, Ségolène Royal well and truly fell into the trap set by her rival.

Whatever type of discourse is involved, it is the analyst's job to try and piece together the interpretative work done by all those likely to be on the receiving end. But depending on the type of discourse, the problem is not posed in quite the same terms.

We might first of all distinguish cases where the analyst is a recipient among others of the discourse they are describing, or situations where the analyst is in the position of "intruder" in relation to the subject involved, which will therefore be impossible to interpret because, as for its official recipients, not all the necessary information is available; this distinction is valid for written texts (an example is an epistolary novel vs. a private correspondence) as well as for oral discourses (an example might be a media debate vs. a conversation one has not taken part in).

But there is a fundamental difference between written and oral productions, which is not always sufficiently borne in mind: like oral speech, written communication develops step by step, not without trial and error and deletions – but it is absorbed by its recipient *after the event*, in the form of a finished text that the analyst can treat as such without scruple, since it is designed for this purpose. It is by no means the same with conversations and other forms of oral interaction, which are made to be absorbed *in real time*, but are analyzed after the event. It is obviously impossible to describe the development of an oral production in real time: the analyst's first task is to *transcribe* it, i.e. to *textualize* it (and decontextualize it at the same time), to turn it into a more or less autonomous and stable object. The analyst might constantly return to the recording, but it is nevertheless from the transcription that one mainly works; however much one tries to follow, by means of the text's thread, the way in which it is constructed dynamically, what one knows of the whole will inevitably influence the sequential analysis:

> It does not seem possible to act as if I did not have 'the whole' [...] before my eyes. I can only assume that I have listened to the cassette time and again, and transcribed the interaction, with the very special sort of listening that this process supposes, and have become permeated with it, to describe what is happening at the T1 moment while knowing what happened at the T2 moment. (Traverso 2003, 30)

The analyst's position is, therefore, in the case of oral still more than in written communication, radically different from that of the "members", that is to say of the participants engaged in the discursive event subject to investigation, as Ten Have (2002, 39 and 41) very rightly recognizes:

> As analysts we can only use our overhearer's perspective, to reconstruct a plausible version of the actually lived participant's perspectives. [...] The relationship between this after-the-fact constitution of the sense of an event, and the lived order of that event, is a problematic one. There are no final solutions to sense-making.

4 Conclusion

With the recent explosion of discourse research (particularly on discourse in interaction), this field of investigation has been considerably extended and diversified – thus the same object of research, such as the Royal-Sarkozy debate, has given rise to a variety of studies in the directions of mathematical linguistics, semiotics, interaction, or political analysis;[11] but these may all be considered to relate to analysis of discourse(s) by virtue of their focus on textual materiality. We should note in conclusion that whatever innovations have taken place in this area of study since the 1970s (when discourse analysis mainly involved the written word – sometimes contrasted, not with conversation analysis as it is today, but with text linguistics), we still come up against the same basic theoretical questions, even though they are no longer phrased in exactly the same terms. Here is a quick, though not exhaustive list of these:

– Given that any description is an interpretation, how far can one go in deciphering markers and cues provided by the textual material? It is certain that analysis cannot be reduced to a simple paraphrase of the type "he says she is worked up and she replies that she is angry". Neither can one be satisfied with statements according to which the participants make themselves "mutually available", in order to be of greatest benefit to the analyst, which is the interpretation it is convenient to give to the utterances they exchange: these utterances are *signifiers* which they "exhibit" in the interaction; moving from signifier to signified always implies a certain "interpretative leap", but insofar as possible with a safety net, and all sorts of other safeguards which still have to be redefined.
– What is the relative importance of the similarities and specificities belonging to each type of discourse and, likewise, to what extent should the methodologies adopted be the same as or different from one another?
– How, today, can the frontier and articulation between language (preexisting conventional "resources") and discourses (which carry out a partial remodeling of the system) be redrawn?
– Is it permissible and desirable to call upon external information for the purposes of description, or should we try to limit ourselves to the text itself (the old debate between partisans of an "immanentist" approach and those condemning the "endogenous illusion" is now undergoing a revival in the field of interaction analysis)?

These are so many questions that still have no definitive answer, and perhaps this is for the best.

---

11 Regarding this debate, see Bertrand/Dézé/Missika (2007); Charaudeau (2008); Fracchiolla (2008); and issues 89 and 90 (2009) of the journal Mots.

References

Barbéris, Jeanne-Marie (ed.), *Le français parlé. Variétés et discours*, Montpellier, Presses universitaires de la Méditerranée/Praxiling, 1999.

Bertrand, Denis/Dézé, Alexandre/Missika, Jean-Louis, *Parler pour gagner. Sémiotique des discours de la campagne présidentielle de 2007*, Paris, Presses de Sciences Po, 2007.

Charaudeau, Patrick, *Entre populisme et peopolisme. Comment Sarkozy a gagné !*, Paris, Vuibert, 2008.

Charaudeau, Patrick/Maingueneau, Dominique (edd.), *Dictionnaire d'analyse du discours*, Paris, Éditions du Seuil, 2002.

Constantin de Chanay, Hugues, *Adresses adroites. Les FNA dans le débat Royal-Sarkozy du 2 mai 2007*, in: Kerbrat-Orecchioni, Catherine (ed.), *S'adresser à autrui. Les formes nominales d'adresse en français*, Chambéry, Éditions de l'Université de Savoie, 2010, 249–294.

Constantin de Chanay, Hugues/Kerbrat-Orecchioni, *100 minutes pour convaincre. L'éthos en action de Nicolas Sarkozy*, in: Broth, Mathias/Forsgren, Mats/Norén, Coco/Sullet-Nylander, Françoise (edd.), *Le français parlé des médias*, Stockholm, Acta Universitatis Stockholmiensis, 2007, 309–329.

Constantin de Chanay, Hugues/Giaufret, Anna/Kerbrat-Orecchioni, Catherine, *La gestion interactive des émotions dans la communication politique à la télévision. Quand les intervenants perdent leur calme*, in: Burger, Marcel/Jacquin, Jérôme/Micheli, Raphaël, *La parole politique en confrontation dans les médias*, Bruxelles/Louvain-la-Neuve, De Boeck, 2011, 25–49.

Cosnier, Jacques, *L'éthologie du dialogue*, in: Cosnier, Jacques/Kerbrat-Orecchioni, Catherine, *Décrire la conversation*, Lyon, Presses universitaires de Lyon, 1987, 291–315.

Fracchiolla, Béatrice, *L'attaque courtoise. De l'usage de la politesse comme stratégie d'agression dans le débat Royal-Sarkozy du 2 mai 2007*, in: Heiden, Serge/Pincemin, Bénédicte, *JADT 2008. Actes des 9ᵉ Journées internationales d'analyse statistique des données textuelles*, Lyon, Presses universitaires de Lyon, 2008, 495–508.

Goffman, Erving, *Façons de parler*, Paris, Les Éditions de Minuit, 1987.

Gülich, Elisabeth/Mondada, Lorenza, *Konversationsanalyse*, in: Holtus, Günter/Metzeltin, Michael/Schmitt, Christian (edd.), *Lexikon der Romanistischen Linguistik*, vol. 1:2, Tübingen, Niemeyer, 2001, 196–252.

Kerbrat-Orecchioni, Catherine, *Le discours en interaction*, Paris, Armand Colin, 2005.

Kerbrat-Orecchioni, Catherine/Traverso, Véronique, *Types d'interactions et genres de l'oral*, Langages 153 (2004), 41–51.

Sacks, Harvey/Schegloff Emanuel A./Jefferson, Gail, *A simplest systematics for the organization of turn-taking for conversation*, Language 50 (1974), 696–735.

Ten Have, Paul, *Reflections on transcription*, Cahiers de praxématique 39 (2002), 21–43, DOI: https://doi.org/10.4000/praxematique.1833.

Traverso, Véronique, *Analyse des interactions: questions sur la pratique. Synthèse en vue de l'obtention de l'habilitation à diriger des recherches*, Lyon, Université Lumière Lyon 2, 2003.

Trognon, Alain/Larrue, Janine, *Pragmatique du discours politique*, Paris, Armand Colin, 1994.

Alain Rabatel
Chapter 5
Enunciator position, positioning and posture

Abstract: This article draws connections between the notions of enunciator position, positioning, and posture, which structure the dialogic, cognitive and interactional co-production of utterances. The notion of *enunciative position* corresponds to the fact that the (first or second) enunciator refers to objects of discourse while positioning him/herself with regard to them, by indicating from what point of view s/he considers them. In view of the dialogic nature of the discourse, two modal subjects and levels of responsibility can be discerned: the first enunciator has the role of agent in charge of the discourse and the second enunciators fulfill internal functions of validation, thus assuming a sort of responsibility which does not necessarily commit the first enunciator. The article then analyzes the dialogic strategies of positioning by enunciative intensification and distancing which account for auto-dialogic and hetero-dialogic situations. Finally, it deals with the enunciative postures of co-enunciation, over-enunciation, and under-enunciation, which refine the notions of enunciative intensification or distancing by specifying the degrees of agreement, according to a dialectic between discordant concordance and concordant discordance.

Keywords: (co-, over-, and under-) enunciation, (first, and second) enunciator(s), positioning, posture (of enunciator), viewpoint

By articulating the position, positioning, and posture of enunciators, I propose to shed light on the agents and operations which structure the dialogic,[1] cognitive, and interactional co-production of utterances. Pursuing a line of thinking begun in 2005, I first of all set out the notion of enunciator borrowed from Ducrot (1984), together with that of *enunciative position*: this is consistent with the fact that the first enunciator refers to objects of discourse while positioning him/herself in relation to them, by indicating from what point of view and in what context s/he considers them [1]. In view of the general dialogic nature of discourse, the positions involve both the first (E1) and second (e2) enunciators who feed the discourse of E1. This means that two different modal subjects and levels

---

[1] In this article, the dialogic dimension is understood in a mainly monologal context, but it is of course possible to account for it in a dialogical context (Rabatel 2005b; 2007; 2008b).

Alain Rabatel, Université de Lyon 1/Université de Lyon 2, ICAR

https://doi.org/10.1515/9783110794434-006

of assuming responsibility (AR) can be discerned: the first enunciator has the role of agent in charge of the discourse while the second enunciators, represented by L1/E1, fulfill internal validation functions (Gosselin 2010), thus assuming a sort of quasi-AR which does not commit L1/E1 [2]. This disassociation between levels of AR highlights the dialogic strategies of *positioning by enunciative intensification* (*"redoublement"*, i.e. showing agreement with the viewpoint expressed by another and making it one's own) and *distancing* (*"dédoublement"*, i.e. distancing oneself from another's viewpoint without actually disagreeing).[2] These come into play when E1 positions him/herself in relation to others of him/herself (*autres de soi*) or others than him/herself (*autres que soi*), since positioning by intensification is auto-dialogic, while positioning by distancing is hetero-dialogic [3]. Finally, the *enunciative postures of co-, over-, and under-enunciation* refine the notion of enunciative distancing and intensification at an interactional level, by specifying all the nuances of agreement, introducing discordance within concordance (and vice versa), according to the cognitive and interactional adjustments that occur as the discourse unfolds [4].

1 Enunciative positions of the first and second enunciators

I define the *locutor* as the first agent to produce utterances materially – which is why the locutor can be compared to the notion of voice, uttered (or written) by a locutor/writer, endowed with materiality, and dependent on sensory experience (Rabatel 2010a; 2012d) – while the *enunciator* is seen as the source of viewpoints (VPs) expressed through the predication of propositional contents (PCs) in an utterance.[3]

---

2 All subsequent translations from other works are by Rosemary Rodwell, the translator of this chapter, unless stated otherwise.
3 The utterance results from an act of enunciation, 'a linguistically structured fragment of experience, actualized in an enunciation situation, which is an individual realization of a system of expression common to all speakers of the same language.' (Neveu 2004, 119: "un fragment d'expérience linguistiquement structuré, actualisé dans une situation d'énonciation, et constituant une réalisation individuelle d'un système d'expression commun à tous les locuteurs d'une même langue.") This structured fragment is of variable size (Maingueneau 2002, 222).

1.1 From propositional contents to viewpoints

PCs do not only refer to the world in a truth-conditional manner; they also indicate the enunciator's position with regard to the objects of the discourse. The notion of enunciative position refutes the commonplace referentialist and objectivist hypothesis, according to which words are deemed to be 'etiquettes placed upon things' (Dubois 2009, 16):[4] the choices of category (nouns and verbs), qualification (adjectives and adverbs), modifier and modalization, word order and predication, together with the choices of what to highlight, all indicate the enunciator's position in relation to the objects of the discourse. In this sense, the notion of position intersects with that of viewpoint (VP), by being part of a strong conception of enunciation/referentiation ("*mode de donation de la référence*", '*means of giving referents*') that is coextensive with language. This is why the referentiation of the PC of a VP is crucial for grasping the enunciative position of the enunciator and for interpreting the meaning of the utterance. The analysis of VPs cannot be limited to the abstract PC; this is what logicians reduce them to, making (1) equivalent to a proposition of the type [man-being-wolf-for-man]:

(1) Man is a wolf for man.[5]

This abstract PC flouts the generic turn of phrase and the metaphor, as well as the choice made by human beings to speak in a certain way, giving "man" a generic meaning that has been accepted for centuries, or even millennia, but is now increasingly contested. People will object that these considerations do not affect the truth of the judgment *sub specie aeternetatis*. No doubt this is true. But extra-linguistic truth does not exhaust either the meaning or the implications of this predication. Furthermore, to understand the whole of the referentiation we must also take intonative phenomena into account (something rarely done, in theory, but not in daily life. . .): all these elements enable us to determine in context whether (1) signifies (1a) or (1b) – the list is not ended. Indeed, the fragments in curly brack of ets, which are not pronounced, explain the meaning demonstrated by the PC, said in the tone an obvious doxic fact[6] in (1a), which is refuted in (1b):[7]

---

4 "[D]es étiquettes posées sur les choses".
5 The entire original corpus (in French) can be found at the end of the chapter.
6 I will not enter here into the stratifications between the common meanings of canon, vulgate, and doxa, nor the distinctions between doxa and ideology. See, in particular, Sarfati (2011, 145–152 and 152–160).
7 See what Recanati (1979) calls the "margins of the text" ("les marges du texte").

(1a) {As everyone knows,} man is a wolf for man.

(1b) {Big deal,} man is a wolf for man.

1.2 The actualization of positions in viewpoints

The enunciator expresses his/her VP through predications in situation, carrying out enunciative operations (Culioli/Normand 2005, 164–165) and actualizing a certain number of enunciative positions (Barbéris/Bres/Siblot 1998). The notion of position refers first and foremost to different operations enabling the speaker to assert the objects of the discourse in relation to the notional categories involved: the enunciator can put these objects at the center of their domain by means of identification ("He's a real wolf"), disconnection ("This is not a wolf"), or differentiation ("This is only remotely like a wolf"). In the preceding examples, the choices of categorization are coupled with choices of quantification, qualification, and modalization which are all significant in terms of the enunciator's position in relation to the object. Furthermore, the enunciator can validate the predications either in relation to him/herself ("Where I'm concerned, Pierre's brother is a real wolf"); or in relation to an interlocutor or a third person ("Where Pierre/I/anyone is concerned, he's a real wolf"); through enunciative deletion ("He's a real wolf"); in relation to a fictitious locutor ("According to the criteria, we're no longer facing a real wolf"); or by being non-assertive ("I'd like to meet a real wolf") (Culioli 1990 ; 1999). Secondly, the notion of position refers to a positioning in an enunciation plan, and to the way in which the primary enunciator (E1) constructs his/her object by referring (or not) to the enunciation situation through a deictic or anaphoric point of reference. Thirdly, the notion of position is indicated by a large number of markers which affect predication. As Verine (2014) reminds us, at the morpho-syntactic level the enunciator uttering a predication chooses between enunciation modalities (assertion, injunction or questioning) and utterance modalities (exclamation, negation, emphasis). S/he can still specify the modal value through the choice of terms, syntactic constructions or circumlocutions relating to the (more or less) necessary, obligatory, possible or probable nature of the process represented, using modal auxiliaries or their adverbial or periphrastic equivalents. S/he can also evaluate the process, and explain this evaluation through a number of metalinguistic comments dealing with the propositional content or its modality, which may be diluted or strengthened. This explains the fact that, for Bally (Ducrot 1989, 181–191), the enunciator can be compared with the notion of modal subject insofar as his/her imprint can be seen not only in the *modus*, but also in the choices that structure the *dictum*, as emphasized by Ducrot (1993).

2 Agent assuming responsibility (L1/E1, l2/e2) and agent of validation (second enunciators) for quasi-responsibility

Just as we cannot limit ourselves to an "abstract" conception of PCs when thinking about enunciation, neither is it possible to confine ourselves to a monological or monologic conception of the enunciative position – see also Desclés/Guibert (2011).

2.1 Locutor and enunciator in syncretism or non-locutor second enunciators

The difficulty increases if we come up against the notion of enunciative position with voices and VPs intertwined, or if we consider that the enunciative positions may correspond to our own (2) or to those of others, and that these others are either the locutor/enunciators at the origin of a VP communicated by a speech act (3)–(5), or second enunciators referring to VPs expressed through 'ways of seeing' or 'attitudes' (6)–(7), according to Ducrot 1984, 204).[8]

When an utterance refers directly to the VP of the first locutor (L1), as in (2), there is syncretism between L1 and E1, coded by a slash between the agents (L1/E1). In the discourses represented, with embedded locutors (l2), who are the source of a VP, there is a dual syncretism, between L1/E1 and l2/e2, as in examples (3) to (5):

(2) I'm coming tomorrow without fail.

(3) Pierre said: "I'll come tomorrow without fail".

(4) Pierre said that he would come tomorrow without fail.

(5) Pierre said that he would come tomorrow "without fail".

This notion of syncretism is crucial: it indicates that, out of all the enunciators who skim through utterances and discourses, one of them is more important than the others – namely, the first enunciator, the one who *forms a body* with L1, whom people address when there is agreement or disagreement, and whom I have

---

8 "Manières de voir", "attitudes".

named the principal (Rabatel 2005a). This is the person who, in syncretism with L1, takes responsibility for E1's successive VPs and the meta-VP which sums up his/her position in the discourse. The notion of taking responsibility, which is variously glossed, corresponds to truth of expression – in a truth-conditional way that is independent of the locutors or linkage to a particular agent, I-truth, you-truth, one-truth – (Culioli 1980, 184; Berrendonner 1981, 59).

In (2), L1/E1 takes responsibility for the VP. In (3)–(5), L1 is the locutor of the PC [Pierre-to come-tomorrow-without fail], but it is Pierre who is the enunciator taking responsibility for the commitment to come. E1 only takes responsibility for the act of reporting that Pierre said something to him yesterday but limits him/herself to taking account of (Roulet 1981, 19) the commitment to come. As soon as one thinks about enunciative positions in dialogism or dialogue, the question of the VPs' origin is posed, as is the position and hierarchy of enunciators in the face of others' VPs (Rabatel 2005a). In this respect, the notion of position corresponds to the notion of AR. In fact, Culioli and Berrendonner's conceptions of AR concern L1 (or E1)[9] and they do not consider complex utterances where autonomous second validation occurs that is not at the origin of a speech act, as in (6) and (7). In (6), the expression "fool of a brother" is opaque:

(6) That's how it is, Pierre loves his fool of a brother.

The utterance consists of an initial predication (Pierre loves his brother) and a second predication (Pierre's brother is a fool): of course, at an argumentative level, the utterance goes further – "That's how it is" indicates that, *although* the brother is a fool, he is loved by Pierre; Carel (2010) would say that this is an utterance in *however*). But if the L1/E1 assumes responsibility for the inexplicable nature of Pierre's love for his brother ("That's how it is"), which agent is responsible for describing the brother as a "fool"? It may be Pierre's judgment ("His fool of a brother, as he says"), a judgment by the primary locutor ("His fool of a brother, as I say"), or shared evidence ("His fool of a brother, as is obvious to everyone"). This doubt about the source affects the question of responsibility for the enunciative position, and leads us to make a distinction between an AR involving enunciators in syncretism with a speech act (L1/E1 or l2/e2) and a presupposed quasi-AR involving enunciators who are not locutors (e2). This is why, in diagram no. 1, (6) is followed by a question mark, and can potentially be interpreted as an agreement ("Pierre and I are agreed in saying that his brother is

---

[9] With regard to this question, I differ strongly from Ducrot (1984): see Rabatel (2005a; 2009; 2010a).

a fool"), an observation ("Pierre says that his brother is a fool, I don't know about that"), or even a disagreement ("I don't think his brother is a fool. He does, but that doesn't stop him loving his brother").

In the same way, in (7), L1/E1 lends his/her voice to a second enunciator, who is at the center of the modal perspective without being the (second) locutor:

(7) The armored column wound its way through the never-ending small town, which was very like those it had crossed amid plowed fields and copses in springtime. It advanced alongside a factory with perforated roofs and broken windows, old-fashioned houses with gaping windows, burned-out vehicles, yet more industrial buildings, and suddenly Ivan realized that this was it. They were in the suburbs of Berlin. (Bergounioux 2010, 30)

In (7), L1/E1, the narrator empathizes with Ivan, putting himself in his place (e2). Ivan himself is given a sort of infra-verbalized inner monologue ("yet more industrial buildings"): the adverb implies that Ivan has seen other buildings before this one and that this series of industrial buildings, together with the houses of a particular style tell him he is entering the suburbs of the capital. L1/E1 reconstructs the VP of e2 empathetically by organizing the referentiation in such a way as to express *the view and thoughts of e2*. The initial implicit inferences are confirmed by the words "this was it", so that "they were in the suburbs of Berlin" is equivalent to "here we are at last in the suburbs of Berlin", communicating the soldiers' emotions. In this sense, responsibility for the VP is taken by e2. However, this assumption of responsibility is not of the same order as that of L1/E1; it is an *imputed, putative AR (a quasi-AR)*. Moreover, the narrator could have followed up this extract with an utterance of the type: "But Yvan was completely mistaken"; it is only because of the pact between realist writers and their readers, concerning belief in a world that exists beyond the text, that this quasi-AR is shared by L1/E1, in the absence of any sign of divergence (Rabatel 2008a; 2009).

2.2 Agents taking responsibility for the utterance, and internal validation of the utterance

From the angle of AR, we therefore need to distinguish first and second enunciative agents, as will be verified in examples (8) and (9):

(8) In general, man is really a wolf for man.

(9) In principle, man is always a wolf for man.

Indeed, the second enunciators of (8) and (9) do not make do with saying that [man-to be-wolf-for-man]; they pose this PC by modalizing it as a certainty ("really"/"always"). Quasi-responsibility for this truth is taken by the doxic second enunciator. As for L1/E1, s/he modalizes this doxic VP with "in general" and "in principle" – and only the co(n)text would enable a declaration to be made *with certainty* about whether the modalization confirms or dilutes the VP or is confined to evoking it without taking sides – even though, out of context, the most *probable* hypothesis is that of agreement. In Gosselin's terms (2010, 127), the doxic VPs of e2 correspond to "agents of validation" that are distinct from the agent of AR role assumed by E1. Only E1, in syncretism with L1, really takes charge of the utterances s/he judges to be true; it is also E1 who imputes a quasi-AR to the second enunciators (at the origin of a VP which can be detected from the choices of referentiation). This is to say s/he presupposes that the e2s do indeed espouse the VPs s/he attributes to them – which then enables E1 to take up a position in relation to the VPs of e2 by marking his/her agreement, disagreement or making do with noting the VP in a more or less "neutral" way. In (7), (8), and (9), L1/E1 marks his/her agreement with the doxic VP. (3)–(5) relate to taking into account, while in (1), (2) responsibility for the VP is directly taken by E1 in the *hic et nunc* of making the utterance. As for (6), the absence of contextual data reinforces the opacity of the speech and the doubt about L1/E1's position in relation to the second predication.

I summarize these different agents and levels of responsibility in the table below (Table 1).

Table 1: Instances of assuming responsibility and validation (quasi-assumption of responsibility).

Responsibility	Quasi-responsibility imputed by L1/E1 to l2/e2 or e2 or (L1')/E1' in another world...		
Agent taking responsibility (L1)/E1	*Agent of validation l2/e2 or e2*		
Syncretism of the AR and validation agents [Auto-VP (VP of L1/E1)]	Presupposed disjunction between agents of AR and validation [hetero-VP (of an interlocutor, a third person, the doxa, or even of (L1')/E1' in another world...)]		
	[others than oneself...	and....	others of oneself]
	Agreement ←→	**Taking into account** ←→	**Disagreement**
	=> Hetero-dialogic fusion of validation agents of E1 and e2 or E1'	∅	=> Refusal of the (con)fusion between validation agents of E1 and e2 or E1'
(1), (2)	(7), (8), (9) (6)?	(3), (4), (5) (6)?	(6)?

There is no room here to show how my analysis of responsibility clearly diverges from traditional views (Dendale/Coltier 2005; Coltier/Dendale/De Brabanter 2009), which place responsibility and non-responsibility on the same level. Let us say that I put both the distinction between responsibility taken by L1/E1 for his/her own VP and the imputation of alter-VP that L1/E1 attributes to second locutors/enunciators or to non-locutor second enunciators on the first level (Rabatel 2009; 2012c). This avoids confusion between the role of agent of responsibility assumed by L1/E1 and that of quasi-AR imputed by L1/E1 to l2/e2. It is only at a second stage, and a second level, that L1/E1 takes up a position in relation to the imputed VPs by marking his/her agreement or disagreement, or by making do with taking them into account without further specifying his/her position (Rabatel 2009),[10] it being understood that these positions in relation to alterity relate as much to the hetero-dialogic as the auto-dialogic dimension of utterances.

3 Enunciative positioning: enunciative intensification and distancing

The distinction between locutor and enunciator and between first (E1) and second (e2) enunciators is crucial, not only for recording the referentiation of the *dictum*, and therefore of its modalities, but also for thinking about modalization phenomena based on auto- and hetero-dialogic positioning.

3.1 Auto- and hetero-dialogism

It is usual to think of the embedding of modality as emanating from two distinct, hierarchical judgments of modality, reflecting the same enunciative source. This is what Gosselin does, when he reminds us that 'within the modal structure of the utterance, an evaluative modality (intrinsic to the predicate) may perfectly well enter the field of an epistemic modality (10) and that the reverse is also true (11):

---

10 For a more complete analysis of the question, at the epistemological level, I refer the reader to Coltier/Dendale/De Brabanter (2009), and to Rabatel (2012a; 2012b).

(10) This soup is certainly good.

(11) Fortunately Pierre is tall.' (Gosselin 2010, 70)[11]

According to this auto-dialogic hypothesis, a single enunciator assumes responsibility for two distinct, but complementary judgments of modality. However, (10) and (11) can also be interpreted in a hetero-dialogic sense, combining an external *modus* expressing the first enunciator's VP ("certainly," "fortunately") and a *dictum* linked to an implicit internal *modus* ("this soup is good," "Pierre is tall") expressing the modal VP of a second enunciator. People often act as if they do not see this second enunciator, and confine themselves to talking of a modality that is intrinsic to the predicate. But if it is true that there is indeed a modality intrinsic to the predicate, in relation to the extrinsic modality expressed in the external *modus*, it does not mean that this intrinsic modality cannot be credited to an internal enunciator/internal modal subject: proof of this lies in the possibility of linking dialogical utterances or embedding a dialogical comment, which paraphrases the intra-predicative modality:

(12) Certainly, as you have said, this soup is good.

(13) This soup is certainly "good", as you say.

(14) You've said it, this soup is certainly good.

I interpret these utterances (12)–(14) in a hetero-dialogic sense, with an *enunciative intensification of two different modal subjects*. The auto-dialogic interpretation is possible, but not on just any condition because (15) produces an artificial effect;[12] for the auto-dialogic interpretation not be forced, *intensification* must be introduced, *with two distinct positions by the same enunciator reconsidering a pre-*

---

[11] "[A]u sein de la structure modale de l'énoncé, une modalité appréciative (intrinsèque au prédicat) peut fort bien entrer dans le champ d'une modalité épistémique (10) et que l'inverse est vrai aussi (11) : (10) Certainement que cette soupe est bonne. (11) Heureusement que Pierre est grand."

[12] This explanation is in line with the work of Roberts (1989), and Proust (2007), on recursive utterances of the type "I know that I know that P", which are difficult to understand beyond the second level, unless there is a change of subject (and then we are in a hetero-dialogic context). If we remain in an auto-dialogic context, there must be a change of tense, mode or aspect. Other markers are possible, if they indicate a change in the enunciative position. I am grateful to R. J. Lavie for these references.

vious statement (16), about customary ways of speaking, in a meta-enunciative commentary (17), (18):

(15) ?? Certainly, as I say, this soup is good.

(16) Certainly, as I have said, this soup is good.

(17) Certainly, as I always say, this soup is good.

(18) Certainly, as I say again and again, this soup is good.

Gosselin interprets (10) and (11) in an auto-dialogic sense, even though he does not phrase his explanation in these terms, and he generalizes his previous comment by pointing out that:

> As there are various institutions [according to Gosselin, subjectivity, reality, and institution] it is quite possible for the same locutor to utter two contradictory axiological judgments on condition, of course, that they are shown to relate to distinct institutions. Lenepveu (1990, p. 154 on) also deals with utterances of the type:
>
> (a) Legally, he is guilty, but, morally, he is innocent.
>
> The axiological values[13] (negative and positive respectively) are here intrinsically marked by adjectives (guilty and innocent), while the institutional sources of these evaluations are indicated by adverbs of point of view (legally: from the viewpoint of the legal institution; and morally: from the viewpoint of morality, which is itself a system of conventions) (Gosselin 2010, 71).[14]

---

13 Gosselin makes a distinction between axiological and appreciative: 'Any institution seeks to transform the axiological into the appreciative (to lead people to love the good and hate the bad) since this is its only way of governing behavior and subjugating individuals.' ("Toute institution cherche à transformer l'axiologique en appréciatif (à faire aimer le bien, et détester le mal) car c'est son seul moyen de régir les comportements, d'assujettir les individus." Gosselin 2010, 72).

14 "Comme il existe diverses institutions [selon Gosselin, la subjectivité, la réalité, l'institution] il est tout à fait possible, pour un même locuteur d'énoncer deux jugements axiologiques contradictoires, à condition bien sûr, qu'ils soient présentés comme relevant d'institutions distinctes. Lenepveu (1990: 154sq) traite ainsi d'énoncés du type:
(a) Juridiquement, il est coupable, mais, moralement, il est innocent.
Les valeurs axiologiques (respectivement négative et positive) sont ici intrinsèquement marquées par les adjectifs (coupable et innocent), tandis que les sources institutionnelles de ces évaluations sont indiquées par les adverbes de point de vue (juridiquement: du point de vue de l'institution judiciaire) ; moralement (du point de vue de la morale, qui est elle-même un système de conventions)."

In this analysis, I find confirmation of the relevance of distinctions between first and second enunciators: if utterances include different frameworks of validation/modalities, they de facto involve different enunciators, on condition that the enunciator or modal subject is not considered as a locutor nor that all VPs are transmitted through an explicit represented discourse.

3.2 Positioning by auto-dialogic intensification and hetero-dialogic distancing

Starting from the diversity of dialogic situations, the notion of enunciative positioning enables us to think about the co-construction of VPs through auto-dialogic intensification (*autre de soi*, 'other of oneself') or hetero-dialogic distancing (*autre que soi*, 'other than oneself'). With intensification, L1/E1 reconsiders one of his/her statements or previous VPs and confirms it (or disassociates him/herself from it or reserves judgment); s/he does the same in cases of distancing, which can lead to agreement, disagreement or neutrality being manifested toward (l2)/e2. According to these positionings, the agents of responsibility and validation are either combined or not. In cases of distancing, L1/E1 constructs his/her discourse by relying on others than him/herself and then takes up a position according to the same mechanisms of agreement, disagreement or neutrality. In short, L1/E1 takes charge of all the utterances, by being the author of the extra-predicative "certainly", in the external *modus*, and by showing agreement with the agent of validation, who corresponds in (12)–(14) to a hetero-dialogic second enunciator and, in (15)–(18), to an auto-dialogic second enunciator, with L1/E1 reconfirming in the hic et nunc of his enunciation a VP expressed by him/her in another situation. (12)–(14) therefore mark agreement. (19) indicates a simple taking into account, while (20) marks a disagreement inferred by the dissonance between the initial VP and the fact that the bowl has not been emptied, despite the proclaimed excellence of the soup...

(19) Perhaps, as you say, this soup is good – but personally, I don't like soup.

(20) Undoubtedly, "the soup is good", but the bowl remains full.

As for (10) and (11), the difference between Gosselin's analysis and my own means that they appear either in the box for responsibility assumed by L1/E1, or in the one for agreement, through intensification or distancing. This is made evident in Table 2, which completes the preceding one by adding the question of positioning by intensification or distancing (underlined in bold) to the problem of responsibility.

Table 2: Instances of assuming responsibility and validation, enunciative intensification ('redoublement') and distancing ('dédoublement').

Responsibility	Quasi-responsibility imputed by L1/E1 to l2/e2 or to e2 or to (L1')/E1' in another world...		
Agent taking responsibility (L1)E1	Agent of validation l2/e2 or e2		
Syncretism of AR and validation agents [Auto-VP (VP of L1/E1)]	Presupposed disjunction between AR and validation agents [hetero-VP (of an interlocutor, a third person, the doxa, or even of (L1')/E1' in another world...)] [others than oneself... and... others of oneself]		
	Agreement ←⎯⎯→ Taking into account ←⎯⎯→ Disagreement		
	=> Hetero-dialogic fusion of validation agents of E1 and e2 or E1'	Ø	=> Refusal of the (con)fusion between validation agents of E1 and e2 or E1'
(10), (11)[15]	(10), (11),[16] (12)–(14), (15) – (18)	(19)	(20)
	Intensification (10), (11), (15)–(18)		
	⎯⎯⎯⎯⎯⎯⎯⎯⎯ *Distancing* ⎯⎯⎯⎯⎯⎯⎯⎯⎯→		
	(10), (11), (12)–(13)	*(19)*	*(20)*

4 From positions and positioning to enunciative postures

Postures correspond to the relationships between enunciators in the linguistic co-construction of a "same" VP, considering that the formulations do not significantly alter the initial VP. At the syntactic and discursive levels, co-construction is mainly based on marks of repetition, quotation, mention, reformulation, and recontextualization: in this context, all the markers involved in the co-construction of VPs (means of giving referents, choice of predication, thematic progression, types of argument, rhetorical processes, etc.) contribute to expressing postures of co-, over- and under-enunciation (Rabatel 2008b; 2010b; 2011a; 2011b).

---

[15] According to Gosselin's analysis.
[16] According to my analysis.

4.1 Postures in the co-construction of viewpoints

Postures enable us to think about the co-construction of VPs according to a continuum, in a more discriminating way than the agreement/disagreement opposition. This is why I have sometimes made reference to Ricœur's (1983) notions of "discordant concordance" and "concordant discordance", and described concordant concordance as the only real form of co-enunciation, discordant concordance as over-enunciation, and concordant discordance as under-enunciation (Rabatel 2002; 2004; 2005b; 2006; 2007; 2008b). These two latter postures indicate a dissymmetry in the co-construction of *a* VP that is more or less assumed by both locutors through its repeats and reformulations, while discordant discordance relates to the manifest and explicit expression of *two* conflicting VPs (Table 3):

Table 3: Enunciative positions and points of view.

concordant concordance	discordant concordance	concordant discordance	discordant discordance
consensus <			> dissension
←			→
co-enunciation of a VP	over-enunciation of a VP[17]	under-enunciation of a VP	enunciation of two opposing VPs

Co-enunciation is the co-production of a common VP shared by two locutors/enunciators. Defined thus, it differs from Jeanneret's (1999) co-enunciation, which is equivalent to a phenomenon of co-locution without the co-constructed VP being effectively shared by both enunciators. It also differs, to a lesser degree, from Morel and Danon-Boileau's (1998) co-enunciation, if co-enunciation is reduced to the locutor's stratagem of anticipating the addressee's reactions in order to produce an utterance that will glean consensus. Since agreements on a VP are limited (without which communication would scarcely advance and would be reduced to an ideal cooperation), co-enunciation is rapidly followed by over- or under-enunciation, which is more able to register the frequent disagreements and inequalities in the dynamic of communication (Rabatel 2007). Over-enunciation is the coproduction of an overhanging VP of L1/E1, who reformulates the VP by appearing to say the same thing while modifying the content's area of pertinence or the thrust of the argument to his/her own advantage. It is

---

[17] From the angle of AR, over-enunciation is close to co-enunciation, and this is why I place it toward the right in table no. 3: there is a fusion of the two enunciators, since there is a dual assumption of responsibility, but the fusion is undermined by a rift, explaining the intermediate position of over-enunciation, which may result in a more or less strong discordance.

a form of agreement modulated by L1/E1 with a view to gaining a cognitive and/ or interactional advantage, as if allotting him/herself the role of completing the initial VP, of giving it its real meaning, its true implication. Finally, under-enunciation is the coproduction of a "dominated" VP, with L1/E1, the under-enunciator, hesitantly repeating, with distance or precaution, a VP from a source to which s/he confers preeminent status.

In examples (21)–(23), the VP of Hobbes and that of L1/E1 are expressed by means of an impersonal enunciation. The choice of an indefinite subject of a deontic in (21), an impersonal turn of phrase in (22), and an infinitive in (23) indicates that L1/E1 agrees with the Hobbesian VP, which is itself expressed in a disengaged form so as to better reinforce the authority of his/her VP. L1/E1 therefore produces an interactional construction of VPs.

(21) One can only share Hobbes' view that man is a wolf for man.

(22) It is often/constantly proved true that man is a wolf for man.

(23) To say that man is a wolf for man has perhaps been a truism ever since Hobbes, but it remains axiomatic.

Depending on the way in which L1/E1 builds his/her relationship to truth and to others, (21) expresses co-enunciation, (22) under-enunciation, and (23) over-enunciation. In (21), L1/E1 explicitly marks his/her agreement with Hobbes' VP (a truth founded in L1/E1 and in Hobbes). In (22), E1's agreement with e2 emanates from the truth of an analysis whose pertinence is perpetually borne out and obvious to all ("constantly"), including E1, who thereby registers that the VP's merit is not due to him/her; it will be noted that with a divergence marker ("often") the under-enunciation testifies to a reservation or precautions which, in any case, do not change the fact that this truth is primarily one from elsewhere, and from another person. . . In (23), E1 takes up the position of over-enunciator insofar as Hobbes' viewpoint is categorized as a "truism", especially since this opinion is confirmed despite reservations and reformulated in a way ("axiomatic") demonstrating the incontrovertible truth of the assertion, which could only be called into question by the simple-minded. L1/E1's VP is the source of a truth which dominates Hobbes and the doxa. The over-enunciation is not based on the derogatory semantic content of "truism", because "truism" can be used in a positive sense, as in (23a), without preventing L1/E1 being in over-enunciation. It is therefore L1/E1's comment that is the validation source of Hobbes' judgment, *despite* its doxic appearance, and *beyond* doxa:

(23a) To say that man is a wolf for man has certainly been a truism since Hobbes, but the doxic nature of the judgment is not sufficient reason to undermine its relevance.

4.2 Postures and scale

These postures can be graded, as we have seen with regard to the variation "constantly" and "often" in (22). They are expressed more or less strongly according to L1/E1's level of commitment. The variability of the commitment is relatively disconnected from the AR (Rabatel 2009, 76), which remains identical where truth is concerned; it does, however, influence posture, in a more or less significant way. Co-enunciation is therefore strongly marked in (24) and less marked in (25):

(24) Man is always/really a wolf for man.

(25) Man is pretty much always a wolf for man.

The over-enunciation of (26) is explained by the fact that L1/E1 seems to say the same thing as the doxic enunciator e2; but in reality s/he is modifying the argumentative force of the VP. Over-enunciation is stronger in (27) because the argumentative reorientation, marked by the presence of "in principle" and "in general" in the *modus*, restricts the pertinence of "always" in the *dictum*. This restriction also exists in (26), but as it does not involve words with the same meaning, it is less contradictory, and also less ironic/polemical (see Rabatel 2012e). This is why we expect that (27), in over-enunciation, will be followed by a comment of the type: "But in this case, it is not true...".

(26) In principle/in general man is really a wolf for man.

(27) In principle/in general man is always a wolf for man.

Scale is also a factor in under-enunciation. From this aspect, the under-enunciation of (28) is less strong than that of (22):

(28) They will say that man is a wolf for man.

Account is taken of the VP, without the intervention of the indefinite to indicate that L1/E1 is really taking responsibility, without restriction, for the doxic VP. There is a kind of distance, without it verging toward disconnection. This is why it appears difficult to determine out of context whether L1/E1 is weakly modalizing that for which s/he is assuming responsibility ("They will say it, I agree, even if it's not quite right") or if s/he is repeating a VP of which s/he is not convinced ("They will say it, since it's the general opinion"). This is why (28) appears in two places in Table 4, as under-enunciation of a split VP, with minimal responsibility taken by L1/E1, or as simply taking account of another's VP, without marking a clear disconnection.

These phenomena apply to cases of enunciative distancing, as we have just seen. But they also concern cases of enunciative intensification, as I have shown with regard to the problem of auto-quotations (Rabatel 2006). Indeed, it is always possible to quote oneself by marking the fact that one shares a previous VP, as in (29), and indicate a co-enunciation between oneself, hic et nunc, and oneself in different circumstances – which are not limited in time and space:

(29) I did say that X, and I repeat it with no changes. = co-enunciation.

But it is possible to over-enunciate one's previous VP, as in (30), or under-enunciate it as in (31), where the postures are due not only to the meaning of the words, but also depend on the choice of verbal inflectional classes and aspectual characters, the way of positing truth in relation to oneself or giving it a general import, and so on:

(30) I did say X, but then I was talking about a particular case; I repeat it now, while making clear that I consider it applies to all situations. = over-enunciation.

(31) I did say X, but I would no longer put it in those terms, and I would restrict the remark to certain situations only. = under-enunciation.[18]

Enunciative postures are therefore interesting from the viewpoint of marking degrees of agreement or taking into account, together with the interactional repercussions that these involve. There are also degrees in the expression of disagreement but here, the co-construction of a shared VP is left behind and a new, alternative VP takes shape. This means that the problem of enunciative postures is no longer there. However, although I am sure that, with disagreement, an alternative VP emerges, I am not certain that this constitutes a definitive argument for dismissing disagreement postures. It is a point I would like to leave open for discussion, because this position could be counterbalanced by concrete examples

---

[18] I refer the reader to Rabatel (2006; 2008a, volume 2, chapter 9) for documented examples.

of emerging alternative VPs which, as the discourse unfolds, are far from always being progressive and clear-cut: when the phrasing of an alternative VP is accompanied by flashbacks, certain reformulations or repetitions might be analyzed in terms of under- or over-enunciation.

The table below sums up all my hypotheses, showing the restriction of the field of postures (in italics) to agreement, and, to a lesser degree, taking into account, through intensification or distancing.

Table 4: Instances of assuming responsibility and validation, enunciative intensification and distancing, enunciative postures.

Responsibility	Quasi-responsibility imputed by L1/E1 to l2/e2 or to e2 or to (L1')/E1' in another world...		
Agent taking responsibility (L1)E1	Agent of validation l2/e2 or e2		
Syncretism of AR and validation agents [Auto-VP (VP of L1/E1)]	Presupposed disjunction between AR and validation agents [hetero-VP (of an interlocutor, a third person, the doxa, or even of (L1')/E1' in another world...)]		
	[others than oneself...	and...	others of oneself]
	Agreement ←——→ **Taking into account** ←——→ **Disagreement**		
	= > Hetero-dialogic fusion of validation agents of E1 and e2 or E1'	Ø	= > Refusal of the (con)fusion between validation agents of E1 and e2 or E1'
	Intensification		
	co-enunciation + (29)		
	over-enunciation + (30)		
	under-enunciation + (31)		
	←—————————— *Distancing* ——————————→		
	co-enunciation + (21), (24), (25)	co-enunciation Ø	co-enunciation Ø
	over-enunciation + (23), (26), (27)	over-enunciation Ø	over-enunciation Ø
	under-enunciation + (22), (28)	under-enunciation + ? (28)	under-enunciation Ø
	Postures		

At the end of this overview, one might, with Ockham, question the relevance of distinguishing positions, positioning and postures. These distinctions are born of practice, out of a concern to account for the interpretative issues and dynamics that are at work in discourse. At a theoretical level, this hotchpotch reflects my approach to enunciation as "problematizing enunciation" (see also Jaubert 2008), linked with the argumentativeness of discourse, insofar as referentiation constructs and justifies interpretations, according to a conception of argumentation that owes as much to Amossy (2006), for the argumentative distinction/dimension intended, as to Meyer (2008), for his conception of argumentation as problematology. These notions help us to *think of interactions in dialogism, and dialogism in interactions*, both from a social and cognitive point of view. Locutors, who are neither paper dolls nor abstract entities, adopt positions, positioning, and postures which reflect communicational, cognitive and (inter)actional issues. Certainly, it is not the job of linguistics to study human beings according to their backgrounds and life histories, events, and systems of production and exchange, but it does befall it to analyze how locutors communicate by taking up a position – when they reflect *in and through* discourse their experience of otherness (in themselves, in others, in language) and their praxis. It is therefore in relation to this linguistic dynamic that positions, positioning and postures are useful. When all is said and done, it is about pursuing the original ambition of Benveniste, of thinking of the subject in language according to a cumulative approach which should be more central to our practice.

References

Amossy, Ruth, *L'argumentation dans le discours*, Paris, Armand Colin, 22006.
Barbéris, Jeanne-Marie/Bres, Jacques/Siblot, Paul (edd.), *De l'actualisation*, Paris, CNRS Éditions, 1998.
Bergounioux, Pierre, *Le baiser de sorcière*, Paris, Argol, 2010.
Berrendonner, Alain, *Éléments de pragmatique linguistique*, Paris, Éditions de Minuit, 1981.
Carel, Marion, Note sur la présupposition, in: Colas-Blaise, Marion/Kara, Mohammed/Perrin, Laurent/Petitjean, André (edd.), *La question polyphonique ou dialogique en sciences du langage. Actes du colloque Metz-Luxembourg 2008*, Metz, Université de Metz/Celted, 2010, 157–174.
Coltier, Danielle/Dendale, Patrick/De Brabanter, Philippe, *La notion de prise en charge. Mise en perspective*, Langue française 162 (2009), 3–27, DOI: https://doi.org/10.3917/lf.162.0003.
Culioli, Antoine, *Valeurs aspectuelles et opérations énonciatives. L'aoristique*, Recherches linguistiques 5 (1980), 182–193.

Culioli, Antoine, *Pour une linguistique de l'énonciation*, vol. 1: *Opérations et représentations*, Paris, Ophrys, 1990.

Culioli, Antoine, *Pour une linguistique de l'énonciation*, vol. 3: *Domaine notionnel*, Paris, Ophrys, 1999.

Culioli, Antoine/Normand, Claudine, *Onze rencontres sur le langage et les langues*, Paris, Ophrys, 2005.

Dendale, Patrick/Coltier, Danielle, *La notion de prise en charge ou de responsabilité dans la théorie scandinave de la polyphonie linguistique*, in: Bres, Jacques/Haillet, Pierre Patrick/Mellet, Sylvie/Nølke, Henning/Rosier, Laurence (edd.), *Dialogisme et polyphonie. Approches linguistiques*, Bruxelles, De Boeck/Duculot, 2005, 125–140.

Desclés Jean-Pierre/Guibert, Gaëll, *Le dialogue, fonction première du langage. Analyse énonciative de textes*, Paris, Honoré Champion, 2011.

Dubois, Danièle (ed.), *Le sentir et le dire. Concepts et méthodes en psychologie et en linguistique cognitive*, Paris, L'Harmattan, 2009.

Ducrot, Oswald, *Le dire et le dit*, Paris, Éditions de Minuit, 1984.

Ducrot, Oswald, *Logique, structure, énonciation*, Paris, Éditions de Minuit, 1989.

Ducrot, Oswald, *À quoi sert le concept de modalité?*, in: Dittmar, Norbert/Reich, Astrid (edd.), *Modality in language acquisition/Modalité et acquisition des langues*, Berlin, De Gruyter, 1993, 111–129.

Gosselin, Laurent, *Les modalités en français. La validation des représentations*, Amsterdam/New York, Rodopi, 2010.

Jaubert, Anna, *Dire et plus ou moins dire. Analyse pragmatique de l'euphémisme et de la litote*, Langue française 160 (2008), 105–116, DOI: https://doi.org/10.3917/lf.160.0105.

Jeanneret, Thérèse, *La coénonciation en français. Approche discursive, conversationnelle et syntaxique*, Berne, Peter Lang, 1999.

Maingueneau, Dominique, *Article énoncé*, in: Charaudeau, Patrick/Maingueneau, Dominique (edd.), *Dictionnaire d'analyse du discours*, Paris, Seuil, 2002, 221–223.

Meyer, Michel, *Principia rhetorica. Une théorie générale de l'argumentation*, Paris, Fayard, 2008.

Morel, Mary-Annick/Danon-Boileau, Laurent, *Grammaire de l'intonation. L'exemple du français*, Gap/Paris, Ophrys, 1998.

Neveu, Franck, *Dictionnaire des sciences du langage*, Paris, Armand Colin, 2004.

Proust, Joëlle, *Metacognition and metarepresentation. Is a self-directed theory of mind a precondition for metacognition?*, Synthese 159 (2007), 271–295.

Rabatel, Alain, *Le sous-énonciateur dans les montages citationnels. Hétérogénéités énonciatives et déficits épistémiques*, Enjeux 54 (2002), 52–66.

Rabatel, Alain, *Stratégies d'effacement énonciatif et posture de surénonciation dans "Le dictionnaire philosophique" de Comte-Sponville*, Langages 156 (2004), 18–33, DOI: https://doi.org/10.3917/lang.156.0018.

Rabatel, Alain, *La part de l'énonciateur dans la co-construction interactionnelle des points de vue*, Marges linguistiques 9 (2005), 115–136 (= 2005a).

Rabatel, Alain, *Les postures énonciatives dans la co-construction dialogique des points de vue. Co-énonciation, sur-énonciation, sous-énonciation*, in: Bres, Jacques/Haillet, Pierre Patrick/Mellet, Sylvie/Nølke, Henning/Rosier, Laurence (edd.), *Dialogisme et polyphonie. Approches linguistiques*, Bruxelles, De Boeck/Duculot, 2005, 95–110 (= 2005b).

Rabatel, Alain, 2006, *Les auto-citations et leurs reformulations. Des surassertions surénoncées ou sousénoncées*, Travaux de linguistique 52 (2006), 71–84, DOI: https://doi.org/10.3917/tl.052.84.

Rabatel, Alain, *Les enjeux des postures énonciatives et de leur utilisation en didactique*, Éducation et didactique 1–2 (2007), 89–116, DOI: https://doi.org/10.4000/educationdidactique.162.
Rabatel, Alain, *Homo Narrans. Pour une analyse énonciative et interactionnelle du récit*, 2 vol., Limoges, Lambert-Lucas, 2008 (= 2008a).
Rabatel, Alain, *Stratégie discursive de concordance discordante dans les ensembles reprises + reformulations (en contexte didactique)*, in: Schuwer, Martine/Le Bot, Marie-Claude/Richard, Élisabeth (edd.), *Pragmatique de la reformulation. Types de discours, interactions didactiques*, Rennes, Presses universitaires de Rennes, 2008, 187–202 (= 2008b).
Rabatel, Alain, *Prise en charge et imputation, ou la prise en charge à responsabilité limitée...*, Langue française 162 (2009), 71–87, DOI: https://doi.org/10.3917/lf.162.0071.
Rabatel, Alain, *Retour sur les relations entre locuteurs et énonciateurs. Des voix et des points de vue*, in: Colas-Blaise, Marion/Kara, Mohammed/Perrin, Laurent/Petitjean, André (edd.), *La question polyphonique ou dialogique en sciences du langage. Actes du colloque Metz-Luxembourg 2008*, Metz, Université de Metz/Celted, 2010, 357–373 (= 2010a).
Rabatel, Alain, *Schémas, techniques argumentatives de justification et figures de l'auteur (théoricien et/ou vulgarisateur)*, Revue d'anthropologie des connaissances 4 (2010), 505–526, DOI: https://doi.org/10.3917/rac.011.0505 (= 2010b).
Rabatel, Alain, *La sous-énonciation comme stratégie de co-construction interactionnelle des points de vue*, in: Verine, Bertrand/Détrie, Catherine (edd.), *L'actualisation de l'intersubjectivité. De la langue au discours. Hommages à Jeanne-Marie Barbéris*, Limoges, Lambert-Lucas, 2011, 157–177 (= 2011a).
Rabatel, Alain, *Des conflits de valeurs et de points de vue en discours*, Semen 32 (2011), 55–72, DOI: https://doi.org/10.4000/semen.9354 (= 2011b).
Rabatel, Alain, *Sujets modaux, instances de prise en charge et de validation*, Le discours et la langue 3–2 (2012), 13–36 (= 2012a).
Rabatel, Alain, *Le rôle du dialogisme et des paramètres textuels dans la notion de prise en charge*, in: Sullet-Nylander, Françoise/Engel, Hugues/Engwall, Gunnel (edd.), *La linguistique dans tous les sens. Hommages à Mats Forsgren*, Stockholm, Vitterhetsakademien, 2012 (= 2012b).
Rabatel, Alain, *Énonciateur, sujet modal, modalité, modalisation*, in: Maury-Rouan, Claire (ed.), *Regards sur le discours. Énonciation, interaction. Hommage à Robert Vion*, Aix-en-Provence, Presses universitaires de Provence, 2012, 55–72 (= 2012c).
Rabatel, Alain, *Les relations locuteur/énonciateur au prisme de la notion de voix*, Arts et savoirs 2 (2012), DOI: https://doi.org/10.4000/aes.510 (= 2012d).
Rabatel, Alain, *Ironie et sur-énonciation*, Vox romanica 71 (2012), 42–76 (= 2012e).
Recanati, François, *La transparence et l'énonciation. Pour introduire à la pragmatique*, Paris, Seuil, 1979.
Ricœur, Paul, *Temps et récit I*, Paris, Éditions du Seuil, 1983.
Roberts, Craige, *Modal subordination and pronominal anaphora in discourse*, Linguistics and philosophy 12 (1989), 683–721.
Roulet, Eddy, *Échanges, interventions et actes de langage dans la structure de la conversation*, Études de linguistique appliquée 44 (1981), 7–39.
Sarfati, Georges-Élia, *Analyse du discours et sens commun. Institutions de sens, communautés de sens, doxa, idéologie*, in: Guilhaumou, Jacques/Schepens, Philippe (edd.), *Matériaux

philosophiques pour l'analyse du discours, Besançon, Presses universitaires de Franche-Comté, 2011, 139–173.

Verine, Bertrand, *Du transfert de sens à la représentation altersensorielle. Peut-on échapper à la structuration visuelle des référents extéroceptifs multimodaux?*, in: Havelange, Carl/Strivay, Lucienne/Molina Marmol, Maïté (edd.), *La lettre et l'image. Enquêtes interculturelles sur les territoires du visible*, Liège, Presses universitaires de Liège, 2014, publication en ligne. DOI: http://web.philo.ulg.ac.be/culturessensibles/les-ateliers-du-sensible/

Original corpus

(1) L'homme est un loup pour l'homme.
(1a) {Chacun sait cela,} l'homme est un loup pour l'homme.
(1b) {La belle affaire,} l'homme est un loup pour l'homme.
(2) Je viens demain sans faute.
(3) Pierre a dit : "Je viendrai demain sans faute".
(4) Pierre a dit qu'il viendrait demain sans faute.
(5) Pierre a dit qu'il viendrait demain "sans faute".
(6) C'est comme ça, Pierre aime bien son andouille de frère.
(7) La colonne blindée n'en finit pas de s'extraire d'une bourgade pareille à celles qu'elle a traversées parmi les labours et les boqueteaux de printemps. Elle longe une fabrique aux toits dentelés, aux verrières brisées, de vieilles demeures rococo aux fenêtres béantes, des véhicules incendiés, encore des bâtiments à usage industriel, et Ivan comprend subitement que ça y est. Ils sont dans les faubourgs de Berlin. (Bergounioux 2010 : 30)
(8) En général, l'homme est vraiment un loup pour l'homme.
(9) En principe, l'homme est toujours un loup pour l'homme.
(10) Certainement que cette soupe est bonne.
(11) Heureusement que Pierre est grand. (Gosselin 2010 : 70)
(12) Certainement que, comme tu l'as dit, cette soupe est bonne.
(13) Certainement que cette soupe est "bonne", comme tu le dis.
(14) Tu l'as dit, certainement que cette soupe est bonne.
(15) ?? Certainement que, comme je le dis, cette soupe est bonne.
(16) (Certainement que, comme je l'ai dit, cette soupe est bonne.
(17) Certainement que, comme je le dis toujours, cette soupe est bonne.
(18) Certainement que, comme je le dis et le redis, cette soupe est bonne.
(19) Peut-être que, comme tu dis, cette soupe est bonne – mais personnellement je n'aime pas la soupe.
(20) Indubitablement, "la soupe est bonne", mais l'assiette reste pleine.
(21) On ne peut que partager le jugement de Hobbes selon lequel l'homme est un loup pour l'homme.
(22) Il se vérifie souvent/constamment que l'homme est un loup pour l'homme.
(23) Dire que l'homme est un loup pour l'homme est peut-être un truisme depuis Hobbes, mais ça reste un axiome.

(23a) Dire que l'homme est un loup pour l'homme est un truisme depuis Hobbes, certes, mais le caractère doxique du jugement n'est pas une raison suffisante pour en saper la pertinence.
(24) L'homme est toujours/vraiment un loup pour l'homme.
(25) L'homme est à-peu-près toujours un loup pour l'homme.
(26) En principe/en général l'homme est vraiment un loup pour l'homme.
(27) En principe/en général l'homme est toujours un loup pour l'homme.
(28) On va dire que l'homme est un loup pour l'homme.
(29) J'avais dit que X, je le redis sans y rien changer.
(30) J'avais dit X, mais alors je visais un cas particulier ; aujourd'hui, je le redis, mais en précisant que je considère que cela vaut dans toutes les situations.
(31) J'avais dit X, je ne le dirais plus en ces termes, et je restreindrais la portée du propos.

Part 2: **Text epistemologies**

François Rastier
Chapter 6
Dissipative units

Abstract: We contrast two paradigms which dominate the tradition: the logical-grammatical paradigm of the sign and the rhetorical-hermeneutic paradigm of the text. We evoke this contrast in order to challenge the weaknesses of sign theory when it attacks textuality, and to establish postulates for a new heuristics with which to think of semantic forms and their dynamics. From there, we show that the text in its complexity is governed as much by the norms of discourse and genre as by the *a priori conjectural character* of interpretation, which is at work in both text and intertext.

Keywords: continuum, fragment, ground, semantic forms, semiosis, transformations

Scholarly tradition has developed a concept of the unit which matches the hypothesis of a logico-grammatical parallelism. But this has proved to be debatable, at both word and sentence levels, and even more so at the level of the text.

On the other hand, units such as themes or narrative functions can be described as semantic and expressive forms, capable of being represented by structured groupings of features. Throughout the text, these forms are the carriers of *metamorphisms*, recurring transformations which determine the direction of the text.

Textual forms stand out against expressive and semantic grounds (isotopies). (In this study, the opposition between form and ground is derived from the figure/ground opposition in Gestaltpsychology.) Throughout the text, the grounds themselves may evolve through *transpositions*. Furthermore, the dynamic of text scanning includes dissolution of the forms through dispersal within the grounds, together with global summations which construct forms from elements of the ground.

The question of units and linguistic rules therefore needs to be reconsidered in light of the text, recognizing how the global is determined by the local and also taking account of the interpretation of software output in corpus semantics.

François Rastier, CNRS Paris

1 From words to passages

Questions about the linguistic unit. – Linguistics has inherited from ancient grammar a notion of unit which has become so evident that it needs to be explained in detail.

(i) The unit is positive, in that it has a persistent substantial content, despite possible variations owing to context or situation. (ii) It is discrete, bordered to right and left, both in time and space. The word remains the typical unit. (iii) It is immediately identifiable according to defining criteria interpreted by a typology, and it appears as a datum, if there is a list of categories available. The parts of speech are perfect examples of this. On this basis, rules take charge of these discrete and typed units to organize them into sentences (comparable to propositions; see Pinker 1999).

This image of the unit, with its ontological presuppositions, is perfectly compatible with the Fregean concept of logical calculus. It nevertheless remains debatable, and has been undermined in various ways: Martinet, for example, with his theory of the *discontinuous signifier*, aimed to account for sequences of agreements and concordances, and posed the problem from the semasiological viewpoint; Pottier, with the notion of *isosemy*,[1] focused on the same phenomena of repetition, but by adopting the opposite, onomasiological approach. We should remember that syntax presents difficulties for listing units, especially since non-discrete units such as prosodic intonations crucially organize the content of sentences and are sufficient, for example, to change an affirmation into an interrogation. They certainly do not correspond to the positive, not to say positivist, notion of the unit.

Is it possible then, to think of textual units as being like lexical or grammatical units? This opinion has prevailed in semiotics, with Hjelmslev envisaging the commutation of textual units in this way. At present, text linguistics and discourse analysis generally suppose that a textual unit, paragraph, sequence, or chapter are identifiable either as a sequence of characters (in the tradition of Harris), or as the trace of an enunciative intention or a macro-act (in the tradition of discursive pragmatics).

The decompartmentalization of sentence limits. Favored by the logico-grammatical tradition, nouns are considered to be words *par excellence*: they are seen to represent material objects and thus to ensure that language is ontologically rooted. By contrast, *passage* has no extra-linguistic reference – and the question of truth has no relevance in linguistics since it has always come under the aegis of metaphysics.

---

[1] All subsequent translations from other works are by Rosemary Rodwell, the translator of this chapter, unless stated otherwise.

We must, however, return to the question, because Saussure's readings of Benveniste attempted to reestablish the prohibitory character of the alleged sentence limit.[2] The preeminence of predication is founded on the ideal of true judgment, which is to say, without being accused of tautology, on the representation of a "state of things". The question of predication will therefore allow us to illustrate the opposition between ontology and praxeology.

What Saussure calls a *syntactic unit* is anything relating to sentence structure, which includes all aspects of syntax. But the span of a syntactic unit is perfectly able to extend beyond the sentence, because the sentence is only a "type of syntactic unit". Thus, unlike Benveniste, Saussure accords no preeminence to the sentence, but brings a fresh perspective to this level of organization: he does not reprise the predicative concept of the sentence, but compares it to a productive activity. If speech is considered as a course of action, it is indeed at sentence level that the problem of praxeology is posed most clearly. Adopting a praxeological viewpoint in an elliptical but distinct way, Saussure then feels the need to distinguish a sentence from a rite – whereas in fact nobody, to my knowledge, outside the domain of sacramental theology,[3] had ever even thought of comparing them: 'A rite, a mass, are not at all comparable to the sentence, since it is only the repetition of a *series of acts*. The sentence is comparable to a musical composer's activity (rather than to that of the performer)' (Saussure 2002, 94–95).[4] In this passage, the sentence is indeed considered as a series of acts (and not a proposition or a representation), and the comment concerns only the constitutive nature of these acts: the sentence is compared not (or not only) to a cultural *object*, but to a creative *activity*.

A contradiction therefore emerges between the sentence, which is normally considered as a closed syntactic unit, and the passage (Saussure's "syntactic construction") defined as a creative compositional activity. This is certainly reminiscent of Chomsky's generativity, but for Chomsky, generativity was completely governed by rules operating on given, preexisting units, while Saussure's syntactic constructions continually create new units. Among these are forms, which are merely moments in a series of transformations: this is how the theory of metamorphisms argues for a transformational conception of the text – while pro-

---

[2] See Benveniste (1966, 129): 'There is no linguistic level beyond the categorematic level.' ("Il n'y a pas de niveau linguistique au-delà du niveau catégorématique." Footnote, page 128: "*catégorématique*: Gr. *katégoréma* = lat. *prædicatum*").

[3] See the excellent work by Irène Rosier (1995).

[4] "Un rite, une messe, ne sont pas comparables du tout à la phrase, puisque ce n'est que la répétition d'une *suite d'actes*. La phrase est comparable à l'activité du compositeur de musique (et pas à celle de l'exécutant)."

posing no transformation of "deep structures" which would give rise to surface structures. The activity itself of developing a text (written or oral) is duplicated by the interpretative activity: the linguistic units are restored or reconstructed by the interpreter, as shown by defrosting phenomena, which increase the number of lexical units. Therefore, far from being a given, any syntactic unit depends on the viewpoint from which it is established, according to textual norms that have never been described as rules. In this way, linguistic units of all sizes are the result of a semiosis rather than its starting point.

Units or forms? – The divergences between problematics are clearly apparent with regard to textual units. The logico-grammatical conception tends to make the unit an element of textual "vocabulary". Like a sentence that is considered as a linking of words, a text is thought to result from a linking of units (propositions, sequences, narrative functions, etc.); text linguistics thus conceives of the text as a structured series of propositions.[5] Even Greimas' narratology represented discourse by a concatenation of narrative functions, with units considered as discrete and able to be localized, or even grouped into *sequences*.[6]

If logico-grammatical ontology attributes discreteness and presence, self-identity, and isonomy to textual units, based on the naive model of physical objects, the rhetorical/hermeneutic conception shared by interpretative semantics acknowledges that the objectivities it constructs are continuous and sometimes implicit, varying over time and according to context; there are qualitative inequalities between them and they do not uniformly obey the same rules. It does not exclusively relate semantic forms to spatio-temporal localizations, because these forms are not objects in the sense of being things; at least, their form of objectification cannot be prejudged by submitting them to the procedures of grammatical analysis: localization, commutation, hierarchical organization with unique connections, univocal typing of relationships, and formal characterization of categorial identity. Indeed, the manifestations of textual unity may remain diffuse (isotopies, isotopic bundles) or rhapsodic (themes). The same form may, incidentally, have diffuse or compact manifestations. In

---

5 Text linguistics goes somewhat beyond the limits recognized by Benveniste, who makes propositions the insuperable horizon of linguistics. Transferring these characteristics of words to propositions, text linguistics has therefore attempted to extend the logico-grammatical problem in a variety of ways: for example, according to Van Dijk/Kintsch (1983), a text could be boiled down to one or several *macro-propositions*.

6 This is used both in text linguistics and in narratology. Defining the unit through spatio-temporal localization and self-identity is characteristic of classical ontology, as maintained by the Aristotelian tradition. Any complex phenomenon is therefore conceived as a combination of units, and scientific description itself is seen as an analysis: through various forms of compositionality, this position supposes that the local determines the global.

short, a form is not a discrete, stable unit that is identical to itself: far from being opposed to evasive substances, forms are *figures* which contrast with grounds.

Since texts present contours of forms, and the purpose of interpretation is to recognize and scan them – identification and scanning processes being inseparable – it is necessary to complete and probably go beyond the distributional conception of the text by means of a *morpho-semantic* conception which takes account of the qualitative inequalities between forms.

The problems of identifying units need to be approached in accordance with the dual nature of the paradigms: for example, the sentence is a logical segmentation (Benveniste defines it as propositional, *categorematic*), whereas the period is a physiological and/or emotional segmentation. Beyond the period, whose span is doubtless measured by our motor and respiratory capacities, the text presents no signifier that can be identified by segmentation procedures, unless it is by strong demarcations, such as long pauses or change of subject. This is a fundamental reason for escaping from the sign model: textual semantic units have no signifiers capable of being isolated as parts of speech; they are composed of connections of significata from the lower levels of the period. These connections do not constitute a uniform network: some of them are given prominence, enhanced, or modalized.

Finally, the opposition between logico-grammatical and rhetorical/hermeneutic conceptions of interpretation finds concrete expression through the differences in the temporal and aspectual regimes of productive and interpretative processes. The distributional and iterative regularity of equal intervals in logico-grammatical time contrasts with the alternations of momentary and durative, perfective and imperfective in rhetorical/hermeneutic time.

Redefining the sign as a passage. – It is therefore appropriate to redefine the sign to suit the textual problem. The unit, whatever its size and level of description, can be redefined as a *passage*: a passage has no fixed boundaries and obviously depends on the point of view which determined its selection.

To define the sign as a passage is to develop a purely relational and therefore contextual definition. Since speech commands language, the sign is first and foremost a "speech segment":[7] at the level of the signifier, it is an *extract* – between two breaks, it involves a chain of characters; between two pauses or punctuations it involves a period, for example. The extract may reflect connected voice ranges, through isophonic rules, for instance, or concordance of morphemes: these are expressive *co-occurring elements*.

---

[7] Remarkably, Saussure uses the expression *speech sign* (see 2002, 265), but not *language sign*.

The apocryphal sign in Saussure's *Course in General Linguistics* can thus be replaced by this figure of the *passage*:

← ⊃ *fragment of the content* ⊂ →

← ⊃ *extract from the expression* ⊂ →

Figure 1: The passage [⊂ →: opening toward the context].

At the level of the signified, the passage is a *fragment* that points toward its contexts to the left and right, close and distant, through isotopies as well as through dialectic or dialogical thematic recurrences. This definition of the fragment holds good in a more restricted way for the content of the lexical items (the *sign system*) as it does for that of the syntactic unit or the period, the section, etc.

Each extract can bring together several written or vocal chains in co-occurrences, and each fragment can assemble several semantic correlates. The extracts and fragments are not necessarily discrete or continuous, and this breaks with traditional semiotic atomism which presents each sign as a closed entity.

The close or distant contexts of a passage are also passages of variable size defined by groupings of expressive *co-occurring elements* and semantic *correlates*:

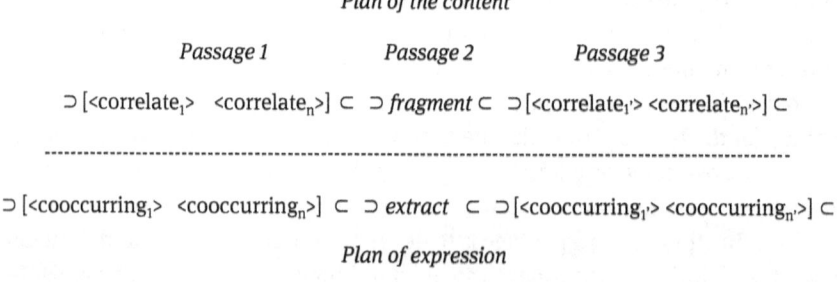

Plan of the content

Passage 1   Passage 2   Passage 3

⊃ [<correlate$_1$> <correlate$_n$>] ⊂ ⊃ *fragment* ⊂ ⊃ [<correlate$_{1'}$> <correlate$_{n'}$>] ⊂

⊃ [<cooccurring$_1$> <cooccurring$_n$>] ⊂ ⊃ *extract* ⊂ ⊃ [<cooccurring$_{1'}$> <cooccurring$_{n'}$>] ⊂

Plan of expression

Figure 2: The passage and its contexts.

The passages are matched, differentiated, or opposed by virtue of their semantic correlates and their expressive co-occurring elements.

In corpus linguistics, co-occurrences and correlates are now accessible by means of probabilistic methods and can, for example, be selected using the reduced deviance test, and then interpreted critically in order to establish co-occurrences of expressions with semantic correlations (see Rastier 2011). The typology of passages obviously varies with the corpora.

Relations between forms and grounds. – The study of semantic forms extends in three directions: links between grounds, in the case for example of genres comprising several generic isotopies, such as the parable; links between forms; and especially the links between forms and grounds, which are crucial for the study of semantic perception.

In general, the semantic ground is not reduced to a single isotopy but consists of a bundle of isotopies. Consequently, it is not homogeneous but naturally includes irregularities (for a bundle, there are differences between isotopies, momentary disconnections, and disappearances of isotopy); these slight heterogeneities in fact enable the semantic ground to be perceived.

All forms are not equal: in addition to the fact that they stabilize and break up in the course of the text, a fortiori diachronically, there are qualitative inequalities between them. Some forms owe their pre-eminence to the value placed on them: for example, in the work of Spinoza, Nature is the semantic form which seems to dominate all others; in *Madame Bovary*, it is Emma; for Bossuet, it is Providence. In theoretical texts, these preeminent forms are the concepts which subsume the others; in stories, it is the agonistes who stand for a class of actors (such as Don Juan). They thus assume the status of *paragons* or typical forms.[8]

2 From forms to textuality

Semantic forms and their dynamics. – The meaning of a text cannot be deduced from a series of propositions, but results from the scanning of semantic forms[9] linked to expressive forms. These may be subject to a variety of descriptions: for example, related to different semantic components, a semic molecule may be described as a theme, an actor, the aim or source of a modal point of view, or as a moment in the linearity of the text.

Although the static description may be appropriate for certain applications, in didactics for example, a more subtle description should restore the dynamic aspect of the production and interpretation of texts. The first stage consists in describing the dynamics of grounds and forms: for example, the construction of

---

[8] See Rastier (1991, 198). These three instances, contents, normal forms, and paragons, are distinguished by their degrees of salience, and the *saillance-prégnance* ('salience-pregnance') opposition borrowed from the biology of perception could therefore be transferred to a theory of semantic forms.

[9] In the understanding of texts, we even find problems similar to those posed by the recognition of noisy or incomplete forms.

semic molecules, their evolution and their possible disintegration. These dynamics and their relative optimizations have different parameters depending on the genre and discourse, because forms and grounds are constituted and recognized according to these various norms. Furthermore, since the production and interpretation regimes associated with genre and discourse guide the scanning of grounds and forms, the semantics of texts has to adapt its descriptions to these regimes.

The perception of semantic grounds appears to be linked to rhythms, while the perception of forms seems to be linked to contours; at the level of expression, prosodic contours can present a similarity. Although semantic grounds are formed by isotopies, generally produced by the recurrence of generic features, the temporalization of these recurrences is provided by semantic rhythms.[10] Since semantic grounds appear to be series of regular points and since forms are rendered non-discrete by their singular points, the productive or interpretative scanning of these forms and grounds supposes a rhythm, which is the basic cell of all action: it determines the regular segments of forms, at the extremities of which the singular points stand out.

At the macrosemantic level, qualitative inequalities mark outstanding places or times that might be called semantic *nodal points*, defined by their high degree of connectivity: the easiest to distinguish are words which connect several areas of meaning (generic isotopies), or responses which change the narrative structure. Over and above a concatenation of symbols, the text can therefore be considered as a semiotic *course of action*, given emphasis at critical moments. Genre codifies the way in which this action is conducted, but what might be called the *ductus* particularizes an enunciator and would enable the *semantic style* to be characterized by particular rhythms and layouts of the contours of forms.

Transformations. – Let us remember that a form is a *family of transformations*: the form and the metamorphosis are two points in the same process. This transformation is diachronically oriented in the time of the text and of tradition. Depending on the components brought into play, it is necessary to distinguish transformations that are thematic, dialectic (narrative), dialogical (modal, according to "points of view" and "speech positions"), and tactical (positional). Among these transformations, I include *mereomorphisms*, defined as relationships between parts of the text which present, in a compact and local manner, forms which else-

---

[10] The fundamental role of rhythms in perception is well known: they have a facilitating effect over the short term, and the linguistic correlation is the creation of zones of pertinence. They thus account for an element of the *presumption of isotopy* which allows the semantic features to be actualized.

where are amplified in a global and diffuse manner: for example, configurations codified as an initial description, the parable, the warning dream, are transposed in the remainder of the text by other, more extended forms. In text linguistics, mereomorphisms express *solidarity of scale* phenomena.

Transformations and transpositions. – The generation of a text consists in a series of metamorphisms and transpositions which, orally, can be shown by studying reformulations and, in the written form, by examining rough drafts. A good part of its interpretation lies in identifying and evaluating metamorphisms: for example, the meaning of a narrative is articulated through thematic and dialectic transformations.

Metamorphisms can give concrete expression to rewriting relationships between passages that are distant from one another. In Flaubert's *Herodias*, my hypotheses about the metaphorical connections between the citadel of Machaerus and the head of Saint John, whose descriptions are separated by the whole extent of the text, were only able to be corroborated by a later reading of the rough drafts (Rastier 1992). The hermeneutic act which consists of selecting parallel passages must of course be problematized; for example, I was able to compare, in the description of the Temple of Jerusalem: "The sun [. . .] shed a dazzling splendor on its walls of snowy marble" with "the tiny drops of perspiration on her forehead looked like dew upon white marble" in the description of Salome's dance at the end of the story.[11] An interpretant is to be found in Folio. 403 of Flaubert's rough drafts: standing on her hands at the end of the dance, Salome awaits her reward, with "a tiny drop of perspiration on her temples like dew upon white marble". The semantic relationship between the Temple and Salome, both of them actors under the Old Law, is duplicated by the word-play on *temple/temples*. The transformations between passages thus pose the problem of recognizing forms, which are both noisy and incomplete.

We can discern the presence of three levels of semiotic morphologies: the salience of the form, notably the salience of singular points which allow it to be recognized; the pregnance of the ground; and, finally, the absence of other forms and other grounds – an absence that can always be revoked and against which they stand out paradigmatically.[12]

---

11 All translated extracts from Flaubert's *Herodias* are from: https://www.gutenberg.org/files/1291/1291-h/1291-h.htm (the Project Gutenberg Ebook) [last consultation: 09.08.2022].
12 I have studied the processes by which forms are diffused into grounds, as well as the reverse process of summation of forms from elements of the ground (Rastier 2006a). When perceptive assimilation dominates, it establishes grounds; when discretization prevails, it discerns forms.

Between forms and grounds, various types of scanning can be observed: from one element of form to another, through synecdoche or metonymy; from one element of ground to another, through presumption of isotopy; from one form to another, through a metamorphism; and from one ground to another, through transposition. This leads us on to the question of intertext.

Diffusions and summations. – Forms and grounds are interdependent and forms can be transported from one ground to another without being changed during this transposition. Indeed, grounds and forms are in a mutual relationship of diffusion and summation: a ground is a "forgotten" form, in the sense that it has lost its salience, and the passage from foreground to background can be understood in this way.

Semantic diffusion accounts for the phenomena of local isotopy: since all semantic features are actualized and a fortiori propagated from and according to the immediate and distant context, contexts show multiple local redundancies. In a corpus of French novels, for example, many forms of the verb *tordre* 'to twist' will be found in the contexts of the word *grimace*: this is a recurrence of a feature/ distortion.

Diffusion phenomena play an important role at text level. For example, in Flaubert's *Herodias*, the first sentence begins with these words: "In the eastern side of the Dead Sea rose the citadel of Machaerus. It was built upon a conical peak of basalt". In this context, we can analyze: (i) 'eastern': /sun/, /inceptive/, /rising/, (/vital/); 'Dead Sea': /maritime/, /terminative/, /descendant/, /funerary/. In the last description of the panorama over the Judean desert, four pages further on,[13] the semes of the 'Dead Sea' molecule are repeated to form a ground: the semes /maritime/, /descendant/, /funerary/ alternate and combine (I note them by their initials): 'great waves' /m/ 'petrified' /f/, 'depths' /m/ /d/, 'black' /f/, 'cliffs' /m/, 'gloomy valley' /d/ 'of the abyss' /f/ /d/, 'buried' /f/ d/ 'deeper' /d/ than the 'river-bed' /m/ of the /d/ 'slow-running' /d/ 'Jordan /m/. In an embryonic

---

13 "Tous ces monts autour de lui, comme des étages de grands flots pétrifiés, les gouffres noirs sur le flanc des falaises, l'immensité du ciel bleu, l'éclat violent du jour, la profondeur des abîmes le troublaient ; et une désolation l'envahissait au spectacle du désert, qui figure, dans le bouleversement de ses terrains, des amphithéâtres et des palais abattus. Le vent chaud apportait, avec l'odeur du soufre, comme l'exhalaison des villes maudites, ensevelies plus bas que le rivage sous les eaux pesantes."

'The mountain peaks surrounding the palace, looking like great petrified waves, the black depths among the cliffs, the immensity of the blue sky, the rising sun, and the gloomy valley of the abyss, filled the soul of Antipas with a vague unrest; he felt an overwhelming sense of oppression at the sight of the desert, whose uneven piles of sand suggested crumbling amphitheatres or ruined palaces. The hot wind brought an odour of sulphur, as if it had rolled up from cities accursed and buried deeper than the river-bed of the slow-running Jordan.'

form, the semic molecule of 'Dead Sea' has thus become a ground: the case links between semes are not preserved, and its semes are manifested in a recurring and rhapsodic fashion. This semantic form will partially reappear over the course of the narrative: for example, John the Baptist's curses are later compared to floods.[14]

At times when diffusion occurs, the suspension of case links has the effect of dissolving the initial form; but they remain paradigmatically present and able to be re-motivated at times of summation.

Movements of diffusion and summation also organize the level of expression. For example, for an author holding as little mystery as Racine, Valérie Beaudouin was able to prove, using statistical methods, that the phonemes in the name of the main character, especially when the latter is eponymous, are significantly diffused in the whole of the text (Beaudouin 2002). Where phonetic summation is concerned, examples can easily be found, such as this sentence from Baudelaire's *Le spleen de Paris* (see Starobinski 1971, 158; I have kept his notation):

Je sentis ma gorge serrée par la main terrible de l'hystérie.
    HY   S   TERI   (HYSTÉRIE)
I felt my throat constricted by the terrible hand of hysteria.

Movements of summation establish qualitative inequalities, by transforming series of regular points into groupings of singular points. From the psycholinguistic point of view, these movements probably correspond to moments when the enunciative gesture is being prepared, following which come phases of diffusion that can be linked to their recent effects in the immediate memory of the course of action.

3 Scanning in the intertext

Intertextual scanning. – The intertext is not that nebulous space in which deconstructionist hermeneutics nimbly move. Privileged scannings first extend between texts of the same lineage, then between those of the same genre, and then between genres of the same discourse. Relationships within the genre dominate the relations between lineages, but also within discourse. The relationships between one genre and another also suppose transpositions (including hyponymies, quotations, etc.).

---

14 Doubtless through the intermediary of the cliché *flots d'insultes* 'floods of insults', which remained implicit even in the rough drafts, whereas *pluie d'insultes* 'shower of insults' figures in the final version. [The Gutenberg translation (chap. 2) gives: 'The captive thundered them forth (i.e. insults) like bolts from heaven'.]

The intertext is therefore structured a minima by degrees of proximity (between the zones of author, genre and discourse); degrees of connectivity and cycles (two texts distant from one another referring to the same text); and, finally, contextual relationships in absentia.

Going beyond the intuitions of Bakhtin, the question of intertext is now found to be linked to the question of corpora and their analysis, whether instrumented or not. A reasoned characterization of genres remains a prerequisite to forming corpora that are fully usable for tasks of linguistic description.[15]

Levels of context and intertext. – Interpretation mainly proceeds by contextualization. It relates the passage being considered: to its vicinity, according to locality zones of increasing size (syntactic unit, period, etc.); to other passages in the same text, referred to either for comparison or contrast; and finally, to other passages in other texts, chosen from the reference corpus, and which enter the working corpus by virtue of this choice. None of these three contextualizations is "determinist" in the received sense of Artificial Intelligence, which indicates word-by-word linear scanning. The first can be retrograde, and the two others are scarcely constrained by the linearity of the text or texts being subjected to comparison. The practice of comparison, whether it contextualizes or recontextualizes, in all cases generates meaning, in a way that is inevitable if not compulsive, according to a *contextuality principle* which might be expressed as follows: two signs or two passages of the same text, put side by side, mutually select or propagate elements of signification (semes). This exchange transforms their *signification* (linked to the word) into *meaning* (belonging to the text).

The principle of contextuality is the basis of the *intertextuality principle*: two passages of different texts, however brief, and even if reduced to the dimension of a sign, as soon as they are set side by side, mutually select semantic features which overdetermine their meaning. At a still higher level, a principle of *architextuality* can be formulated: any text placed in a corpus is semantically determined by it and potentially modifies the meaning of each of the texts that compose it.

In the non-ontological, indeed the "de-ontological" perspective being used here, meaning is made up of differences (not references) – in the same way as any real categorization is contrastive. If the meaning of a text can be characterized by contrasting its different parts and passages, it is also examined in contrast to other texts. Indeed, if the intention is to restore interpretative scanning based on

---

[15] Whatever the criteria chosen, nothing much can be gained from a heterogeneous corpus, because the specificities of genres cancel each other out, and the disparate elements that remain can hardly be interpreted to characterize texts.

transformations, in order to pass from one word to another, and from one passage to another, it is often necessary to pass through one or several other texts. To this extent, the intertext is included and invoked through the interpretation of the text.

The four intertexts. – A text is developed through internal and external rewritings, transformations which affect the expression and content of the passages in progress, both at the same time.

Literary works are distinguished by corpora of elaboration and interpretation which constitute their intertext. Four privileged corpora give concrete expression to as many intertexts:

(i) The external genetic intertext of "sources" is made up of "ascending" texts from which the text is produced (usually texts of the same genre, and even by the same author).

(ii) The internal genetic intertext of the versions integrates these sources and transforms them by successive rewritings.

These first two intertexts generally undergo reverse processes: the first are destructive, while the second are constructive; but locally, after destroying its sources by erasures and changes, the text destroys its own previous states.

(iii) The internal hermeneutic intertext is composed of texts included through citation or allusion, of which knowledge is required in order to interpret them.

(iv) The external hermeneutic intertext, made up of derived or "descendant" texts (in the sense of being the "offspring" of other texts), differs according to whether or not these "descendant" texts are of the same genre. If the derived texts are of the same genre, they belong to the same lineage as the text being considered; if they are of different genres, they belong to its commentaries, whether "metalinguistic" or not. Interpretations are thus partly derived from the texts they comment upon, and partly derived from other interpretations. Translations are subject to the same set of problems.

The "final" text for genetic phases becomes an initial text for hermeneutic phases; to put it more precisely, in genetic phases, hermeneutics is dominated (self-corrections, rectifications), while in hermeneutic phases, genetics is dominated, or at least limited to the production of descendant texts.

These four series of intertexts succeed one another in a non-determinist manner, for what one might call the textual *transit*, the moment in a tradition made up of preservations and breaks. Genetic and hermeneutic intertexts in fact maintain relationships which are all the closer because the ultimate aim of interpretation is to restore the text's genesis.

A unified theory of metamorphisms might make the concepts of textuality and intertextuality jointly operative. Indeed, the study of textuality controls that of intertextuality, since the text selects its intertext; in this way, we move from the macro-semantics of the text to the "megasemantics" of corpora.

Passages and intertextual rewritings. – The passage is a "unit" of writing, interpreting, and rewriting, all at the same time.[16] Where the genetic regime is concerned, it is the unit of removal and the place of development, when for example a passage is extracted from a text in order to be rewritten in a text relating to another genre.

The way in which in which semiotic forms are composed and developed, and then given concrete expression by passages, determines the text's mimetic regime. Where the hermeneutic regime is concerned, the passage is the unit of interpretation and commentary, but also of translation.

In order to study each of the intertextuality phases, one cannot limit oneself to replacing words: they are semiotic forms (localizable pairings of expressive forms and semantic forms). It is a known fact that the French school of literary genetics has patiently collated replacements, insertions, and suppressions. However, identifying changes of expression is only useful if at the same time one studies the processes governing semantic grounds and forms which concern very diverse dimensions and relationships, from the phonetic distinctive feature and the seme to the prosodic contour or the period.

Despite their diversity, the internal transformations defining textuality are no different in principle from the external transformations defining intertextuality, whether they are monolingual or multilingual. Thus, paths within the text or between texts can be problematized and described according to the same principles. At least, I have never yet observed any notable difference between the rewriting processes within and without the text, even in the case of translation:[17] the same general procedures of compensation, diffusion, and summation are found everywhere, and probably base the regimes under which semiotic forms develop on principles of semantic and expressive perception.

This hypothesis needs to be confirmed or invalidated by a program of comparison. If it can be validated, this would show both the relative nature of textual closure and the autonomy of the text considered as level of complexity: the study of textuality and intertextuality would thus go hand in hand, in the same way as do textual linguistics and corpus linguistics.

---

16 I am here neglecting the perceptive and memorial foundations of that dimension: the extent of this zone of locality can be linked to questions of recentness.
17 See Rastier (2006b). There is every reason to consider translators as writers.

I shall now give an example of each of the principal intertextual relationships. For genetic rewriting, we might refer to the analysis of the beginning of *Herodias* and of its links with *The Land of Moab* by H. B. Tristram (Rastier 1997); for the transformations between passages in works by the same author, we have seen how Atala Judici in *La Cousine Bette* rewrites Judith in the *Médecin de campagne* (see Rastier 2007).

An example of commentary as rewriting. – A commentary is a text derived from the text it is commenting upon, usually with a change of genre, or even of discourse. By way of example, let us take the theme of fixation, which has a prominent place in the work of Flaubert: "Quelque chose, de plus en plus, s'épaissit en moi, qui a peine à couler" 'Something within me increasingly thickens, struggling to flow', he wrote.[18] Proust's (1971, 269) famous judgment is well-known:

> Dans le style de Flaubert, par exemple, toutes les parties de la réalité sont converties en une même substance aux vastes surfaces, d'un miroitement monotone. Aucune impureté n'est restée. Les surfaces sont devenues réfléchissantes. Toutes les choses s'y peignent mais par reflet, sans en altérer la substance homogène. Tout ce qui était différent a été converti ou absorbé.
>
> In Flaubert, for example, all the parts of reality are converted into the same substance, of vast surfaces, of a monotonous series of reflections. No impurity remains. The surfaces become reflections. Everything is portrayed therein, but by means of reflection, without altering the homogenous substance. Everything which was different has been transformed and absorbed.[19]

These sentences could well rewrite the images of petrification at the beginning of *Herodias*:

> Cependant le Jourdain coulait sur la plaine aride. Toute blanche, elle éblouissait comme une nappe de neige. Le lac, maintenant, semblait en lapis-lazuli (. . .) Tous ces monts autour de lui, comme des étages de grands flots pétrifiés. . .
>
> The Jordan wound its way through the arid plains; white and glittering under the clear sky, it dazzled the eye like snow in the rays of the sun. The Dead Sea now looked like a sheet of lapis-lazuli. . . The mountain peaks surrounding the palace, looking like great petrified waves. . .

This is about relationships between writers, but Prévost speaks of a *petrified* discourse; De Biasi notes that Flaubert's project seems "achevé, figé par le démon

---

18 Letter to Louise Colet, April 15, 1852; in relation to this, observers lost no time in recalling the thrombosis that killed Flaubert twenty-eight years later.
19 Proust (1971: 269). English translation from Wood (1993, 155, footnote 2).

de l'achèvement" ('complete, frozen by the demon of completion'); and Genette speaks in the name of "glacis syntactico-rhétorique" ('syntactic-rhetorical glacis'). Critical discourse thus appears, in a remarkable mimesis, to rewrite Flaubert.

An example of intertextual scanning: local citations and rewritings. – A citation, especially when it is claimed as such, derives its meaning from being re-contextualized in the target text, just as much as from its immediate context in the source text; this continues to act allusively by virtue of a *displacement* principle, which appears to be one of the great laws of relationships between texts.

As a first example, I shall take an antithetical repetition in a poem where Primo Levi rewrites Catullus. The poem, *Il tramonto di Fossoli*, finishes with these lines: 'Suns may sink and return: / We, when the brief light is exhausted, / Are destined to sleep for never-ending night'.[20] The plural *soli*, or suns, allusively reveals its origin, confirmed in a note, in three lines by Catullus: 'Suns may disappear and return: / We, when the brief light is extinguished, / Are destined to sleep for never-ending night'.[21] Although this plural is found again in Levi's poem, it takes on a quite different poetic quality. The Latin poem begins with *Vivamus, mea Lesbia, atque amemus*, but the narrator of Levi's poem addresses a person who is dead.[22] The ancient poet's evocation "lacerates the flesh" (verse 5), although the poem quoted is a playful banter, in which he gives up counting the number of kisses and where the never-ending night simply reinforces the dictum to "enjoy the present moment". Levi does not mention the kisses, but these surround the quotation because, in the text, the presence of the other poem functions in the fashion of an absence indicated, and what surrounds the quotation signifies as much, if not more, than the quotation itself. We thus pass from the kisses explicitly demanded in life to those implicitly given beyond death.

More technically, we might question the contextual regimes of the erasure from text to text, whether it is implicit or explicit. Although the limits of the extract are generally indisputable, those of the fragment obviously remain critical areas. In the reprised text, the semantic activation is endocentric at the place

---

[20] *Possono i soli cadere e tornare: / A noi, quando la breve luce è spenta / Una notte infinita è da dormire* (lines 6–8). [English translations on this page are by RR, the translator of the present text.] So as not to overload this bibliography, I refer the reader to the bibliography of *Ulysse à Auschwitz* (see Rastier 2005).
[21] *Soles occidere et redire possunt; / Nobis cum semel occidit breuis lux / Nox est perpetua una dormienda* (Catullus, *Liber*, V, 4, lines 3–6).
[22] The poetic plural, which in Catullus had the power to passionately intensify (see 'Give me a thousand kisses, and then a hundred more' [*Da mi basia mille, deinde centum*], here marks the period of mourning.

of the quotation, which is re-contextualized. Conversely, in the source text, it is exocentric at the place of the erasure, which has meaning by virtue of its contexts: what is not said in the quotation must be looked for in its context.

Within the reprised text, the passage introduced by the quotation is re-contextualized by global determination. Between the reprise and the source, a relationship of intertextual "significance" is established: the quotation continues to point to the source, where the initial context can continue to act. Furthermore, the areas either side of the erasure can, in their turn, indicate other points in the quoted text, thus outlining an elementary cycle of interpretation.

4 Toward a schedule

Recognizing complexity. – We cannot demand that texts be divided into discrete units and obey rules in the grammatical sense: units are replaced by forms and grounds, while rules are supplanted by transformations and transpositions grasped in enunciative and interpretative scanning; calculation is replaced by recognition of forms, and deduction by the inference of probability.[23]

This being the case, and without offering a miraculous solution, the methods of corpus linguistics enable us to approach these textual forms as zones of locality, as well as the grounds, which are characterized in contrast to them (see Rastier 2011).

As with all cultural objects, the text is a complex one, on account of the multiplicity of norms (of discourse, genre and style) as well as in the domain of performances because of the a priori conjectural character of the relationships between passages, both within the text and the intertext.

Textual complexity derives from the semiotic principle itself, because there is no term-to-term correspondence between content and expression; these two levels do not accord with one another (in the Hjelmslevian sense): a compact expression may correspond to a diffuse content, or a compact content may correspond to a diffuse expression. Semiosis therefore needs to be problematized: all the scannings which establish it are complex, because they introduce a minima the two poles of the content/expression duality. What is more, for each dimension resulting from the analysis, the context *constitutes,* and no longer merely determines: it does not modify signs already given, but allows them to be estab-

---

[23] In fact, the lower levels of the text, from the paragraph to the syntactic unit, still need to be reconsidered in the light of this morpho-semiotic conception; but I cannot develop this here owing to lack of space.

lished as signs. It is therefore no longer possible to think of scientific activity as a search for causes: it becomes impossible to establish an etiology, because the regimes of causality are to be revised; nor even to lay down rules which are valid everywhere. This was demonstrated forty years ago by the debate which, in *Cognitive Science*, concluded that text "grammars" were technically impossible.

Finally, the variability of situations is expressed by the impact of external parameters, which are difficult to foresee. The relationship between external and internal linguistics can doubtless be partially modeled, and I have made proposals in the area of lexical diachrony using the dynamic systems theory (see Rastier 1999): in this, internal linguistics has the status of a state space and external linguistics the status of control space; any disruption in the control space (for example, in the doxa) would cause major disruptions of what is able to be observed in the state space.

References

Beaudouin, Valérie, *Mètre et rythmes du vers classique. Corneille et Racine*, Paris, Honoré Champion, 2002.
Benveniste, Émile, *Problèmes de linguistique générale*, Paris, Gallimard, 1966.
Pinker, Steven, *Words and rules. The ingredients of language*, New York, Harper Perennial, 1999.
Proust, Marcel, *Contre Sainte-Beuve. Pastiches et mélanges. Essais et articles*, Paris, Gallimard, 1971.
Rastier, François, *Sémantique et recherches cognitives*, Paris, Presses universitaires de France, 1991.
Rastier, François, *Réalisme sémantique et réalisme esthétique*, Théorie, littérature, enseignement 10 (1992), 81–119.
Rastier, François, *Stratégies génétiques et destruction des sources. L'exemple d'Hérodias*, in: Le Calvez, Éric/Canova-Green, Marie-Claude (edd.), *Texte(s) et intertexte(s)*, Amsterdam/Atlanta, Rodopi, 1997, 193–218.
Rastier, François, *Cognitive semantics and diachronic semantics. The values and evolution of classes*, in: Blank, Andreas/Koch, Peter (edd.), *Historical semantics and cognition*, Berlin, De Gruyter Mouton, 1999, 109–144.
Rastier, François, *Ulysse à Auschwitz. Primo Levi, le survivant*, Paris, Cerf, 2005.
Rastier, François, *Formes sémantiques et textualité*, Langages 163 (2006), 99–114, DOI: https://doi.org/10.3917/lang.163.0099 (= 2006a).
Rastier, François, *Traduction et genèse du sens*, in: Lederer, Marianne (ed.), *Le sens en traduction*, Paris, Minard, 2006, 37–49 (= 2006b).
Rastier, François, *Indices et parcours interprétatifs*, in: Thouard, Denis (ed.), *L'interprétation des indices*, Villeneuve-d'Ascq, Presses universitaires du Septentrion, 2007, 123–152.
Rastier, François, *La mesure et le grain. Sémantique de corpus*, Paris, Honoré Champion, 2011.
Rastier, François, *Faire sens. De la cognition à la culture*, Paris, Classiques Garnier, 2018.

Rosier, Irène, *La parole comme acte. Sur la grammaire et la sémantique au XIIIe siècle*, Paris, Vrin, 1995.

Saussure, Ferdinand de, *Écrits de linguistique générale*, edd. Bouquet, Simon/Engler, Rudolf, Paris, Gallimard, 2002.

Starobinski, Jean, *Les mots sous les mots. Les anagrammes de Ferdinand de Saussure*, Paris, Gallimard, 1971.

Van Dijk, Teun A./Kintsch, Walter, *Strategies of discourse comprehension*, New York, Academic Press, 1983.

Wood, Philip R., *The transformation of the quest from modernity to postmodernity and the third industrial revolution*, in: Arkinstall, Christine (ed.), *Literature and quest*, Amsterdam/Atlanta, Rodopi, 1993, 145–155.

Driss Ablali
Chapter 7
Corpus semantics, the unfinished project of Greimas' *Structural semantics*

Abstract: This paper focuses exclusively on the specific nature of the semiotic project developed in Greimas' *Structural semantics*, a project which needs to be distinguished from the rest of the semiotician's work. The aim, in short, is to establish that the driving force of this text, from both the epistemological and heuristic viewpoints, is based on three descriptive categories: text, genre and corpus, which open up the perspective, not of textual or discourse semiotics, but of corpus semantics.

Keywords: corpus, genre, semiotics, structural semantics, text

1 Preamble

What I will try to show in this paper relates to the specific nature of the semiotic project contained in the Greimas' *Structural semantics* (henceforth referred to as *SS*). This was an uncompleted project – unlike the one which would be developed from *Du sens*, accompanied by theoretical renunciations or "acts of force" – which involved corpus semantics, intersected by ontology, perception and the physical world, and was rooted in reflection about texts as being an integral part of discourse genres.

To describe the intellectual coherence of the *SS* project from the basis of three descriptive categories, corpus, text and genre, I will proceed in three stages: the first part will be mainly focused on the question of the corpus, a concept that is rarely, or never, associated with Greimas; the second will deal with the holistic concept of meaning as it is used in *SS* thanks to the text/corpus linking; the third, in the wake of the two preceding parts, will show that there exists in *SS*, contrary to what is still thought, a semiotic reflection on the category of genre, which is indispensable to the category of narrative.

Driss Ablali, Université de Lorraine, CREM

https://doi.org/10.1515/9783110794434-008

2 The question of data: Variables in the corpus

As will be seen in what follows, *SS* is a semiotic project not of text or discourse, but of the corpus. Before dealing with the fate reserved by Greimas for these three notions (text, discourse, corpus), it would probably be advisable to take a look at how they fare in *SS*, and by this means venture a way of appreciating his semantic theory of corpus. Despite many criticisms which are not always founded, Greimas' thinking about the nature of observables, to describe signification, was frequently linked in *SS* to corpora and the conditions under which they were compiled. Nowadays, however, it seems that work on corpora readily bypasses any reference to *SS*. This statement should nevertheless be qualified: although Greimas is neglected by specialists in linguistics or Corpus linguistics, we should, to put the record straight, recall that the word "corpus" is used 109 times in *SS*. It is not a minor issue. This at least is what stands out, in my eyes, from comments of the following type: from the first occurrence of the word on page 43 ('We will take the liberty of dividing up *this corpus* as we see fit'),[1] one clearly sees the direction that Greimas wished the semiotic project to take, namely to construct an objective semantic theory. Greimas judged that the data to be analyzed had to be organised in accordance with well-founded linguistic and extra-linguistic criteria, among them criteria of "homogeneity" and "representativeness". We must here insist on the fact that, in the 1960s, the word "corpus" was not yet a preoccupation among linguists. In France, it was not until the late 1970s that a new trend appeared in linguistics, notably in the context of discourse analysis – a trend which was officialised by a crop of works explicitly aiming to extract the discipline from the phrasal straitjacket. Before attempting to understand the reasons for favoring corpus over other types of data, like sentence, text and discourse, let us recall the delicate issues linked to the difficulties of deciding whether to keep or reject texts in a corpus. For Greimas, collecting a corpus was not about considering just any set of texts with no relation to one another. Aware of this fact, Greimas instituted what he called the "non-linguistic homogeneity of the corpus" (Greimas 1966, 94)[2] which was necessary for data collection. The corpus was not a simple juxtaposition of independent and disparate fragments; according to Greimas, its collection had to meet very specific selection criteria in order to constitute a "homogeneous" entity that he defined as follows:

---

[1] "Nous prendrons la liberté de diviser *ce corpus* à notre gré." (All subsequent translations from other works are by Rosemary Rodwell, the translator of this chapter, unless stated otherwise.)
[2] "[H]omogénéité non linguistique du corpus".

> One clearly sees what should be understood, in this particular case, by *non-linguistic homogeneity of the corpus*; what allows fifty or so non-individual responses to be gathered together in a collective corpus is a set of characteristics shared by those being tested: the fact that they belong to the same linguistic community and the same age range; and also that they share the same level of culture, the same "situation of examinees". (1966, 94)[3]

Certain forms of expression provide indisputable evidence of this – statements such as:

> The homogeneity of the corpus appears to depend on a set of non-linguistic conditions, on a situational parameter relating to perceptible variations either at the level of the speakers, or at the level of communication volume. (1966, 144)

Greimas is aware here of the impact of collected data on the analysis results; he therefore draws attention to the fact that analysis of the textual data is supremely dependent on the initial choices of what makes up the corpus, which guarantee an intrinsic basis to the analysis. He indicates this in plain language:

> The idiolectal character of individual texts does not allow us to forget the eminently social aspect of human communication. It is therefore necessary to widen the problem by introducing the principle that a certain number of individual texts, on condition they are chosen according to *non-linguistic criteria guaranteeing their homogeneity*, may be formed into a corpus and this corpus may be considered as sufficiently isotope. (1966, 93)[4]

A set of semiotic objects is therefore assembled, clearly announcing that the *SS* intellectual project is limited neither to signs, nor to phrases, nor even to the text. A close reading shows us that the semiotician must go beyond the text in order to be able to construct a corpus, corresponding to the widest semiotic world in which each element finds its semantic value.

Among "The conditions of a scientific semantics"[5] set up by Greimas, he considers the sign as part of the phrase, the phrase as a passage in a text, and the text

---

[3] "On voit bien ce qu'il faut entendre, dans ce cas précis, par *homogénéité non linguistique du corpus* ; ce qui permet de réunir une cinquantaine de réponses individuelles en corpus collectif, c'est un ensemble de caractères communs aux testés : leur appartenance à la même communauté linguistique, à la même classe d'âge ; c'est aussi le même niveau culturel, la même 'situation de testés'."

[4] "Le caractère idiolectal des textes individuels ne nous permet pas d'oublier l'aspect éminemment social de la communication humaine. Il faut donc élargir le problème en posant comme principe qu'un certain nombre de textes individuels, à condition qu'ils soient choisis d'après des critères non linguistiques garantissant leur homogénéité, peuvent être constitués en corpus et que ce corpus pourra être considéré comme suffisamment isotope."

[5] This is the title of the first chapter in *Structural semantics* ("Les conditions d'une sémantique scientifique").

as sample of a corpus. On this point, we can only partly share Rastier's criticism when he reproaches Greimas for his conception of the text as a sign:

> The simplest way of evading the question is to consider the text as a sign. It is the solution chosen by Peirce, as it is by Greimas and Eco (cf. 1988, p. 32: 'the Message is equivalent to the Sign'). This evasion obviously takes little account of the difference in level of complexity between the sign and the text, but it especially avoids thinking about the effect of the global upon the local, in this instance of the text upon each of the signs which go to make it up. (Rastier 1997, 147)[6]

Why "partly share"? Because this remark requires a few clarifications. Yes, it is quite true that Greimas, and what is called the "Paris School" (L'École de Paris), accord no place within the transformational progression to levels that are above the text; but, with respect to analysis categories, the *SS* project is not the same as Greimas' later work. Greimas is completely Rasterian in *SS*, and Rastier, in relation to the *SS* project, is entirely Greimassian, as we shall see later. They are both in complete agreement here.

To return to *SS*, we will follow it a little further to emphasise that Greimas never thinks of the text as the sole product issuing from use of the linguistic system, but as interaction between this system and other norms. He expresses it very lucidly, as we have seen:

> As far as linguistics is concerned, on the other hand [...] what allows fifty or so non-individual responses to be gathered together in a collective corpus is a set of characteristics shared by those being tested: the fact that they belong to the same linguistic community and the same age range; and also that they share the same level of culture, the same "situation of examinees". (Greimas 1966, 93–94)[7]

One cannot therefore say that there is no semiotic thinking about corpus in *SS*. Greimas even devotes a section in it to what he entitles "Forming the corpus", where we can read explicitly how this semiotician conceives the question of relationship between global and local dimensions in textual analysis – by introducing, for the first time in the history of textual and discursive theories, complexification

---

[6] "La manière la plus simple d'éluder la question consiste à considérer le texte comme un signe. C'est la solution que choisissent Peirce, comme Greimas ou Eco (cf. 1988, p. 32 : 'le Message équivaut au Signe'). Cette esquive fait évidemment peu de cas de la différence de niveau de complexité entre le signe et le texte, mais surtout empêche de penser l'incidence du global sur le local, en l'occurrence du texte sur chacun des signes qui le composent."

[7] "Sur le plan linguistique, en revanche, ce qui permet de réunir une cinquantaine de réponses individuelles en corpus collectif, c'est un ensemble de caractères communs aux testés : leur appartenance à la même communauté linguistique, à la même classe d'âge ; c'est aussi le même niveau culturel, la même 'situation de testés'."

factors of signification which show that the digital did not invent the corpus. Four semiotic categories are introduced here to define signification in its trans-phrasal dimension (within a single text) and its intertextual dimension (from one text to another within a corpus): "corpus", "discourse", "text" and "genre". Four levels are set up, with the need to distinguish between them in order to better articulate them. I have chosen this passage from among the more explicit:

> The procedure which, logically, follows upon the formation of a *corpus* consists in the transformation of the corpus into *text*. The text, in fact, is a determined sequence of the *discourse* and, as such, can only be a manifestation of logomachy, from which only one of the chosen isotopies should be retained. We will therefore understand *text* (and, what comes to the same thing, meta-text) to mean all the signification elements situated on the chosen isotopy and enclosed within the limits of the corpus. (1966, 145)[8]

First of all, one fact is blatant here: Greimas is opposed to the idea of a compositionality of signification. Signification is not constructed phrase by phrase, still less sign by sign, as the whole of formal tradition makes out, but by associative links formed by different linguistic operations allowing different aspects of the semantic contents to be revealed. There are effects of semes, and of isotopies of narrative actions, not only within a single text, but between different texts in the same corpus. An intertextual dimension, hidden by linearity, appears here, and on it rests the holistic aspect of signification which is constructed as a totality and is more than the sum of its parts. In fact, for Greimas, no text is seen in isolation. Access to signification emerges against a background of other texts in locality zones directly contributing to the construction of significance. As we can read in several passages of *SS*, the linguistic system is insufficient to account for the semantic regularities of any phenomenon. What unequivocally stands out here is the establishing of the corpus over the text, of the "global" over the "local". Greimas therefore admits that the procedures for describing the modes of existence and manifestation of the semantic world must take account of the relationships between one text and another, something which is only possible within a corpus. Greimas explains this clearly:

---

8 "La procédure qui, logiquement, suit la constitution du corpus consiste dans la transformation du corpus en texte. Le corpus, en effet, est une séquence délimitée du discours et, en tant que tel, ne peut être qu'une manifestation logomachique, dont il ne faut retenir qu'une des isotopies choisies. Nous entendrons donc par *texte* (et, ce qui revient au même, par *métatexte*) l'ensemble des éléments de signification qui sont situés sur l'isotopie choisie et sont enfermés dans les limites du corpus."

> This means that, if the actors can be set up within a story-occurrence, the actants, who are classes of actors, can only be so if based on a *corpus* of all stories: an articulation of actors constitutes a particular story; a structure of actants constitutes a *genre*. (1966, 175)[9]

This redundant correlation in *SS* between local textual descriptions and global description in a corpus enables us to understand the issue of articulation between the problematic of the sign and the problematic of the corpus, by always linking the first to the second. We should remember here that Bernanos is not the only corpus described by Greimas. Other types of discourse are subject to the scalpel of semiotic analysis, an analysis which always favors the global dimension of signification. Before any semantic analysis, a prior phase is necessary for the semiotician, namely the formation of the corpus. In other words, for Greimas, no text is seen alone: there is not the meaning of the text but the meaning of texts. This is the most valuable epistemological implication of *SS*, linking all the observables to be analyzed to the corpus as global authority. It is the case for the "popular tale" (1966, 147), the "psychodrama narrative" (214), the "Littré dictionary" (43), the "play" (177), the "game of chess" (184), and a "questionnaire" collected from philology students at the University of Poitiers (93) – all these show that textual corpora is the semiotician's true activity. And this conception of the corpus or corpora is very far removed from what Rastier calls a "logico-grammatical" conception where "the corpus boils down to a sample of language, a pool of examples or attestations" (2010, p. 35).[10] Here, Greimas develops a "rhetorical-hermeneutic" conception which "takes account of the relations between text and text, which is not possible within a discourse" (Rastier 2011, 35).[11] The passage which appears below makes Greimas a sort of indisputable precursor of corpus semantics, at the time of 1960s semantic and linguistic research, when the corpus was relegated to a back seat in favor of examples and phrases, cut off from their contextual and discursive terrain. Above all, these questions show that the term corpus, for Greimas, was the only language observatory where the signification of semes, actants and figures could be constructed. And Rastier clearly has this passage in mind in the distinctions he makes today between "reference corpus",

---

9 "Il en résulte que, si les acteurs peuvent être institués à l'intérieur d'un conte-occurrence, les actants, qui sont des classes d'acteurs, ne peuvent l'être qu'à partir du corpus de tous les contes : une articulation d'acteurs constitue un *conte* particulier ; une structure d'actants, un *genre*."
10 "Le corpus se résume à un échantillon de la langue, un réservoir d'exemples ou d'attestations."
11 "[Conception qui] tient compte des rapports de texte à texte, ce qui n'est possible qu'au sein d'un discours."

"study corpus" and "virtual corpus" (Rastier 2011, 16),[12] hence the plurality of realities he points to in Greimas' writing:

> The practical question thus raised is knowing what signification should be attributed to the three possible corpora respectively: the corpus having *the dimensions of a novel*, the corpus of *all the writings of Bernanos* and, finally, the corpus of *all the novels in a given society and historical period*, and what structural correlations one can reasonably hope to find between the models that can be made explicit from such corpora. (1966, 148; my underlining)[13]

For the heuristic bases of *SS*'s scientific project, the consequences of these choices are evident: to affirm that "signification does not pre-exist discourse" (Greimas 1966, 33)[14] is to affirm that there can be no semantics without a corpus: "no seme or semic category, even if its designation is borrowed from the French language, is identical in principle to a lexeme manifested in discourse" (Greimas 1966, 34).[15]

Or, a little further on: "Discourse, considered as a manifestation of language, is, as we have seen, the unique source of information about the significations immanent in this language" (Greimas 1966, 39).[16] But Greimas does not only insist upon the impact of the corpus for access to signification. He also ensures that the delimitations and defining criteria of textual corpora as entities are rethought. Modes of cohesion are therefore necessary for a set of texts to be able to constitute a textual corpus. This is what the following passage allows us to glimpse:

> A certain number of precautions and practical advice should therefore accompany this choice, so as to reduce, as far as possible, the element of subjectivity manifest in it. We shall say that a corpus, to be well formed, should satisfy three conditions: it should be representative, exhaustive and homogeneous. (Greimas 1966, 143)[17]

---

12 "Corpus de reference", "corpus d'étude", "corpus virtuel".
13 "La question pratique ainsi soulevée est de savoir quelle signification il faut attribuer respectivement aux trois corpus possibles : le corpus ayant les dimensions d'un roman, le corpus de la totalité des écrits de Bernanos et, enfin, le corpus de tous les romans d'une société et d'une période historique données, et quelles corrélations structurelles on peut raisonnablement espérer retrouver entre les modèles qu'on pourra expliciter à partir de tels corpus."
14 "La signification ne préexiste pas au discours."
15 "Aucun sème ou catégorie sémique, même si sa dénomination est empruntée à la langue française, n'est identique en principe à un lexème manifesté dans le discours."
16 "Le discours, considéré comme manifestation du langage, est, nous l'avons vu, l'unique source de renseignements sur les significations immanentes à ce langage."
17 "Un certain nombre de précautions et de conseils pratiques doivent donc entourer ce choix, afin de réduire, autant que possible, la part de subjectivité qui s'y manifeste. On dira qu'un corpus, pour être bien constitué, doit satisfaire à trois conditions : être *représentatif, exhaustif* et *homogène*."

And a few lines earlier in *SS*, this is confirmed:

> Forming a corpus does not therefore simply mean preparing a description, because the value of the description depends, in fact, on this prior choice, and, conversely, one can only judge the value of the corpus once the description has been completed. (1966, 142–143)[18]

This conception of corpora, which would remain exclusive to *SS*, prefigures what we would read half a century later in Rastier's *La mesure et le grain*. The same criteria advanced by Greimas in 1966 are now essential when configuring a mass of data as a corpus. The following passage is clearly in the wake of, and an extension to Greimas' thinking on the status and weight of the data gathered. Without taking into account here the development of Greimas' thinking, this decisive fragment by Rastier should be quoted:

> The very notion of corpus must be refined, for a corpus is not a set of data, still less a collection with no defined principle, embellished with the name of linguistic resource: as always in cultural sciences, the point of view which governs the formation of a corpus naturally conditions subsequent research. If a corpus' *representativeness* has nothing objective about it and depends on the type of use planned, its *homogeneity* also depends on the type of research. (Rastier 2011, 80)[19]

And to return to the fourth category of genre, mentioned above, still in relation to the levels of globality above the text, we might recall that in all the corpora described or mentioned in *SS*, Greimas does not forget to link genre and signification.

3 Textual genres and levels of textual complexity

Following in the wake of Hjelmslev, the figure of Greimas has always been linked to the question of text. However, as I have attempted to show above, in *SS* there is no text without a corpus. At the level of the analysis data, the text in itself

---

[18] "Constituer un corpus ne signifie donc pas simplement se préparer à la description, car de ce choix préalable dépend, en définitive, la valeur de la description, et, inversement, on ne pourra juger de la valeur du corpus qu'une fois la description achevée."
[19] "La notion même de corpus doit être affinée, car un corpus n'est pas un ensemble de données, encore moins une collection sans principe défini parée du nom de ressource linguistique : comme toujours dans les sciences de la culture, le point de vue qui préside à la constitution d'un corpus conditionne naturellement les recherches ultérieures. Si la *représentativité* d'un corpus n'a rien d'objectif et dépend du type d'exploitation prévue, son *homogénéité* dépend aussi du type de recherche."

does not exist. It is being inscribed in a corpus which gives it observable status, and this status is often referred to by Greimas in *SS* in direct association with the notion of "genre". Semiotics has always been reproached with having made genre the unthought element in its signification theory, as indeed Greimas and Courtés wrote in the *Dictionary of Semiotics*, claiming that it was 'founded on implicit ideological premises' (Greimas/Courtés 1979, 164).[20] Here, once again, we must clearly distinguish the semiotic project specific to *SS* from the new perspectives taken by the semiotic project as a whole after 1966. Why make this distinction? For two reasons directly related to the genre category. Before examining them, let us first stress that this category crops up a hundred or more times in *SS*, while being completely absent from Greimas' other semiotic analyses (from *Maupassant* to *Sémiotique des passions*, with *La soupe au pistou* and *L'imperfection* in between).

The first reason concerns the place of the "genre" variable in compiling corpora which, in order to satisfy the homogeneity principle, must be built up according to certain variables allowing different sets of texts to be compared. In this conception of the corpus, as shown by the diagram below, which distinguishes several levels of complexity, the genre variable is essential to a holistic description of meaning:

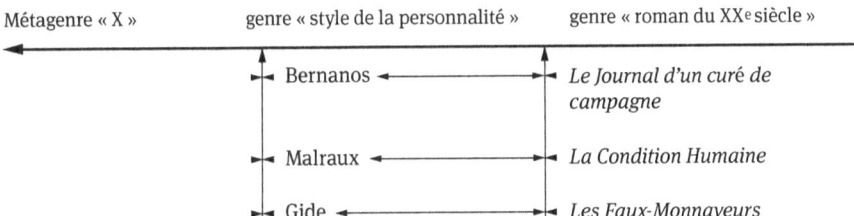

Diagram 1: The "genre" variable (Greimas 1966, 148).

Gide, Malraux and Bernanos did not only write novels, so if Greimas includes them together in this diagram, it is first of all because they all wrote in the same genre, the novel, and because secondly, they wrote novels dating from around the same period. By solely targeting twentieth-century novels, and not the novel alone, Greimas is clearly showing he is sensitive to the diachronic nature of genres, which are continually evolving, both synchronically and diachronically. This grouping of their texts to form a corpus has to take account of a more encompassing variable than the "author" one, which is judged to poorly represent the

---

20 "[F]ondée sur des postulats idéologiques implicites".

genre variable – hence the need to contrast texts by different authors which relate to the same generic category. A second point about the diagram, on which I would like to insist here, concerns the cultural dimension of genres. Greimas considers that analyzing a corpus of texts belonging to the same genre enlightens us in two respects: the first relates to the types of language activities peculiar to each novelist, what he calls "personality 'style' genre" (Greimas 1966, 148);[21] and the second to the novel genre in twentieth-century French society. Here, Greimas starts from three texts (Gide's *Les Faux-Monnayeurs* 'The Counterfeiters', Malraux's *La Condition Humaine* 'The Human Condition' and Bernanos' *Le Journal d'un curé de campagne* 'Diary of a Country Priest') in order to describe what he calls a "meta-genre", which is none other than "an inventory of genres typical of a given linguistic or cultural community" (Greimas 1966, 148).[22] The question of genres is so crucial that any semantic modelling of the story's structure depends on it. To put it another way, Greimas relies on analysis of the genres in a corpus for the purpose of showing the specific way each genre becomes a narrative, a specificity necessary to the setting up of the narrative from all textual genres. By relating the generic specificities of texts to actantial, thematic and figurative invariants, Greimas' analyses attempt to fix the rules of the story within a body of epistemological principles; to start out from the "story-tale" genre as "story-occurrence" (Greimas 1966, 217)[23] and move towards a "meta-genre", defined as a concatenation of generic micro-stories.

On these two points, one might reproach the Greimas of *SS* with anything other than forgetting the genre category, given the decisive role this plays in modelling the story's overall structure, as can be seen from this passage:

> If an inventory of models is a stage on the way to constructing a genre of models, description can just as well be applied to the establishment of a text which is an inventory of genres. Insofar as one succeeds, for example, in defining the popular story as a genre, an inventory of all comparable genres can give rise to the description of a common meta-genre which would be the story, considered in its generality, or else some sort of sub-set of stories. (1966, 147)[24]

---

21 "[G]enre 'style' de la personnalité".
22 "[U]n inventaire de genres caractéristiques d'une communauté linguistique ou culturelle donnée".
23 "Récit-conte", "récit-occurrence".
24 "Si un inventaire de modèles est une étape vers la construction d'un genre de modèles, la description peut tout aussi bien viser l'établissement d'un texte qui serait un inventaire de genres. Dans la mesure où l'on réussit, par exemple, à définir le conte populaire comme un genre, l'inventaire de tous les genres comparables peut donner lieu à la description d'un méta-genre commun, qui serait le récit, considéré dans sa généralité, ou un sous-ensemble quelconque de récits."

It is not the structure of the textual narrative alone which counts for Greimas, but the structure of the genre. Analysis of the genre must lead to setting up the story, and the story, like 'a unique signification structure' (Greimas 1966, 213–214),[25] is the consequence of the contrastive analysis of the different genres. In short, the genre of texts takes precedence over all the other variables with a view to making the descriptive models capable of being generalised – hence the multiplicity of genres described, evoked or quoted in *SS*: "popular Russian tales" (147), "detective stories, Chinese tale, tales of espionage", "analytical psychodrama" (213–214), "theatre dramas" (175), "longer stories, in verse or prose, de Vigny's *Moïse*, Camus' *La Peste*" (97–98), "play" (176), "poetry" (58), and "literary genre" (70).

A story's structure must take into account the effect of genres on the semantic, actantial and figurative codifications. Because, Greimas insists, 'semantics, which aims to be a social science, seeks to describe values and not to postulate them' (Greimas 1966, 58).[26] And in this description, analysis of the story is conducted in such a way as to be able to formulate the rules whose application is conditioned by the effect of genre on the text. One remark is necessary here: when Greimas refers to the texts analyzed, or to be analyzed, he often calls them by their genre and not by their title. For example, he speaks of the popular Russian tale, rather than naming a specific tale. With the novel, he speaks of "Bernanos' novel", and not the novel in general, just as, in his descriptions, he always insists on the novel's subject, on the "novels of a society", of "a given historical period", "twentieth-century novels" and "novels-occurrences". Genre is at the heart of the modelling of the story's structure. It is the partial modellings of each genre which form a coalition and thus define the story's global structure as "meta-genre". The heuristic power of this procedure is due to the fact that it enables the researcher to start from the regularities observed in a corpus to then unify multi-level invariants through defined norms within a class of genre: the genre here is what retains and qualifies the collected data to restore the story's complexity in all genres. At the level of mass data collection, Greimas cannot do without genre, just as he cannot do without it to construct the 'the achronic organisational model of contents, that we thus meet with in areas that are very far distant from one another' (Greimas 1966, 233).[27]

As we saw earlier, in different passages of *SS*, analysis of the story is not envisaged without the complementary upper levels like text, genre and corpus. To con-

---

25 "[U]ne structure de signification unique".
26 "[L]a sémantique, qui se veut une science humaine, cherche à décrire des valeurs et non à les postuler."
27 "[M]odèle d'organisation achronique de contenus, que nous rencontrons ainsi dans des domaines très éloignés les uns des autres."

struct a theory of the story, the text alone, cut off from the other levels, makes no sense in Greimas' eyes. This, inevitably, raises a question: what became of this complementarity in Greimas' other writings after *SS*? The answer, without further ado, is: in the case of Maupassant, up to *La soupe au pistou*, there is no further place for the complexity of levels above the text in the analysis of a story's structure. This is the point at which to recall that the work on Maupassant involves only one short story, *Les deux amis*, and the analysis of a recipe involves only one text, *La soupe au pistou*. This method of analyzing texts heralds a quite different approach on the part of Greimas, an approach which posits that the text is the only upper level of complexity, governing the lower levels like the narrative, the figurative, the thematic and the enunciative. By focusing the analysis on a single text, Greimas abandons the narrow articulation between text and corpus, which he himself had implemented and justified by reasoned argument, in *SS*. If this present article was concerned with giving a detailed history of the development of Greimas' thinking on these points, attention would be drawn to the substantial change in his view of the relationship between text, genre and corpus, and consequently of the semiotic project as a whole.

In *Du sens*, the work published five years after *SS*, and which brings together articles written from 1966 onwards, there appears a conception of the text showing that the text's meaning no longer has need of textual configuration on several levels in order to be described. As we read in the introduction to *Du sens*, formalisation has become the true path to analyzing texts: 'It is through a narrow gate, between two indisputable skills – philosophical and logical-mathematical – that the semiotician is obliged to conduct his investigation into meaning' (Greimas 1970, 12).[28] And this investigation of meaning is only defined in *Du sens* in order to describe the text, the text alone, and not the texts grouped according to whether they belong to a particular genre, as we saw before in *SS*. Greimas now situates meaning in the text itself and not in the interaction between different texts in the corpus. This hypothesis is confirmed in the Maupassant, which involves analysis of a single short story. We have thus moved from the signification of an actant, of a figure or seme described from a corpus, to a conception of signification which understands the text as a "closed world". To quote Greimas himself: 'It nevertheless remains true that certain figurative values which we shall seek to describe can be apprehended *thanks to their recurrence in the closed text*' (Greimas 1976, 55).[29]

---

[28] "C'est par une porte étroite, entre deux compétences indiscutables – philosophique et logico-mathématique –, que le sémioticien est obligé de conduire son enquête sur le sens."
[29] "Il n'en reste pas moins vrai que certaines valeurs figuratives que nous chercherons à décrire peuvent être appréhendées *grâce à leur récurrence dans le texte clos.*"

Only the text makes sense, therefore, in Greimas' eyes. The other levels of complexity, evoked in *SS*, no longer have a legitimate place in the analysis of stories, recipes or passions, such as defiance or anger. The central consideration, of data relating to the text alone, in any analysis by Greimas of literary, anthropological, architectural or pictorial discourse, provides an instant and unambiguous sign of a particular conception of meaning and signification: it is one that is strictly interested only in the close relations which the actants and actors, the semes and figures have with one other, within a closed textual configuration, independently of any other attachment, whether of corpus or genre. Because if *Structural semantics* imposes on the analysis an overall unity which is broader than the text, in Maupassant's *Deux amis*, Greimas follows the semes and figures step by step in their immediate environment, favoring a return to the text which ignores the links establishes between *Deux amis* and Maupassant's other short stories. This allows us to discern the concept of meaning which Greimas chooses to adopt by wishing to consider this notion within the close relations observed in a narrow, limited context. This premise is not explicitly formulated in Greimas' analyses, but it is presupposed in the way the problem is dealt with. This should be explained further. It was in the *Dictionary of Semiotics* that the Greimassian concept of textual analysis appeared in its entirety. With regard to the notion of genre, a problem then aroses: unlike other entries in the *Dictionary*, genre was not defined, by Greimas and Courtés, as a key concept of semiotics. This, at least, is how it appears in the entry in question, as it does in many others – because, unlike the premises in *SS*, which linked text, genre and corpus, from the 1970s onwards primacy was clearly accorded to the specific structure of the text. Moreover, the dictionary entry under "genre" makes a complete tabula rasa of *SS*'s most significant premises, with the entry under "genre" being defined in a general way which excludes it from the conceptual system of semiotics. The main lines are developed of what is called 'the theory of genre in the European cultural context' (Greimas/Courtés 1979, 164),[30] but without it being linked to the global unit levels of description of meaning, which are the corpus and discourse, as was the case in *SS*. This also holds true for the entry under "corpus": the authors, having recalled its different meanings in linguistics, wish to show that it is an operating notion, not only for syntactic theories, but also semantic ones:

> Thus it is possible to speak of syntagmatic corpora (all of an author's texts) or paradigmatic corpora (all the variants of a story), while taking account of the fact that they are never

---

30 "[L]a théorie du genre dans contexte culturel européen".

closed or exhaustive, but only representative, and that the models which help to try and explain them will be hypothetical, projective and predictive. (1979, 74)[31]

Now, as regards Greimas' analysis, from *Maupassant* to *La soupe au pistou*, only the correlations in a single text have meaning. The text is therefore perceived in isolation, cut off from other texts in the corpus in relation to which it acquires meaning. Furthermore, in the sub-entries of "corpus", Greimas and Courtés refer neither to discourse, nor to genre, nor to text. It is rather the notions of "generation", "lexicon" and "verification" which figure. This is of no small importance, because it is about isolating the text from its contours and upper levels in favor of an immanentist conception of meaning. Texts are therefore confined within their internal logic, cut off from exogenous determinations. This means that all the theoretical and epistemological advances of *SS* have remained, for Greimas, at the stage of virtualisation. For Greimas and his followers, it led to the idea of a total autonomy of signs pleading for uniqueness of meaning, as Rastier rightly remind us in this passage:

> It would seem that the text in itself does not exist, and that textuality is an abstraction (as, in fact, is language) [. . .] The universals in the matter are only [. . .] universals of method which appear useful for describing discourse, genres and texts. (1994, 6)[32]

This is the stance which Rastier takes when, in the late 1980s, and in line with his work over the preceding decades,[33] he proposes studying the meaning of texts, in the *SS* tradition of Greimas, Pottier and Coseriu, while taking account of global determinations (corpus, discourse, genre, text) over the local (sign). It was therefore Rastier's semantics which were destined to build on the initiatives and legacy of Greimas' *Structural semantics*, a work 'whose program has not yet been sufficiently developed' (Rastier 2008, 2).[34]

---

31 "Ainsi on peut parler de corpus syntagmatiques (ensemble de textes d'un auteur) ou de corpus paradigmatiques (ensemble de variantes d'un conte), tout en tenant compte du fait qu'ils ne sont jamais fermés ni exhaustifs, mais seulement représentatifs et que les modèles à l'aide desquels on cherchera à en rendre compte seront hypothétiques, projectifs et prédictifs."
32 "Il nous semble que le texte en soi n'existe pas, et que la textualité est une abstraction (comme d'ailleurs le langage) [. . .] Les universaux en la matière ne sont que des catégories descriptives, en d'autres termes des universaux de méthode qui paraissent utiles pour décrire les discours, les genres, et les textes."
33 Particularly "La signification chez Mallarmé" (1966), "Les niveaux d'ambiguïté des structures narratives" (1971), cf. Rastier (1972; 1973).
34 "[D]ont le programme n'a pas été encore suffisamment développé. . ."

References

Ablali, Driss, *La sémiotique du texte*, Paris, L'Harmattan, 2003.
Ablali, Driss/Ducard, Dominique (edd.), *Vocabulaire des études sémiotiques et sémiologiques*, Paris, Honoré Champion, 2009.
Ablali, Driss, *Malaise dans les frontières*, in: Normand, Claudine/Estanislao, Sofia (edd.), *Espaces théoriques du langage. Des parallèles floues*, Louvain-la-Neuve, Academia, 2013, 301–317.
Greimas, Algirdas Julien, *Sémantique structurale*, Paris, Presses universitaires de France, 1966.
Greimas, Algirdas Julien, *Du sens*, vol. 1, Paris, Seuil, 1970.
Greimas, Algirdas Julien, *Maupassant. La sémiotique du texte: exercices pratiques*, Paris, Seuil, 1976.
Greimas, Algirdas Julien, *La soupe au pistou ou la construction d'un objet de valeur*, in: Greimas, Algirdas Julien, *Du sens*, vol. 2, Paris, Seuil, 1983, 157–169.
Greimas, Algirdas Julien, *Débat entre Greimas et Ricœur*, in: Hénault, Anne (ed.), *Le pouvoir comme passion*, Paris, Presses universitaires de France, 1994, 195–216.
Greimas, Algirdas Julien/Courtés, Joseph, *Sémiotique. Dictionnaire raisonné de la théorie du langage*, Paris, Hachette, 1979.
Greimas, Algirdas Julien/Fontanille, Jacques, *Sémiotique des passions. Des états de choses aux états d'âme*, Paris, Seuil, 1991.
Rastier, François, *Idéologie et théorie des signes. Analyse structurale des "Eléments d'Idéologie" d'Antoine-Louis-Claude Destutt de Tracy*, The Hague, Mouton, 1972.
Rastier, François, *Essais de sémiotique discursive*, Tours, Mame, 1973.
Rastier, François, *Sémantique interprétative*, Paris, Presses universitaires de France, 1987.
Rastier, François, *Sémantique pour l'analyse*, Paris, Masson, 1994.
Rastier, François, *Les fondations de la sémiotique et le problème du texte. Questions sur les "Prolégomènes"*, in: Zinna, Alessandro (ed.), *Hjelmslev aujourd'hui*, Turnhout, Brépols, 1997, 141–161.
Rastier, François, *Entretien sur les théories du signe et du sens. Réponses à Peer Bundgaard*, Texto! 13:3 (2008), www.revue-texto.net/docannexe/file/1735/bundgaard_rastier.pdf. [last consultation: 10.02.2019].
Rastier, François, *La mesure et le grain. Sémantique de corpus*, Paris, Champion, 2011.
Rastier, François/Cavazza, Marc/Abeillé, Anne, *Sémantique pour l'analyse. De la linguistique à l'informatique*, Paris, Masson, 1994.

Bernard Combettes
Chapter 8
Suggestions for a diachronic text linguistics

Abstract: The objective of this paper is to examine how *diachronic text linguistics* can constitute a specific discipline when, on the one hand, it studies the development of notions which relate to discursive coherence and, on the other, the changes that can affect the linguistic facts which ensure this coherence. Insofar as the first part of the objective is concerned, it is necessary to avoid applying notions and frameworks of analysis used in synchronic studies. Furthermore, there is a need to consider the development of phenomena concerning textuality, along with textual competence and, more generally, the linguistic consciousness of speakers.

Keywords: referential continuity, diachrony, historical linguistics, textual typology

1 General problematic

My principal objective in this contribution is to examine how text linguistics may form a specific discipline when it takes the diachronic dimension into consideration; when its specific aim is to study how notions relating to discursive coherence have evolved, as well as the changes that can affect speech acts ensuring the coding of this same coherence. It is relatively easy to see that most areas of the language sciences recognize the specific nature of the diachronic approach. Whether it involves phonetics, morphology, or syntax, the description and analysis of change are made up of specific disciplines, with their own concepts, problems, and methods. This is why, for example, the idea that morphosyntactic categories are not immutable but, on the contrary, subject to change, demands that notions leading to the adoption of analysis frameworks able to account for this particularity should be relativized. The same goes for semantics and lexicology or, where studying the "external" causes of evolution are concerned, for sociolinguistics. Consequently, there appears to be quite widespread recognition that the diachronic approach demonstrates sufficient specificity for the methods implemented in synchronic analyses to be applied, just as they are, to studying

---
Bernard Combettes, Université de Lorraine, ATILF

https://doi.org/10.1515/9783110794434-009

how the linguistic system has evolved. Why, under these circumstances, should text linguistics have a different status from other components of the language sciences? Even if it only concerns the "material" aspect of this question, it seems quite significant that compared with historical grammar or historical phonetics textbooks, which have long occupied an acknowledged and well identified place in the disciplinary field, it should be difficult to pinpoint an equivalent text claiming to be a work on "historical text linguistics". One could no doubt point out that text linguistics is a recent approach, which does not have the long history of a tradition going back to comparative grammar, and that it can therefore have neither the same stability nor structuring as other disciplines; however, it seems to me that, in its theoretical thinking, analyses, and results, it shows evidence of sufficient development for us to consider that this is now a well-established scientific field where it is possible to deal with the problem of diachrony.

An explanation is in order here: by making these observations, I do not mean that text linguistics has only been interested in modern synchrony. A number of high-quality studies relating to former periods have already been carried out from a diachronic perspective, in several sub-domains of the textual approach. Subjects as varied as the functioning of anaphoric expressions, the role of verb tenses, represented discourse, modal constructions or connectors, to name just a few examples, have been the subject of research aiming to determine what type of development they have undergone. It might also be noted that symposia devoted to historical linguistics – I am thinking, for example, of the "Diachro" series of symposia – accord a not-insignificant place to textuality among the themes they offer. It has to be said, however, that this interest in "what is beyond the sentence" does not actually result in analyses which might be considered to relate to text linguistics. This research falls within the theoretical and methodological framework of grammaticalization and pragmaticalization, which is perfectly consistent with its objectives; insofar as change in the level of analysis is linked, in a defining way it could be said, to the very concept of grammaticalization, it is quite natural that the textual domain should be involved when the process of reanalysis is observed. Let us take the example of the continuum proposed by E. Closs Traugott, who hypothesizes that forms subject to the process of grammaticalization evolve in a particular direction, from the "referential" domain to the textual domain and finally to the pragmatic-enunciative domain. Although, from this standpoint, the textual dimension can obviously not be ignored, it will nevertheless be noted that these studies do not enable coherence phenomena to be treated globally, since they are concerned with observing particular cases; and more important still, because the focus is on the question of grammaticalization and not on coherence of the text and discourse, priority is given to analyzing change mechanisms, and the problem of text linguistics becomes a secondary matter. I shall therefore attempt here to set out a few points which merit discussion and should be taken into consideration if we believe that the moment has come to introduce a fully-fledged discipline that is autonomous and well identified.

2 The language/text relationship

Before tackling the various distinct aspects of this problem, I would like to quickly touch upon a general point of order, which concerns the relationships it is appropriate to establish between the evolution of the linguistic system and that of textuality. Since the elements of the language system are subject to variation and constant development, what does this mean for text linguistics, which is based precisely on the notion of coding categories of a textual order, through forms of the linguistic system? Can we try to determine causes and effects, modifications in one domain leading to changes in the other? We should note that this question is posed independently of the diachronic approach; synchronic text linguistics cannot avoid coming up against it, explicitly or implicitly. Unlike the studies just mentioned, which take the textual dimension into consideration but in fact aim to study the linguistic system, a different position would be to account for discursive coherence and its coding using the tools provided by a given language system; the forms and syntactic constructions are then, in a way, subordinated, in the analysis, to the tendencies governing the functioning of the textuality. This approach, which corresponds to what seems to be the appropriate method to follow in order to develop a diachronic text linguistics, must however avoid the stumbling block of over-systematic application of the notions and frameworks of analysis used in the synchronic studies involving contemporary texts. Through what might be considered the abuse of a certain type of reasoning, observation of the coding leads, rather paradoxically, to neglecting the specific nature of the text; since the implementation of linguistic markers is related to the speaker's competence, the object of study is no longer really the language/text relationship, but the language/cognition relationship; and since categories of a cognitive order are considered to be universal, it means that the textual dimension has therefore been sidelined and is no longer considered in its specificity, in the particular structuring of the categories belonging to it. The way in which the foreground/background opposition is generally treated offers a good example of this – probably over-quick – generalization. In many studies dealing with this opposition, it is as if the supposed universality of the form/content distinction at the cognitive level inevitably led to a universal alternation of levels, both as regards definition and characteristics, which is a matter of textuality.

It would appear essential to recall that relating linguistic systems, in all their variety, with coherence phenomena, cannot be done without evaluating the specific nature of this same textual field; and this is all the more important because it involves taking the diachronic dimension into account. In the same way as we accept that linguistic systems evolve, it is necessary to consider that categories relating to textuality also change over time and that speakers' competence does not remain immutable – that this "feeling" is focused on the text, textuality, and coherence, together with the units and notions that this competence implies.

3 The question of textual competence

A particularly complex problem then arises: to what extent is it possible to attain this discursive competence, this feeling for the textuality, when we are dealing with the past? It has to be admitted that researchers almost always find themselves faced with the physical impossibility of gaining access to information that is essential for evaluating the various aspects of speakers' intuition. It would therefore clearly be useful to have precise and reliable documentation available on types of reading – reading aloud or reading silently – and the way these evolved during the Middle Ages and the Renaissance. Although there are a few documents enabling us to gain a fairly accurate picture of the way Latin was read in religious communities, it is completely different where the reading of French texts is concerned: for these there is no reliable evidence on which to base an evaluation. So we are forced to approach the problem in reverse, by trying to rediscover, by analyzing linguistic forms and, possibly, punctuation and segmentation also, certain characteristics of production activity at its different levels – whereas, in fact, we should be able to rely on psycholinguistic data in order to determine, without too many anachronisms, how the coding of discursive coherence phenomena worked. One might, for example, think that a notion such as "discursive memory", which seems appropriate to describe the functioning of anaphoric relations or of framing expressions in modern texts, could also be pressed into service for analyzing ancient texts. However, the features of this psycholinguistic reality still remain to be defined as precisely as possible. When, for example, we examine the evolutionary tendencies of the thematic progression system, the changes occurring in the way anaphoric relations work, and the modifications affecting the framing of adverbial modifiers, we are able to perceive the transition from reading based on a coherence applying to stages of treatment of restricted dimension, in relatively narrow contexts, and with short-distance memorization processes, to a style of reading that favors fuller treatment units based on anticipation processes relating to the right-hand context. To somewhat complicate the problem, I would add that it is necessary to distinguish as precisely as possible those aspects which concern production and those concerning reception. We have to admit that we are as poorly informed about the creation of texts as we are about reading them. For example, the fact that authors dictated their texts, as was the usual practice in the Middle Ages, probably had an impact on coding and on textual coherence. There is no doubt about the importance of establishing these links, even though it has to be acknowledged that relying on ample, well-founded data often proves difficult.

When taking diachrony into account, it seems that one of the first tasks of text linguistics is therefore to replace in their context the notions and categories on which the analysis will be based. Whether it involves cognitive processes with, for example, the functioning of discursive memory or managing the presentation and identification of referents; the units in which these same processes are implemented; the typology of texts and discourses; or lateral notions covering several language events such as the narrative/discourse opposition – in all these cases, variation, as the essential driver of development, should be accorded the same fundamental place as the one it occupies when change in the language system is being reported. Over the past few years, emphasis has been placed on the importance of grammaticalization in the diachronic approach and, along with other advances this has led to a revitalization of thinking about the development of notions in the area of morphosyntax and categories. Such categories include nominal determiners or adverbs, for example, but also relations, such as transitivity, or functions undergoing change at the same time as the properties fitting into their definition are being modified. Insofar as an identical perspective can be adopted in the area of discursivity, with recognition of a diachronic variation in the different components of a text grammar, analysis of the evolution of coherence coding then consists in establishing relationships between two levels – that of the language system and that of text structure, which are in constant movement and characterized by a situation of variation.

I now propose to illustrate this general approach, whose main principles are outlined above, by means of a few examples. It may seem somewhat artificial to separate points which have close relations, but specific studies are necessary before the interactions can be analyzed and examination of the cause and effect sequence envisaged. I will tackle the questions of relevant units and textual typology in turn, before making observations on certain aspects of the functioning of referential expressions.

4 Stages of treatment

Most aspects of text coherence seem as if they should be contingent upon notions being relativized in this way, which might allow anachronisms to be avoided when applying certain frameworks of analysis. In this respect, the question of relevant units and stages of treatment becomes crucial, since it conditions the observation and interpretation of the rules governing the way most linguistic markers function. Whether it concerns phenomena such as anaphoric relations or the scope of framings or connectors, it is important to determine whether the tendencies guiding their management are exercised at the level of the clause, the "modern" sentence, or the period, for example. Examining the development of these stages appears indispensable and the changes observed in this domain must be taken into account when analyzing coherence markers; it would be particularly useful if the thinking of a researcher like Seguin (1993), who studied the emergence of the sentence in the classical period, not only as an idea, but also as a unit of linguistic competence, could be extended to the most ancient states of language – from Old French to Pre-Classical French. The rarity or absence of evidence from grammarians should not be an obstacle to observing speech acts which enable developments in linguistic feeling to be defined in the areas where activities of a cognitive order apply. If, for example, we consider the case of narrative prose as it is presented in Old French texts, we can see that it is characterized by the catenation of relatively brief units, constructed on the second verb pattern, with a subject, noun or pronominal, which immediately follows the verbal form. The important feature of all the elements which could be described as the "basic cell" of the utterance appears to reside in the close association it implies between two elements of the production act, namely predication and the identification of a referent. In thirteenth-century texts, it is as if identification of the referent could not be left to wait, could not be effected before the main predication was carried out. This latter could precede identification, but only in cases where the subject was postposed. In cases where the utterance contained a second predication of an "apposition" type, this constraint could doubtless be interpreted as a means of avoiding the cognitive overload formed by the catenation, in the same propositional cell, of two predicates whose subject is not clearly identifiable. It is timely, here, to raise the question of the pertinence of the sentence unit, insofar as we are able to observe the presence of events that an unduly-modern interpretation of the texts might identify as anacoluthons. In reality, two processes are involved – the maintenance of referential continuity, and change of topic – which are disassociated and divided over two different segments of the utterance. Thus, in examples such as:

(1) [puis en son langaige dist (= Jean de Saintré): . . .] En disant ces paroles, le roy qui tresfort me regardoit puis me dist. . . (Antoine de La Sale, *Le Roman de Jean de Saintré*, 1453)

'then Jehan de Saintré said to me in his language. . . While saying these words, the king, who was gazing at me attentively, said to me. . .'[1]

(2) lors damps Abbés fust sur piez et, en riant a Madame, Madame lui dist (id.)

'then monsieur Abbé rose and while laughing to Madame, Madame said to him. . .'

the gerunds: *while saying these words* and *while laughing to Madame* unambiguously refer to salient referents in the previous context (*Jehan de Saintré, damps Abbés*), but are not subjects in the clause forming the right-hand context. In the first example, the participial group which, from the temporal viewpoint, serves as a context for the clause following it, still manages to summarize the discourse preceding it. In the second case, the effect of simultaneity between the second predication and the main predication is less clear, and the participle refers to an event which might relate to the foreground, thus enjoying a certain degree of autonomy. These reduced clauses formed by the gerunds thus behave as units which are not yet very integrated into the sentence structure, maintaining relationships with the context that are identical to those that a syntactically independent unit would establish. This has the particular advantage of enabling referential continuity to be guaranteed. Development of the initial zone of the utterance from the Middle French, with patterns of the S(X)(X)V type, will not only be a surface modification concerning the order of constituents, but will correspond, more deeply, to a change in the very concept of the "clause" as a stage for dealing with the referential identification.

5 The typology of texts: The case of the descriptive text

In order to illustrate the questions raised by the distinction of text types, which should not be thought of as immutable frameworks adaptable to any period, I

---

[1] All subsequent translations from other works are by Rosemary Rodwell, the translator of this chapter, unless stated otherwise.

will take the example of the descriptive text – a type of text that is thought to have appeared during the Middle French period. The emergence of this kind of text should be seen in relation to the development of certain linguistic markers, as I shall attempt to show. This development made it possible for descriptive passages to acquire generic autonomy and thus be freed from the foreground on which they were highly dependent. In Old French texts, description is usually reduced to isolated clauses in the flow of the narrative sequence, whether it is independent or relative subordinate clauses that are involved. One of the links enabling us to unite the marking of the descriptive text's coherence with the domain of linguistic forms appears to consist in the organization of information, particularly the various types of thematic progressions. By way of example, let us consider the following extract:

(3) Et neporec tant a allé que il vint a une croiz de pierre qui ert au departement de deus voies en une gaste lande. Et il regarde la croiz quant il fu pres et voit par dejoste un perron de marbre ou il avoit lettres escrites [. . .] et il resgarde vers la croiz et voit une chapelle mout ancienne [. . .] et troeve a l'entree unes prones de fer [. . .] et voit la dedenz un autel qui [. . .] (*La Queste del Saint Grall*, 13th century.)

'And however he rode for so long that he arrived at a stone cross at the junction of two paths on a deserted heath. And he looked at the cross when he came near to it and saw a marble block by the side on which letters were written [. . .] and he looked toward the cross and saw a very ancient chapel [. . .] and found iron bars at the entrance [. . .] and he saw an altar inside which [. . .]'

The progression with its constant theme, systematized in this type of sequence to express the narrative foreground, matches what one might call the subordination of the background and its low quantitative importance. This progression consists in according the role of theme in the discourse to a salient referent, while the function of syntactic subject is found in successive clauses. This form of organization that ensures the passage's coherence is maintained. The combination of this actantial choice of verbal forms reflecting perception processes (*il regarde, voit*) or actions (*il vint, troeve*) enables referents presented as new to be introduced – referents which will be the possible subject of a description or, more broadly, a commentary. Insofar as the syntactic subject is not necessarily expressed, the initial zone of the utterance is often occupied by a marker (*si, or, lors*) 'if, now, when' which is on the same lines as "close" coherence that is managed "step by step". We can see how, in such sequences, it is the narrative skeleton, with temporal catenations in the foreground, which dominates the description and, one might say, confines it to relative subordinate clauses or adjectival phrases. A fundamental change was to come about with the development of hypertheme and derived-theme progression. This alternative way of presenting and linking referents was a decisive factor in changing the description's status, which could then evolve toward composing a specific type of text. Progression by hypertheme is not unknown in texts of the Old French period, but it usually only takes place in catenations by enumeration, when compiling lists, which cannot be considered as belonging to descriptive texts. Yet again, in this respect Middle French appears to belong to a time of innovation. Even though the "tightened" coherence, typical of narration in the preceding period, is maintained in certain texts, it is evident that progression with derived themes was starting to be used. This, particularly in one of its variants, permits a construction of the text that is radically removed from the former system of writing; the sub-themes are not necessarily attached to a hypertheme conveyed in a referential expression, such as a NP, but can refer to previously evoked propositional content. A transition thus occurs from "close" coherence, at short distance, to broad coherence, which presupposes a feeling of specific textual units, distinct from those composing the foreground. Let us consider, for example, the following extract. It is a descriptive passage taken from Molinet's *Chroniques*, dating from the last quarter of the fifteenth century.

(4) Dès l'année précédente, avoit esté le tempz d'yver tant aspre et angoisseux que [. . .] Petis enfans estoyent trouvéz mors en leurs repos de berceaux, plusieurs gens à cheval s'engeloyent par les champs [. . .] Pelerins, pietons, bosquillons et ceulx qui hantoyent les bois reindirent leurs esperis [. . .] Les oyseaulx du ciel estoyent recoeulliéz morz [. . .]; pluseurs arbrez morurent geléz et steriles (Molinet, *Chroniques*, 1490).

'Since the previous year the winter weather had been so harsh and bitter that [. . .] Little children were found dead in their cribs, several who travelled on horseback were caught by the frost in the countryside [. . .] Pilgrims, those travelling on foot, those living in the woods breathed their last [. . .] The birds from the sky were gathered up dead [. . .]; several trees died frozen and bare.'

It is the content conveyed by the first sentence (*avoit esté le tempz d'yver tant aspre et angoisseux*) which serves as a kind of hypertheme to the development which follows this incipit, since no other nominal phrase in the passage can play this role. If we observe the relations that can be established between the various themes of successive clauses, we will indeed see that there is no relation that could belong to hyperonymy, for example, or to associative anaphora. It is in fact each of these clauses, in its entirety, that is attached to the initial predicate of which it is an illustration. Organized in this way, the progression by derived themes does not take place at the level of referents expressed in nominal syntactic units, but at clause level. In this kind of evolution, the syntactical organization of the utterance – in this instance the system of linearizing constituents – is also changed. The development of hypertheme systems, accompanied by a new conception of the background, led to the creation of textual sequences demanding memorization processes and anticipation of broader dimensions than simple inter-sentence catenation. It was indeed, as we have just seen, at the origin of referential "disconnections", insofar as no element can be reattached to the context and where the whole of the clause is interpreted as rhematic. At the syntactic level, it is no longer the V2 order which constitutes the unmarked turn in the narrative discourse, but the direct order, since any sequence of the SV(X) type can appear in a context independently of the values of its constituents on the scale of communicative dynamism. We then go from a type of utterance defined by clear marking of the theme/rheme distinction – a dichotomy that had its *raison d'être* in a textual system with tightened coherence – to a type of utterance that put this distinction in the background and, instead, privileged predication, which intervened as such in the informational structuring of descriptive sequences.

The Middle French period thus witnessed the emergence of portions of text which had a specific form of organization and were independent of the narrative foreground; they were sometimes announced as such, as can be seen in the following extract where the beginning and end of the description are indicated (*le conte s'entremectra d'en diviser... s'en taira atant*):

(5) Et combien qu'il n'est langue qui peust fournir a diviser les grans richesses, merveilles et beaultez du beau chastel, touttefoiz le conte s'entremectra d'en diviser aucunes choses, non pas toutes, car il ne savroit, mais partie.

Ce tresbel chastel de Plaisance estoit fondé sur une roche d'esmeraude [...] Les quatre pans des murs dudit beau chastel estoient de cristal [...] Et estoit ledit beau chastel ensaint tout autour de murailles faites de gros saphirs [...] Combien que pas ne vous a divisé la moictié de la beaulté du beau chastel, mais s'en taira atant, car tout diviser ne savroit, et revendra a nostre matiere, a parler des trois compaignons (René d'Anjou, *Le Livre du Cuer d'Amours Espris*, 1457).

'And though there is no language able to tell of the great riches, marvels and graces of the beautiful castle, this tale will nevertheless devote itself to recounting certain things, not all, for it would not be able, but a part of them.

This very fine castle of Plaisance was built on an emerald rock [. . .] The four walls of this fine castle were of crystal [. . .] And this castle was surrounded by walls made of large sapphires [. . .] Although the tale has not recounted one half of the beauty of this fine castle, it will stop here, for it could not tell all, and will return to our subject, to speak of the three companions.'

The combination of two types of evolution – that of the informational structure with the development of specific progressions and the change in the theme/rheme dichotomy's status, together with the syntactic position, where the V2 order has been replaced by direct order as the basic pattern – is no doubt favored by external factors, but leads to the creation of a type of text identified as a particular genre and with its own characteristics.

It therefore appears necessary, when studying the coding and relating speech acts to textual structures, to take account of the specific nature of speakers' "feelings" about the type of text, insofar as it can be understood for a given period. The indicators that may represent the syntactic position, the different degrees of communicative dynamism, but also other speech acts – the play of verbal tenses springs particularly to mind – are to be rethought, not only in the linguistic system of a particular period, but also in relation to the specific textual notions whose coding they ensure.

6 Dealing with referential expressions

Managing events linked to referentiation, whether it involves presenting and introducing a new referent, establishing chains of co-reference, or renaming a referent, does not raise the same problems as the textual typology just mentioned; even if the question of units and stages of treatment is always present, it is mainly linked here to the functioning of discursive memory and to taking account of "shared knowledge". Examining states of language that preceded modern French reveals the tendency already indicated above, which consists in not expressing the core of the predication, in this instance the conjugated verbal form, before the subject referent is identified. The exception to this lies in schemata with a postposed subject, but in this case the order of priority is (X)VS(X), with the subject in immediate proximity to the verb. The changes affecting the preverbal zone from Middle French onward, while favoring the "retreat" of the verb toward the end of the utterance, do not fundamentally change this tendency to link the identification of referents to the predication process. It may therefore be considered that cataphoric events – that there is an explicit anaphoric form in a subordinate clause or that there is an implied "subject" of the reduced clauses represented by appositions or gerunds, for example – were not usual before the modern period. It can happen, in Old French and particularly Middle French, that some occurrences of subordinate clause + main clause catenations appear to illustrate a cataphoric relationship; but an examination of the preceding context usually shows that it already contains the information necessary for identifying the referent to which the main predication refers, and that the co-reference relationship is in fact an inter-sentential anaphoric relationship; what should then be explained are the factors leading to a renaming of the referent by a "full" NP, in situations where a pronominal form or ellipsis of the subject would seem sufficient to ensure comprehension. This is the case, for example, in the following extract, where the referent *messires Gauvains*, the theme of the passage, is repeated with the pronominal form *il* in the subordinate clause opening the final sentence. However, this does not prevent it being renamed by a proper noun in the main clause that follows it:

(6) Apres allerent oïr messe, si çaint messires Gauvains au vallet l'espee et chauce le destre esperon si com il estoit costume. Mais ainçois li demanda son nom, et li dist qu'il avait nom Helain. Quant il ot donee l'ordre de chevalier si com droiture le requiert, et il orent oï le service, si demande messires Gauvains ses armes (*Lancelot du Lac*, 13th century).

'They then went to mass, and Gauvain buckled the sword on to the young man, and put the spur on his right foot, according to custom. But before that, he asked him his name and the other man said he was called Hélain. Once he had conferred the order of knighthood as demanded by proper procedure, and they had heard mass, Monseigneur Gauvain called for his arms.'

In this kind of system, anaphoric relations do not appear to be subject to sentential constraints, as their functioning belongs to the level of the text; this can lead to catenations that would be considered as breaks in construction by a system of interpretation that is probably too modern and too prescriptive. The following two passages amply demonstrate how, in this type of writing which continues the system of the classical period, managing co-reference is not determined in the context of the sentence but at the level of a broader discursive sequence. In each of the extracts, the initial detached constructions (*surpris*. . .; *m'attirant*. . .) have a reach that is not limited to the boundaries of the sentence they appear to belong to. The controller function does not play a part and it is only at the end of the sequence that it takes the form of a subject pronoun (*j'aurai affaire*; *elle m'a dit*):

(7) – D'un autre côté, ses lettres! . . . ils peuvent croire que je les ai sur moi. Surpris dans sa chambre, on me les enlève. J'aurai affaire à deux, trois, quatre hommes, que sais-je? (Stendhal).

'– On the other hand, her letters!. . . They may think I have them on me. Caught in her room, they would take them away. I would be dealing with two, three, or four men, what do I know?'

(8) – Atala [. . .] elle devenait triste [. . .] Souvent elle tressaillait [. . .] Toujours m'attirant et me repoussant, ranimant et détruisant mes espérances, quand je croyais avoir fait un peu de chemin dans son cœur, je me retrouvais au même point. Que de fois elle m'a dit: "O mon jeune amant, je t'aime comme l'ombre des bois [. . .] Eh bien, pauvre Chactas, je ne serai jamais ton épouse!" (Chateaubriand).

'– Atala [. . .] she became sad [. . .] Often she quivered [. . .] Always enticing me and pushing me away, reviving and destroying my hopes, when I thought I had made some progress into her heart, I found myself at the same point once again. How many times did she say to me: "O my young lover, I love you like the shade in the woods [. . .] Ah well, poor Chactas, I shall never be your wife!'

One might legitimately think it is the formation of the modern "sentence", characterized by a strong internal hierarchy of constituents that results in a series of phenomena among which the cataphora is one of the most significant. But it was only during the nineteenth century that linearization became systematized, and in which anaphoric expressions, placed at the beginning of a sentence, could precede a controller referring to a supposedly new referent which had not yet been evoked. This "true" cataphoric relationship appears just as much with pronominal anaphora, such as the form *il* in the following example:

(9) Quand il vint, l'ouragan les poussa au sud, vers le golfe de Gascogne (M. Schwob, 1891).

'When it came, the hurricane pushed them southward, toward the gulf of Gascony.'

as with the implied subjects of second predications, which is the case with the detached constructions *la face contre terre, raide et immobile*, in:

(10)   la face contre terre, raide et immobile, une femme était couchée, les mains enfoncées dans ses cheveux, pareille à une statue (Dumas, 1839).

'face down, stiff and immobile, a woman lay with her hands thrust into her hair, just like a statue.'

This development of cataphoric turns corresponds to a modification of the stage dealing with referential continuity, the sentence thus occupying the role which, until then, had been assumed by the discursive sequence.

7 Conclusion

By way of conclusion, I would like to emphasize that a textual approach of the type just outlined can also be of interest to other areas of diachronic linguistics. Research that adopts a framework of grammaticalization theories prioritizes the process of reanalysis and, consequently, accords particular importance to studying the contexts that favor this process. In the same way, establishing a direction for grammaticalization, which would lead expressions from the text level to the pragmatic-enunciative level is, without a shadow of doubt, a relevant and fruitful strategy, but textual specificity at any given period needs to be taken into account, since speakers' competence is subject to variation and does not remain immutable; the evolution of this textual competence concerns general notions such as the typology of texts as much as the way the forms themselves function. Earlier, I drew on the example of order of constituents and anaphora, but it might be considered that any category or construction, if it plays a part in marking coherence, should be resituated in the particular textual context of a given period. The contributions of well-understood text linguistics will be truly enriching only if the analyses it proposes take account of the relativization I have described, and which I consider essential.

Reference

Seguin, Jean-Pierre, *L'invention de la phrase au XVIIIe siècle. Contribution à l'histoire du sentiment linguistique français*, Paris, Éditions Peeters, 1993.

Corpus

All examples are taken from Frantext (https://www.frantext.fr/), except:

(4)   Molinet, Jean, *Chroniques*, ed. Doutrepont, Georges/Jodogne, Omer, Bruxelles, Palais des Académies, 1938.
(5)   René d'Anjou, *Le livre du cuer d'amour espris*, ed. Wharton, Susan, Paris, UGE, 1980.
(10) Dumas, Alexandre, *Acté*, Paris, Press-Pocket, 1984.

Lita Lundquist
Chapter 9
40 years of text linguistics and its didactic application in teaching French as a foreign language

Abstract: The article traces the history of Scandinavian text linguistics as it evolved over a 40-year period, together with its didactic application in teaching French as a foreign language. Different structural and procedural approaches will be presented, to arrive at a model focusing more particularly on learning to read academic texts in French. At the same time, the author will show how analyzing and understanding texts does not stop with linguistics and the text itself, but links up naturally with cognitive and cultural aspects. This is illustrated by a systematic comparison of Danish and French, belonging to Germanic and Romance languages respectively; a comparison that reveals interesting differences in the way the Danish and French think and make texts. It also demonstrates the capacity of text linguistics to face fresh demands in the area of foreign language teaching, while at the same time clarifying the relationship between language, text, cognition, culture, and society.

Keywords: anaphora, cognitive perspective, contrastive text linguistics, French as a foreign language, mental model, (procedural, structural) perspective

The fortieth anniversary of the journal Pratiques[1] offered an ideal opportunity to simultaneously celebrate the appearance and establishment of text linguistics in France, both as a linguistic discipline and as language-teaching practice(s). The present chapter sets the evolution of text linguistics over these four decades in a Scandinavian perspective and looks at it "from the outside" as a means and practice of *didactic application* for the teaching of French as a foreign language (FFL) (part 1). Considering a taught language from the point of view of its foreign aspect naturally leads to broadening the models, concepts and phenomena belonging to text linguistics to embrace a contrastive perspective, comparing an L1 and an L2, which, in this case, will be Danish and French (part 2). It is from just such a com-

---

[1] Pratiques 169–170 (2016) : https://journals.openedition.org/pratiques/2925.

Lita Lundquist, Handelshøjskolen i København/Copenhagen Business School

https://doi.org/10.1515/9783110794434-010

parison that the teaching of an L2 to a given L1 needs to be conceived. I shall illustrate this through an example of teaching learners how to read academic texts in FFL, since these types of texts are now one of the main purposes for learning FFL at university level in Denmark (part 3). But this will not be the end point, because research comparing the different linguistic productions of textual coherence in these two languages have shown that the different ways of "making a text" (making an academic text) also reveal different ways of "thinking" (in the related disciplines); the thought processes which prevail in Danish culture diverge from those dominating in French culture (part 4). Conceived in this way, contrastive text linguistics goes beyond purely linguistic concerns and becomes open to comparisons at a cognitive or even cultural level; expression and linking of thoughts in a particular language are, after all, rooted in a specific culture, language, and cognition which mutually influence one another. It is with these considerations that the article will conclude (part 5).

1 Three stages of text linguistics. A brief personal history

There have been three decisive turning points in the history of text linguistics. The first, characteristic of the period around the 1970s, saw texts and textual coherence from a structural perspective, in which textual coherence was studied as a "texture" structured by different types of coherence. The second, inspired by the procedural grammar of the 1980s, marked a cognitive turning point influenced by the cognitive sciences in general and by psycholinguistics in particular; in this context, the text was studied in its progression, from a procedural perspective, taking account of the reader's (and speaker's) prior knowledge of the world and the construction of a mental representation of the text (Johnson-Laird 1993; Ehrlich/Tardieu 1993). The final phase had greater didactic emphasis, combining the two previous structural and procedural phases in a procedural on-line model of processing, where knowledge of the structures of language and texts were taken into consideration equally as much as knowledge of the world. From this overview of the three pivotal stages we can see how "non-linguistics", in the form of previous knowledge possessed by partners in communication, as well as their knowledge of language, texts, and the world, was introduced into text linguistics.

1.1 Structural perspective

In order to set this evolution, with its three different phases, in a Scandinavian perspective, I offer the following model as an aid to tracing my own history as a "text linguist", which began in 1976.

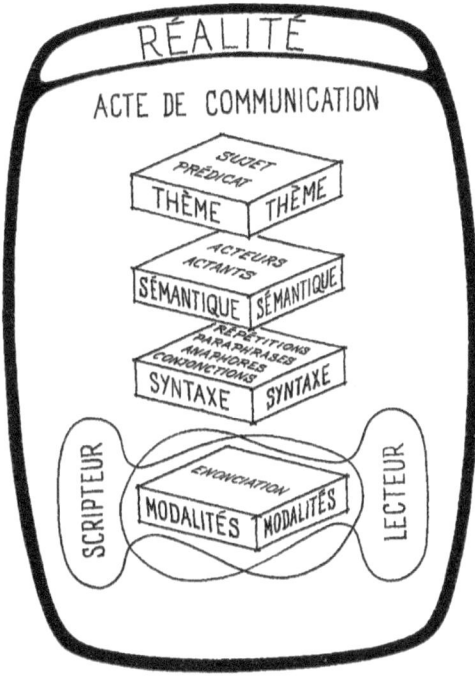

Figure 1: The structures of text linguistics (Lundquist 1976, 63).[2]

This model illustrates the attempt, on the one hand, to situate text linguistics within traditional linguistics, with its three-part division between syntax, semantics and pragmatics ("enunciation"), while at the same time adding the supplementary level of the "theme", pertaining to the sentence's communicative organization; and, on the other hand, to introduce into this structural compartmentalization the key phenomena of text linguistics, namely those that contribute to textual coherence. Examples of these are "modalities" at the "enunciation"

---

2 The analysis relates to a journalistic text, which appeared in Le Figaro (28.06.1976): *Les absurdités de l'urbanisme* ('The absurdities of urbanism'; all subsequent translations from other works are by Rosemary Rodwell, the translator of this article, unless stated otherwise.)

level (Benveniste 1970), anaphora and conjunctions at the "syntax" level (Halliday/Hasan 1976), actors and actants at the "semantic" level (Greimas 1966; Fillmore 1968), and subject and predicate, which is to say word order, at the "theme" level, with a view to the sentence's communicative dynamic (Daneš 1974a; 1974b). Although eclectic in its desire to bring a variety of linguistic phenomena from different linguistic "schools" under the umbrella of a "unitary" textual model, Figure 1, beneath the "reality" heading, appears to contain in embryo the subsequent development of text linguistics, with its ever greater insistence on extra-linguistic factors such as knowledge of the addressee's world. These were necessary for grasping the textual coherence intended by the addresser and would lead to the construction of a corresponding mental model. To go further still, as we shall do toward the end of this article, the "reality" layer will also prove to contain elements of a sociocultural order, such as ways of "making a text" and of thinking that are characteristic of a given society.

Another way of approaching textual coherence has been proposed in Lundquist (1980), where the notion of speech act is used to account for three different types of coherence which "weave" a text. According to J. Searle (1969), there are three speech acts which form part of any sentence uttered:

(illocutionary act (act of reference + act of predication))

In the catenation of sentences, each of these three acts engenders a specific type of coherence between the sentences. Thus, the act of reference engenders a *thematic* coherence, the act of predication a *semantic* coherence and the illocutionary act a *pragmatic* coherence, with each type of coherence being manifested in particular linguistic expressions, as shown in Figure 2.

The detailed analysis offered by Lundquist (1980) demonstrated the possibility of establishing a typology of texts according to criteria outlined under each type of coherence. Thus, for example, a necrology was classed as a type of narrative text by reason of its continued reference to a single referent appearing in the case role of AGENT, governed by a series of verbs of action in the past historic tense and framed by adverbs of time chronologically indicating events in the life of the deceased.[3]

---

[3] Among other types of text included in Lundquist's (1980) analysis according to the three types of coherence, a persuasive text was found (a description of France in a geography textbook used in French secondary schools) together with an explanatory text (a civil law textbook).

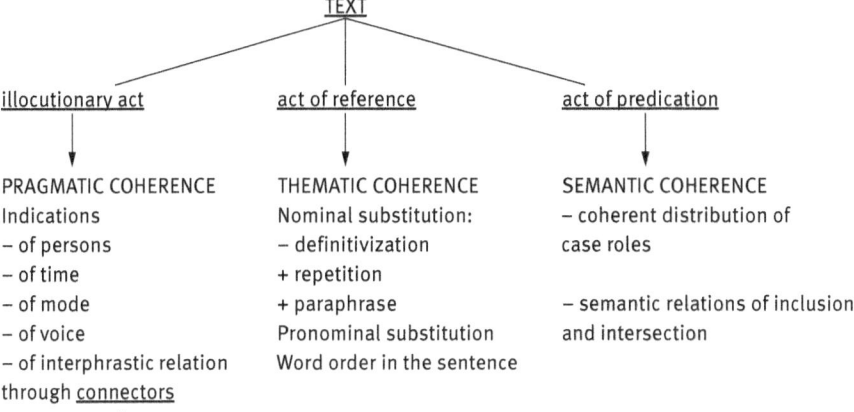

Figure 2: The three structures of textual coherence (from Lundquist 1980, 185).

1.2 Procedural perspective

Although the structural principle clearly emerges from models 1 and 2, the following model, borrowed from the procedural grammar proposed by Winograd in 1983, distinctly marks the transition toward the procedural perspective.

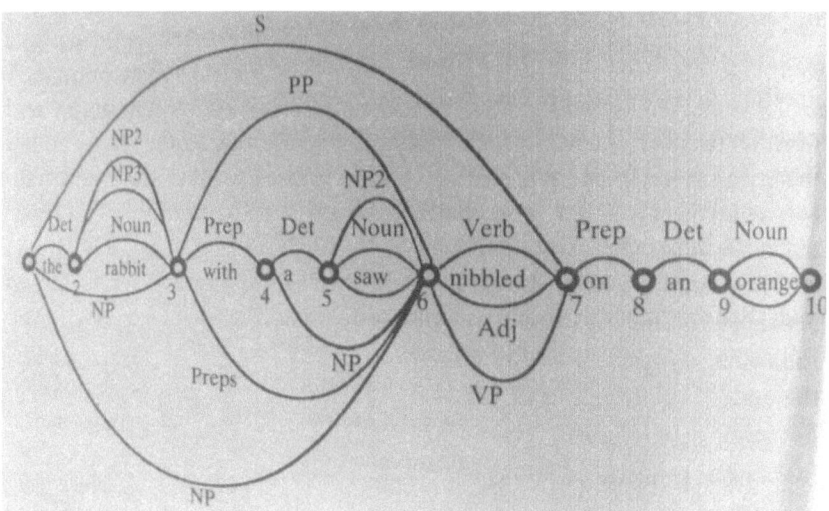

Figure 3: Procedural processing, *on line parsing*, of a sentence (Winograd 1983, 117; quoted in Lundquist 1990, 108).

In the procedural analysis which simulates the processing of the sentence on line, from left to right, the rules governing word order and parsing, according to their type (nominal group, verbal group, and prepositional group – NP, VP and PP in Figure 3), and function (subject, verb, etc.) take on a crucial importance. In my opinion, the basic principle of procedural analysis can be effectively transferred to the level of the text. I have demonstrated this (Lundquist 1990) by means of a pragmatic coherence analysis constructed from modalities (modalities of enunciation yet again!) contained in the opening sentence of a journalistic text (Krop, *Les Nouvelles*, 1983) with the title "Les curieuses méthodes du père Duchesne" 'The Curious Methods of Père Duchesne': "À en croire l'opposition, le syndicalisme serait roi en France" 'If we are to believe the opposition, trade unionism reigns in France'.

The title already appeals to knowledge shared by French people, because of the reference to "père Duchesne",[4] and then contains modalities in the opening sentence (of divergence, with the word *curieuse* preposed; *à en croire*; the conditional *serait*) and these will "control" what appears next. It is an idea supported by the theory of enunciation – or argumentation – in language, which was gaining a foothold in the 1980s. Indeed, in the chapter "Analyse de texte et linguistique de l'énonciation" of *Les Mots du discours* (Ducrot/Bourcier/Bruxelles 1980), Ducrot sought to establish 'a logic of language', 'which is to say rules that are internal to discourse, and which order its catenation' (Ducrot 1980, 12).[5] According to Ducrot, 'the sense of an utterance contains an allusion to its possible continuation: it is essential for it to call forth a particular type of follow-up, to claim to orient the subsequent discourse in a particular direction' (Ducrot 1980, 11).[6] In fact, in the text subjected to procedural analysis, the opening modalities would indeed prove to be followed, over the course of the text, by others which, "incrementally", constructed local links between two sentences (the lower arcs in Figure 4), and between increasingly extended segments (the higher arcs), to finally establish a coherence encompassing the whole of the text. Figure 4 traces the interpretation of the text, of its 39 sentences distributed over seven paragraphs. The small arrows at the front indicate the predictions, based here on modalities, of "what is going to come in the text", predictions of which cognitive linguistics has shown the quite crucial importance for a successful reading flow (Kintsch 1998). The

---

[4] 'A popular figure [...] who, from the beginning of the Revolution, was a kind of spokesman for the masses.' (Petit Robert)

[5] "[U]ne logique du langage [...] c'est-à-dire des règles internes au discours, et commandant son enchaînement."

[6] "Le sens d'un énoncé contient une allusion à son éventuelle continuation : il lui est essentiel d'appeler tel ou tel type de suite, de prétendre orienter le discours ultérieur dans telle ou telle direction."

illustration is supposed to contain an arc encompassing the whole in a coherent and global mental representation of the text's content.

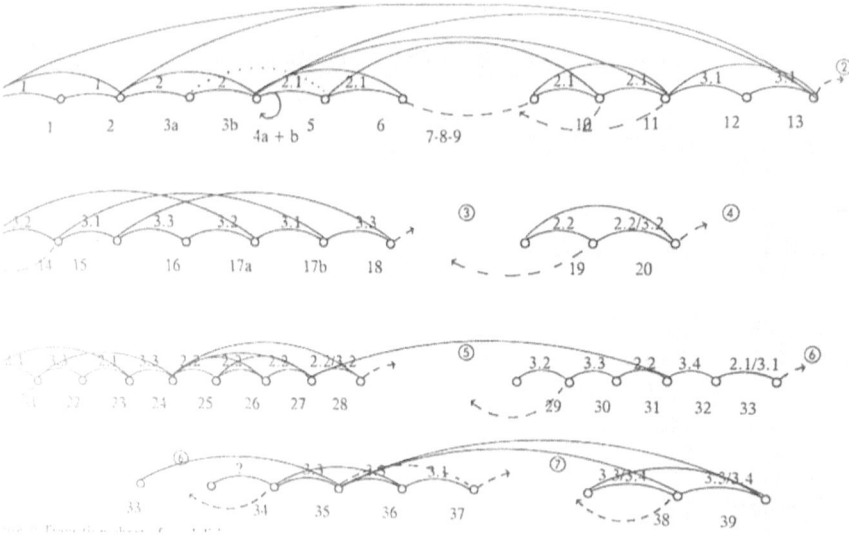

Figure 4: Procedural processing of a text (Lundquist 1983, 115).

1.3 The dynamic perspective of reading

The third phase of my personal journey toward a better-defined didactic application of FFL combines both perspectives, the structural and the procedural, in a 'dynamic model of reading' (Couto/Lundquist/Minel 2005), in which reading is seen as 'textual navigation' (Lundquist 2008).[7] As Figure 5 shows, reading is seen as an alternative movement between top-down procedures which use global and structured knowledge of the world (both general and specific parts "of the world") and texts (discourses, genres, and types of text). It is these top-down procedures that enable predictions to be made about what will follow in the text. These predictions will subsequently have to be confirmed, or invalidated and redefined through bottom-up procedures, which include knowledge of the structure of the language in question, that is to say its morphosyntactic and other rules.[8]

---

[7] "Modèle dynamique de lecture" (Couto/Lundquist/Minel 2005); "navigation textuelle" (Lundquist 2008).
[8] For further details, see Lundquist (2013).

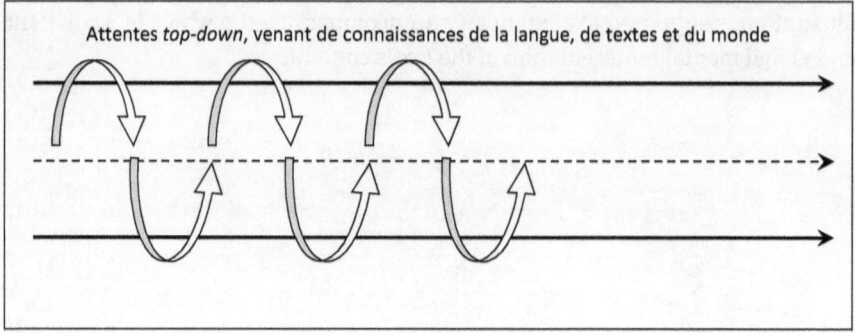

Figure 5: Dynamic model of reading (Lundquist 2013, XVII).

A single example is used to illustrate how these types of top-down knowledge interact when interpreting a text horizontally. The text is presented as a book with the title on the front, followed by the names of the author and publisher:

Claude Hagege	Claude Hagege
Combat	Battle
pour le francais	for French
Au nom de la diversite des langues et des cultures.	In the name of linguistic and cultural diversity
Odile Jacob. Poches	Odile Jacob. Poches

And on the back:

> Claude Hagège, linguiste, est professeur au Collège de France et lauréat de la médaille d'or du CNRS. Il est l'auteur de nombreux grands succès... (Hagège 2008).

> Claude Hagège is a linguist and a professor at the Collège de France. He has also been awarded the gold medal of the CNRS, and is the author of many outstanding works... (Hagège 2008)

The box below imitates a "reasoned reading" based on initial segments, divided into reading units in the left-hand column; in the right-hand column, I have reproduced the thoughts prompted by the text's successive segments. The predictions are indicated by "THEREFORE".[9]

---

[9] Extract from Lundquist (2013, 38–39). In the remainder of the reasoned reading, "BNGOS" also appears for identifications, and "REVIS" for the revised predictions.

Box 1: Example of reasoned reading

Claude Hagège	The author: I know/don't know him; but I learn by reading the information on the back, that he is a linguist and professor. THEREFORE: need to access an already-existing mental image of *linguistics*, or be prepared to create one.
Battle for French	I identify *linguistics*, and am able to relate it in my mental image to *the French language*; I add the complement of *battle*, which makes me predict a *type of argumentative text* in which the protagonist defends French against an enemy; the antagonist – I am expecting – will be the English language.
In the name of diversity	The protagonist is going to defend the linguistic and cultural diversity of languages and cultures
Odile Jacob	The publisher: I know/don't know them
Poches	Wide circulation
2008	Topical

From this initial information, I can therefore begin to construct a mental model containing two central topics: (1) linguistics with French as hyponym and (2) linguistic and cultural diversity, which are both put (3) into a text with an argumentative purpose (*battle*). Based on this initial model and drawing upon my knowledge of the world (the status of English as the current dominant language), I will be able to form predictions saying that the author will probably be defending French against English, and linguistic and cultural diversity against the hegemony of this language – predictions which will only be confirmed over the course of the later text.[10]

2 Contrastive text linguistics and FFL

In the actual process of reading (imitated in the horizontal Figures 3 and 4), it is necessary to implement different types of coherence markers outlined in the structural, vertical model (Figures 1 and 2): *anaphora, connectors, word order*, etc. In the same way, these key notions may be considered as pivots used by *contrastive* or *comparative text linguistics*, whose objective is precisely to compare the linguistic means by which two different languages achieve these pivots, and thereby ensure textual coherence, organization of information, and a specific way of sentence-linking.

---

[10] Procedural analysis of the text is continued in Lundquist (2013, 40–44).

Indeed, it is by comparing French as a foreign language with another language, in this case Danish, a Germanic language derived from the East Nordic branch (with Swedish – Norwegian, Icelandic, and Faroese belonging to the western branch of Nordic languages), that the particular features of each language appear, in the way they "make a text". Several comparative studies between Danish and French – and, more generally, between Romance languages and Germanic ones (Herslund 2012) – have led to a recognition of how systematic differences at the lexical and morphosyntactic levels of the two languages are reflected at the text level. This applies, among other things, to the sentence's communicative dynamic, in which French, with its flexible word order, often resorts to preposing often very complex constituents. Danish, by comparison, is a strict V2 language,[11] appearing to prefer a regular communicative dynamic, with the word order "subject (theme) + Verb (rheme)" (Lundquist 2009). For rhetorical relationships, which include not only connectors but also the construction of sentences in coordination or subordination, the latter (*hypotaxis*) can be seen to dominate in French texts, organized in a nucleus with many satellites (Matthiessen/Thompson 1988); in Danish, on the other hand, construction by coordination (*parataxis*) predominates, with coordinated nuclei and fewer satellites (Lundquist 2006). Finally, with regard to anaphoric relationships, Danish texts contain a greater number of pronominal anaphora compared to French texts,[12] which favor nominal anaphora.

This difference between the two languages with regard to establishing anaphoric relationships[13] is attributable to a systematic difference at the level of nominal lexicalization, where nouns in French have a tendency to be more specific in terms of their semantic features than do nouns in Danish. Closer comparative studies have shown that for verbs, the reverse is true: Danish verbs (among which, verbs of movement inevitably include the MANNER feature) are more specific than French verbs. It is this "reverse" complementarity between nouns and verbs in Danish and French which justifies the two languages being typed as "endocentric" and "exocentric" respectively (Baron 2003; Herslund/Baron 2003; Baron/Herslund 2005). The Danish language is therefore endocentric, with the semantic weight of the sentence encoded in the verbal core; while French is an

---

11 That is to say with inversion of the subject if there is preposing: $Prepos^1 + V^2 + Subject^3 + Compl^4$.
12 For Italian texts, see Korzen (2007).
13 It also applies to co-referential (faithful and unfaithful, Lundquist 2005), associative (Lundquist 2003), evolving (Lundquist 2007a), and resumptive (Lundquist 2007b; Lundquist/Couto/Minel 2012) anaphora.

exocentric language where the semantic weight is conveyed by nominal clusters, organized around the verb, as shown in Figure 6:[14]

Danish: Endocentric sentence	Noun------------VERB-------------Noun
French: Exocentric sentence	NOUN----------verb-------------NOUN

Figure 6: Endocentric and exocentric sentence.

3 Reading academic texts in French as a foreign language

By more specifically comparing academic texts in the two languages, I have been able to observe that the general differences are even greater, which can pose a problem for Daneš reading FFL. The example below enables us to put ourselves in the place of the Danish reader-learner, having to read on line, in real time, following the direction of left to right. It is the sentence (ii) which presents an obstacle:

> (i) Le discours sur la langue a beaucoup évolué au Canada. (ii) Longtemps pensée comme un aspect parmi d'autres des critères de distinction entre groupes culturels ou "raciaux", distinction servant de principe de stratification sociale dans l'économie coloniale canadienne, la langue devient le terrain central de lutte contre la marginalisation économique chez les francophones au milieu du XXe siècle.

> (i) Discourse about language has undergone much development in Canada. (ii) Long thought of as one aspect among others of the criteria distinguishing cultural or "racial" groups, a distinction serving as a principle of social stratification in the Canadian colonial economy, language became the focus in the fight against economic marginalization for French-speakers in the mid-twentieth century.

The identification and syntactical processing of the long, detached preposed construction (Combettes 1998) in (ii) demands knowledge and application of the morphosyntactic rules (of agreement, among other things), in order to make the link backwards between (*longtemps*) *pensée* and *langue*, and to expect to see a singular feminine subject appear – which will in fact be the case, with *la langue* (*devient*), but only after twenty or so words, organized into constituents of different types

---

[14] Upper case signifies the density of semantic features and lower case the rarity of semantic features.

(GN, GP) and at several levels (complements and apposition, for example). Figure 7 illustrates the degree to which the preposed participial construction presents "a huge effort" in terms of procedural interpretation, demanding the linear implementation of a considerable range of grammatical rules, with a safeguard in the memory of the content already processed and the anticipation of the content still to come.

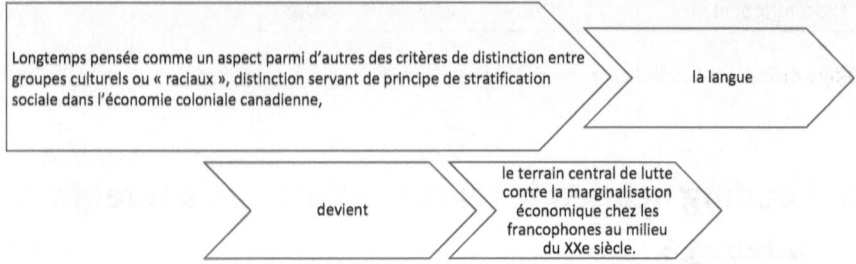

Figure 7: Processing of a French sentence into main constituents, from left to right (Lundquist 2013, 70).

Figure 7 thus exemplifies the tendency of (academic) French to prepose (to the subject and verb) heavy, accumulated constituents, in a construction that is "front heavy" and can seem difficult to decipher, "in-tractable" even, for Danish readers. One imagines them desperately searching for the subject and verb: these are often found at the beginning in Danish, which is generally "back heavy", i.e. Subject–Verb–Complements.

Another difference is the high number of nominalizations found in French academic texts. As these nominalizations are often derived from abstract verbs, a sentence structure with a high level of abstraction is the result; whereas Danish verbs, which are usually more "concrete", give rise to nouns that are also more "concrete" (NV), and vice versa in French (nv), as summarized in Figure 8:[15]

| Danish: Endocentric sentence with verbal nominalizations | NV----------VERB--------VN |
| French: Exocentric sentence with verbal nominalizations | nv-----------verb---------nv |

Figure 8: Verbal nominalizations and abstraction.

What is more, the nominalizations derived from abstract verbs in French are often part of expanded nominal groups: abstract nouns are thus accumulated, attain-

---

[15] A reminder that upper case signifies density of semantic features, and lower case, rarity of semantic features.

ing a level of abstraction which, for a Danish reader, risks appearing detached from a context of action where actors are removed; to put it in more technical terms, academic Danish tends to prefer *instantiation* of patterns of action; while in academic French, actions are often *converted* into facts (Lyons 1977, 442), as in the example below:

> La défiscalisation des heures supplémentaires et son exonération de cotisations sociales sont centrales dans le dispositif du nouveau gouvernement.
>
> Tax exemption for overtime and its dispensation from social security contributions are central to the strategy of the new government.

To end with, we should mention this little list of notable differences between academic French and academic Danish, together with the frequent use in French of unfinished verbal forms (participles, gerunds, and infinitives). These too contribute to condensing a great deal of information, while at the same time organizing this information in the foreground and background[16] within the same sentence. The following example thus contains a whole series of reduced clauses, whose content will have to be unraveled by the reader as they go along; this same reader will only see the main verb, *risqué*, appear once they have processed a good thirty or so words:

> L'incapacité des ministres des finances européens, réunis samedi 17 septembre à Wroclaw (Pologne), à se mettre d'accord sur la mise en œuvre du plan de secours à la Grèce décidé en principe le 21 juillet risque d'enflammer de nouveau les marchés.
>
> The inability of European finance ministers, gathered in Wroclaw (Poland) on Saturday September 17, to arrive at an agreement for implementing a rescue plan for Greece which was decided in principle on July 21 risks igniting the markets once again.

Figure 9 summarizes the main differences between the creation of an academic text in Danish and French.

---

16 Which corresponds to the "core" and "satellite" in terms of rhetorical relationships ("noyau", "satellite", Lundquist 2006).

Danish	French
Language V2: Fixed word order Subject-Verb-Complements (preposing) – Verb – Subject – Complements	Flexible word order (Preposing) – Subject – Verb – Complements
Nominalizations of concrete verbs More concrete	Nominalizations of abstract verbs High level of abstraction
Less expanded nominal groups	Highly expanded nominal groups
Instantiation of patterns of action (with actors)	Conversion of actions into facts (with "removal" of actors)
Parataxis	Hypotaxis
Complete clauses, finished verbal forms	Reduced clauses, unfinished verbal forms

Figure 9: Characteristics of academic texts in Danish and French.

4 From ways of "making text" to ways of thinking

More in-depth comparative studies of academic texts in Danish and French have enabled us to open up text linguistics toward a cognitive perspective, by moving from the way of "making text" in the two languages, to the way "of thinking" in the two cultures. A comparison of texts belonging to the same discipline and dealing with the same type of theme enables us to identify substantial differences in the way of presenting information, connecting sentences, and fixing the content in a concrete or abstract framework. The two extracts below showing the opening sentences of two sociology papers, which deal with problems in French and Danish society respectively (Lundquist 2014a), will serve as an illustration.

Box 2: Michel Crozier & Bruno Tilliette: *Quand la France s'ouvrira* (2000)

Reconnaître la réalité. Le principe de réalité est le premier principe de gouvernement de tout ensemble humain, qu'il s'agisse d'une entreprise, d'une ville, d'une famille ou d'une société tout entière. On peut avoir les meilleures idées et la meilleure dialectique du monde, on ne prépare pas l'avenir en ignorant les réalités du présent et les tendances lourdes qui se dessinent déjà. Certes, on doit combattre les erreurs et les injustices qui ternissent ce présent, craindre les dangers que recèlent les tendances dominantes et essayer d'y parer. Mais on ne saurait infléchir la réalité que si on la connaît et la comprend. Le premier signe du mal français, c'est le refus de la réalité.

'Recognizing reality. The reality principle is the first principle of government for any human organization, whether it is a company, a town, a family, or a whole society. One may have the best ideas and the best dialectics in the world, but it is not possible to prepare for the future while ignoring present realities and the ominous trends already on the horizon. Certainly, it is necessary to combat the errors and injustices that tarnish the present, to fear the dangers concealed by dominant trends, and try to remedy them. But it is only possible to change reality by knowing and understanding it. The first sign of the French malaise is the refusal of reality.'

Box 3: Lars Bo Kaspersen: *Danmark i verden* **'Denmark and the world' (2008)**

Det går jo godt i Danmark! Siden midten af 1990'erne har de fleste socioøkonomiske oversigter og tabeller vist, at Danmark klarer sig fornemt internationalt. [. . .] Sammenlignet med de fleste andre 191 lande i verden er Danmark en succeshistorie. Vi klarer os godt økonomisk, og vi anerkendes stadig som en autonom stat med selvbestemmelse. Hvorfor gør vi det? Hvordan kan et lille land overleve så succesfuldt i en staerkt globaliseret verden?

'But, as you know, all is going well in Denmark! Since the mid-1990s, most socioeconomic reports have shown that Denmark is doing remarkably well internationally. [. . .] Compared to most of the other 191 countries in the world, Denmark is a success. We are doing well economically, and we are still recognized as an independent state with self-determination. How do we manage this? How can a small country survive so successfully in a thoroughly globalized world?'

The French text opens with an infinitive construction, *reconnaître*, with an abstract object, *la réalité*. Following this is a sentence in which the grammatical subject repeats this notion in a composite GN, *Le principe de réalité*. This, followed by the GV and its complements, *est le premier principe de gouvernement de tout ensemble humain*, raises the content to an ever-higher level of abstraction, which will continue in the subsequent sentences (*idées, dialectique, réalités, tendances, erreurs, injustices*), and will only be rooted in the lived experience of (French) readers by the reference to the – still abstract – (*le*) *mal français*. Compared with this, the Danish text is immediately fixed in the experience of (Danish) readers, partly by its explicit reference to the country (*in Denmark*), and partly by creating a closeness with readers through its opening remark, *Mais, comme vous savez*. This is a paraphrastic translation of the Danish monosyllabic adverb, *jo*,[17] which, with the exclamatory form, implicitly evokes a former political context, that is to say knowledge that is believed to be shared. The reference to Denmark is maintained, both by repetition of the proper noun or paraphrases (*a small country*), and by the pronoun *we*, which regularly occupies the place of the grammatical subject, that is to say the focus. Addressing and involving the readers is ensured not only by the *we*, but also by the exclamatory and interrogative forms of the sentences. In comparison with this, the French text, instead of linking the content directly to the readers by addressing them personally, presents it in an imper-

---

17 The use of such adverbs "of connivance" is extremely frequent in Danish. See a more extensive discussion in Lundquist (2014b).

sonal (*on*) and assertive form (*est*, *c'est*), organizing it in rhetorical relationships of negation and concession (*certes – mais*).[18]

I have linked the features of each of these texts to more general "ways of thinking", characteristic of each of these cultures. Thus, the reasoning based on abstract ideas and the analysis presented impersonally and assertively in *argumentative* relationships that are evident in the French text, I see as closely linked to the Cartesianism so typical of French culture – a Cartesianism[19] which advocates analysis based on general ideas and, if need be, the "reality principle". By comparison, Danish reasoning in the above text follows *inductive reasoning*, starting from a concrete, individualized case: "Denmark", as seen from the viewpoint of socioeconomic studies. This method of presenting a subject can be seen as *pragmati(cis)m*, a philosophical method directed toward the real world.[20] Set within a personalized form of inferences and complicity, the inductive method shown above also nurtures *human relations*. In Figure 10, I have summarized the main cognitive divergences observed by comparing text-producing processes in Danish and French.

Pragmati(ci)sm in Danish academic texts	*Cartesianism in French academic texts*
Induction (from experience of actual cases)	Deduction (from general principles)
Rational figurations	Argumentative figurations

Figure 10: Two ways of thinking and reasoning.

---

18 For a more detailed analysis, see Lundquist (2014b).
19 'Rational deduction is an operation by which we understand any necessary conclusion from other things known with certainty, although not self-evident, so long as they are deduced from principles known to be true by a continuous and uninterrupted movement of thought, with clear intuition of each point.' (René Descartes, *Regulae ad directionem ingenii* [*Rules for the direction of the mind*], 1628, règle [rule] III: "La déduction rationnelle est une] opération par laquelle nous entendons tout ce qui se conclut nécessairement d'autres choses déjà connues avec certitude, bien qu'elles ne soient pas elles-mêmes évidentes, pourvu seulement qu'elles soient déduites à partir de principes vrais et connus par un mouvement continu et ininterrompu de la pensée qui a une intuition claire de chaque chose.")
20 The term describes a philosophical movement according to which truth is based only on what has practical consequences in the real world.

5 Language, text and society

I wondered where the difference I had observed in the way of creating a text and of thinking stemmed from, and I believe I have found the explanation in the fundamental differences between the two languages. French, because of the abstract relationships introduced by abstract verbs and nominalizations based on this type of verb, is a language suited to expressing ideas and making deductions from principles; whereas Danish, with its concrete verbs, which sanction actors in semantically denser relationships, is therefore much more fitted to describing actions and events. Furthermore, the connivance particles, *ja, jo, vel, nok, bare*, etc., which are more frequently used, even in academic texts, link these facts "intimately" to the circumstances of readers.[21]

However, I am going to offer a more speculative additional explanation, of a sociocultural order, by considering that the two cultures, Danish and French, were formed by totally different "civilization processes". In fact, in the wake of the sociologist N. Elias and his historico-sociological approach (Elias 1969), especially his astute and insightful description of the civilizing process followed by France (Elias 1974), we might describe France as a "société de cour" ('court society'), characterized by hierarchical relationships and dominated by an elitist mind-set of refinement, psychological analysis and calculation, elegant conversation, and so on: this governed ways of being together and infiltrated, in a top-down process, the whole of French society. Denmark, by contrast, was a great state reduced (in 1814 and 1864) to a small country, having to fight for its survival as an autonomous national unit. It was formed from the bottom-up, partly by assiduous efforts to train the peasant classes; and partly because political parties and social partners needed to cooperate and act together to create a consensus and obtain political results to ensure the country's survival. It was this civilizing process, determined by the historical context and specific to Denmark, which led to the formation of a collectivist society and welfare state, but also to a "tribal" spirit. In fact, Denmark has been described as a *campfire* society (Jespersen 2004).

Two illustrations demonstrate this cultural – and mental – difference between a *court society* and a *campfire* society. A picture painted by François Marot (1710), showing the Sun King raising courtiers in the "First Class of the Knights of the

---

[21] These adverbs "of connivance and intimacy" abound in the stories of Hans Christian Andersen, the representative par excellence of "the soul of the Danish people", as Adam/Heidmann (2009) have eminently shown, dealing with the translation problems inherent to this type of adverb (*rigtig* and *virkelig*).

Order of Saint-Louis" (cf. Saule 2005),[22] is a perfect illustration of the courtly hierarchy and attitude. Compared with this, the drawing of a joyful campfire society by Per Illum (cf. Lundquist 2016),[23] shows the participants all seated at the same level around the fire, their backs turned toward the outside, in a convivial setting, where there is probably an abundance of connivance particles!

6 Conclusion

Without venturing too far in these speculations about the relationship between language, text, and society,[24] and especially without positing causal relationships, I think I can say, by way of conclusion to this overview of text linguistics throughout 40 years of theory and practice, that the two languages, French and Danish, each have specific features which lend themselves particularly well to expressing the dominant modes of thinking in the two linguistic communities, and even to regulate and shape these modes of thinking.

I hope to have outlined the way in which text linguistics, while maintaining coherence and its solid roots in linguistics, now offers the possibility of opening up wider and more interesting perspectives, of a cognitive and cultural order.

References

Adam, Jean-Michel/Heidmann, Ute, *Le texte littéraire. Pour une approche interdisciplinaire*, Louvain-la-Neuve, Bruylant-Academia, 2009.
Baron, Irène, *Catégories lexicales et catégories de pensée. Une approche typologique du danois et du français*, in: Herslund, Michael (ed.), *Aspects linguistiques de la traduction*, Bordeaux, Presses universitaires de Bordeaux, 2003, 29–53.
Baron, Irène/Herslund, Michael, *Langues endocentriques et langues exocentriques. Approche typologique du danois, du français et de l'anglais*, Langue française 145 (2005), 35–53, DOI: https://doi.org/10.3917/lf.145.0035.
Benveniste, Émile, *L'appareil formel de l'énonciation*, Langages 17 (1970), 12–18, DOI: https://doi.org/10.3406/lgge.1970.2572.
Combettes, Bernard, *Les constructions détachées en français*, Paris, Ophrys, 1998.

---

22 Direct link: https://journals.openedition.org/crcv/docannexe/image/132/img-11.jpg [last consultation: 23.08.2022].
23 Direct link: http://journals.openedition.org/pratiques/docannexe/image/2949/img-8.png [last consultation: 23.08.2022].
24 See Lundquist (2014a; 2014b) for more solidly supported argumentation.

Couto, Javier/Lundquist, Lita/Minel, Jean-Luc, *Navigation interactive pour l'apprentissage en linguistique textuelle*, in: Tchounikine, Pierre/Joab, Michelle/Trouche, Luc (edd.), *Environnements informatiques pour l'apprentissage humain. Proceedings of the EIAH 2005 conference*, Montpellier, Université Montpellier 2/INRP, 2005, 45–56.

Daneš, František, *Functional sentence perspective and the organization of the text*, in: Daneš, František (ed.), *Papers on functional sentence perspective*, Prague, Academia, 1974, 106–128 (= 1974a).

Daneš, František (ed.), *Papers on functional sentence perspective*, Prague, Academia, 1974 (= 1974b).

Descartes, René, *Regulae ad directionem ingenii (1628–1629)*, edd. Adam, Charles/Tannery, Paul, Paris, Librairie philosophique J. Vrin, 1965 [1930].

Ducrot, Oswald, *Les échelles argumentatives*, Paris, Éditions de Minuit, 1980.

Ducrot, Oswald/Bourcier, Danièle/Bruxelles, Sylvie, *Les mots du discours*, Paris, Éditions de Minuit, 1980.

Ehrlich, Marie-France/Tardieu, Hubert, *Modèles mentaux, modèles de situation et compréhension de textes*, in: Ehrlich, Marie-France/Tardieu, Hubert/Cavazza, Marc (edd.), *Les modèles mentaux. Approche cognitive des représentations*, Paris, Masson, 1993, 47–79.

Elias, Norbert, *Über den Prozeß der Zivilisation*, 2 vol., Bâle, Haus zum Falken Verlag, 1939; *The civilizing process*, vol. 1: *The history of manners*, transl. Jephcott, Edmund, Oxford, Blackwell, 1969.

Elias, Norbert, *La société de cour*, transl. Kamnitzer, Pierre/Etoré, Jeanne, Paris, Calmann-Lévy, 1974 [1969].

Fillmore, Charles J., *The case for case*, in: Bach, Emmon/Harms, Robert T. (edd.), *Universals in linguistic theory*, London, Holt, Rinehart & Winston, 1968, 1–25.

Greimas, Algirdas Julien, *Sémantique structurale. Recherche de méthode*, Paris, Larousse, 1966.

Hagège, Claude, *Combat pour le français. Au nom de la diversité des langues et des cultures*, Paris, Odile Jacob, ²2008.

Halliday, Michael Alexander Kirkwood/Hasan, Ruqaiya, *Cohesion in English*, London/New York, Longman, 1976.

Herslund, Michael/Baron, Irène, *Language as world view. Endocentric and exocentric representations of reality*, in: Baron, Irène (ed.), *Language and culture*, Copenhagen Studies in Language 29, Copenhagen, Samfundslitteratur, 2003, 29–42.

Jespersen, Knud J. V., *A history of Denmark*, Basingstoke/New York, Palgrave, 2004.

Johnson-Laird, Philip N., *Introduction. La théorie des modèles mentaux*, in: Ehrlich, Marie-France/Tardieu, Hubert/Cavazza, Marc (edd.), *Les modèles mentaux. Approche cognitive des représentations*, Paris, Masson, 1993, 1–22.

Kintsch, Walter, *Comprehension. A paradigm for cognition*, Cambridge, Cambridge University Press, 1998.

Korzen, Iorn, *Linguistic typology, text structure and anaphors*, in: Korzen, Iorn/Lundquist, Lita (edd.), *Comparing anaphors. Between sentences, texts and languages*, Copenhagen studies in language 34 (2007), 93–109.

Lundquist, Lita, *La cohérence textuelle. Syntaxe, sémantique, pragmatique*, Copenhagen, Nyt Nordisk Forlag, 1980.

Lundquist, Lita, *L'analyse textuelle. Méthode, exercices*, Copenhagen, Samfundslitteratur, ²1990.

Lundquist, Lita, *L'anaphore associative en danois et en français, sur quoi roule-t-elle? Étude contrastive et expérimentale*, in: Herslund, Michael (ed.), *Aspects linguistiques de la traduction*, Bordeaux, Presses universitaires de Bordeaux, 2003, 105–124.

Lundquist, Lita, *Noms, verbes et anaphores (in)fidèles. Pourquoi les Danois sont plus fidèles que les Français*, Langue française 145 (2005), 73–91, DOI: https://doi.org/10.3917/lf.145.0073.

Lundquist, Lita, *Lexical anaphors, information packing, and grammaticalisation of textual relations*, in: Nølke, Henning/Baron, Irène/Korzen, Hanne/Korzen, Iorn/Müller, Henrik H. (edd.), *Grammatica. Festschrift in honour of Michael Herslund/Hommage à Michael Herslund*, New York, Peter Lang, 2006, 311–323.

Lundquist, Lita, *Comparing evolving anaphors in Danish and French*, in: Korzen, Iorn/Lundquist, Lita (edd.), *Comparing anaphors. Between sentences, texts and languages*, Copenhagen Studies in Language 34 (2007), 111–126 (= 2007a).

Lundquist, Lita, *Academic discourse as social control and system(s), seen through the use of demonstrative noun phrases in French scientific texts*, in: Fløttum, Kjersti (ed.), *Language and discipline. Perspectives on academic discourse*, Newcastle, Cambridge Scholars Publishing, 2007, 219–242 (= 2007b).

Lundquist, Lita, *Navigating in foreign language texts*, Frederiksberg, Samfundslitteratur, 2008.

Lundquist, Lita, *Adverbiaux initiaux en danois et en français. Langue, texte, mentalité*, in: Korzen, Iorn/Lavinio, Christina (edd.), *Lingue, culture e testi istituzionali*, Florence, Franco Cesati Editore, 2009, 141–162.

Lundquist, Lita, *Lire un texte académique en français*, Paris, Ophrys, 2013.

Lundquist, Lita, *Danish humor in cross-cultural professional settings. Linguistic and social aspects*, Humor 27 (2014), 141–163 (= 2014a).

Lundquist, Lita, *Pragmatic danes and cartesian French. Language and culture, text and cognition*, in: Korzen, Iorn/Ferrari, Angela/De Cesare, Anna-Maria (edd.), *Between romance and Germanic. Language, text, cognition and culture*, Bern, Peter Lang, 2014, 315–335 (= 2014b).

Lundquist, Lita, *40 ans de linguistique textuelle et didactisation du français langue étrangère*, Pratiques 169–170 (2016), DOI : https://doi.org/10.4000/pratiques.2949.

Lundquist, Lita/Couto, Javier/Minel, Jean-Luc, *La navigation discursive. Anaphore résomptive et mouvement discursif*, in: Pugniere-Saavedra, Frederic/Sitri, Frédérique/Veniard, Marie (edd.), *L'analyse du discours dans la société. Engagement du chercheur et demande sociale*, Paris, Honoré Champion, 2012, 347–365.

Lyons, John (ed.), *Semantics*, 2 vol., Cambridge, Cambridge University Press, 1977.

Matthiessen, Christian/Thompson, Sandra A., *The structure of discourse and "subordination"*, in: Haiman, John/Thompson, Sandra A. (edd.), *Clause combining in grammar and discourse*, Amsterdam/Philadelphia, John Benjamins, 1988, 275–329.

Saule, Béatrix, *Insignes du pouvoir et usages de cour à Versailles sous Louis XIV*, Bulletin du Centre de recherche du château de Versailles (2005), DOI: https://doi.org/10.4000/crcv.132.

Searle, John R., *Speech acts. An essay in the philosophy of language*, Cambridge, Cambridge University Press, 1969.

Winograd, Terry, *Language as a cognitive process*, vol. 1: *Syntax*, Boston, Addison-Wesley, 1983.

Part 3: **Epistemologies of discourse – and beyond**

Patrick Charaudeau
Chapter 10
A socio-communicational model of discourse (between communication situation and individuation strategies)

Abstract: The author identifies three questions to pose to a discipline interested in discourse, namely (1) the limits within which it can be effective as a result of the theoretical positions of the analyst, (2) the link that exists between the speech act and the inseparable activity extraneous to language which enables it to be interpreted, and (3) the interpretation to be given to the analysis. In the text that follows, he proposes to examine the second point in greater depth.

Keywords: communication contract, situation of communication, discursive instructions, identity of the speaker, discursive strategies

1 Presentation of the problems

In my view, a discourse discipline is confronted with three types of problem: (1) defining the field of study, in accordance with the objectives declared to be those of the analysis, which can be perceived through the theoretical presuppositions and methodological instrumentation that have been made known; (2) that of the relationship between what might be called the interior and exterior of language, between the speech act[1] proffered and what is outside language – which is perhaps language if one refers to what Lacan says of the unconscious – but which is not verbalized at the very instant of its utterance, not identifiable in the forms of what has been uttered, but is necessary to the interpretation of this; (3) and finally, the problem of interpretation, that is to say of the meaning given to the results of our analyses. This resides in the question of knowing by what process the texts and their discourse are interpreted when one is in the position of the analyzing subject: what is the interpretative practice and what is its possible theorization?

---

[1] In this exposition, *speech act* – sometimes known as *communication act* – will be used in the generic sense of speech production act, and not as in the theory of speech acts.

Patrick Charaudeau, Université Sorbonne Paris Nord

It is not possible here to deal with all these questions, which each merit a study of their own; I shall therefore focus on the second problem – that of the relationship between the speech act and its exteriority – and will only allude to the two others.

2 Determining the field of study

When reading studies claiming to be discourse analyses,[2] a wide diversity of approach becomes apparent: some are focused on discursive markers (either grammatical or lexical) and others on modes of organization of the discourse (narrative, argumentative); some adhere to an utterance grammar while others relate to argumentative rhetoric, and still others study language rituals as an interactional device; and some, finally, seek to describe the systems of ideas (ideologies) contained in discourse.

One might attempt to group these various trends around major research problematics. A problematic is not a theory but a place of general questioning which gathers together a series of given propositions that are seen as provisionally (or hypothetically) true,[3] according to certain parameters. In a sense, it defines an epistemological positioning within the discipline.

The problematics will be defined here according to three parameters: the nature of the *object of study* constructed by each of these problematics; the way in which the *subject of the discourse* is seen as regards his or her activity as the producer of speech acts; and, consequently, the type of corpus that has to be assembled in order to undertake the analysis, which, at the same time, is presumed to correspond to the memory of the subject of discourse. We have thus arrived at three basic problematics, each of which corresponds to a type of approach to discourse analysis.

2.1 A cognitive and categorizing problematic

The *object* of study is considered as a series of *discursive devices* whose existence and mode of organization within any discursive production (text or random utterances) need to be identified. It is a problematic that has been developed in the

---

[2] I base these remarks on Charaudeau/Maingueneau (2002).
[3] It should be remembered that, for Kant, a problematic is a "proposition that expresses a simple possibility".

tradition of linguistic pragmatics for which Austin, Searle, and Ducrot are noted: speech acts, presuppositions, and so on; studies relating to interplays of coherence and cohesion in text organization also correspond to this, as too does the work of certain psycho-cognitivists of language who seek to determine "down" or "up" movements of discursive realization of patterns, scripts or scenarios, in order to describe the mode of production or comprehension of texts; and studies focusing on the use of certain words in discourse (connectors, modalities, etc.). From all these cases, there have emerged instrumental categories of analysis that serve to identify or produce discursive configurations.

The *subject* concerned by the determination of such an object will be called *cognitive* insofar as the only factor taken into account is his or her ability to produce or identify discursive articulation operations: anaphoric or cataphoric relations, coordinate or subordinate conjunctions, coherent conditions of repetition, progression and non-contradiction, rules of argumentation, and so on.

The *corpus* constructed in the context of such a problematic has no need to be finalized in accordance with a particular communication situation. From this viewpoint, it might be called *random*, and limited only by the linguistic contexts in which these devices appear.

2.2 A communicational and descriptive problematic

The *object* of study here is empirical, or more precisely it is determined by the observation (more or less naïve) of manifestations in the phenomenal world. Acts of communication can thus be determined according to a certain number of variables: the *identity* of the partners in the exchange, the actional *purpose* (aim) of the situation in which they find themselves, and the *material circumstances* of the communication. Consequently, the object of study emerging from this empirical analysis can be structured into *ideal types* of communication enabling diverse typologies to be established, known as discourses, texts, genres, or communicative situations, but which all presuppose a theorization of these *ideal types* of communication.[4]

The *subject*, here, is linked to this empirical analysis of communicative exchanges, but is also constructed and theorized according to the way in which these exchanges are constructed and theorized. The subject is therefore a subject of communication defined by their psychological and social identity, by a com-

---

[4] On the notions of *Idealtypus* (Weber) or *type idéal* (Durkheim), see Coenen-Huther (2003). (All subsequent translations from other works are by Rosemary Rodwell, the translator of this article, unless stated otherwise.)

portment that is finalized both by the constraints he or she experiences if they wish to interpose themselves into the exchange (from this point of view they are a "that") and by their own intentions vis-à-vis the other (from this point of view they are an "I"). Various theorizations of this subject are possible, but whatever they may be, the subject is considered to be in a relation of inter-subjectivity with regard to the other of language (alterity principle).

The *corpus*, too, is affected by this empirical view of the object of study. It is generally composed of texts that are grouped according to whether they belong to a particular type of communicative situation: advertising, journalistic, administrative texts; school textbooks and political agendas, as well as various conversational texts (telephone conversations, requests for information, interviews, discussions, debates, etc.).

2.3 A problematic known as representational and interpretative

The *object* of study of this problematic is defined through the hypotheses of socio-discursive representations that are presumed to be dominant at a given moment in the history of a society (they are therefore socio-historical) and are thought to characterize a particular social group. In this they are interpretative, since a hypothesis is required, from the outset, on what "social positionings" are in relation to "discursive practices" and the "types of subjects" that relate to them. The difficulty with this problematic lies precisely in the fact that it is necessary to make these hypotheses and that, in order to do so, one must rely upon extremely diverse discursive manifestations – ones that are not always explicit, and may even be diffuse or vague. This poses the problem of how to assemble the corpus.

From this perspective, the *subject* also raises a problem, which has often been discussed. Because the subject initiates the discursive practices that construct representations, he or she may be considered an *active* subject. But because these practices are shared by others in the social group, and they recur in that group in the form of representations of value systems which overdetermine it, it could be said that this subject is *passive* and is diluted in the group consciousness. This has led to two positions defended by various analysts:
- One is radical, and grants this subject no other existence than that of an "illusion", since he or she is held to be entirely overdetermined by what Pêcheux calls the 'pre-constructed' of 'discursive formations' (Pêcheux 1975, passim);[5]

---

[5] "Pré-construits", "formations discursives"; see also Amossy in this book, ch. 12.

the subject is not an "I" but a "that" (ideological or unconscious) which speaks through them;
– The other is less generalized, which is not to deny that the subject may be overdetermined, but rather than considering them an illusion, this position creates a positive view of the subject, saying that they are all partly the bearers of discourses that overdetermine them (often without their knowledge), but at the same time they seek to position themselves in relation to these discourses. It might therefore be said that these subjects are in some way "responsible" (of course this needs to be in inverted commas) for their representations. This is a position that I will call sociological, which is defended in France by certain sociologists who work on analyzing representations of public space in the media (L. Quéré), and has an affinity with the viewpoint of constructivist sociology as conceived by Bourdieu.

The *corpus*, therefore, varies in accordance with one or the other position. However, both positions have a common problem: the social representations – for this is what they are – that are formed by these discourses run across situations and genres, and can thus only be identified transversally, making it particularly difficult to build the corpus. It should nevertheless be pointed out that the corpus is sometimes formed from a series of archival texts, chosen for their emblematic value of dominant discourse, and sometimes from a series of symptomatic signs (verbal or iconic) symbolically representing value systems (racism, immigration, women in publicity, use of certain formulae in the media, and so on).

These three problematics define the *field of discourse*. It is a field that can be ploughed in different ways, but with a common purpose: to discover how social interactions are structured through language and, by doing this, to see how social relations are organized and social links established. It means that insofar as this is achieved by and through language as the geometrical center of social organization, discourse analysis as a discipline sets itself apart from others (sociology, social psychology, anthropology, etc.) while still being linked to these.

3 Connection between the speech act and its environment

It must be said that the meaning of a speech act (or communication) does not reside solely in its verbal manifestation nor only in the explicit meaning contained in the utterance produced (a meaning that is verifiable by recourse to the dictionary or to a language grammar). If we limited ourselves to this meaning only, we would always fall short of the meaning of the speech act, if indeed we wish to consider this as an act of psychological and social exchange. This exchange is always made in accordance with a certain concern, namely the concern for significance. Speech acts are always interpreted on the basis of the utterances produced and in relation to a concern, or at least the concern that is presumed to be that of the exchange, and which corresponds to the question: "what does he want to say to me?". This leads us to perceive what is unsaid, that is to say the hidden, implicit meaning; this does not appear in the simple combination of words that make up the utterance, which we ourselves have constructed by *inference*. What is an inference? It is a mental process by which a subject relates what is said explicitly to something else that is in its environment – an elsewhere, something outside language which is nevertheless relevant to the construction of this implicit: hence the hypothesis that the speaker, on their side, creates their utterance to accord with a certain concern, by distributing in the speech act meanings that are both explicit and implicit according to the inferential possibilities that they attribute to their interlocutor.

In other words, the words and utterances produced do not in themselves have meaning; they can only be interpreted in relation to an "elsewhere" that is more or less overdetermining, a place of conditioning that must be shared by the partners in the exchange: all speech acts are produced and interpreted in accordance with the conditions that govern their production and interpretation. In order for the utterance "he is thirty years of age" to mean that the person being spoken of is "too old", both the locutor and interlocutor need to know that they are talking of a football player; in other words, they need to share a certain knowledge which is one of the requirements of the communication act.[6] The question is how to deal with this issue of linguistic environment in terms of relevance in relation to the speech acts produced.

For this, we need both a theory of "discourse subject" and a theory of the "communication situation": of discourse subject because this is what is at the center of the process in which the speech act is produced and interpreted, and it is partly conditioned by the communication situation; and communication situation because it is this that structures the relevant language environment. This dual theory must be exclusively linguistic – neither sociological nor psycho-sociological – which does not prevent elements of a sociological and/or psychological order being included.

A model will therefore be proposed which distinguishes *three places of relevance* for construction of meaning; at the same time, this means that the subject

---

[6] It is "the theory of mutual knowledge" defended by Sperber/Wilson (1986).

will be defined according to a dual *social and discursive identity*; that the conditions of production and interpretation will be determined in terms of *effects*; and that a position will be adopted on the *subject's mode of existence* in the midst of these places of constraint.

3.1 The place of production

This is the place of a social practice in which the subject producing the communication act is situated. But it is a communicative social practice, which is therefore structured according to the conditions relating to what we shall call a *communication situation*. This communication situation has a particular structure that will be explained below, but we can already say that it is the place where the issue of the communicative exchange is defined, which permits an answer to the question: "What is the purpose dictated by this situation?". That being the case, the speaker (in the generic sense)[7] who is in this situation is *overdetermined* by the status and roles assigned to them by that situation. In each communication situation the subject defines themselves through the *social identity* that the situation dictates to them.

But this social identity has to be considered in relation to its relevance to the communication act, for this is what establishes the speaker's legitimacy, that is to say it is what enables the speaker to answer the question: "What authorizes me to speak?". For example, such a person's status as a doctor is irrelevant if they go and knocks on their neighbor's door to ask for a piece of bread. In this scenario, it is the person's social identity as a neighbor that is relevant to the situation in which a favor is being asked; it is this identity that authorizes them to make such a request. On the other hand, it is their role as a doctor that will be relevant in the situation of a medical consultation, and will authorize them to ask their patient: "Are you sleeping well?". Conversely, it is obvious that this utterance cannot be made by a passer-by who stops another passer-by in the street, because the situation in which information is requested by one stranger from another stranger does not authorize it.

If we are interested in analyzing different types of discourse, it will be necessary to question the social identity of the subject at the origin of each of them. In a press discourse, for example, what are the relevant features of social identity

---

7 The "speaker" in the generic sense is the person who produces the speech act in whatever form it may be – oral, written and in whatever locutive relationship it may be, interlocutive or monolocutive. I also name it "communicating subject" in contrast to "enunciating subject". For these designations of the speaker, see Charaudeau/Maingueneau (2002), under the entry *Sujet parlant*.

that relate to the text being produced: are we dealing with a journalist from the newspaper, a correspondent or special envoy, or is it an occasional columnist, a person unrelated to the newspaper, etc.? If it is a political discourse, does it involve an electoral candidate, an elected representative, a minister, a head of state, a member of the majority or a member of the opposition?

If we base the speech act on a principle of influence and regulation of social interactions, due to the problem that the alterity principle poses to all speakers (sharing with the other/being different from the other), its concern could be defined as relating to the effects to be produced upon the other and, on the part of this other, a concern to perceive these effects: effects of causing to act, making known, making believe, and so on. However, since the speaker cannot be sure that these effects are also perceived by the interlocutor, we shall name them *intended effects*. Of course, it is desirable that these effects should be perceived by the interlocutor since they are a condition of the success of the verbal exchange; but, as we shall see, the interlocutor has their word to say in any verbal interaction. In any event, the place where conditions of production exist will be defined as a place where the data of the communication situation are amassed, which partly overdetermine the identities of the subjects present and the purpose of the interaction in terms of intended effects.

3.2 The place of interpretation

This is also the place of a social practice in which the subject receives the communication act and has to interpret it. This activity is dependent, at least in part, on the same conditions as those of production insofar as the subject in this situation is the partner in an act of communication whose concern they must recognize: "What is the purpose dictated by this situation?", "what social identity does it assign to the speaker?", "what social identity does it assign to me, the interlocutor?"; this is the condition for attempting to reconstruct the meaning proposed by the speech act received.

However, this interlocutor subject[8] is a social actor with his or her own autonomy as far as interpretation is concerned; they devote themselves to this activity in accordance with their own social identity, the social identity of the speaker as they perceive it, the intentions they attribute to the speaker, their own knowledge of the world, and their own beliefs. From this perspective, it might be said that the speaker does not totally control the interlocutor; the former might be

---

8 I will call this person the "interpretant subject".

able to imagine what the latter is, but cannot be sure that the interlocutor will interpret their speech act as they envisage it. This is because the interlocutor in turn constructs a meaning; they are not a simple recipient whose activity consists in decoding the message emitted by the speaker, as in the traditional pattern of communication: they are an *interpretant who constructs meaning*.

It signifies that this place is one where effects of meaning belonging to the interlocutor are realized, which is what enables us to speak here of *effects produced*. And we must accept that intended effects and the effects produced do not necessarily coincide. Of course, non-coincidence, even distortion between these effects varies according to the characteristics that the situation assigns to each of the partners in the communicative exchange. One might think that in a face-to-face conversation, the interactors are more able to adjust what they say to the reactions of the other, to rectify them and therefore to bring intended effects and the effects produced closer together (of course, this depends on the degree of knowledge and familiarity that characterizes their relationship, as well as their psychological state). But in all cases of communication where the interpreting subject is plural, represented by a group, a public, or an audience, there is a strong possibility that these two types of effects will coincide only slightly. This is the case with political discourse, information media discourse, publicity discourse, and, to a lesser extent, didactic discourse. The more heterogeneous and ill-defined the public, the less coincidence there will be.

I will define the place of interpretation conditions as a place where the specific data of the interpretant subject are assembled, and revealed by the effects produced, which are then added to the conditions of the communication situation.

3.3 The place of construction of the text

First and foremost, let us be clear that what we call *text* refers to all speech production configured in a visual or verbal fashion or by any other signifying semiological system: it results from the speech act in its semiological manifestation, whether this is open or closed, oral or written, long or short, continuous as in a written production or fragmented in a succession of speakers' turns as in a conversation.

We are therefore now in the place where a text is constructed from data imposed by the place of production. Its organization depends on the way in which certain categories of discourse are chosen and arranged in a combination of argumentative, narrative, or descriptive structures at the service of a certain theme regarding the world, which is to say a certain construction of meaning.

But here, the subjects implied by the text are not those of the place of production or of interpretation. They are, as Barthes says with regard to the narrative of "speech beings",[9] beings who exist only by and through the linguistic event. Thus we are dealing on the one hand with an *enunciating subject*, the one who emerges from the verbal utterance; and on the other with an *addressee*,[10] the one who is implied by the text itself. They are defined in terms of *discursive identity*.

Both the enunciator and the recipient are constructed by the speaker. It is the speaker who through their speech act forms a discursive image of themselves (a kind of ethos), and an ideal image of the person they think they are addressing. Although, as we have seen, the speaker does not control their interlocutor, they do on the other hand control the recipient who depends entirely on the speaker. Of course, the speaker can be mistaken in their calculation because they produce their utterance according to what they know of the interlocutor and create an image of that person which matches their own taste, but it may turn out that the interlocutor does not correspond to this ideal image. In this way, misunderstandings, misconstructions, false interpretations, or quite simply other interpretations are made.

The meaning of a text does not depend solely on the intention of the person who produces it; all is not settled in advance because of the speaker's status, as Bourdieu appeared to say.[11] The discursive identities of the protagonists in the speech act also construct meaning which then, in return, proceeds to confirm or modify the speaker's intention with regard to the interpretant subject. In the same way as in a narrative, people will not confuse *author* with *narrator* on the one hand, or mistake the *reader constructed* by the narrative (the "lector in fabula" of whom Umberto Eco speaks)[12] for the *effective reader* on the other hand, since, in both cases, the latter provide a certain image of the former. Similarly, and more generally, the speaker will not be confused with the enunciator, nor the recipient with the interpretant, since one constructs images of the other and vice versa. It can therefore be seen that, from the point of view of meaning, a text is the bearer both of the effects intended by the speaker and the effects produced by the interpretant; it is filled with this sum of effects of meaning that are so many *possible effects*. Every text is the result of a co-construction of meaning effectuated by the two partners in the communication act.

This explains why we might consider a text to be both *closed* and *open*. It is closed around the interpretation made by a particular type of interpretant subject; its meaning is the result of an interpersonal encounter between the two partners in the exchange. It is open if one considers the diverse interpretations

---

9 See Barthes (1966).
10 See Charaudeau/Maingueneau (2002), under the entry *Sujet parlant*/'Speaker'.
11 See Bourdieu (1982).
12 See Eco (1979).

given it by different types of interpretant subject, and the interpretant subject can vary over time (we do not read Molière as Molière's contemporaries did); over space (we do not read a novel by García Márquez as a Columbian reader would and, in France, the warmongering declarations of George W. Bush were not read in the way the average American would have read them); according to age bracket (a child does not read television advertisements in the same way as an adult); according to gender (women will consider an advertisement sexist whereas men will consider it sexy); according to *social class* (there are those who like popular television programmes of the talk-show type, games, or reality shows like Love Island, and those who detest them); and also according to the type of link that exists between this and the speaker (not everyone experiences the same emotions when seeing images of an air disaster, at least not those who have a close relative in the aeroplane).

The text may therefore be considered in two ways:
- From the viewpoint of its linguistic configuration, as a constructed materiality becoming the object of the verbal interaction, but at the same time consistent with an intentional aim, in accordance with the "intentionality postulate" defined by Searle. This intentionality postulate does not indicate what the speaker's communicative intent might be, but the fact that all speech acts are based on an intention, on what enables us to say that the act has a meaning,[13] without the particularities of this meaning being envisaged;
- From the point of view of its content, as a text "full of meanings", meanings which depend on those provided by the situation, the speaker, and the interpretant subject, all at the same time. We can therefore say that every text has multiple meanings, plural meanings, encompassing a series of "possible meanings" as the result of various encounters which each give rise to a specific co-construction.[14] In this respect it is open, but it is an opening with a succession of closures. It is sufficient to recall the multiple interpretations occasioned by the expression "fracture sociale" ('social fracture'), used by Jacques Chirac during the 1995 presidential campaign: for some this was an *appropriation* while for others it was a *winner*, for still others a *hope*, and so on.

---

13 This notion of Searle's is very often misinterpreted; see Searle (1983).
14 To echo what Roger Odin (2006) has pointed out, I would say that a camera that rolls freely without being placed anywhere, because people have forgotten to unplug it, does not participate in the premise of intentionality and cannot produce a text. But it is enough for sequences recorded by this camera to be taken and put in a television report or feature film for them to acquire a meaning (postulate of intentionality) and they become "inflated" with meaning by virtue of the encounter between the director's intention and that of the spectator.

This hypothesis of places of relevance (see Diagram 1) highlights several things:
- The meaning of a text involves both process and structure. It is a process because of the fact that there is a co-construction between the occurrences of production and interpretation, a construction that varies according to the variation in the relationship between these two occurrences; it is structural due to the closure presupposed by the encounter between a part of the speaker's planned meaning and the construction of meaning by a *particular recipient-interpretant*. And, undoubtedly, we all need to believe that our interpretation of a text is the right one, just as we all need to believe that a text does not remain fixed in a single interpretation.
- The subject of the discourse is not Singular. Supposing that he or she is constructed according to a principle of alterity, they split in a variety of ways. They split according to the roles they play with regard to the speech act itself: sometimes they are a communicating subject, sometimes an interpreting subject. But every speaker knows that while they are the producer of the speech act, they are also an interlocutor because they cannot help imagining what the interpretative activity of their interlocutor might be; the interlocutor, for their part, knows that at the same time as interpreting, they are also the producer because they cannot help imagining the productive activity of the speaker. Furthermore, the linguistic subject splits according to their nature as a psycho-social being (social identity) and as a speaking being (discursive identity). Thus, the speaker, through the enunciator's discursive staging, proceeds to make a selection from the multiple filiations of which this is composed, and the interlocutor, through their interpreting activity, starts to create their own discursive scenario.

PRODUCTION	TEXT	RECEPTION
Place of production conditions	Place of text construction	Place of interpretation
Social identity →	← **Discursive identity** →	← **Social identity**
of the	of the	of the
Speaker	Enunciator Recipient	Recipient-Interpretant
in the social practice	in the discursive	in the social practice
(status, roles)	organization(categories of discourse)	
Intended effects →	Possible effects	← **Effects produced**
↑	↑	↑

--------------------------------Co-construction of meaning--------------------------------

Diagram 1: The three places of relevance.

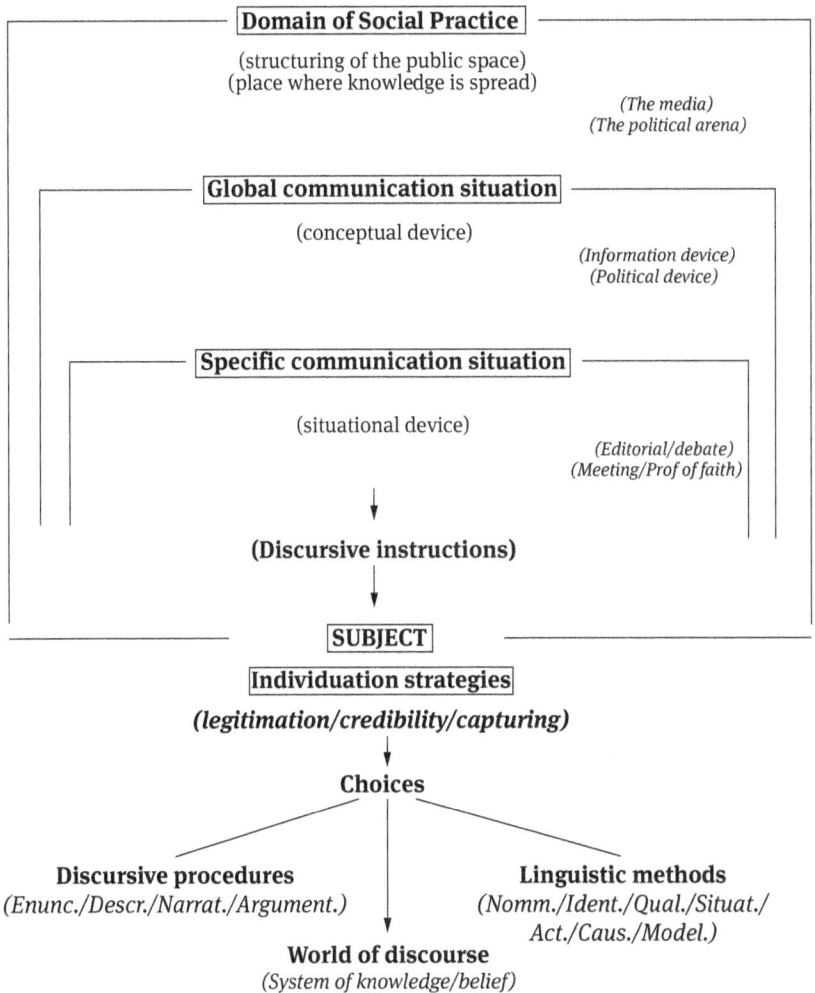

Diagram 2: The communication situation.

– Finally, these three places, defined in relation to their relevance to speech acts, at the same time establish a possible link between different disciplines (sociology, ethnography, anthropology, social psychology, etc.) that are interested in the places of production and reception. But interdisciplinarity is not a simple gathering of several disciplines, or of their concepts or results. It is not by bringing together various results relating to the same object (in fact is it the same object?), nor by citing particular concepts or theories here or there, that this ambition can be satisfied. In order to achieve interdisciplinarity, there needs to be a geometrical center, a place from which other concepts and other results are questioned. In my case, for example, it is from the place of discourse analysis that concepts and results from other disciplines will be reconsidered; but one might imagine that the same stance would be taken by sociology, social psychology, and other disciplines, each of them becoming the geometrical place of this questioning. This is what I call *focused* interdisciplinarity. I consider this to be the necessary condition for the human and social sciences to enter into dialogue. But it also requires the will to achieve it.

4 The communication situation

In all acts of human communication, there are therefore conditions of production and conditions of reception that partly overdetermine the act of producing meaning by each of these subjects. And for a certain mutual comprehension between these two subjects to be possible, we might make the assumption that they have to share some of these conditions: the speaker must be aware of them (this awareness may be unconscious), and the interpretant subject must be able to recognize them. We will name this shared part "communication situation": it represents all the unuttered situational conditions that partly determine the meaning of the speech act and make this a contractual exchange between the two parties concerned. This communication situation constitutes a place of constraint for the production and interpretation of utterances, thereby giving advance instructions to the producing and interpretant subjects for the construction/interpretation of meaning.

One might think that this is trivial since, in most writing, there are so many references to the need to resort to context in order to interpret the meaning of an utterance. But it is not sufficient simply to say this. One cannot make do with simply referring to it from time to time, on the occasion of this or that interpretation. We have to show how this situation is structured, how it imposes its constraints, and how, itself, it becomes a place where meaning is constructed.

4.1 "Spheres of practice" (SP)

Spheres of practice are the place where social interactions are produced, organized into sectors of social activity defined by a set of finalized practices. They result from an interplay which regulates the power relations developed there, and introduce a division of the social space as the symbolic place of an ordered activity by social actors for a purpose implying rules of interaction. In Bourdieu's terms we might speak of "fields" of social practice.

Each SP results from an apportioning of the social space:[15] the political (and not politics), the legal (and not justice), the religious (and not religion), the media (and not one medium in particular), the economic (and not this or that commercial act), the educational (and not this or that form of education), and so on.

The sphere of practice[16] belongs to no discipline exclusively, and therefore possibly belongs to all of them. It is the empirical place of organization for the phenomenal world, which can be made into an object of study by each discipline: sociology, social psychology, anthropology, history, discourse analysis, and so on. But at the same time, by virtue of being recognized as a field of practices, it is the place where different disciplines can meet and share some of their concepts. For example, there are social actors in this sphere of practice who belong in relational contexts, but without any of these yet being determined. It will be up to each discipline to define them as "subjects", "action situations", and "rules of conduct".

4.2 The "global communication situation" (GCS)

The *global communication situation* is a prime place for constructing the sphere of social practices in a sphere of communicational interaction. We are therefore now in the field of communication acts. This situation is defined conceptually by the number of communication instances that are present: this legitimates their role and status, the types of relationship established between them, the discursive purpose intended, and the thematic domain relating to it, all organized according to a system that will itself be called conceptual because it does not prejudge the specific nature of these constituents.

For example, the global communication situation in politics is characterized by four instances: the "political" instance, the "adversarial" instance, the "citizen" instance, and the "mediation" instance;[17] the *discursive intention* is "an incitement to share an idea for a project and for social action"; the macro-thematic domain deals with a "social ideal". The GCS of publicity, on the other hand, brings

---

[15] I shall name this with the aid of the definite article *the*, to indicate that it remains a vague object that has not yet become an object of study.
[16] It appears to correspond with what Dominique Maingueneau calls the "global scene" (in: Charaudeau/Maingueneau, 2002), under the entry *Scène d'énonciation*/'Utterance scene') and what Van Dijk (1999) calls the "domain".
[17] See Charaudeau (2014).

together a "publicity" instance and a "consumer" instance (it is its own mediation instance), a discursive intent "to encourage ownership of a consumer product", and a macro-thematic domain "of individual ideality". As for the global communication situation of the news media, this brings together an "information" instance, a "public" instance (it is also its own mediation instance), a discursive intention to "communicate and comment on world events" and a thematic domain of "events occurring in the immediate public arena",[18] which explains the collusion that can occur between political discourse and the news media discourse.

The global communication situation[19] is therefore the place where social actors in the practical sphere are constructed in *communication instances*,[20] where the interplay of regulation is constructed into *discursive intentions* and the world of knowledge concerned with it into a *macro-thematic* domain. Although in the SP there is a blurred division between the political, the legal, the educational, the media, etc., in the GCS we are dealing with the conceptual devices of political, legal, educational, and media communication. But here, the concrete communication situation is not yet specified.

4.3 The "specific communication situation" (SCS)

The *specific communication situation* is a second place of structuring the sphere of practice where the physical conditions of linguistic staging are determined, and the terms of the global communication situation specified. Although, in this latter, we were dealing with globally defined communication instances, here we are concerned with subjects participating in the exchange, who have a social identity and very precise communicational roles. The same can be said of the exchange's intention and of the thematic domain, which are specified according to the "material circumstances" in which the latter takes place. Thus, the conceptual device of the GCS is transformed into a signifying *material device*. It is a kind of "mediologization"[21] of the conceptual device. This concerns both the materiality of the semiological system (written, phonetic, iconic, visual, gestural, etc.), and that of the medium of transmission (paper, audio-oral, audio-visual, electronic, etc.).

---

18 See Charaudeau (1997).
19 Also named "generic scene" by Maingueneau (cf. Charaudeau/Maingueneau 2002).
20 Van Dijk (1999) speaks here of "global participants".
21 See Debray (1994).

This place[22] is one where communication situations are typified as variants of the GCS. For example, one might say that a political candidate for election who is male belongs to a specific "electoral candidature" situation by having assumed the identity of electoral candidate and appealing to electors; he is led to produce a discourse that charms and persuades in the diverse sub-situations represented by political meetings, leaflets stating his political position, declarations made to the staff of large companies, etc., each time with a change of discursive register. But this same politician, once elected, becomes part of other SCSs, depending on whether he is addressing his fellow citizens during televised party political broadcasts, journalists at press conferences, ministers at Cabinet meetings, and so on. The discourses produced in each of these particular situations will obviously be different.

If, therefore, the GCS is the place of conceptual devices, the SCS is the place of material communication devices as so many sub-sets of the former: specific situations involving "candidacy", "meetings", "press conferences", "parliamentary questions", etc., as sub-sets of the "political" conceptual device; specific situations of "class", "school textbook", "teaching syllabuses and instructions", etc., as sub-sets of the "educational" conceptual device; specific situations of "radio news bulletin", "television news", "newspaper headline", press "editorial" or "report", etc., as sub-sets of the "media information" conceptual device.

Of course, linguistic interactions are always carried out in specific situations. There is no global situation that does not take shape in a specific situation, but I would also suggest that there is no specific situation that does not depend on a global situation. This distinction does not claim to be ontological (although it might claim to be so) but it at least has an operative virtue enabling two types of question to be answered: what is a genre? And how does a genre change?

The question of discourse genres is too vast to be dealt with here, but part of the answer might lie in the fact that genre is not determined by the formal characteristics of the discourse – as is often said – but rather by the situation that sets up the conditions for producing it: a discourse is political, promotional, administrative, religious, legal, media-related, and so on, primarily because of its production conditions: genre is first and foremost *situational*. The nature of the discursive features corresponding to it remains to be seen, which is why I propose to make a distinction between situational genre and discursive genre.

At the same time, this distinction enables us to understand the set of variants established within the same situational genre, since a specific situation produces

---

22 Called "scenography" by Maingueneau (cf. Charaudeau/Maingueneau 2002) and "scene" by Van Dijk (1999).

several variants as part of the same global situation. Thus, to the often-posed question of whether it is possible to speak of a political discourse or whether one should speak of different political discourses, the answer is that there are a number of specific situations of political discourse; and that these all comply with the conceptual device defined in relation to the global communication situation of politics: there are *several* political discourses within *the* political discourse. The same is true of all types of discourse.

Also at the same time, this distinction enables us to understand that SCSs are more unstable, that they may change or new ones may appear in accordance with shifts in the material circumstances of their devices, which may end up influencing the GCSs. This is the case with the appearance of internet technology, which created specific new conditions for information, and these had the effect of gradually modifying media devices. In the toing and froing between these two types of situation, changes in genre are thus produced over time. But this happens through the interventions of subjects staging their discourses, as we shall see in what follows.

In conclusion, we can say that global and specific communication situations form the framework that overdetermines linguist subjects (communicating subject and interpretant subject). This framework is itself made up of a set of constraints that are imposed upon the speaker by providing them with *discursive instructions* which they must take into account in their utterance. It is this set of constraints that I call *communication contract*[23] because it is the condition for establishing mutual understanding between the two partners in a speech act.

These instructions are said to be *discursive* because they determine linguistic behaviours without necessarily prejudging the specific linguistic forms that may be used: they are not linguistic or semiological instructions dictating which words or grammatical construction to use; or what image, script, colour, or gesture to employ – these are the speaker's choices. Instead, they are ways of organizing the discourse (descriptive, narrative, argumentative), its textual or paratextual composition, and the thematic selection and organization with which to shape speech. For example, the instructions given by the situation of a publicity poster tell the subject displaying it that they must, somehow or other, show the product and present or suggest its benefits to the public, in a thematic domain that concerns the problems an individual might encounter in their quest for wellbeing (youth, prestige, health, bodily appearance, satisfaction of exerting charm, etc.). But these instructions do not say whether the slogan must be configured in allocutive or delocutive form; if the product's qualities should be suggested through

---

[23] See this same entry in Charaudeau/Maingueneau (2002).

a particular type of argument; or if the product should be iconically represented in a particular manner.

A communication situation will therefore not be confused with an utterance situation. The former brings together data that are external to the speech act, whereas the latter concerns the discursive arrangement of the speech act. As Bakhtin says and J.-P. Esquenazi has reminded us, it is the situation that shapes the utterance.

5 Positioning of the subject

I do not intend to develop this point unduly because my intention, in the context of this exposition, was to demonstrate the type of communication model through which one might attempt to articulate the speech act with an element outside language conditioning it, and to show this by defining three places of relevance together with a theory of the communication situation. But since both of these imply a joint theory of the subject of discourse, I am bound to follow this conception of the subject through to its end – a conception which says that the subject is both constrained by the particular facts of the communication situation and at the same time relatively free to position him- or herself in relation to it. I will therefore limit myself to outlining this second aspect.

It should be stated from the outset that the linguistic subject, as we have said, can only be conceived of if based on a principle of otherness which says that the Self can become aware of its existence only insofar as it recognizes the existence of another, who is both similar and different from the Self. To this might be added the paradox that the more this other resembles the Self, and even merges with them, the less the Self exists; and the more the other is differentiated from the Self, the more the Self exists, but in an antagonistic relationship which means that the other may present a threat to the Self. This means that an ambivalent relationship of attraction and rejection is established between the Self and the other and, in a verbal interaction, this becomes a relationship between I and You: sometimes in an I-You partnership which leads the subjects to make common cause, configured as a We, and sometimes to make a differentiation between I/You, leading the subjects into a process of individuation configured as an I, which is different from everything that is non-I.[24]

---

[24] This perhaps relates to a comment by Bernard Stiegler on Gilbert Simondon, when he said something in the vein of "the I can only think of itself in relation to the We, assuming a collective history in which it recognizes a plurality" and "the I is a process of individuation that tends to become One (ideal of the Self), but is not One".

It is therefore as I-We that the subject becomes part of a communication situation and has to fulfil its instructions, and it is as I/non-I that the subject implements a linguistic process of *individuation*. The discursive staging demonstrates this dual tension between respect for the facts of the situation and differentiation within these facts. Having seen what the constraints of the communication situation were, how these were organized into different levels of embedding, and how they were converted into discursive instructions, we now face the problem of knowing how the subject is able to differentiate him- or herself.

Let us then assume that the subject, in the linguistic phenomenon, is both a subject of knowledge and a relational subject, without our really knowing the interactive relationship established between the two. The linguistic subject is therefore caught between two stools: whether to position themselves in relation to knowledge or in relation to the other.

With regard to knowledge, the subject is confronted by the issue of perception and the conceptual understanding of the world through the different thought systems that organize knowledge of the world. I propose to consider that these thought systems can be of two orders: the order of "cognizance" as objectivized knowledge, exterior to the subject, whether it comes from a widely shared experience (if I throw an object into the air, it falls down again) or from erudite knowledge (the law of gravity); the order of "belief" as subjectivized knowledge, interior to the subject, implying a polarized judgment of the world (it is good not to humiliate an enemy). The subject has to position themselves in relation to these different forms of knowledge by using the systems of recognition available to them and activating the belief systems that they carry within them. These systems are conveyed by the discourses that circulate in social communities and are just as much a part of collective memory as of each individual memory. Understanding these discourses is to plunge into an intertextuality such as that described by Bakhtin's dialogism.

With regard to the other, the subject is confronted with the question of the validity of the communicational exchange according to its constraints. I propose to consider that the subject acts by attempting to answer three types of question: (1) does the other perceive what authorizes me to speak (what legitimates me)? If not, I will have to try to legitimate myself in the other's eyes; (2) does the other believe me? If not, I will have to try to make myself credible; (3) does the other agree to enter into a relationship with me and are they ready to subscribe to my world of discourse? If not, I will have to try to be amiable towards them, to persuade and move them. In other words, the subject, in order to become individuated, has to implement strategies of *legitimation*, *credibility*, and *capturing* by means of a certain discursive staging.

Legitimation strategies are not to be confused with legitimacy which is granted in advance and attributed by the communication situation (see the instances and identities established by the GCSs and SCSs). These strategies are put in place when the speaker is not certain of the communication situation or when they think that it has not been sufficiently legitimized in their interlocutor's eyes. Depending on the case, the speaker may then insist on their own trustworthiness, their knowledge of a particular domain, their experience or filiation, as politicians often do when in an electoral campaign situation.

Credibility strategies are implemented when the speaker wishes to be believed. They can then construct an image of themselves, an ethos,[25] as a serious person who reasons calmly, is level-headed, knows how to weigh advantages and disadvantages, proves what they say, reports known facts, and so on. They then have to resort to all the power of persuasion of which they are capable.

Capturing strategies are implemented when the subject, because they are not in a position of authority over their interlocutor (in the opposite case, it would be sufficient for them to give orders), tries to ensure that the latter finds what they say interesting, shares their opinion, or adheres irrationally to their own feelings. In order to achieve this, they may resort to using a discourse that touches their interlocutor's emotions by creating affects in them (effects of pathos)[26] that give the subject the upper hand.

6 Conclusion

I will conclude by saying that this socio-communicational model[27] is a hypothesis about the functioning of the speech act and that breaking it down into its component parts enables its different aspects to be analyzed: the subject of the speech act has their identity split between the social and the discursive, but they are also constrained by situational factors; they then tend to become individuated by employing discursive strategies whose linguistic staging produces a text carrying possible effects of meaning, the results of a series of co-constructions of effects intended and effects produced (see Diagram 2).

---

25 On this question, see Charaudeau (2014).
26 On this question, see Charaudeau (2014).
27 I should say "socio-semio-communicational" to be precise, since it takes account of the significance of signs in the various semiological systems brought into play in order to carry out a speech act.

To end with I will clarify what has previously been sketched out, namely the back and forth interplay between the global communication situation, the specific situation, and individuation strategies.

The publicity discourse has changed from its beginnings, when the challenge was mainly to ensure the existence of a product, to the 1970s-1980s when the concern was to promote the product's qualities and benefits around a desire, a dream, or a fantasy; by the contemporary period it had evolved again so that, now, the staging of the advertisement itself predominates, independently of the product. It might be said that the general conditions of the publicity discourse, in its conceptual operation, are still the same but that what has changed, because of differentiation strategies, are the conditions of the specific communication device.

The information discourse has also changed and Bernard Miège has well described its different phases.[28] In the eighteenth century the aim of the press was to foster engagement between élites so that opinions could be shared; in the nineteenth century, a mass commercial press aimed to transmit information exalting the values of social progress; and in the twentieth century, the mass audio-visual media were caught in a financial trap that made them approach viewers with a concern to influence their emotions rather than their reason. And I myself have shown through a joint study of the conflict in the countries of the former Yugoslavia[29] that television develops a dual discourse, of dramatization with an excessive use of pathos on the one hand, and moral awareness on the other, with its calling out of political authorities. It will be said that capturing strategies have gradually become dominant in a communication contract that, ideally, should be "to inform". And one might add that, due to a rise in the power of televised media, current political discourse is wondering what discursive capturing strategies to use: this may well end up transforming the global communication situation in politics in such a way that the purpose is no longer to offer citizens an "ideal social plan" but identical images of both politicians and citizens.

---

[28] See Miège (1995).
[29] See Charaudeau/Croll/Fernandez/Lochard/Soulages (2001).

References

Barthes, Roland, *Introduction à l'analyse structurale des récits*, Communications 8 (1966), 1–27.
Bourdieu, Pierre, *Ce que parler veut dire*, Paris, Fayard, 1982.
Charaudeau, Patrick, *Discours d'information médiatique. La construction du miroir social*, Paris, Nathan/INA, 1997.
Charaudeau, Patrick, *Discours politique. Les masques du pouvoir*, Limoges, Lambert-Lucas, 2014.
Charaudeau, Patrick/Croll, Anne/Fernandez, Manuel/Lochard, Guy/Soulages, Jean-Claude, *La télévision et la guerre. Déformation ou construction de la réalité? Le conflit en Bosnie (1990–1994)*, Bruxelles, INA/De Boeck Université, 2001.
Charaudeau, Patrick/Maingueneau, Dominique, *Dictionnaire d'analyse du discours*, Paris, Éditions du Seuil, 2002.
Coenen-Huther, Jacques, *Le type idéal comme instrument de la recherche sociologique*, Revue française de sociologie 44 (2003), 531–547, DOI: https://www.cairn.info/revue-francaise-de-sociologie-1-2003-3-page-531.htm?contenu=article.
Debray, Régis, *Manifestes médiologiques*, Paris, Gallimard, 1994.
Eco, Umberto, *Lector in fabula*, Bompiani, Milano, 1979; trad. Bouzaher, Myriam, Paris, Grasset, 1985.
Miège, Bernard, *L'espace public. Au-delà de la sphère politique*, Hermès17–18 (1995), 49–62.
Odin, Roger, *La sémio-pragmatique, un modèle heuristique*, Médias et culture, "Discours–outils de communication–pratiques : quelle(s) pragmatique(s) ?", numéro spécial en hommage à Daniel Bougnoux (janvier 2006), 55–70.
Pêcheux, Michel, *Les Vérités de La Palice. Linguistique, sémantique, philosophie*, Paris, François Maspero, 1975.
Sperber, Dan/Wilson, Deirdre, *Relevance*, Oxford, Blackwell, 1986; *La pertinence*, trad. Gerschenfeld, Abel/Sperber, Dan, Paris, Les Éditions de Minuit, 1989.
Searle, John R., *Intentionality. An essay in philosophy of mind*, Cambridge University Press, Cambridge, 1983; *L'intentionalité. Essai de philosophie des états mentaux*, trad. Pichevin, Claude, Paris, Les Éditions de Minuit, 1985.
Van Dijk, Teun A., *Context models in discourse processing*, in: Van Oostendorp, Herre/Goldman, Susan R. (edd.), *The construction of mental representations during reading*, Mahwah, Lawrence Erlbaum, 1999, 123–148.

Dominique Maingueneau
Chapter 11
Discourse, discourse analysis, and discourse genres

Abstract: This paper questions the notion of *discourse* both in its particularities and its vagueness: it can be thought of as outside communication ("discourse structures our beliefs") and on the other hand as referring to genres ("the discourses around publicity"). Having distinguished discourse from text (such-and-such a *text* relates to political discourse), discourse from sentence (the former being a *discourse-level* matter), and discourse from language (according to the language/speech distinction), we examine the diversity of discourses. Finally, we look at two discourse regimes which do not fall under traditional textuality: the Internet and aphorizing utterances.

Keywords: aphorizing vs textualizing (utterance), auctor, author, conversational regime, genre, scenography

1 Different regimes

1.1 Discourse

The position of discourse studies appears to be both strong and weak. Strong, because it is through discourse that social reality is constructed, and all semiotic activity – including discourse study itself, and the criticisms directed at it – is subject to its order. But it is also weak, because there is a temptation to see discourse as an area of study as unclear as it is useless, a latecomer to other well-established disciplines such as sociology, history, psychology or linguistics.

It has to be said that the very term "discourse" does not make the task any easier, since it seems to defy all definition. We should therefore avoid two particular stances, one of which might be called "skeptical", and the other "therapeutic". The first involves refraining from giving "discourse" any semantic consistency, making do with recording its uses and explaining them according to the interests of its users. The second, by contrast, disqualifies those of its meanings

Dominique Maingueneau, Sorbonne Université

that are not "strictly" defined, which, in reality, means most of them. The fact that it is used as a *non-countable* noun ("discourse structures our beliefs") as well as a *countable* noun ("the discourses around publicity") therefore means it can refer to empirical objects as well as transcend any particular act of communication. This favors a dual appropriation of the notion: (a) by theories of a philosophical order, and (b) by analyses of corpora. Even within (b), the relationship between *text* and *discourse* is very different depending on whether one links a discourse to *each text* or a single discourse to *a set of texts*: the "discourse of psychiatry", for example, covers a more or less vast series of texts of very different genres (theoretical works, hospital rules, consultations, and so on). Used in this way, "discourse" may refer to extremely diverse entities: the discourse of geography, communist discourse, discourse about security, discourse about Africa, journalistic discourse, nurses' discourse, etc.

If we now turn to linguistics, we see that "discourse" is part of two major antitheses: between *discourse* and *sentence*, and between *discourse* and *language*.

When we contrast *discourse* and *sentence*, discourse is considered as a discourse-level linguistic unit. It was in this sense that Harris (1952) was able to speak of "*discourse* analysis". It is also on this interpretation of "discourse" that many researchers in textual linguistics base their work today. The journal *Discours*, for example, focuses on the following themes:

> Structuring of discourse, cohesion, co-referencing, linearization, indexation, informational structure, word order, segmentation markers, integration markers, discourse relationships, cognitive processes at work when understanding and producing texts and other related themes.[1]

When *discourse* and *language* are opposed to one another, it is the system and its use in context that are being opposed. We find here certain aspects of Saussure's "language"/"speech" pairing.

It is noteworthy that the concept of "language in use", which appears frequently in Anglophone literature as a paraphrase for "discourse", combines these two oppositions.

These linguistic meanings of "discourse" have interacted with a number of ideas emanating from theoretical trends that run through all the human and social

---

[1] Cf. https://journals.openedition.org/discours/: "Structuration du discours, cohésion, co-référence, linéarisation, indexation, structure informationnelle, ordre des mots, marqueurs de segmentation, marqueurs d'intégration, relations de discours, processus cognitifs à l'œuvre lors de la compréhension et de la production des textes et autres thèmes reliés." [last consultation: 02.09.2018] (All subsequent translations from other works are by Rosemary Rodwell, the translator of this article, unless stated otherwise.)

sciences: the philosophy of ordinary language (Wittgenstein), the theory of language acts (Austin, Searle), the inferential conception of meaning (Grice), symbolic interactionism (Mead), ethnomethodology (Garfinkel), the Palo Alto school (Bateson), Bakhtin's dialogism, Vygotsky's psychology, the archaeology and theory of power of Foucault, who himself was part of a "poststructuralist" trend (along with Derrida, Deleuze, Lacan, Laclau, Butler...), and certain constructivist tendencies, particularly Berger's and Luckmann's sociology of knowledge.

When we speak of "discourse", we are, in a diffuse manner, activating an open set of leitmotivs and key ideas: in particular, that discourse socially constructs meaning; discourse is a form of action and not a representation of the world; discourse is interactive; discourse is contextualized; discourse is governed by norms; discourse is part of an inter-discourse, and so on. We are then dealing more with a principle of "family likeness" than with a core of stable meaning that is common to all uses. This means that the notion of discourse forms a kind of standard envelope for positions that sometimes strongly diverge.

However, even if it is very unstable, the use of "discourse" is not empty of meaning. It allows us both to indicate *subjects* for analysis ("the press discourse", "doctors' discourse", and so on) and to show that we are adopting a certain *point of view* about them. Saying, for example, that this leaflet or that newspaper is a discourse is implicitly saying that we consider them *as* discourse. By speaking of the "leaflet discourse", we are indicating that we not only intend to analyze the contents, the organization of the text, and its stylistic devices, but that we are going to relate this utterance to communication methods, to the norms of an activity, to groups which derive their legitimacy from it, to a certain mode of circulation, and so on.

1.2 Discourse analysis

Most of those who claim to be practitioners of discourse do not subscribe to the "theory of discourse" but present themselves as discourse *analysts*. They study corpora, trying to maintain a balance between thinking about the way discourse works and understanding phenomena of a socio-historical or psychological order.

In didactic works at the international level, the term "discourse analysis" is most often used. There is also a growing tendency to use the term "discourse studies", taking its cue from the Anglo-Saxon notion of "studies". The plural, *studies*, is not insignificant, because the research concerned is extremely diverse. Faced with this diversity, people usually content themselves with speaking of a multitude of "approaches". Discourse studies then appear as a vast market from which one can pick and choose according to need. However, to speak of "approaches" risks giving the illusion that there are stable data independent of any approach, whereas, in reality, each "approach" makes a decisive contribution to building the relevant corpus. Furthermore, these "approaches" cover very different realities: real disciplines (such as semiotics or stylistics), discourse study trends (ethnography of communication, critical discourse analysis, etc.), models of language functioning (for example, systemic-functional linguistics), units of all verbal interaction (proxemics, politeness, language acts. . .), conceptions of language that do not belong to any particular trend (pragmatics), and so on.

Rather than accepting this abundance of "approaches" without closer inspection, it would appear preferable to use the distinction between "discourse studies" and "discourse analysis" to assign a specific space to discourse analysis, conceived as a discipline within discourse studies (Maingueneau 1995). From this perspective, discourse is not a given but becomes an object of knowledge only if it is assumed by a particular discipline, which is characterized by a specific *interest*.

The existence of disciplines is linked to the fact that research is a fundamentally cooperative activity which – over and above any particular trend or school – requires social spaces where scientific results can be shared by communities of researchers interested in the same sets of problems, where they can exchange information, have privileged access to the same groups (networks, mailing lists, symposiums, study days, PhD examining boards, etc.), and figure in the same networks of bibliographical references. Here, we can count on the contributions of social science studies since the 1970s.

The specific interest underlying discourse analysis is to relate the structuring of texts to the social locations that make them possible and which they make possible. In this context, the notion of "social location" should not be understood in a literal way: it may, for example, involve the positioning in a discursive field (for example, a political party, a religious or philosophical doctrine. . .). The object of discourse analysis, therefore, is neither the functioning of texts, nor the communication situation, but what binds them together through a process of utterance production that involves both the verbal and institutional realms. Under these conditions, thinking about locations independently of speech (sociological reduction), or thinking of speech independently of the locations to which they belong (linguistic reduction), means to fall short of the demands which form the basis of discourse analysis.

Even if there are no materials that belong exclusively to a discipline of discourse, each discipline has its favored corpora. A discourse analyst will automatically be ill-equipped to study ordinary oral interactions, which are difficult to link to an institutional location or an identifiable ideological position. An analyst of conversation, on the other hand, will hardly have a penchant for philosophical treatises or telephone directories.

To say that discourse studies are an area where different disciplines interact does not mean that all research conducted in this area belongs to a discipline. Indeed, much of the research undertaken has a very descriptive aim. Since it does not privilege debate over the methods, concepts or theoretical presuppositions of the research practice, it would be artificial to want to link it to a particular discipline. The results of such research can be made to serve a variety of disciplines. Even though many researchers follow a particular path without worrying about whether it belongs to a discipline, it is disciplines which ensure the stability of the field by establishing *shared* objects of research.

Furthermore, as is the rule in human and social sciences, disciplines are themselves places of confrontation between multiple "trends" which associate a certain conception of discourse and the purpose of its study with a specific conceptual and methodological system. These different trends do not necessarily allow themselves to be confined to a single discipline. For example, a specialist of rhetoric (Amossy 2012)[2] working in discourse analysis belongs to the field of rhetoric as well as discourse analysis.

1.3 The heterogeneity of discourse

In principle, discourse analysis is duty bound to deal with verbal productions in all their diversity. In reality, the great majority of scholars who work in the area of discourse studies prefer to study "ordinary" conversations or texts relating to politics, the media, education, health, or the business world. In their eyes, this restriction does not appear to be detrimental because they tacitly admit that discourse is fundamentally homogeneous, and that it can be unified around two postulates: one is that the prototype of discursive activity is oral interaction, while the other is that the basic unit of discourse analysis is the text/genre pairing. Each of these postulates can be related to a specific tradition. North-American research tends to favor oral interaction, whereas many European researchers place the emphasis on the text/genre duo. But these two postulates are constantly linked and contaminate one another: a large number of conversation analysts consider conversation as a genre or covering a considerable number of genres, while those who work on genres linked to institutions favor oral genres. Furthermore, the great majority of researchers share a certain conception of discourse as being a set of practices where, in well-defined contexts, individuals of flesh and blood interact and develop strategies for influencing others according to their interests.

---

[2] See also the next chapter of this book.

This restriction of corpora can be explained. Discourse analysis appeared in the West in certain historical circumstances, i.e. in the 1960s, at a time when television had become the dominant medium and when, for the first time in history, researchers had the technical means available to record spontaneous oral speech easily and cheaply. It also developed in the world of social sciences, outside departments which until then had studied prestigious texts: literature, law, philosophy, and so on. Being a discourse analyst therefore implied that corpora previously considered as peripheral were studied using sophisticated methods. Furthermore, these corpora had the not inconsiderable advantage of making it easier to relate textual phenomena to social ones, something which was much less evident with scientific or religious texts.

Certainly, discourse analysts are aware of the diversity of discursive practices. They are constantly insisting on the difference between written and oral, formal and informal contexts, monological and dialogical, etc. In the English-speaking world, the supporters of corpus linguistics (Biber 1988; Sinclair 1991), closely linked to functional systemic linguistics, seek to identify the multiple "registers" of the same language. But in this type of approach, to say that language is "heterogeneous" is simply another way of saying that the system varies according to different situations. For example, when they define literature or religion as a "register" (Crystal/Davy 1969), it is because these are considered as specific areas of language usage, and not because there is a "religious discourse" or a "literary discourse", whose functioning does not relate to the categories used to analyze television or education.

It would appear more realistic to defend a robust conception of discourse heterogeneity – to distinguish different regimes which correspond to different modes of communication, and need to be analyzed using specific concepts and methods. It is impossible to deny the fundamental role played by conversation in constructing subjectivity and the social order, or the role played by discourse genre in the licensing and structuring of speech, but this does not mean that conversation forms the center and the prototype of discursive activity, nor that the concepts and methods of analyzing discourse have to be based on it. And, as we shall see, the universality of the discourse genre category can also be contested.

1.4 The enunciation scene and modes of genericity

To begin with, it is already possible to distinguish two discourse regimes, which constantly interweave but are subject to different constraints: these are *conversational* and *instituted* (Maingueneau 2014). Conversations are not closely linked to institutions which prescribe stable contexts, roles, and scripts; their context is constantly changing and the participants are continually negotiating their status and methods of exchange. It is in the instituted regime that the notion of discourse genre is truly relevant; speakers take part in communicational rituals where they are given particular roles. The whole difficulty consists in not setting up a hierarchy between these two regimes, any more than would be the case between a written and oral regime.

However, the notion of genre should be refined, since there are various types depending on the way speech is staged. The enunciation scene (Maingueneau 1998) can be broken down into three components:

– The *enclosing scene*, corresponding to what is generally understood by "type of discourse". When you find a leaflet in your letter box, you need to decide whether it belongs to a religious, political, administrative, advertising, or other type of discourse – in other words, within what enclosing scene does it need to be set in order to be interpreted; on what grounds is it appealing to the reader, and what is its ultimate aim? A political utterance, for example, implies that a citizen is addressing other citizens. This is certainly a vague identification, but it defines the status of each partner within a certain context of space and time.

– An enclosing scene covers a variable number of discourse genres, which may be understood as so many *generic scenes*: a candidate appealing to electors in an electoral campaign leaflet, a teacher addressing pupils in a class, and so on. The generic scene does not only assign roles to the actors; it also prescribes the right place and time, the medium, the organization of the text, its mode of circulation and reception, etc.

– Texts that belong to the same generic scene can give rise to very varied *scenographies*. A sermon, for example, can be uttered by means of a prophetic, meditative, or other kind of scenography. The scenography is not simply a framework, a décor, as if the discourse were taking place within an already-constructed space that was independent of that discourse; it is the act of enunciation itself which, as it develops, strives to gradually implement the appropriate setting for speech, to fit the world it is evoking. Indeed, taking part in speech is, to various degrees, to take risks, and all discourse, by its very essence, institutes the scenography that licenses it.

On this basis, a distinction can be made between four types of genericity, commensurate with the relationship between generic scene and scenography:

– Mode (1): this concerns very limited genres, including the way they are phrased: commercial flyers, weather forecasts, telephone directories, exchanges between air pilots and control towers, administration forms, legal transactions, etc. These are genres in which the speakers are, in principle, replaceable.

- Mode (2): this covers genres that follow routines, but have some room for maneuver. Examples of these are television news or university courses: they are subject to specific requirements, but these are not rigid. Generally speaking, their generic scene calls for a particular scenography, but nothing prevents the speaker occasionally departing from what is expected, and having recourse to more original scenographies. A travel guide, for example, may be presented as a narrative or as a friendly conversation.
- Mode (3): in this case, the genre obliges the speaker to invent an original scenography, because the generic scene does not call for a particular scenography. By way of example, we might cite advertisements, songs, television entertainment programs, etc. Although we may know that a specific text is an advertisement, this does not enable us to anticipate the scenography through which it will be uttered. If advertisements or entertainment programs had scenographies defined in advance, it would be difficult for them to gain the attention of consumers. Creativity is nevertheless exercised within frameworks that are pre-established by the generic scene, and advertisements do not call into question the genre to which they belong.
- Mode (4): these are genres where a single *author* must not only invent a personal scenography but also take part in categorizing his or her own verbal production by deciding on its name: whether it is an "essay", a "fantasy", "thoughts", "story", and so on. These names cannot be replaced by others, or be disassociated from the meaning that the authors intend to confer upon their utterance.

The genres in modes (3) and (4) possess similarities in that they all need to create stimulating scenographies that are likely to appeal to their audience; to do this they have to set a scene for speech to take place which is in keeping with the message being conveyed. But while advertising texts (mode (3)), for example, have a specific purpose (to make people buy their product), and they look for the appropriate strategy to achieve this objective, the aim of religious writers or novelists is fundamentally an open one: there is literature or religion only because their aim is not set in stone and accepted by all.

As one might expect, most discourse analysts focus on the genres in modes (1), (2), and (3) – with a marked preference for (2) – and abandon mode (4), which is linked to types of discourse that fit ill with their theoretical and methodological presuppositions. However, if one wants to embrace generic diversity, then the specific character of mode (4) has to be accepted and, along with it, 'self-constituting discourses' (philosophical, scientific, religious, etc.) (Maingueneau/Cossutta 1995;

Maingueneau 1999)³ that are *paratopic*, in that they must show they both "belong" and at the same time do not "belong" to ordinary society. Being limited by the inexpressible, they have to negotiate the paradoxes that this position implies. There are also *atopic* utterances (pornography for example, cf. Maingueneau 2007) which cannot really occupy a place in society.

In other words, discourse does not develop over a uniform space from which any utterance might emanate – from the most spontaneous conversations to the most sophisticated written texts with television programs in between –, but the way in which different speech regimes relate to the space is what forms their identity.

2 Beyond discourse genre

If there is a discourse regime that develops in its own space, it is certainly the internet. The new communication technologies are forcing us to rethink many categories: textuality, speaker, addressee, memory, circulation, etc. We can no longer see technology as an element of the "context", but as an actor in the communication process. The problem is that most discourse analysts appear to live in a world where traditional face-to-face conversation is still the normal way to communicate. They accord a marginal role to corpora produced with the aid of new technologies, unless they can study them with the tools for conversation analysis. This is particularly the case where forums, emails, and text messages are concerned.

This lack of interest is largely linked to the fact that the concepts and methods of discourse studies are ill-adapted to these types of data. This applies, for example, to the notion of discourse genre. When considering the functioning of the internet, it is indeed possible to contest the premise that all utterances, written or oral, belong to a genre of discourse.

2.1 The challenges of the internet

As we have seen, genre is structured by hierarchy: Enclosing scene > generic scene > scenography. We also need to take account of categories such as "interview", "dialogue", "relationship", etc. which I call "hypergenres" (Maingueneau 1998) and Fairclough (2003, 68–70) calls "disembedded genres": these are very

---
3 "Discours constituants".

poor formattings which cover extremely varied genres. In fact, this strategy is not relevant to the Web, where the enclosing scene and the generic scene no longer play a key role. The primary preoccupation of website designers is to coordinate communication and develop scenographies, rather than conform to the norms of discourse genre. In fact, all these productions are sites, and as such they are subject to strict technical constraints. There is a homogeneity about them that enables people to navigate from one site to another. Of course, sites can be graded into broad categories (blogs, social networks, commercial sites, etc.), but they are not discourse genres in the sense that we understood earlier. They are more like hypergenres. A blog, for example, has minimal features: someone talks about him/herself to the visitor of their site. Within the constraints imposed by the hypergenre, it is then a question of mobilizing verbal, sound, and visual resources to invent appropriate scenographies, giving meaning to the activity by fashioning a certain image of the enunciator, his/her addressees, and the relationship between them according to the objective of the site.

The Web also has a major effect on the other aspect of genre, which is textuality. Whereas the traditional conception of discourse genre is focused on specifically verbal scenography, on the Web this is part of a "digital scenography" with two inseparable components: "iconotextual" (the site contains images and offers itself as an image, bounded by the screen) and "reticular" (a site is a network of pages and creates links with other sites). The very notion of "page" becomes problematic: on the Web a screen displays only a part of a whole that can never be taken in with a single look. On many sites one mostly sees medleys of heterogeneous modules: advertisements, videos, quotations, beginnings of articles, diagrams, images, and so on. The digital world is increasingly becoming a world of decontextualized fragments that can be combined in countless ways. The very stability of the content poses a problem, because what is seen on the screen only exists at a specific moment: a certain number of modules are constantly being refreshed while others change more slowly, but we can never be certain that the combination of signs we see was identical ten minutes or three days previously. This calls into question what is commonly considered as a main feature of written texts, namely their stability.

Thus, while the usual conception of discourse genre implies that there is a map of verbal activity (the world of discourse can be divided into various main areas, which in turn can be divided into distinct speech institutions and genres), the Web, by giving a key role to scenography and hypergenre, implies a "de-differentiation" of speech areas. On the screen one cannot see texts, in the traditional sense of the term –texts that can be allotted specific places within well-marked institutional territories – but multimodal medleys of modules that are more or less transitory and are so many nodes in an infinite network.

3 Detached utterances

It is not only the Web which questions the premise that all utterances belong to a discourse genre. For very different reasons, it is also the case with thoroughly traditional practices, which relate to "detached" utterances, *aphorizations* and *Works*.

3.1 Aphorizing utterances

There are many utterances circulating in society which do not belong to a text. One thinks of slogans or mottoes, which are designed to stand alone; but to these may be added all the phrases that have been extracted from texts: titles of press articles, maxims, famous quotes, etc.

As a general rule, the fragment extracted differs from its original wording, even when the original is placed next to it – as happens, for example, in this title from an article in the free daily newspaper *20 Minutes*:

> My vote will go to whoever is most persuasive.

But the text below it is different: 'My vote will go to whoever is most persuasive, who will seem most prepared to change things in France.'[4] Omitting the end of the sentence has substantially changed the meaning of the original utterance.

Such alterations are normal if we assume that detached utterances do not imply the same type of verbal act as usual utterances, and if we make a distinction between an "aphorizing" enunciation (or "aphorization") and a "textualizing" enunciation. Whereas in textualizing enunciations speakers produce texts belonging to genres, in aphorizing enunciations we are not dealing with texts or fragments of texts but with utterances for which the notion of text is irrelevant. One might object that aphorizations do in fact figure in texts: for example, the title of an article is part of the article, and a proverb is inserted into a conversation. No doubt this is so, but their authority is based on the fact that they claim to be free from textualizing enunciations, and we should note the tension between their insertion in a text and their constitutive rejection of textuality.

Unlike texts, aphorizations are not attributable to "speakers" in the usual sense of the term. The responsibility for primary aphorizations (slogans, mottoes,

---

[4] "Mon vote ira à celui qui sera le plus persuasif."/"Mon vote ira à celui qui sera le plus persuasif, qui me semblera le plus motivé pour bouger les choses en France." (20 Minutes, 2 May 2007, page 7)

etc.) is attributed to an anonymous authority (for example, "the Wisdom of nations" for proverbs). As for secondary aphorizations, which have been extracted from a text, these are not attributed to real speakers, but to *aphorizers* who have been created by the very act of detaching the words. Aphorizers are supposed to speak independently of any genre of discourse, in an absolute way, as Subjects with full right. In Latin, the precise meaning of *sub-iectum* is something that does not vary. In the aphorizer, the Subject who is the medium of linguistic activity coincides with the ethical Subject: through their utterance, aphorizers express their values to the world, without calling for any response from an addressee placed at the same level. They are addressing a 'universal auditory' (Perelman/Olbrechts-Tyteca 1958),[5] the whole community for which their utterances are supposed to be fully meaningful.

3.2 "Works"

Like that of aphorizer, the notion of author cannot be reduced to that of speaker. Since authorship is a question traditionally confined to literary theory, it has no assured status in discourse analysis, being neither the enunciator – a linguistic authority – nor a flesh-and-blood human being, situated outside language. Rather it is a function that closely links agency (X is the cause of an utterance) and legality (X must answer for it): to any monological utterance one must be able to attribute an author, even if this author is a group.

There are very few authors of utterances who are associated with "Works", that is to say a unit bringing together very diverse texts which are supposed to express a particular view of the world (Foucault 1994). Some of these authors, who have become part of the heritage, gain the status of "great authors", and their whole gamut of texts is published, no matter what they are: private correspondence, intimate diaries, school work, and so on. We might refer to this type of author by the Latin noun *auctor*, to distinguish it from ordinary authors who have definite descriptions: "the author of this pamphlet", "of that response", "of this article"... Works is a category that discourse analysts leave to specialists of literature, philosophy, or religion. This lack of interest may seem surprising if we think that all culture depends on a restricted number of personalities, who are the sources of major utterances which are constantly quoted and commented upon.

As with aphorization, Works relegates text genericity to the background. As a fragment of their works, an author's text is no longer read as the product of a

---

[5] "Auditoire universel".

situated speech activity, but as the expression of an extra-ordinary Subject. If, in the complete works of Balzac, published in La Pléiade collection, we read letters that he wrote to his publisher, we do not read them as utterances embedded in a context, a social practice, but as relics of an exceptional creative career belonging to the literary canon. The addressee of these texts is no longer the one specified by their genre, but an indeterminate audience.

As we can see, aphorizers and *auctors*, each in their own way, are freed from the constraints imposed by genericity. *Auctors* escape it upwards, so to speak, since their texts are converted into fragments of a higher unit, the "Works". Aphorizers are freed from below, with their texts being broken down into aphorizations. And in both cases, the usual notion of "speaker" becomes problematic. Both Works and aphorization are foreign to the logic of ordinary exchange. Like aphorizers, *auctors* cannot establish themselves as such: it requires the intervention of a third party who has detached a particular utterance or utterances and made it part of a new configuration.

4 Conclusion

By organizing their field around conversations and the text/genre pairing of discourse, discourse analysts give some homogeneity to the space in which they work, but they marginalize those manifestations of discourse which fit ill with these presuppositions. However, there is an alternative conception that might be adopted, which is to consider that the world of discourse has neither center nor margins and that we need to take note of its fundamental heterogeneity, with all the difficulties that this implies.

References

Amossy, Ruth, *L'argumentation dans le discours*, Paris, Armand Colin, ³2012.
Biber, Douglas, *Variation across speech and writing*, Cambridge, Cambridge University Press, 1988.
Crystal, David/Davy, Derek, *Investigating English style*, London, Addison-Wesley Longman, 1969.
Fairclough, Norman, *Analysing discourse. Textual analysis for social research*, London, Routledge, 2003.
Foucault, Michel, *Qu'est-ce qu'un auteur ?*, in: Foucault, Michel, *Dits et écrits 1954–1988*, vol. 1: *1954–1969*, Paris, Gallimard, 1994, 789–821.
Harris, Zellig Sabbetai, *Discourse analysis*, Language 28 (1952), 1–30.
Maingueneau, Dominique, *Présentation*, Langages 117 (1995), 5–11.

Maingueneau, Dominique, *Analyser les textes de communication*, Paris, Dunod, 1998.
Maingueneau, Dominique, *Analysing self-constituting discourses*, Discourse studies 1 (1999), 175–199.
Maingueneau, Dominique, *La littérature pornographique*, Paris, Armand Colin, 2007.
Maingueneau, Dominique, *Discours et analyse du discours. Introduction*, Paris, Armand Colin, 2014.
Maingueneau, Dominique/Cossutta, Frédéric, *L'analyse des discours constituants*, Langages 117 (1995), 112–125, DOI: https://doi.org/10.3406/lgge.1995.1709.
Perelman, Chaïm/Olbrechts-Tyteca, Lucie, *Traité de l'argumentation. La nouvelle rhétorique*, Bruxelles, Éditions de l'Université de Bruxelles, 1958.
Sinclair, John, *Corpus, concordance, collocation*, Oxford, Oxford University Press, 1991.

Ruth Amossy
Chapter 12
Integrating argumentation in discourse analysis? Problems and challenges

Abstract: This paper justifies the need for Discourse Analysis to fully integrate argumentation as a constitutive element of discourse. A global presentation of the theory of argumentation in discourse, drawing upon New Rhetoric and Discourse Analysis as developed in France, shows how it differs from the new version of CDA (Critical Discourse Analysis) which is inspired by a normative approach to argumentation based on pragma-dialectics. It also endeavors to resolve the theoretical tensions between conceptions of argumentation borrowed from Aristotle and Perelman, and trends in Discourse Analysis based on contemporary views of the subject and the social and institutional constraints imposed upon discourse. The theoretical synthesis is followed by a concrete example – the micro-analysis of a polemical web post on the *burqa* in France. The paper concludes with a discussion about the ways in which analysis dealing with social discourse and social issues authorizes or excludes political or ethical engagement by researchers.

Keywords: argumentation, Discourse Analysis, subject, descriptive vs. normative analysis, commitment

Introduction

We know that Discourse Analysis, on the one hand, and theories of argumentation or rhetoric on the other, have not always sat happily together. The art of persuasion seemed too tainted with intentionality, and not sensitive enough to power relationships to attract the attention of early discourse analysts.[1] Indeed, these latter, in the wake of Pêcheux (1969), sought to discern the ideology at work in the

---

[1] For more details on the early French school of Discourse Analysis, see Dominique Maingueneau's chapter in this book.

Translated from: *Faut-il intégrer l'argumentation dans l'analyse du discours ? Problématiques et enjeux*, Argumentation et Analyse du Discours 9 (2012), DOI: https://doi.org/10.4000/aad.1346

Ruth Amossy, Tel Aviv University, ADARR, אוניברסיטת תל אביב

text, while condemning the mirage of the subject as controller of significations. Influenced by Foucault and Althusser among others, they could not but ignore Perelman/Olbrechts Tyteca's New rhetoric of Aristotelian inspiration, even though it was published as early as 1958. Although this first "French school" was gradually eclipsed in favor of less ideological approaches, those espousing the Discourse Analysis trends which appeared in France in the 1980s, and especially the 1990s, continued to show their mistrust of the rhetorical tradition, even though rhetoric was at the origin of the study of language considered from the angles of action, enunciation, and communication. Dominique Maingueneau expresses this mistrust when he notes in his important 1991 summary:

> There is an irreducible split between rhetoric and its modern extensions (the multiple techniques for effective communication, for persuasion...) and DA: while the former supposes a predominant subject 'using' 'processes' to fulfil an explicit aim, for the latter the forms of subjectivity are implied in the very conditions for possible discursive formation. (1991, 234)[2]

We can see that the question of agency which is dear to rhetoric is largely at the source of this split.[3] Furthermore, rhetorical argumentation[4] is rejected insofar as, in the great Aristotelian tradition, it is founded on universals and delights in taxonomies that are, by definition, timeless.

However, attempts to bring together the two fields of study are becoming ever more apparent. I should point out that the complementarity (or fusion) of rhetoric and argumentation, on the one hand, and Discourse Analysis on the other, is part of a more extensive area of studies which establishes a close link between linguistics and rhetoric. The first work dates from the pioneering articles by Jakobson (1963) and then the μ Group (1970), which are essentially devoted to the linguistic analysis of figures from the structuralist perspective that was then

---

[2] "Il demeure une coupure irréductible entre [la] rhétorique et ses prolongements modernes (les multiples techniques de la communication efficace, de la persuasion...) et l'AD : alors que la première suppose un sujet souverain 'utilisant' des 'procédés' au service d'une finalité explicite, pour la seconde les formes de subjectivité sont impliquées dans les conditions mêmes de possibilité d'une formation discursive." (All subsequent translations from other works are by Rosemary Rodwell, the translator of this article, unless stated otherwise.)

[3] The question of agency has been the subject of numerous debates in American rhetoric in the light of contemporary theories of subjectivity. We find traces of it in Geisler (2004), among others.

[4] I am dealing here with rhetoric defined in the Aristotelian tradition as the art of persuasion, which is to say as argumentation. The two terms are therefore synonymous, as in the work by Perelman/Olbrechts-Tyteca titled *Traité de l'argumentation. La nouvelle rhétorique*. The English translation has reversed the order of the titles, putting *La nouvelle rhétorique* first. We can therefore speak equally of argumentative rhetoric (in contrast to the rhetoric of figures, for example) or rhetorical argumentation (in contrast to Ducrot's linguistic argumentation, for example) depending on the trend one wishes to differ from. For further clarification, see Amossy/Koren (2009).

dominant. However, even though the argumentative nature of figures is possibly recognized by the trends stemming from language studies, these mainly examine *elocutio* and do not concern themselves with persuasion. Moreover, the notion of argumentation has been introduced wholesale into language studies by the trend known as argumentation in language, which was started by Anscombre/Ducrot (1988). We know that this was a pragmatic-semantic theory which intended to show how the line of argument determines the sense of utterances. In this sense, argumentation is a constitutive element of language, and not of discourse. Furthermore, Ducrot (2004) insists on the fact that he is interested in linguistic argumentation as a sequence of utterances, and not as *logos* with the aim to persuade, in which speech is also reason. These two trends – the linguistic study of figures, and argumentation in language – open up fertile fields of research, which are not however relevant to the present undertaking, which is to articulate the linguistics of discourse and, more specifically, the French Discourse Analysis trend and rhetorical argumentation.

1 Theoretical insights

1.1 The place of discourse in argumentation theories: The new rhetoric and pragma-dialectics

It is perhaps not superfluous to recall that it was argumentation specialists who were initially interested in the linguistic aspect of their discipline. Indeed, faced with studies focused on argument and its logical validity (such as informal logic), we find trends whose central preoccupations were the communicational and linguistic aspect of rhetorical argumentation. The most notable example of this is the New rhetoric of Perelman/Olbrechts-Tyteca (1969). The authors start from the dynamic which links an orator and a listener, and they devote a major part of their study to the verbal aspect of techniques designed to elicit agreement. This study of the language elements which relate to the enunciative framework, to the addressee, the lexicon, hedges, qualifications, etc. – are highly valuable for analyzing persuasive discourse. However, as I have shown elsewhere (Amossy 2002), the study is nonetheless based on a notional system derived from a very traditional conception of linguistics and grammar. Furthermore, the chapter titled "Présentation des données et formes du discours" ('Presentation of data and forms of discourse') is not structured around a classification of arguments and topics which take pride of place; the two enterprises remain separate and autonomous. Consequently, the exploration of the role of language only indirectly casts light on the overall functioning of persuasive discourse and does not lead to a practice of analysis. In fact, this undertaking, as such, was of little interest to Chaïm Perelman; as a philosopher and a philosopher of law, he had only an occasional interest in language.

It was not the same for pragma-dialectics, which was based on the advances in the philosophy of language developed by Austin and Searle, and designed to adapt it to a normative view of argumentation. This was perceived as a verbal process which aimed to resolve differences by means of critical discussion, itself founded on the norms of rationality:

> Such an analysis is 'pragmatic' in viewing the discourse as essentially an exchange of speech acts; it is 'dialectic' in viewing this exchange as a methodical attempt to resolve a difference of opinion. (Van Eemeren/Grootendorst/Snoeck-Henkemans 1996, 29)

More precisely, in the critical discussion, the two parties together examine the acceptability of antagonistic viewpoints in a confrontation according to the rules; they verify the extent to which the positions put forward appear plausible to the two parties, in the light of the counter-arguments provided by each of them. The exchange takes place in four stages, or phases by which the argumentative process develops: the confrontation (emergence of the disagreement), the opening (engagement in a resolution procedure based on a minimal number of shared premises), the argumentation (defense and refutation of points of view), and the conclusion (both parties determining the results, which must lead to the difference being resolved). This four-stage critical discussion is subject to a set of ten rules which guarantee that the rational exchange proceeds smoothly, and where any breach of the rules is considered as a fallacy. To reconstruct the argumentation from the basis of empirical data (and therefore of the discourse in its materiality), it is necessary to identify the different speech acts which occur at each of the numbered stages (Van Eemeren/Grootendorst 1984). These are of four types: the assertive, the commissive, the directive, and the declarative, each one playing a particular and more or less decisive role in each phase of the critical discussion (a synoptic table of this is shown on page 289 of Van Eemeren/Grootendorst/Snoeck-Henkemans 1996). Identifying these speech acts and analyzing how they are linked and structured enables us to deal with the demands of pragma-dialectic description; while assessing how far the critical rules have been respected or infringed enables us to guarantee the normative dimension of pragma-dialectics – to judge the argumentative exchange by seeing whether the rational and ethical norms necessary to resolve conflicts of opinion have been respected. In short, this is an approach which considers that the theory of argumentation must be firmly rooted in the pragmatics of speech acts. At the same time, it is meant to be deliberately normative: it is not simply about describing the way in which the verbal argumentation takes place on the ground but, on the contrary, about assessing how well the critical discussion proceeds and provide criteria which can ensure its success.

These two important models – New rhetoric and pragma-dialectics – are certainly not exclusive, but they are potentially fruitful both because of their widespread dissemination and because they present two very different ways of adopting linguistic approaches that are likely to provide a rhetorical argumentation theory with one of its constitutive dimensions. The two approaches doubtless show common features. Both of them accord pre-eminence to an exchange founded on reason, which may enable the interlocutors to reach a point of agreement. The person presenting the argument appears as someone endowed with reason who consciously and deliberately pursues strategies of persuasion or engages in a critical exchange for the purpose of finding an agreement based on what is reasonable – i.e. what can appear plausible and acceptable to the various interlocutors. However, the New rhetoric relates to different enunciative, lexical, grammatical, and other elements that are likely to contribute to a descriptive study of the way argumentation functions in a communicational context. It highlights the attributes of various discursive elements which, combined with the deployment of arguments and topics, and used advisedly, can prove effective in the attempt to win minds over to a particular theory. As for the Amsterdam school, its pragma-dialectics draw on the theory of speech acts to provide its discursive foundations to a normative model of argumentation. It is in relation to this dual model that I will attempt to outline the methods of integrating argumentation into Discourse Analysis, which is what distinguishes the theory known as "Argumentation in Discourse" (Amossy 2021 [2000]). This will be done by comparing it with the new, fascinating enterprise of "Critical Discourse Analysis" proposed by Fairclough/Fairclough (2012).

1.2 The place of argumentation in Discourse Analysis

When the question of argumentation and language arises, Discourse Analysis modifies the perspectives and inverts the hierarchies – provided it wishes to take account of the argumentative element. Indeed, Discourse Analysis is not concerned to explore the linguistic dimensions of argumentation in order to enrich the theory of argumentation. It is rather about seeing how analysis can integrate the argumentative element to cast light on the functioning of discourse in given situations as exhaustively as possible. The purpose of the investigation thereafter is to look at language in use and in situations in its socio-discursive aspects, and at the many functions it can fulfil in the social arena.

It was in this perspective that Dominique Maingueneau devoted a place to argumentation in his work on *L'analyse du discours* (1991, 228–250), defined as an investigation of the 'verbal act mechanism which links the organization of a text to a specific social location' (Maingueneau 1991, 13).[5] He included it in a chapter on discursive coherence of which, according to him, argumentation was a privileged factor. To my knowledge, this was the first attempt in the French field to think of argumentation in the context of Discourse Analysis[6] – an interesting attempt which was not followed up in Maingueneau's later work. He underlined the problem raised by any analysis of arguments taken alone – namely, an "atomiste" ('atomistic') argumentative analysis (Plantin 1995, 258):

> It is not difficult to reveal a logical structure in such utterances [i.e. advertising], but to stop there means remaining well short of the effective complexity of discourse. Indeed, it is not sufficient to extract a logical framework from it; one must study what its function is in the discourse being considered, plunge it into the archive that gives it meaning; in what type and genre of discourse does this argumentation appear? At what stage of the text's development? Of what linguistic structures is it a part? What are the pragmatic effects? What norms, what premises are invoked? Are they explicit? And so on. (Maingueneau 1991, 230)[7]

Approaches taking account of linguistic materiality therefore stress that arguments are constructed in the thickness of discourse and only make sense within the interdiscursive network and communicational framework of which they are part. Consequently, we need to see how they are woven into the text; how the text includes them in a dynamic where the attempts to influence the other person call upon the most diverse verbal resources; the modalities according to which the discourse is situated within a global exchange in tune with pre-established arguments; and what social functions it fulfils in a particular sociocultural space.

From this perspective, the analysis of arguments or the verbal ordering of logical reasoning cannot be separated from the total discourse in which they are constructed. A first stage certainly consists in detaching them from the materiality of this discourse: an abstract pattern is detected by the reader/analyst from the linguistic traces and connected to a known model. In this way a pattern can

---

5 "[D]ispositif d'énonciation qui lie une organisation textuelle et un lieu social determiné."
6 I am not taking into account here the early work of Moeschler (1985) which studies argumentation in the context of conversational analysis, whose conceptual and methodological framework differs considerably from that of DA.
7 "Il n'est pas difficile de mettre à jour une structure logique dans de tels énoncés [i.e. publicitaires], mais à s'en tenir là on reste bien en deçà de la complexité effective du discours. Il ne suffit pas en effet de dégager une armature logique, il faut étudier quelle est sa fonction dans le discours considéré, la plonger dans l'archive qui lui donne sens ; dans quel type et quel genre de discours intervient cette argumentation ? à quelle phase du développement textuel ? dans quelles structures linguistiques s'inscrit-elle ? quels en sont les effets pragmatiques ? quelles normes, quelles prémisses sont invoquées ? sont-elles explicites ? etc."

be reconstructed which reflects that of argument by analogy, enthymeme, argument by consequence, or rule of justice. Once this pattern is reconstructed, it is still important to see how it is taken up by a discourse which confers upon it its meaning and force. In short, it is not a question of identifying and labelling arguments by means of a prior taxonomy, still less of assessing them, but of seeing how they are put into words. We might note that, in this procedure, the *logos* as reason and discourse finds its ideal unity. It is by taking account of both the abstract patterns of reasoning (to which discourse analysts give barely a thought) and the material procedures of putting into words (neglected by argumentation theorists) that it is possible to highlight the ways language is used in context while integrating its intentions to exert an influence on the audience.

1.3 A socio-discursive approach to argumentation

In the socio-discursive perspective unanimously adopted by discourse analysts of all allegiances, emphasis is placed not only on the way arguments are put into words, but also on the institutional constraints, doxic and ideological encumbrances, and power relations. Analysis therefore has to isolate the constitutive elements of verbal argumentation by relating them to a situation of discourse, to relationships of place, and to an inter-discourse full of received ideas and pre-formed arguments. This is tantamount to saying that argumentation appears to be shaped by social constraints, and, in its turn, shapes society.

Arguers can therefore only exercise their wishes in the social and institutional frameworks within which their words are spoken – even though these constraints are often concealed from them through habit (if not habitus) and the self-evident beliefs which naturalize and mask underlying socio-political forces. Doubtless, from this perspective one might question what fate is reserved for the notions of purpose, project, choice, strategy, free adherence of listeners, and thus for agency, which are at the root of rhetorical argumentation. The solution to this problem seems to have been well formulated by Charaudeau (2007, 15): if 'the communication situation partially over-determines the actors, giving them instructions for producing and interpreting speech acts' and is therefore 'constructive of meaning', nevertheless 'any speech act is under the responsibility of a *subject* who is both *limited* by the situation and free to proceed to put into discourse what he judges to be fitting for his speech plan'.[8] Marc Angenot (2012, 67)

---

8 "La situation de communication surdétermine en partie [l]es acteurs, leur donne des instructions de production et d'interprétation des actes langagiers [...] constructrice de sens [...] tout

offers a more robust and extreme expression of this position. According to him, recognizing the limits of the thinkable and describable in a given society should not lead us to see 'humans as mystified and conditioned by their environment and ultimately as illusory subjects, like puppets or parrots, of a social [world] reduced to needs and interests...'[9] In other words, social regulation and determination do not bar the possibility of an exchange where subjects engage in a scheme to mutually influence one another, and where the speaker makes free choices for which he is fully accountable. We then rediscover the agency at the heart of rhetoric, which supposes that the speakers are capable of initiative and action, through which they endow themselves with a certain power to influence reality; and that this freedom carries with it a responsibility.

A triple movement is thus performed: one which reintroduces abstract reasoning into the global functioning of discourse without being dissolved in it; one which reintroduces argumentation into a social space that includes norms, institutional constraints and power relations which limit without diluting the endeavor to persuade; and one which deprives the arguer of absolute control by causing the social forces conditioning him to re-emerge, without removing his freedom and responsibility. It is in this perspective that Discourse Analysis can resume responsibility for rhetorical argumentation by ironing out the incompatibilities which at first sight seemed to irremediably separate the two disciplines.

1.4 Argumentation in discourse and rhetoric

Among discourse analysts, Patrick Charaudeau appears closest to this program when he speaks of a "problématique d'influence" ('problem of influence', Charaudeau 2008, I), by decreeing that 'argumentation is part of a general problem of influence: any speaker seeks to make the other share his world of discourse' (2007, 14).[10] He undertakes to study linguistic processes "by taking the viewpoint of the subject of the discourse", that is to say by examining the "problems presented to him when he seeks to persuade someone: how to enter into contact with the other, what position of authority to adopt toward the other,

---

acte de langage se trouve sous la responsabilité d'un *sujet* qui est à la fois *contraint* par la situation et libre de procéder à la mise en discours qu'il jugera adéquate à son projet de parole."
9 "Les humains comme mystifiés et conditionnés par le milieu et au bout du compte comme des sujets illusoires, comme des marionnettes ou des perroquets d'un social réduit à des besoins et des intérêts..."
10 "L'argumentation s'inscrit dans une problématique générale d'influence : tout sujet parlant cherche à faire partager à l'autre son univers de discours."

how to affect the other, and, consequently, how to order his speech".[11] The discourse analyst thus insists on the need to examine verbal attempts to act upon the other which are not limited to the use of arguments or to models of argumentative linking. In this approach, he sees argumentation to be fully integrated into Discourse Analysis, as he clearly says in the conclusion to his 2008 article.

However, Charaudeau sees in rhetoric an obsolete discipline, and suggests replacing it with contemporary human sciences. Furthermore, Charaudeau's analyses of political discourse mainly underline the ways in which the listener is caught in the trap of the coercive project of the arguer. Argumentation as making-believe then appears destined to control the other rather than engage with him/her in a partly restricted dialogue in which the partner could play a role and manifest his/her freedom. This is to say that for the Discourse Analysis expert, exploring argumentation enables him/her primarily to identify the power relations involved, and to stress the relationship between discourse and power.

Although it intersects with this work, the theory of Argumentation in Discourse that I have been developing since its first synthesis in 2000, proclaims the rhetorical legacy loud and clear (particularly that of Chaïm Perelman). It reprises the view of rhetoric as a negotiation of difference (Meyer 2004, 11) which is achieved by the exchange between socially situated individuals who are responsible for their choices. Furthermore, the theory of Argumentation in Discourse clearly borrows its conceptual framework from Aristotle. It is really a matter of examining the way in which humans interact and mutually influence each other by bringing to bear all verbal means relating to the *logos*, the *ethos*, and the *pathos*; it is also a question of repositioning these exchanges within institutional contexts and genres of discourse, even if the tripartite division into legal, deliberative, and epideictic now appears too perfunctory in relation to the very wide diversification of discourses circulating in the contemporary world. The investigation is nevertheless led, as has been said, by means of an analytical process exploring *logos*, *ethos*, and *pathos*, thanks to the tools developed by contemporary language studies: linguistics of enunciation (*linguistique de l'énonciation*), pragmatics, argumentation in language, the study of verbal interactions, and so on.

---

[11] "En prenant le point de vue du sujet du discours [. . .] les problèmes qui se présentent à lui lorsqu'il cherche à persuader quelqu'un : comment entrer en contact avec l'autre, quelle position d'autorité adopter vis-à-vis de l'autre, comment toucher l'autre, et, conséquemment, comment ordonnancer son dire."

1.5 Argumentation as the constitutive dimension of discourse

At the same time, we should stress that attempts to interact and to elicit agreement do not necessarily occur in discourses that are designed to persuade, where clearly identifiable argumentative sequences are manifest. Here, the notion of argumentation is extended to its maximum insofar as it covers discourse genres that explicitly defend or refute a theory, as well as those which make do with directing ways of seeing and thinking. All speech tends toward sharing a point of a view, a way of reacting to a situation, or a feeling about a state of affairs. Its patterns of reasoning are more or less developed and more or less visible. Often, the direction given to the discourse appears in linguistic traces (hedging, axiological marks, connectives, etc.) without, however, a formal argument emerging. Sometimes, that argument is only uttered in an elliptical form which requires recourse to inter-discourse in order to be reconstructed. It is to distinguish discourses with a persuasive purpose from those intended simply to orient, problematize, share, etc. that I have established a difference between the argumentative goal and the argumentative dimension of discourse (Amossy 2005; 2010; see also Amossy 2018). It is interesting to note that this distinction (often controversial) echoes a remark by Dominique Maingueneau (1991, 228) of which little use has been made, about the definition of properly argumentative utterances:

> Do not all utterances possess an argumentative dimension, to various degrees? To resolve this difficulty, we usually need to make a distinction between *direct* and *indirect* argumentation, as only the first produces sequences which present themselves as argumentative.[12]

And Maingueneau adds that 'the division between the two is not very easy when it comes to the detail' (1991, 228),[13] an issue that merits deeper investigation.

This conception of argumentation, in its own particular way, reprises that of Grize (1990), who sees in it a way of acting upon the representations of the other, and through this on his opinions and attitudes, with the help of schematizations; or perhaps of Vignaux, who considers that 'to utter means to argue, owing to the simple fact that one chooses to say or put forward certain meanings rather than others' (Vignaux 1981, 91).[14] However, this is rejected by some who, like Christian

---

[12] "Est-ce que l'ensemble des énoncés ne possèdent pas, de près ou de loin, une dimension argumentative ? Pour résoudre cette difficulté on doit en général faire intervenir une distinction entre argumentation *directe* et *indirecte*, la première seule produisant des séquences qui se présentent comme argumentatives."
[13] "[L]e partage des deux n'est guère aisé dans le détail."
[14] "[É]noncer revient à argumenter, du simple fait qu'on choisit de dire ou d'avancer certains sens plutôt que d'autres."

Plantin, condemn it for 'breaking up the notion of argumentation in language' (Plantin 2005, 34),[15] a break-up that Plantin attempts to prevent by proposing a dialogical model based on 'the confrontation of contradictory points of view in response to the same question' (Plantin 2005, 53).[16] This model certainly complies with the Aristotelian tradition which only conceives of argumentation around a controversial question. We can, nevertheless, see in it one scenario among others. Indeed, in a dialogical conception inspired by Bakhtin (1977), discourses answer, oppose, and reinforce one another; they form moving constellations proposing divergent, complementary or similar points of view on questions debated by the members of a given society. Strong and explicit opposition in discourses is then only one of the poles of argumentative communication. There are also other modalities, such as the reinforcement of agreement in the epideictic (Perelman/Olbrechts-Tyteca 1970), or the co-construction of responses. One might say that the confrontation of viewpoints, especially when it is polemical, is one of the poles of argumentation, the other being the argumentative dimension of discourses which reorient ways of thinking, seeing, and feeling, without explicitly revealing themselves as attempts to persuade.

To be specific, the wider definition of argumentation leads us to detect in it a constitutive dimension of discourse. By this we understand that if the discourse comprises indispensable elements which make it such, argumentation belongs to it in the same way as do enunciation as the use of language by a speaker, or dialogism – which postulates that every word is always a response to the word of the other. The trend initiated by the work of Émile Benveniste has clearly highlighted the constituents and functioning of enunciation, to be inserted in the context of an exchange between enunciator(s) and enunciatee(s). In his wake, the question of subjectivity has been rethought in discursive terms in order to see how it was embedded in language in evaluative or axiological terms, up to and including the enunciative deletion practices which attempt to erase it (known in French as "effacement énonciatif"). Moreover, the Bakhtinian notion of dialogism, taken up and extended by the concepts of inter-text and inter-discourse, has enabled the text to be grasped in the circulation of discourses in which it participates, showing how it is constructed in relation to the speech of the other and woven into the weft of what has already been said. Pragmatics, on the other hand, has insisted on the fact that saying is also doing: speech is action. It is where all these constituents meet – the use of language in situation, dialogism, speech as action – that Argumentation in Discourse is situated, understood as a constitu-

---

15 "[D]issolution de la notion d'argumentation dans le langage".
16 "[C]onfrontation de points de vue en contradiction en réponse à une même question".

tive dimension not of language (Ducrot 2004) but of discourse: verbal exchange clarifies things in a certain light, reinforcing or modifying the viewpoint in the same way as it reinforces, reorients or modifies the common values underlying it.

1.6 Descriptive and normative approaches

Broadly speaking, we can therefore say that the theory of Argumentation in Discourse proposes to integrate rhetorical argumentation into Discourse Analysis and is expressed through a certain analytical practice. This practice is neither normative, nor "critical" in the sense that it is not proposing to evaluate or condemn the discourses it scrutinizes. Unlike CDA, which sees itself as an integral part of a critical project developed within social sciences, the contemporary French trend of Discourse Analysis (which differs in this from the early French school of Discourse Analysis) has no preconceived ideological program. Because it is seen in this perspective, the theory of Argumentation in Discourse is linked to the theories of argumentation in a totally different way from that recently proposed by Fairclough/Fairclough (2012a; 2012b). Indeed, the supporters of CDA revitalize the discipline by drawing on argumentation theories, and particularly on pragma-dialectics, in their normative aspect. Reconstruction of the argumentation that takes place in political discourse enables them to assess the logical validity of the reasoning presented to the other and to detect anything that departs from the strict rules of the debate; this is understood in both a Habermassian and an Aristotelian sense, linking rationality to the ethics of discussion. Argumentation based on debate as a reasoned exchange about the choices and collective action to be taken in view of the common good, then enables CDA supporters to investigate an essential dimension of political discourse in a critical fashion. It also allows them to judge discursive practices in terms of pre-established argumentative norms.

The intention of Argumentation in Discourse, in its close relation to the French trend of Discourse Analysis, is, on the contrary, to account for the way in which discourse works and fulfils certain functions on the ground, without making a judgment about it. Although it draws on a theory of argumentation, it is not on the normative viewpoint of pragma-dialectics, but on rhetorical argumentation as a study of the communication system and discursive techniques which persuade somebody to espouse a certain position. Unlike the work of Norman Fairclough, which is part of a venture in social criticism that exposes the manipulative practices and harmful political ideologies in discourse, it has no predetermined mission, and does not set out to be ideologically or politically engaged.

We might speak of a "descriptive" method in the sense that it intends to report on the very complexity of a process, without comparing it to an ideal norm: here, "descriptive" acquires its meaning from its opposition to "normative". But it is first and foremost an analytical practice. Indeed, this practice deconstructs the discourse in order to discover its constituents and to reconstruct, behind the material concretization on the surface, the underlying model and the logic which animates it in a given socio-institutional situation. In doing this, it reveals a discursive functioning in its very regulation, and highlights a system that is not apparent to the naked eye. Its intention is to identify the particular logic that presides over the development of concrete discourse, without judging it in terms of universal standards of validity. It takes account of the variety and differences in discourse, and the links and ruptures established between them. Indeed, if we consider that argumentation is 'not an empty space in which a demonstration might be constructed', but an 'intervention in a saturated and cacophonic social discourse' (Angenot 2012, 67),[17] putting things into words and the management of reasoning vary according to the social settings, the cultures, and the times in which they are used. Marc Angenot (2012, 42) clearly highlights this aspect by adopting a historical perspective: he notes the extent to which the 'reasoning through which a human in the past invited a particular audience to admit as credible and 'adopt' [a] theory'[18] can seem shocking to contemporaries. Perelman said that the notion of reasonable – what appears plausible and acceptable to a given group – is relative and changing. There are therefore no criteria of absolute validity enabling the other person to be taxed with irrationality and his methods of reasoning to be condemned; there are alternative rationalities that should be assessed in terms of the belief systems and prevailing ways of thinking in the space to which the examined discourse belongs.

These are the principles that I would now like to exemplify by means of a concrete analysis based on the recognized advances in language studies and argumentation theories.

---

17 "[N]on un espace vide où se construirait une démonstration [. . .] une intervention dans un discours social saturé et cacophonique."
18 "[R]raisonnements par lesquels un humain du passé invitait un auditoire déterminé à admettre pour crédible et à 'adopter'[une] thèse."

2 Argumentative and discursive analysis: The example of a post on the burqa

2.1 An argumentative and evaluative analysis

Let us take a concrete example to briefly test this practice of analysis, in the context of a micro-analysis that will enable us to demonstrate the different points referred to above. I have chosen a message posted in an on-line discussion forum which does not comply with classical canons of argumentation, but nevertheless has a persuasive objective in the context of a verbal exchange between several participants. It is a post reacting to an article in the left-wing magazine Marianne, condemning the wearing of the burqa in France and calling for legislation on the subject. An opposing demand is forcefully expressed by an internet user, claiming that Muslims should be free to wear the full veil: "For freedom of expression and the rite of woman to ware what they desir. When you see men in djellabas in the street, no-one says nothing to them!!!!" (sic) 'Pour la liberté d'expression et le droit aux femme de se vêtir comme elles le désir. Les hommes en djelaba dans la rue ont leurs dit rien !!!!' (sic).

What happens when we attempt to make a purely argumentative analysis of this text, concentrating only on its argumentative content? At the level of pure reasoning, we find a dual construction in this post. The first is an enthymeme. Its major premise is implicit: freedom of expression is an important (democratic) value. The minor premise suggests that dress (in this case the burqa or the djellaba) is an individual or collective mode of expression; the conclusion is that women have the right to express themselves by wearing a burqa. The second construction involves an argumentation by analogy: A – the burqa – is analogous to B – the djellaba – in that they share the same characteristic C: they are both (over)garments worn by Muslims in public spaces. What is legitimate for B should also be so for A. In other words, if the djellaba is allowed to be worn in the French street, then the burqa should also be acceptable by virtue of the similarity C between them.

If we remain at the level of informal logic, paying close attention to the reasoning and being careful to evaluate its logical validity separately from its verbal formulation, we can conduct a standard analysis in terms of fallacies. It is thus possible to detect the fallacious character of the argument in the poor use of analogy. It is a matter of seeing whether the similarity between A and B justifies applying the same assessment criteria to them, or if differences appear, demanding that they should not be treated similarly. Thus, for example, one can argue that the burqa, unlike the djellaba, is not a simple item of clothing but a religious sign (it claims to be a response to divine precepts). Furthermore, it is unique to women, its purpose being that they should be hidden from the male gaze; while the djellaba is a long, sleeveless, occasionally hooded coat that is an Eastern fashion (with no relationship to religious customs) and can be worn by either men or women. These differences, which concern the divergent relationships of A and B to religious practice and the female sex, would be seen to prevail over the similarity at the basis of the initial analogy. Analysts would then condemn an "amalgam", that is to say a false analogy which wrongly justifies the unequal treatment applied to the burqa and the djellaba in France. We can see that, in doing this, they would become engaged in the debate as they refute the argument put forward by one of the parties by negatively evaluating its logical validity.

We are able to perceive here the meaning of analysis. It consists of a dual process. On the one hand, it extracts abstract patterns from the materiality of the utterances in order to reconstruct the reasoning. It finds them by drawing them out from underneath the veneer of verbal formulations, and then turns the utterances into logical propositions, paraphrasing them at the cost of diluting the discourse. One might say that argumentation specialists look for the framework rather than the texture, or flesh of the text. In fact, the supporters of informal logic do not deny this. The process seems to them not only acceptable, but necessary insofar as it appears to be the sole means of extricating the structure of the argument for the purpose of reconstructing and evaluating it. Indeed, the second part of the procedure here is of a normative and evaluative order. It aims at measuring the argument's logical validity according to established criteria. Theoreticians of argumentation belonging both to informal logic and to pragma-dialectics then act as censors: they defend the rights of reason by measuring the argumentation put forward against the standards of good reasoning and try to maintain an ideal that is likely to guide humans in their attempts at debate and rational exchange. Analysis is then defined both by the reconstruction of arguments and the assessment of their validity in the light of established criteria.

2.2 An argumentative and discursive analysis of utterances in situation

What happens when we examine not arguments in themselves, but utterances in their situational contexts? First of all, we need to refer to the genre of discourse in order to grasp speech in action, in all its possibilities and constraints. In this case, it happens to be a post – an electronic message posted on a discussion forum, which is in principle open to everyone. This explains the faults of style in the message, which does not mean it is ipso facto disqualified. The internet user is indicated, as is common practice, by a pseudonym, and takes part in an on-line debate about a controversial question of public interest: the forum is a virtual agora where opinion is formed by the exchange, or even confrontation, of divergent or adverse opinions. The speaker's objective is therefore to intervene in the debate about the authorization or legal prohibition of the full veil in public places, which it is suggested should be sanctioned by law.

In fact, this post is openly polemical insofar as it is presented as a counter-discourse participating in the polarization of antagonistic positions. It does not only offer a more or less valid process of reasoning; it also takes up a strong position in a debate where conflicting views are opposed and where the internet user takes the side of those who violently object to the position adopted by the Marianne journalist against the wearing of the burqa in France. The text is then subject to two sets of rules: that of the electronic forum genre, which authorizes brief and almost elliptical comments, acquiring its meaning against the background of a general argument circulating in the public space; and that of the polemical discourse, often expressed in the form of "flames" or a virulent and unbridled attack against the adversary in cyberspace.[19] It is in this particular situation and this framework of communication (a polemical discourse on the web, in the genre of an on-line discussion forum) that *logos* – discourse as language and reason – is constructed.

Now, the post is composed of three juxtaposed elements: an appeal with the value of a slogan, a justification, and a hyperlink.

The polemical reaction of the internet user to the Marianne article is virulent, and what must first be underlined is the vehemence, and even verbal violence, that is used. It is linked to the character of the acknowledgment made by the utterance through the syntactic form: "For X", a phrase which indicates that a position is adopted in a situation where a choice has to be made (for/against). The presupposition is therefore that the opponent (the Marianne journalist and all her followers, who are hostile to the wearing of the burqa) are against freedom of expression. It reprises a parallel that is already used in the argument about the veil in France, namely that the banning of the burqa = an assault on the freedom of expression which is the foundation of democracy.

The phrase also acts as an appeal for militancy. In this context, it is not a matter of giving reasons, but of defending a cause that has been attacked and of brandishing a phrase which appears as a slogan. This phrase – "for X" – has to

---

[19] This analysis is based on a vast literature concerning the regulation of discussion forums, the "flames" phenomenon, and the question of polemics, which I will not cite here for reasons of economy.

present a widely shared value in order not to require immediate justification and be able to dispense with presenting any proof. The fact that it draws on a familiar argument gives it this secure foundation. The readers – and other internet users – are summoned: they are called upon not to let themselves be convinced by arguments, but to rally around a banner, and to defend an already-known cause that is presented as their own. In short, the utterance is an act asserting a demand, and an implicit act of protest. That it partakes of an action is strongly emphasized by the link given at the end of the post, to a petition to sign against a law said to be Islamophobic. It is a matter of making speech a weapon that is able to gather all readers together in the same civic action.

As for justification, we might note that what is put forward is primarily the idea of the great principle flouted: freedom of expression is here elevated to the rank of supreme value. It is followed by the concrete example of this principle in the case at issue – in this instance, freedom consists in letting the individuals dress as they like, and not imposing limitations on it. Choice of clothing is an individual decision that cannot be subject to constraints. By using the word "and" to link the two phrases, "For freedom of expression" *and* "the rite of woman to ware what they desir", the post presupposes that the two things are intimately connected – the "and" introduces a parallel between the two segments. What is more, the second segment, "to ware what they desir", appears as the continuation and consequence of "freedom of expression" (the second is deduced from the first – the right to dress as one wants is an example of individual freedom of expression). From this perspective, wearing the burqa appears as one way of dressing just like another; it is an innocuous form of clothing resulting from a personal choice. However, if one remembers that the burqa is interpreted as a mark of allegiance to Islam, it means that, at the same time, the post is defending – albeit implicitly – the freedom to assert one's religious or community identity in the public space ("in the street"). This aspect is partly covered by the principle of individual freedom, so that the community demand (taken up in the link) only appears indirectly.

Finally, freedom of expression supposes the possibility of a choice made from the heart, which is reinforced by the selection of the word "desir". It evokes women's free will to adopt the burqa which also, in its connotations, refers back to "desir" (emphasized by the faults of grammar): "the rite of woman to ware what they desir". The inversion of the notion of "desire" is flagrant here: the act of completely concealing the face and body becomes synonymous with (amorous) desire, reflecting pleasure. What is implicitly suggested is that women satisfy their desire by wearing this form of dress which conceals them from the eyes of the public – and from men. The suggestion runs counter to what is said elsewhere, namely that this accoutrement is imposed upon women and deprives them of their liberty, autonomy and a free relationship with their body. Here, the polemic is at its height, without the opposition between the two conceptions of freedom – that of dressing as one wants, and that of freely exposing oneself to the gaze of others – being clearly stated. The counter-argument is not dealt with and is therefore not refuted in accordance with the rules. The speech offered in the name of important principles and the act of appeal both authorize and cover the absence of real counter-argumentation by playing on what seems obvious. At the same time, they suggest that the women whom secular French people are quick to aid find their satisfaction in another way of life, and that it is inappropriate for those who do not understand it to condemn this by ignoring the free will and wishes of the women involved.

The speaker embeds his/her affectivity in the discourse by means of punchy elliptical syntax, but also in the numerous exclamation marks following the second utterance. These manifest his/her revolt in the face of an injustice; it is an explosion of indignation in which s/he wishes the readers to participate. The effect of pathos now comes in to support the reasoning. It is allied to the argument by the analogy already mentioned, and to what Perelman calls the rule of justice: what is valid for X is also valid for Y, when there is equality between two parties. The clumsy style indicates that this is not a trivial infringement of the rule of justice, which should be the norm, but a shameful and revolting transgression which should be publicly condemned.

The presupposition of the on-line appeal is that men and women are equal, and that what is due to one is automatically due to the other. The refusal to let women wear a (local) item of clothing would be an infringement not only of the rule of justice, but also of women's right to liberty and equality. The internet user thus constructs an alternative ethos as a defender of women's rights, which is opposed to the ethos of those who defend the right of women not to hide their faces from the gaze of passers-by and to own and control their own bodies. S/he demands an identification that is both rational and passionate on the part of his/her listeners, who are supposed to be appalled by the fact that "when you see men in djellabas [...] no-one says nothing to them" whereas "they" want to prohibit women wearing burqas. In doing this, the internet user projects the image of an audience s/he supposes to be similar to him/her: imbued with the principle of sexual equality and the right of women to own their own bodies – feminist and republican principles which are precisely those defended by the weekly magazine, Marianne, in which the forum is situated. S/he thus attempts to turn his/her own weapons against the adversary by a process of rhetorical retorsion.

The appeal therefore appears as a defense of the individual liberties of both sexes, but primarily those of women. The post genre and the compulsory fictitious name play an important role here, because we do not know if the internet user is a man or a woman. "Alier", which means nothing in French, is unisex. The fact that the discourse shows no sign of feminization allows the uncertainty to remain. The post appears as a message that is universal in scope and does not differentiate between the sexes. It even neutralizes the impact of belonging to a "gender" in a quarrel that deals with female clothing and behavior. It deliberately remains at the level of principles that each and every one should accept and recognize.

The neutrality of this ethos of a principled citizen who refuses to be categorized in terms of "gender" is, however, blurred by the particularly poor level of language, which immediately signals the internet user's lack of education. The numerous and crude faults of grammar and spelling tell us that this is an individual without much schooling, who does not know how to use language well. The digital message conveys a working-class voice, which does not bother about well-developed reasoning. It is therefore interesting to see that the internet user exploits a major characteristic of the genre, which is the possibility of links and hypertexts: at the end of the post s/he adds a link to a petition "against a new Islamophobic law". Probably, as we have already said, the insertion of the link to the petition reinforces the character of the discourse as an act – an appeal and a demand. On the other hand, the text of the petition forms an extreme contrast to the post because it offers an elaborate argumentation that the signatories accept. What is more, it shifts Alier's argument. In fact, the petition presents the law against the burqa as an attack against Muslims and a mark of Islamophobia – which the post does not. The internet user thus makes the reader pass from defending women's liberty to defending the Muslims of France, from feminism to antiracism. S/he also makes sure his/her brief and terse post adjoins a closely reasoned text based on clearly explained logic.

But there is more still: the petition, which begins with "We, citizens of the French Republic, teachers, elected representatives, intellectuals, company directors, and members of civil society of all confessions", insists not only on the assembly of citizens, but also on the intervention of people of letters, and individuals of intellectual standing and social prestige. As we have said, the internet user employs very simple language that is full of mistakes. The ethos that is involuntarily but probably consciously projected, of an uncultivated man or woman without education is thus offset by the figure of the signatory constructed by the petition given in the hypertext. In fact, the image of Alier is capable of producing a dual effect. The ignorance of the man or woman defending the great principles of liberty and equality could act against him/her: how would s/he be fit to judge in a public controversy? But this untutored image may also project the ethos of a simple person emitting a *cri de cœur*, who speaks to others in everyday language, the language of the street – an almost childlike language: "when you see men in djellaba in the street, no-one says nothing to them" is reminiscent of the recriminations of children when they feel they are victims of an injustice: "No-one says anything to *him*!".

3 By way of conclusion: The analyst's position

The question posed here is not how an analysis of this brief fragment from an on-line forum enables us to assess its logical validity or to judge its deliberative value in the democratic sphere. The argumentative and discursive micro-analysis consists in highlighting the way the selected post works, in order to better understand how a *quidam*, especially one with little education, participates in a public exchange about a social issue; the way in which popular reasoning of a polemical type – the logic of which needs to be understood – is constructed in a certain culture; and the means by which a polemical discourse can fulfil the function of protesting and rallying support on the internet. It also enables us to reconstruct the system of reasoning and justification which supports the position expressed, by reintroducing the elliptical utterance into its inter-text, and indexing it to the arguments it feeds on. Showing that reasoning, strongly infused with affectivity, is of the order of feeling and not only of rational conviction, is not to invalidate it, but to highlight the way in which *pathos* and *logos* are connected in moral emotions such as indignation. This process underlines the passionate nature of the commitment that leads people to militate in favor, not only of freedom of expression, but also of the Muslims (both male and female) of France whose ways of life and religious practice are attacked. Generally speaking, it appears that the argumentative value of a selected discourse cannot be measured in itself, according to abstract criteria of rationality. The post defending the wearing of the burqa is in tune with all the opinions, beliefs, and conflicts that go to make up the social discourse of the moment, and it is in this sociocultural space that its peculiar logic is developed.

From this perspective, analysts do not condemn the defense of the full veil and neither do they accuse the opponent of irrationality. They find, at both the argumentative level (patterns) and the discursive level (putting into words) the elements composing the discourse that is designed to be read in the public space of the internet; they examine the way these elements are organized in order to produce their meaning and effects; they relate them to the inter-discourse to see what sustains the post and what it produces in return. By doing this, they expose the social determination that weighs upon the discourse as well as the possibilities for adopting a position or taking civil action that it offers to the speaker.

An analysis that dissects and then reconstructs a discursive object in order to understand its functioning, internal logic, and implications, is an undertaking that breaks entirely with the normative theories of argumentation and critical approaches to Discourse Analysis. From a certain point of view, however, this "disengagement" is not without its problems. Indeed, normative theories of argumentation, which sort the wheat from the chaff and establish the logical validity of arguments, have a social mission. They teach citizens to detect fallacious reasoning, to make sure that debates proceed correctly, and to defend the democratic values on which their regime is founded. Their critical and prescriptive approach has an educational purpose. What is more, it aims to play a social role by improving our ability to construct a public space in which the affairs of the city can be discussed rationally in order to arrive at a negotiated agreement. In this sense, argumentation theories are not purely scientific undertakings. Their aim is to contribute to conflict resolution, to the good management of human affairs, and to the implementation of governance that is worthy of its name. This is why they are compatible with Critical Discourse Analysis, which announces its social objectives right from the outset and puts its expertise at the service of an existing ideal – for example, the criticism of neo-liberalism, thought to be destructive for our democratic societies.

However, the theory of Argumentation in Discourse does not submit to these normative and critical objectives; it has no prescriptive vocation. It attempts to construct a (discursive) object that it highlights from the inside, in order to understand ways of saying, which are also ways of doing. It acknowledges diversity, plurality, and the existence of alternative rationalities. It allots itself the task of revealing and comprehending, which leads it to investigate a variety of discursive phenomena. Its corpora are always situated and examined in the social context that gave rise to them, where they fulfil functions that are important to determine. In this sense, it adopts the detached attitude of the ethnographer, who explores cultural phenomena that reveal the belief systems and ways of thinking of a particular human group; or perhaps the attitude of the historian attempting to piece together lifestyles and interactions, "mentalities" and cultural practices, in their socio-cultural conditions. The micro-analysis of the post on the burqa enables us to see how opponents of the legal ban on wearing the full veil reason and act verbally in the midst of a polemic that is tearing France apart. It also reveals the ways in which private citizens deprived of formal education think and communicate, and the use they make of the internet as a platform for expression, protest, and a call to rally over a controversial question.

At the same time, analysts can select corpora – such as the post about the burqa – that are in tune with the social issues being highlighted, and for which they provide tools for critical reflection. Although analysts do not directly adopt a position in the polemics as researchers, they nevertheless choose to play a part, in their own fashion, in the society to which they belong: they highlight problems, reveal the nature of the differences between social groups, and expose doxic foundations and divergent, often incompatible modes of reasoning. By doing this, they do more than offer their knowledge – they attempt to stimulate thinking by raising it above the level of the verbal confrontation in which the actors are trapped. "Ethnographers" or historians of contemporary life who describe their own societies have no intention of cutting themselves off from these: by analyzing the discourses that construct it, they attempt to look at it from a distance, thus enabling it to be considered more objectively. They are then free, in the subsequent stage, to pose as citizens who take a stand for or against what has been revealed, since it is now a matter of playing a part in the public sphere and of fighting for a collective decision (combating or promoting the bill against wearing the burqa in public spaces, for example).

Indeed, Discourse Analysis, and the related Argumentation in Discourse, is used for various purposes. The first is scientific, in the sense of making new knowledge part of common knowledge and casting new light on social phenomena in their discursive aspect (in Nathalie Heinich's definition, this is the role of the researcher, cf. Heinich 2002). The second may be pragmatic, in the sense of the use that different actors – institutions, companies, professionals, etc. – can make of the knowledge contributed by the discourse analyst (who then becomes an "expert" who is called upon; cf. Heinich 2002). City halls, decision-makers, and business leaders increasingly call upon the skills of discourse analysts in order to carry out concrete tasks. The third and final one is sociopolitical. It concerns the use made of Discourse Analysis to condemn ideologies considered to be harmful, and to combat positions considered as contrary to ethics. Heinich speaks of "thinker" with regard to this – a word synonymous with the notion of intellectual, as someone who tries to criticize or justify a situation in the way any citizen would do, but with the aid of his/her intellectual skills and prestige (Heinich 2002, 118). I would prefer to see in this a direct extension of the work of researchers, authorized by the actual results of their research. For analysts as researchers, knowledge helps to "understand the world and encourage mutual understanding"; for analysts as individuals involved in society, this same knowledge can contribute to "changing the world", producing a declared commitment based on this knowledge (Fleury-Vilatte/Walter 2003, 101). Rather than an opposition, it is about a distinction which aims to maintain the possibility for analysts to investigate their subject without bias, and to discern all its aspects in their complexity, not to say their tensions and aporias, without any ideological a priori.[20]

---

[20] The question of whether the rejection of axiological neutrality is vital in cases of flagrant attack on values or fundamental rights (Koren 2003, 276) nevertheless remains open. It is difficult to imagine that Discourse Analysis does not allow racism or texts of a fascist nature to be condemned. This problem is more extensively dealt with in the issue of Argumentation et analyse

References

Amossy, Ruth, *Nouvelle rhétorique et linguistique du discours*, in: Koren, Roselyne/Amossy, Ruth (edd.), *Après Perelman: quelles politiques pour les nouvelles rhétoriques? L'argumentation dans les sciences du langage*, Paris, L'Harmattan, 2002, 53–171.

Amossy, Ruth, *The argumentative dimension of discourse*, in: Van Eemeren, Frans H./Houtlosser, Peter (edd.), *Practices of argumentation*, Amsterdam, John Benjamins, 2005, 87–98.

Amossy, Ruth, *La dimension argumentative du discours littéraire. L'exemple de* Les Bienveillantes, in: Maingueneau, Dominique/Östenstad, Inger (edd.), *Concepts et démarches de l'analyse du discours littéraire*, Paris, L'Harmattan, 2010.

Amossy, Ruth (ed.), *Repenser la "dimension argumentative" du discours*, Argumentation et analyse du discours 20 (2018), DOI: https://doi.org/10.4000/aad.2492.

Amossy, Ruth, *L'argumentation dans le discours*, Paris, Armand Colin, ^{4}2021.

Amossy, Ruth/Koren, Roselyne (edd.), *Rhétorique et argumentation*, Argumentation et analyse du discours 2 (2009), DOI: https://doi.org/10.4000/aad.206.

Angenot, Marc, *La notion d'arsenal argumentatif: L'inventivité rhétorique dans l'histoire*, in: Frydman, Benoît/Meyer, Michel (edd.), *Chaïm Perelman (1912–2012). De la nouvelle rhétorique à la logique juridique*, Paris, Presses universitaires de France, 2012, 39–68.

Anscombre, Jean-Claude/Ducrot, Oswald, *L'argumentation dans la langue*, Liège, Mardaga, ^{2}1988.

Aristote, *Rhétorique*, edd. Ruelle, Charles-Émile/Meyer, Michel/Timmermans, Benoît, Paris, Le Livre de Poche, 1991.

Bakhtine, Mikhail (Volochinov, Valentin N.), *Le marxisme et la philosophie du langage*, trad. Yaguello, Marina, Paris, Éditions de Minuit, 1977.

Benveniste, Émile, *Problèmes de linguistique générale*, 2 vol., Paris, Gallimard, 1966/1974.

Charaudeau, Patrick, *Le discours politique. Les masques du pouvoir*, Paris, Vuibert, 2005.

Charaudeau, Patrick, *De l'argumentation entre les visées d'influence de la situation de communication*, in: Boix, Christian (edd.), *Argumentation, manipulation, persuasion*, L'Harmattan, Paris, 2007, 13–35.

Charaudeau, Patrick, *L'argumentation dans une problématique d'influence*, Argumentation et analyse du discours 1 (2008), DOI: https://doi.org/10.4000/aad.193.

Ducrot, Oswald, *Argumentation rhétorique et argumentation linguistique*, in: Doury, Marianne/Moirand, Sophie (edd.), *L'argumentation aujourd'hui. Positions théoriques en confrontation*, Paris, Presses Sorbonne Nouvelle, 2004, 17–34.

Fairclough, Isabela/Fairclough, Norman, *Political discourse analysis. A method for advanced students*, Abingdon/New York, Routledge, 2012 (= 2012a).

Fairclough, Isabela/Fairclough, Norman, *Analyse et évaluation de l'argumentation dans l'analyse critique du discours (CDA). Délibération et dialectique des Lumières*, Argumentation et analyse du discours 9 (2012), 5–28 (= 2012b).

---

du discours 11 (2013) that Roselyne Koren, the author of several works on the subject (cf. Koren 2002) devotes to it.

Fleury-Vilatte, Béatrice/Walter, Jacques, *L'engagement des chercheurs (2)*, Questions de communication 3 (2003), 99–108, DOI: https://doi.org/10.4000/questionsdecommunication.7465.

Fleury-Vilatte, Béatrice/Walter, Jacques, *L'engagement des chercheurs (3)*, Questions de communication 4 (2003), 241–249, DOI: https://doi.org/10.4000/questionsdecommunication.5525.

Geisler, Cheryl, *How ought we to understand the concept of rhetorical agency? Report from the ARS*, Rhetoric Society quarterly 34 (2004), 9–17.

Grize, Jean-Blaize, *Logique et langage*, Paris, Ophrys, 1990.

Groupe µ, *Rhétorique générale*, Paris, Larousse, 1970.

Heinich, Nathalie, Pour en finir avec l'engagement des intellectuels, Questions de communication 5 (2004), "Sur l'engagement des chercheurs", 149–160, DOI: https://journals.openedition.org/questionsdecommunication/7106

Heinich, Nathalie, *Pour une neutralité engagée*, Questions de communication 2 (2002), 117–127, DOI: https://doi.org/10.4000/questionsdecommunication.7084.

Jakobson, Roman, *Essais de linguistique générale, vol. 1: Les fondations du langage*, Paris, Éditions de Minuit, 1963.

Kerbrat-Orecchioni, Catherine, *L'énonciation de la subjectivité dans le langage*, Paris, Armand Colin, 1980.

Koren, Roselyne, La "nouvelle rhétorique": "technique" et/ou "éthique" du discours? Le cas de "l'engagement" du chercheur, in: Koren, Roselyne/Amossy, Ruth (edd.), *Après Perelman: quelles politiques pour les nouvelles rhétoriques? L'argumentation dans les sciences du langage*, Paris, L'Harmattan, 2002, 197–228.

Koren, Roselyne, *L'engagement dans le regard de l'autre. Point de vue d'une linguiste*, Questions de communication 4 (2003), 271–277.

Koren, Roselyne, *Sur la critique du constructivisme en communication*, Questions de communication 5 (2004), 203–211, DOI: https://doi.org/10.4000/questionsdecommunication.7110.

Koren, Roselyne, *Ni normatif ni militant. Le cas de l'engagement éthique du chercheur*, Argumentation et analyse du discours 11 (2013), DOI: https://doi.org/10.4000/aad.1572.

Maingueneau, Dominique, *L'analyse du discours*, Paris, Hachette, 1991.

Meyer, Michel, *La rhétorique*, Paris, Presses universitaires de France, 2004.

Moeschler, Jacques, *Argumentation et conversation. Éléments pour une analyse pragmatique du discours*, Paris, Hatier/Crédif, 1985.

Pêcheux, Michel, *Analyse automatique du discours*, Paris, Dunod, 1969.

Perelman, Cham/Olbrechts-Tyteca, Lucie, *Traité de l'argumentation. La nouvelle rhétorique*, Bruxelles, Éditions de l'Université de Bruxelles, 1958. Transl. Wilinson, John/Weaver, Purcell, *The New Rhetoric. A Treatise on Argumentation*, London, University of Notre-Dame Press, 1969.

Plantin, Christian, *L'argument du paralogisme*, Hermès, La Revue 15 (1995), 245–262.

Plantin, Christian, *L'argumentation*, Paris, Presses universitaires de France, 2005.

Van Eemeren, Frans H./Grootendorst, Rob (edd.), *Speech acts in argumentative discussions. A theorical model for the analysis of discussions directed towards solving conflicts of opinion*, Dordrecht, Foris, 1984.

Van Eemeren, Frans H./Grootendorst, Rob/Snoek Henkemans, Francesca (edd.), *Fundamentals of argumentation theory*, Mahwah, Lawrence Erlbaum, 1996.

Vignaux, Georges, *Énoncer, argumenter. Opérations du discours, logiques du discours*, Langue française 50 (1981), 91–116, DOI: https://doi.org/10.3406/lfr.1981.5093.

André Petitjean
Chapter 13
Linguistics and literature: Style in question

Abstract: We question the notion of *style* and the links that exist between literature and linguistics, particularly since the 1960s. The first part of this paper provides a history of stylistic studies which, from the 1940s to 1950s, defined *style* as an expressive and aesthetic marker, and therefore through its intentional markers, which confined it to the literary field. In a second part, we examine the "textualist" period of the 1960s to 1970s, which were particularly noted for linguistic theories such as intertextuality or dialogism. Finally, we propose a linguistic "overhaul" of literary stylistics, in which it would be up to the specialists of literature to reconstruct the context of literary works in their intertextual and interdiscursive dimensions.

Keywords: dialogism, interdiscursivity, intertextuality, (aesthetic, intentional) markers, (linguistic, literary, textual) stylistics

Introduction

I dedicate this paper to Jean Peytard, the person who, through a symposium held at Cluny in 1968 which was published in a special edition of *La Nouvelle Critique*, enabled me to discover – at almost twenty years of age – that there were theories of language and of literary texts whose existence had been completely hidden from us students during our university training.

If I had to justify my choice of today's presentation, I would say that it was based on a dual observation:
- On the one hand, the fact that author, style and genre are so many integrating concepts which are a continuing source of fascination for literary studies;
- and on the other, the no less evident fact that, during recent years, these ideas have been the subject of numerous theoretical investigations, particularly of a linguistic type.

This is why, in order to gain some perspective on the relationships between *Literature* and *Linguistics*, I have chosen to concentrate on the notion of *style*.

André Petitjean, Université de Lorraine, CREM

In the first part I shall give a rapid overview of the history of linguistic theories of style which were present in the context of the 1960s. I have limited this to style in literature; and in the second part, I shall offer a brief panorama of recent work on the theory of style.

1 The linguistic theorization of literary style in the 1960s

A re-reading of the proceedings of the 1968 Cluny symposium, published in a special edition of *La Nouvelle Critique*, makes it clear that, by the 1960s, the notion of *style* had lost its theoretical validity. This was how Arrivé highlighted the ectoplasmic character of stylistics: 'As for stylistics, I believe it would be still more dangerous to seek to give a definition that was general enough to encompass all its manifestations' (Arrivé 1969a, 171).[1] He proposed instead to combine it with "literary" semiotics, on condition that this latter (and Greimas 1962/1963 is implicit here) provided itself with the means of 'accounting for the apparently non-functional details of the literary text' (1969a, 173).[2] At the same period, but without success, Gérald Antoine was attempting at the Cerisy symposium (1966) to save stylistics from disaster by annexing certain trends from the new criticism, which was not asking for so much.

To understand what was at stake at that particular moment, we have to remember the quarrel that took place in the early 1950s between Spitzer (1952) and Bruneau (1951), which pitted those in favor of a hermeneutic conception of style against supporters of the philological tradition; and we should also bear in mind that during these same years French stylistics was dominated by Marouzeau (*Précis de stylistique française*, 1941) and Cressot (*Le Style et ses techniques*, 1947 [1959]) who, over and above their differences, considered that its distinctive features were to be mannered, intentional, expressive and atomist.

These theoretical premises and presuppositions were to become the targets of radical criticism, whether they focused on the intentionality and illusion of the subject as developed by Foucault or by Derrida deconstruction; on the description of style in terms of gaps (see Gueunier 1969, for a critique) compared with

---

[1] "Quant à la stylistique, il serait croyons-nous, plus périlleux encore de chercher à en donner une définition suffisamment générale pour en englober toutes les manifestations." (All subsequent translations from other works are by Rosemary Rodwell, the translator of this article, unless stated otherwise.)

[2] "[R]endre compte des détails apparemment non fonctionnels du texte littéraire".

a norm judged indefensible when account is taken of the polylectal aspect of all languages and the constitutive heterogeneity of discourse (Authier-Revuz 1995); or on the restriction of style to the sole domain of literature.

It follows that at this period stylistics saw itself, at best, as paired with new paradigms such as structural semantics, narrative semiotics and poetics, which were beginning to take the place of those 'Auxiliary sciences of stylistics": for Cressot, these were represented by "phonetics, lexicology, normative grammar, historical grammar, psychology, sociology, aesthetics and ancient rhetoric' (Cressot 1947 [1959, 10]).[3] However different they were, these theories shared common ground with the postulates elucidated by P. Guiraud (1963) in his work entitled *Essais de stylistique*: the literary text is a linguistic object; it is a language of connotation; and it must be the subject of immanent study... This emerging textualism was in line with the stylistics of the period in the English-speaking world ("Stylistics is a branch of linguistics, but one concerned especially with the treatment of variables in the entire text" observed Roger Fowler in his *Essays on style and language*, 1966). He also found theoretical justifications in the work of Russian formalists; see, for example, Vinogradov (1922) in Todorov (1966). It would very soon experience competition from generativist models (the text as productivity which changes the rules) and the influence of Bakhtinian theories (the text as "dialogic space"). In all cases they led to a re-examination of style (its definition, its purpose, its methods of analysis, and so on) – even leading to a proclamation of "the death" of stylistics, as Arrivé affirmed in Langue française no. 3 (1969b), entitled "Stylistics". And this was despite the epistemological and methodological salvage operation attempted by Antoine (1959) in an article that remains of great interest.

2 Towards a radical reform of literary stylistics

The pertinence of Antoine's article is all the greater because, in the thirty years following its publication, the wave of structural stylistics has gradually receded and literary stylistics has experienced the successive influences of textual linguistics, enunciation theories and textual pragmatics without, however, having been able to assume a disciplinary identity that was not institutional (Bordas 2007). This has meant that Dominique Maingueneau (1994, 189), for example, has more than one argument to justify his 'suspicion of style'[4] and to question what

---

3 "[L]a phonétique, la lexicologie, la grammaire normative, la grammaire historique, la psychologie, la sociologie, l'esthétique, l'ancienne rhétorique".
4 "[S]uspicion à l'égard du style".

he calls 'the obscure logic which governs use of the notion of style'[5] as it exists in universities and schools.

I would add that the questions concerning the status of literary stylistics can be much better understood because, in the interim, style has been subject to multiple definitions and attempts at objectification, depending on whether these emanate from theoretical domains whose borders themselves are shifting: semio-poetic (Genette 1991; Schaeffer 1997), semio-linguistic (Fontanille 1999), textual semantics (Rastier 1994), textual genetics (Herschberg Pierrot 2005), aesthetics (Goodman 1992; Vouilloux 2005), literature (Jenny 1993; 1997; 2000; Combe 1991; Saint-Gérand 1995; 1996; Compagnon 1998).

Limiting my observations to the field of language sciences, I would say that the abundant research that has been carried out is not all of equal interest in terms of the questioning to which literary stylistics has been exposed.

- There are those who exploit stylistics by making literary texts a place in which to experiment and to apply linguistic descriptions, without questioning the way in which the linguistic event being studied represents a stylistic trait nor what aspect of style it exemplifies. See, for example, the study devoted by Gary-Prieur (2005) to demonstrative nominal groups.
- There are those who are interested in the corpora of literary fictions, less to apply theories than to resolve the mysteries posed by certain "unusual" uses of language, whether at the level of utterance production of fictional texts (Philippe 2000; 2005), of deixis (Kleiber 2005), of verbal tenses (Vuillaume 1990), or of the demonstrative in contemporary fiction (Gary-Prieur/Noailly 1996).
- There are those who devote themselves to the linguistic study of the way speech is formed in fiction according to literary genre (see Rabatel 1998, for points of view in fictional accounts, and Achard-Bayle 2001 for the "référents évolutifs" ('evolving referents') constituted by a novel's characters) and/or according to the "creative methods" which characterize an author: Pétillon (2006) for the origin of adjectival characterization in a work of Jabès; Gollut and Zufferey (2000) for the establishment of a fictional referent in Balzac's incipits; Corblin (2005) for the functioning of proper names in Flaubert and Balzac; and Serça (2004) for the role of the parenthesis in Proustian acts of utterance.
- There are those who endeavor to linguistically problematize the phenomena of subjectivation identifiers, whether they do so in terms of voice (cf. Philippe 2005) or idiolect (cf. Neveu 2001; 2005; Détrie 2005; Rabatel 2005; 2007), of discursive ethos (cf. Maingueneau 2002; Rabatel 2007) or scenography (cf.

---

5 "[L]'obscure logique qui préside à l'usage de la notion de style".

Maingueneau 2002 and Géraud 2004 for its application to Marivaux, Rousseau and Beaumarchais).
- There are those who, in the tradition of the founding programme outlined by Larthomas (1964), aim to develop a stylistics of genres, either fictional (Frédéric 1999; Combe 1999) or non-fictional (Rinck 2007).
- Finally, there are those who, like Adam (1994; 1996; 2002; 2005), have for several years been undertaking a "re-conception of stylistics" with the aim of summing up what the notion of literary style might cover, both in its development and understanding.

We should bear in mind that style is shot through with tensions between a singularizing pole ("a" style, as a set of genetic features, or "the" style, as a singular form) and a universalizing pole ("some" style), without there being any contradiction between the pluralizable singular ("a style") and the mass singular ("some style"), since both meanings are articulated in language use (Jaubert 2005).

The notion of style is helpful precisely for thinking about these tensions (style can be changed more easily than idiolect) whereas idiolect is an aid to thinking about the processes of singularizing tension that are shaped by the social dimension of language material and by the interactional play in co-constructing identities and linguistic singularities.

The basic essentials to retain are therefore:
- That, particularly for literature relating to what Bourdieu (1991, passim) calls the 'restricted' field,[6] there exists a whole series of accommodations and assimilations between the resources made available to authors through language and genres, the stylistic innovations produced by writers, and their retroactivity in the form of new genres (cf. Jaubert 2004; 2007).
- That, in the same way as all speakers have multiple styles, all fiction (whether it consists of novels or plays) is dialogic and polyphonic in the sense that it uses a variety of styles in the same work (voices, and the turns of phrase given to different characters). This takes place under the guidance of an all-encompassing process of stylization which itself is dependent on the historical conditions of the literary environment (cf. Petitjean/Privat 2007 for the implications and ways of stylizing the effects of ordinary voices in fiction).
- That authors' styles gain, as geneticists suggest, by being thought of as a way of shaping writing through an objectivization of writing styles, which themselves can be examined from the perspective of the writing process (cf. Grésillon 1994; Contat/Ferrer 1998; Herschberg-Pierrot 2005).

---

6 "Sous-champ de production restreint".

Between extreme positions of the type 'I would say that stylistics does not exist but that everything is grammar' (Gardes-Tamine 2005) and '"The phenomenon of style" is speech itself' (Genette 1991) or 'Style is everywhere' (Adam 2005),[7] it is understandable that the concept of style is a delicate matter, and even an impossible one other than in the guise of an empirical notion.

It is true, as Saint-Gérand (1995, 22) reminds us, that 'the style of a work extends beyond the simple itemizing of its language constituents'[8] and implies a 'world view', which is to say 'political, ideological, ethical and aesthetic values'.[9] It is also true that 'Semiological, linguistic and aesthetic characteristics are combined in the process of textual signification' (1995, 22).[10] This is why – but time should now be allowed to play its part – some linguistic research is focused on problematizing the concept of style. Anna Jaubert (2007), for example, is concerned to describe the modes of speech stylization as a progression, at the conclusion of which the "style" value is the outcome of an aim to both requalify and particularize: this in turn opens the way to a study of stylistic properties that are pertinent from the viewpoint of the aesthetic function at work in literary texts.

3 Conclusion

To conclude my remarks on the links between literature and linguistics where *style* is concerned, and more particularly style in literature, I would say that the demanding model of the stylistician envisaged by Saint-Gérand would be a historian, philosopher, aesthetician, moralist, linguist and semiologist all at the same time – in other words, a Renaissance all-rounder of the modern era. On the other hand, stylometric studies, whether they are applied to literary or scientific writing, may or may not be valued (Rinck 2007): they have statistical precision on their side but rather weak indicators (length of words or sentences, frequency of function words, lexical fields and so on). Of more interest are Danielle Bouverot's (1996) suggestions when she explains the ways of using Frantext for the purpose of determining an author's style, genre, or period: these might involve choosing an invariant (for example, an author), using the alphabetical index for words and

---

[7] "Je dirais que la stylistique n'existe pas mais que tout est grammaire." (Gardes Tamine) ; "'Le fait de style', c'est le discours lui-même." (Genette) ; "Le style est partout." (Adam).
[8] "Le style d'une œuvre déborde la seule énumération des constituants de son langage."
[9] "Vision du monde"; "valeurs politiques, idéologiques, éthiques, esthétiques".
[10] "Les caractéristiques sémiologiques, linguistiques et esthétiques se combinent dans le procès de signification du texte."

their presence, and the hierarchical index for their frequency or their concordance with key words in other contexts. In keeping with this, she is interested, among other things, in signs of usage or connotation, the intricacy of lexical fields, the processes of trope re-categorization and analogies. The database also makes it possible to carry out interpretation work.

All this implies that stylistic studies are subject to multidisciplinary approaches that bring together researchers of literature (both historical and comparative) and linguists. As Genette (1991) suggests, this should enable intentional stylistic features to be distinguished, as consciously desired by the author or not, and as part of the text's operal identity and attentional stylistic features, as dependent on the theoretical viewpoint adopted by the stylistician. This distinction is akin to the one that Schaeffer (1997) makes between stylistic properties which relate to the native identities of literary works and those produced over time by their decontextualization/ recontextualization through repeated acts of reading. It is therefore the responsibility of those working in the field of literature to reconstruct the stylistic landscapes of literary works in their contexts, particularly with regard to their intertextual and interdiscursive seriation. The task of linguists, whether they specialize in poetics, genetics, semiology or discourse analysis, is to develop coherent models of stylistic events. They should take account of the fact that style can assume different conceptual forms, depending on the status, collective or individual, that is attributed to it and upon which depends the nature of observables. As for idiolectal singularity, which is particularly represented in the "restricted" field of literature, it cannot be described other than through an interpretative process, and gains from being thought of not in terms of disparity but as a set of tensions, between the general and the specific, variation and repetition, continuous and discontinuous, stability and movement – according to the proportion of "stylistic codes" and the linguistic level of their description: the transformation of a recognizable *style event* into a typical *style trait* to create a *style indicator*, at the culmination of a process of interpretative abduction.

The challenge is to put an end to the division of intellectual labor that exists between external studies (historical, sociological, etc.) and internal ones (linguistic, semiotic, and so on) by making *style* – but one might equally say *genre* or *author* – the subject of multi-disciplinary research.

These are strategies which will open the way to establishing and processing the *corpus* which is essential if we wish to *configure* the contributions of individual speech within a kaleidoscopic interplay between language norms, the norms imposed by the literary world on what may be said and written, and multiple intertextual relationships or interdiscursive exchanges.

References

Achard-Bayle, Guy, *Grammaire des métamorphoses*, Bruxelles, Duculot, 2001.
Adam, Jean-Michel, *Style et fait de style. Un exemple rimbaldien*, in: Molinié, Georges/Cahné, Pierre (edd.), *Qu'est-ce que le style? Actes du colloque international*, Paris, Presses universitaires de France, 1994.
Adam, Jean-Michel, *Stylistique littéraire. Un "retour" ambigu*, Le français aujourd'hui 116 (1996), 90–101.
Adam, Jean-Michel, *Le style dans la langue. Une reconception de la stylistique*, Lausanne, Delachaux et Niestlé, 1997.
Adam, Jean-Michel, *Le style dans la langue et dans les textes*, Langue française 135 (2002), 71–94, DOI: https://doi.org/10.3406/lfr.2002.6463.
Adam, Jean-Michel, *Stylistique ou analyse textuelle? L'exemple du fragment 128 des "Caractères"*, in: Gouvard, Jean-Michel (ed.), *De la langue au style*, Lyon, Presses universitaires de Lyon, 2005.
Antoine, Gérald, *La stylistique française, sa définition, ses buts, ses méthodes*, Revue de l'enseignement supérieur 1 (1959), 42–60.
Antoine, Gérald, *Stylistique des formes et stylistique des thèmes, ou le stylisticien face à l'ancienne et à la nouvelle critique*, in: Poulet, Georges/Ricardou, Jean (edd.), *Les chemins actuels de la critique. Actes du colloque de Cerisy-la-Salle, 2–12 septembre 1966*, Paris, Plon, 1967, 289–303.
Arrivé, Michel, *Stylistique littéraire et sémiotique littéraire*, La nouvelle critique (numéro spécial, 1969): *Linguistique et littérature. Colloque de Cluny, 16–17 avril 1968*, 171–174 (=1969a).
Arrivé, Michel, *Postulats pour la description linguistique des textes littéraires*, Langue française 3 (1969), 3–13, DOI: https://doi.org/10.3406/lfr.1969.5429 (=1969b).
Authier-Revuz, Jacqueline, *Ces mots qui ne vont pas de soi. Boucles réflexives et non-coïncidences du dire*, 2 vol., Paris, Larousse, 1995.
Bordas, Éric, *La "stylistique des concours"*, Pratiques 135–136 (2007), 240–248, DOI: https://doi.org/10.3406/prati.2007.2166.
Bourdieu, Pierre, *Le champ littéraire*, Actes de la recherche en sciences sociales 89 (1991), 3–46, DOI: https://doi.org/10.3406/arss.1991.2986.
Bouverot, Danielle, *La base Frantext au service de la stylistique*, L'information grammaticale 70 (1996), 38–42, DOI: https://doi.org/10.3406/igram.1996.2990.
Bruneau, Charles, *La stylistique*, Romance philology 5 (1951), 1–14.
Combe, Dominique, *La pensée et le style*, Paris, Éditions universitaires, 1991.
Combe, Dominique, *Pour une stylistique des genres. Le lyrique et le dramatique dans "L'après-midi d'un faune"*, Le français moderne 67 (1999), 81–92.
Compagnon, Antoine, *Le démon de la théorie. Littérature et sens commun*, Paris, Éditions du Seuil, 1998.
Contat, Michel/Ferrer, Daniel (edd.), *Pourquoi la critique génétique ? Méthodes, théories*, Paris, CNRS Éditions, 1998.
Corblin, Francis, *Les chaînes de référence de la conversation et les autres*, in: Gouvard, Jean-Michel (ed.), *De la langue au style*, Lyon, Presses universitaires de Lyon, 2005.
Cressot, Marcel, *Le style et ses techniques*, Paris, Presses universitaires de France, 1947 [²1959].
Détrie, Catherine, *La dynamique idiolectalisante, entre singularisation et réitération*, Cahiers de praxématique 44 (2005), 51–76, DOI: https://doi.org/10.4000/praxematique.1652.

Fontanille, Jacques, *Le style*, in: Fontanille, Jacques, *Sémiotique et littérature*, Presses universitaires de France, 1999, 189–221.
Fowler, Roger (ed.), *Essays on style and language*, London, Routledge, 1966.
Frédéric, Madeleine, *Palingénésie de la stylistique. Intergénéricité et récit de guerre*, Le français moderne 1 (1999), 15–33.
Gardes Tamine, Joëlle, *De la grammaire à la stylistique. À propos de l'ordre des mots*, in: Gouvard, Jean-Michel (ed.), *De la langue au style*, Lyon, Presses universitaires de Lyon, 2005.
Gary-Prieur, Marie-Noëlle, *La référence démonstrative comme élément d'un style*, in: Gouvard, Jean-Michel (ed.), *De la langue au style*, Lyon, Presses universitaires de Lyon, 2005, 255–277.
Gary-Prieur, Marie-Noëlle/Noailly, Michèle, *Démonstratifs insolites*, Poétique 105 (1996), 111–121.
Genette, Gérard, *Style et signification*, in: Genette, Gérard, *Fiction et diction*, Paris, Éditions du Seuil, 1991, 95–151.
Géraud, Violaine, *Trois scénographies singulières. Les "Journaux" de Marivaux, les "Rêveries" de Rousseau, et les "Mémoires contre Goëzman" de Beaumarchais*, in: Amossy, Ruth/ Maingueneau, Dominique (edd.), *L'analyse du discours dans les études littéraires*, Toulouse, Presses universitaires du Mirail, 2004, 267–277.
Gollut, Jean-Daniel/Zufferey, Joël, *Construire un monde. Les phrases initiales de "La Comédie humaine"*, Lausanne, Delachaux et Niestlé, 2000.
Goodman, Nelson, *Le statut du style*, in: Goodman, Nelson, *Manières de faire des mondes*, Paris, Jacqueline Chambon, 1992.
Greimas, Algirdas Julien, *La linguistique statistique et la linguistique structurale*, in: Le français moderne 30 (1962), 242–252; Le français moderne 31 (1963), 55–68.
Grésillon, Almuth, *Éléments de critique génétique*, Paris, Presses universitaires de France, 1994.
Gueunier, Nicole, *La pertinence de la notion d'écart en stylistique*, Langue française 3 (1969), 34–45, DOI: https://doi.org/10.3406/lfr.1969.5432.
Guiraud, Pierre, *Essais de stylistique*, Paris, Klincksieck, 1963.
Herschberg Pierrot, Anne, *Le style en mouvement. Littérature et art*, Paris, Belin, 2005.
Jaubert, Anna, *Genres discursifs et genres littéraires. De la scène d'énonciation à l'empreinte stylistique*, in: Amossy, Ruth/Maingueneau, Dominique (edd.), *L'analyse du discours dans les études littéraires*, Toulouse, Presses universitaires du Mirail, 2004, 279–291.
Jaubert, Anna, *La diagonale du style. Étapes d'une appropriation de la langue*, Pratiques 135–136 (2007), 47–62, DOI: https://doi.org/10.3406/prati.2007.2155.
Jenny, Laurent, *L'objet singulier de la stylistique*, Littérature 89 (1993), 113–124, DOI: https://doi.org/10.3406/litt.1993.2633.
Jenny, Laurent, *Sur le style littéraire*, Littérature 108 (1997), 92–101, DOI: https://doi.org/10.3406/litt.1997.2455.
Jenny, Laurent, *Du style comme pratique*, Littérature 118 (2000), 98–117, DOI: https://doi.org/10.3406/litt.2000.1679.
Kleiber, Georges, *Démonstratifs et pratique des textes littéraires*, in: Gouvard, Jean-Michel (ed.), *De la langue au style*, Lyon, Presses universitaires de Lyon, 2005, 279–297.
Larthomas, Pierre, *La notion de genre littéraire en stylistique*, Le français moderne 3 (1964), 185–193.
Maingueneau, Dominique, *L'horizon du style*, in: Molinié, Georges/Cahné, Pierre (edd.), *Qu'est-ce que le style? Actes du colloque international*, Paris, Presses universitaires de France, 1994, 187–199.
Maingueneau, Dominique, *Problèmes d'ethos*, Pratiques 113–114 (2002), 55–67.

Marouzeau, Jules, *Précis de stylistique française*, Paris, Masson, 1941.

Neveu, Franck, *Singularités linguistiques du discours. L'idiolecte: fiction ou réalité?*, in: Neveu, Franck (ed.), *Styles. Langue, histoire, littérature*, Paris, Sedes, 2001.

Neveu, Franck, *L'idiolecte, entre linguistique et herméneutique*, Cahiers de praxématique 44 (2005), 25–50, DOI: https://doi.org/10.4000/praxematique.1641.

Pétillon, Sabine, *Genèse de la caractérisation adjectivale dans le manuscrit de "Récit" d'Edmond Jabès*, L'information grammaticale 108 (2006), 14–19, DOI: https://doi.org/10.3406/igram.2006.3795.

Petitjean, André/Privat, Jean-Marie (edd.), *Les voix du peuple et leurs fictions*, Metz, Université Paul-Verlaine, 2007.

Philippe, Gilles, *Les divergences énonciatives dans les récits de fiction*, Langue française 128 (2000), 30–51, DOI: https://doi.org/10.3406/lfr.2000.1007.

Philippe, Gilles, *Le style est-il une catégorie énonciative?*, in: Gouvard, Jean-Michel (ed.), *De la langue au style*, Lyon, Presses universitaires de Lyon, 2005, 145–156.

Rabatel, Alain, *La construction textuelle du point de vue*, Lausanne/Paris, Delachaux et Niestlé, 1998.

Rabatel, Alain, *Idiolecte et représentation du discours de l'autre dans le discours d'ego*, Cahiers de praxématique 44 (2005), 93–116, DOI: https://doi.org/10.4000/praxematique.1664.

Rabatel, Alain, *La dialectique du singulier et du social dans les processus de singularisation. Style(s), idiolecte, ethos*, Pratiques 135–136 (2007), 15–34, DOI: https://doi.org/10.3406/prati.2007.2153.

Rastier, François, *Le problème du style. Pour une sémantique du texte*, in: Molinié, Georges/Cahné, Pierre (edd.), *Qu'est-ce que le style ? Actes du colloque international*, Paris, Presses universitaires de France, 1994, 263–282.

Rinck, Fanny, *Styles d'auteur et singularité des textes. Approche stylométrique du genre de l'article en linguistique*, Pratiques 135–136 (2007), 119–136.

Saint-Gérand, Jacques-Philippe, *Styles, apories et impostures*, Langages 118 (1995), 8–30, DOI: https://doi.org/10.3406/lgge.1995.1712.

Saint-Gérand, Jacques-Philippe, *Le style et ses mesures. Méthodologie, critique, historicité*, L'information grammaticale 70 (1996), 31–37, DOI: https://doi.org/10.3406/igram.1996.2989.

Schaeffer, Jean-Marie, *La stylistique littéraire et son objet*, Littérature 105 (1997), 14–23.

Serça, Isabelle, *La paratopie de l'écrivain Proust*, in: Amossy, Ruth/Maingueneau, Dominique (edd.), *L'analyse du discours dans les études littéraires*, Toulouse, Presses universitaires du Mirail, 2004, 295–307.

Spitzer, Leo, *Les théories de la stylistique*, Le français moderne 20 (1952), 160–168.

Todorov, Tzvetan (ed.), *Théorie de la littérature*, Paris, Éditions du Seuil, 1966.

Vinogradov, Viktor, *Des tâches de la stylistique (1922)*, in: Todorov, Tzvetan (ed.), *Théorie de la littérature*, Paris, Éditions du Seuil, 1966, 109–113.

Vouilloux, Bernard, *Les prédicats stylistiques*, in: Gouvard, Jean-Michel (ed.), *De la langue au style*, Lyon, Presses universitaires de Lyon, 2005, 319–355.

Vuillaume, Marcel, *Grammaire temporelle des récits*, Paris, Les Éditions de Minuit, 1990.

Index nominum

Ablali, Driss 10–13, 15, 92, 153, 167
Achard-Bayle, Guy 7, 9, 11, 15, 77, 92, 276
Adam, Jean-Michel 7, 9–11, 15, 16, 21–52, 78–85, 92, 93, 201–203, 273–276
Althusser, Louis 246
Amossy, Ruth 10, 14, 15, 97, 125, 210, 235, 243, 245–268, 277, 278
Angenot, Marc 251, 257, 267
Anscombre, Jean-Louis 247, 267
Aristotle 14, 245, 253
Arrivé, Michel 16, 270, 271, 276
Athanasiadou, Angeliki/Dirven, René 91, 93, 94
Austin, John Langshaw 85, 209, 233, 248
Authier-Revuz, Jacqueline 271, 276

Bakhtine (Bakhtin), Mikhaïl 5, 11, 84, 93, 144, 225, 226, 233, 255, 267
Barthes, Roland 5, 215, 216, 229
Bateson, Gregory 233
Beaudouin, Valérie 143, 150
Béguelin (Reichler —), Marie-José 27, 29, 55
Benveniste, Émile 2, 5, 16, 37, 53, 55, 85, 125, 135–137, 150, 188, 202, 255, 267
Berger, Peter Ludwig 233
Bernanos, Georges 158, 159, 161, 162, 163
Berrendonner, Alain 21, 27, 34, 53, 112, 125
– see also Groupe de Fribourg
Biber, Douglas 236, 243
Bourdieu, Pierre 211, 216, 221, 229, 273, 276
Brown, Gillian/Yule, George 83, 93
Bruneau, Charles 270, 276
Butler, Judith 233

Camus, Albert 163
Carel, Marion 125
Charaudeau, Patrick 10, 14, 15, 99, 105, 106, 126, 207–229, 251–253, 267
Charolles, Michel 7, 9, 11, 16, 26, 43, 53–75, 79, 86, 88, 93
Coenen-Huther, Jacques 209, 229
Coltier, Danièle 115, 125, 126
Combe, Dominique 272, 273, 276

Combettes, Bernard 10, 13, 22, 53, 84–93, 169, 195, 202
Compagnon, Antoine 272, 276
Conte, Maria-Elisabeth 29, 59
Corblin, Francis 272, 276
Coseriu, Eugenio 53, 166
Cossutta, Frédéric 238, 244
Courtés, Joseph 165, 166, 167
Crystal, David 236, 243
Culioli, Antoine 53, 63, 75, 110, 112, 125, 126

Dancygier, Barbara 86
Daneš, František 22, 53, 80, 83, 93, 188, 195, 203
Danon-Boileau, Laurent 53
– see also Morel
Davy, Derek 236, 243
Debray, Régis 222, 229
Deleuze, Gilles 233
Dendale, Patrick 115, 125, 126
Derrida, Jacques 233, 270
Desclés, Jean-Pierre 75, 111, 126
Dijk, Teun van —, 5, 7, 8, 16, 17, 22, 23, 55, 136, 151, 221–223, 229
Dirven, René, see Athanasiadou
Doury, Marianne 267
Dubois, Danièle 126
Ducrot, Oswald 12, 16, 107, 111, 112, 126, 190, 203, 209, 246, 247, 256, 267

Eco, Umberto 33, 44, 53, 156, 216, 229
Eemeren, see Van Eemeren
Elias, Norbert 201, 203

Fairclough, Norman 239, 241, 257
Fairclough, Isabela/Fairclough, Norman 249, 256, 257
Fauconnier, Gilles 63, 75, 79, 86–88, 93
Fauconnier, Gilles/Sweetser, Eve 63, 75, 87, 88, 93
Fillmore, Charles J. 86, 93, 203
Firbas, Jan 22, 54
Fleury (-Vilatte), Béatrice/Walter, Jacques 266, 268

Foucault, Michel 233, 242, 243, 246, 270
Fontanille, Jacques 16, 272, 277
François, Jacques 69, 76

Garfinkel, Harold 233
Gary-Prieur, Marie-Noëlle/Noailly, Michèle 272, 277
Gaulle (Général de —) 24 ff.
Geisler, Cheryl Grize 246, 268
Genette, Gérard 48, 54, 148, 272, 274, 275, 277
Gibbs, Raymond 86, 93
Gide, André 161, 162
Givón, Talmy 54
Gollut, Jean-Daniel/Zufferey, Joël 272, 277
Goodman, Nelson 272, 277
Greimas, Algirdas Julien 5, 9, 12, 13, 16, 17, 29, 54, 136, 153–167, 188, 203, 270, 277
Grésillon, Almuth 53, 277
Grice, Herbert Paul 57, 75, 233
Grize, Jean-Blaise 254, 268
Grootendorst, Rob 248, 268
Groupe de Fribourg 22, 27, 34, 54
– see also Béguelin
– see also Berrendonner
Groupe Mu (Groupe µ) 32, 54
Guillaume, Gustave 6–10
Guiraud, Pierre 271, 277
Gülich, Elisabeth/Mondada, Lorenza 100, 106

Halliday, Michael Alexander Kirkwood (M.A.K.) 54
Halliday, M.A.K./Hasan, Ruqaiya 5, 22, 24, 75, 82, 83, 93, 203
Harris, Zellig Sabbetai 22, 54, 134, 232, 243
Hasan, Ruqaiya, see Halliday
Heinich, Nathalie 15, 266, 268
Hjelmslev, Louis 4–6, 10, 16, 134, 160, 167
Humboldt, Wilhelm von —, 87
Huumo, Tuomas 63, 76

Jakobson, Roman 5, 6, 246, 268
Jenny, Laurent 53, 272, 277
Johnson-Laird, Philip 203

Kerbrat-Orecchioni, Catherine 9, 11, 95–106, 268
Kintsch, Walter 136, 151, 203

Kleiber, Georges 75, 272, 277
Koren, Roselyne 246, 266–268
Kristeva, Julia 5, 55

Lacan, Jacques 207, 233
Lacheret-Dujour, Anne 60, 76
Laclau, Ernesto 233
Lakoff, George 85
Lakoff, George/Johnson, Mark 86, 87, 94
Larthomas, Pierre 273, 277
Le Draoulec, Anne 65, 68, 75, 76
Lundquist, Lita 10, 13, 75, 185–204
Luckmann, Thomas 233

Maingueneau, Dominique 10, 14, 45, 51, 52, 54, 78, 92, 93, 97, 99, 106, 108, 126, 208, 213, 216, 221–229, 231–244, 245, 246, 249, 250, 254, 267, 268, 271–273, 277, 278
Malraux, André 161
Martin, Robert 7–9, 16, 55, 63, 76, 79–85, 87–89, 94
Mathesius, Vilém 22, 54
Matthiessen, Christian/Thompson, Sandra A. 194, 204
Maupassant, Guy de —, 164–166
– see also Greimas
Mead, George Herbert 233
Meyer, Michel 125, 126, 253, 267, 268
Miège, Bernard 228, 229
Moignet, Gérard 89, 94
Mondada, Lorenza, see Gülich
Morel, Mary-Annick/Danon-Boileau, Laurent 120, 126

Neveu, Franck 42, 53–55, 108, 126, 272, 278
Noailly, Michèle, see Gary-Prieur

Odin, Roger 217, 229
Olbrechts-Tyteca, Lucie, see Perelman

Pêcheux, Michel 3, 210, 229, 245, 268
Perelman, Chaïm 15, 245, 248, 253, 257, 262
Perelman, Chaïm/Olbrechts-Tyteca, Lucie 242, 244, 246, 247, 255, 268
Péry-Woodley, Marie-Paule 59, 68, 75, 76
Pešek, Ondřej 80, 85, 94

Pétain (Maréchal —) 30 ff.
Petitjean, André, 10, 15, 125, 127, 269–278
Philippe, Gilles 272, 278
Pinker, Steven 134, 150
Plantin, Christian 250, 255, 268
Prague (Circle, — linguistics, — School) 8, 22, 54, 77–80, 82–85, 87, 92, 203
– *see also* Second Prague Circle
Prandi, Michele 22, 25, 55
Proust, Joëlle 116, 126
Proust, Marcel 147, 150, 272, 278

Rabatel, Alain 9, 12, 92, 107–127, 272, 278
Rastier, François 9, 11, 12, 16, 133–150, 156, 158–160, 166, 167, 272, 278
Recanati, François 109, 127
Reichler-Béguelin, *see* Béguelin
– *see also* Groupe de Fribourg
Ricœur, Paul 5, 85, 92, 94, 120, 127, 167
Riffaterre, Michael 5
Roulet, Eddy 112, 127

Saint-Gérand, Jacques-Philippe 272, 274, 278
Sarda, Laure 66, 68, 75, 76, 92
Saussure, Ferdinand de —, 2–4, 10, 11, 15–17, 135, 137, 138, 151, 232
Schaeffer, Jean-Marie 272, 275, 278
Searle, John 85, 188, 204, 209, 217, 229, 233, 248
Second Prague Circle 22, 80, 85

Seguin, Jean-Pierre 174, 182
Skalička, Vladimir 80, 94
Sinclair, John 236, 244
Slakta Denis 22, 55
Sperber, Dan/Wilson, Deirdre 57, 76, 212, 229
Spitzer, Leo 270, 278
Starobinski, Jean 3, 17, 143, 151
Sweetser, Eve 86
– *see also* Fauconnier/Sweetser
– *see also* Sweetser/Fauconnier
Sweetser, Eve/Fauconnier, Gilles 87, 94
Szondi, Péter 5

Tesnière, Lucien 8–10, 17
Thompson, Sandra, *see* Matthiessen
Todorov, Tzvetan 5, 271, 278

Van Eemeren, Frans 248, 267, 268
Vigier, Denis 68, 75, 76, 92
Vignaux, Georges 255, 268
Vuillaume, Marcel 272, 278
Vygotski, Lev 1, 233

Walter, Jacques, *see* Fleury
Weinrich, Harald 21, 38, 47, 55
Wilson, Deirdre, *see* Sperber
Winograd, Terry 189, 204
Wittgenstein, Ludwig 1, 233

Zufferey, Joël, *see* Gollut

Index rerum

Abstract, see "THE TEXT as —/empirical object" (according to Adam)
Academic text 186
Access (Principle of —) 87
Actuality or actualization (in Prague linguistics) 80
Adverbials, see Framing adverbials
Agency 242, 246, 251, 252, 268
Analogy 251, 258, 259, 262
Anaphora 13, 28, 57, 74, 82, 100, 127, 177, 181, 182, 185, 188, 193, 194
Aphorization/Aphorizing enunciation 241
Argumentation 10, 11, 14, 35, 49, 52, 95, 125, 126, 190, 202, 209, 243, 244–267, 269, 271
– Argumentative dimension of discourse 245
Assemblages (Circumstantial —/Referential —/Rhetorical —) 59
Atopic (Paratopic) discourse 239
Attitude (Propositional —/Predicate of —) 90, 91, 99, 101, 202, 254, 265
Auctor/Author 231, 242

Blend/Blending 77
"Beyond the sentence" (according to Benveniste) 135

Case grammar 86
Clause (Inter- —) 25
Co-/Over-/Under-enunciation 107
Cognition 77–92
Cognitive perspective 198
Coherence (Discursive —) 13, 169, 250
Coherence/cohesion 57, 79, 83, 209
Cohesion (Enunciative/semantic/textual —) 30, 31, 34, 42, 44, 46
– Markers of textual — 82
– Modes of — 159
– Progression of — 84
Communication:
– contract 99
– Global/specific — 219
– Situation of — 212
– Subject of — 209

Competence (Textual —) 169, 172, 182
Complexity (Textual —) 12, 21, 149, 160
Conceptual metaphor 86
Connectives 30, 31, 40, 57, 59, 64, 65, 74, 254
Connectivity 28, 30, 140, 144
Consciousness (Linguistic —) 169
Constructions (Syntactic —) 110, 171
Continuity (Referential —) 169, 174, 175, 182
Contrastive text linguistics 185
Conversational regime 231
Corpus semantics 133, 153, 158
Counterfactuality 91
CDA (Critical Discourse Analysis) 234, 249, 256, 267

Debate (on TV) 97, 98, 210, 219, 256
Descriptive:
– discourse 215, 224
– text or sequences 175–178
Detached utterance 241
Diachronic text linguistics 169–183
Dialogism 112, 226, 233, 255, 269
Digital scenography 240
Disconnections 47, 139, 178
Discourse:
– analysis 7, 14, 15, 51–55, 79, 83, 85, 93, 95, 99, 102, 105, 134, 154, 208, 211, 220, 221, 231, 232, 245, 275
– genre(s) 45, 85, 153, 223, 237, 254
– markers 57
– Paratopic — (Atopic—) 239
– studies 233
– topic 63 (see Theme/rheme)
Discursive:
– coherence 169, 250
– strategies 207
Dissipative units 133 ff.
Dual integration (syntactic and conceptual) 77
Dynamic(s) 23, 38, 40, 51, 120, 125, 133, 139, 150, 188, 191, 194, 247, 250
– perspective of reading 191

Empirical ("THE TEXT as — vs. abstract object", Adam) 84
Enclosing scene 237
Enthymeme 251
Enunciation 31, 32, 80, 95, 187, 246, 255, 271
– First and second — 107–116
– Co- —/Over- —/Under- — 107
Enunciation scene 237
Enunciator (Posture of —) 125–127, 278
Epideictic 253, 255
Ethos 97, 103, 216, 227, 253, 262, 263, 272, 277, 278

Fragment 138
Frame(s) 62
Framing adverbials/structure 57, 59, 65, 70, 74
French:
– FFL (French as a foreign language) 185
– Middle/Old/Pre-classical French 175
French Resistance 21

Generic scene 222, 237
Genericity 51, 84, 85, 236, 242, 243
– Mode of — 237
Global/Specific communication situation 219
Grammar:
– Case — 86
– Text — 7, 39, 95, 173
– Transformational and generative — (TGG) 7
Grammaticalization 170
Ground 133

Historical linguistics 169
Hypergenre 239
Hyperlink 260
Hypertheme 178
Hypotheticality 91

Iconotextual component 240
Internet 239, 258–265
Instituted regime 237
"If" (percontative, hypothetical) 63, 89–93
Immanent/Immanentism 105, 166
– Implicit (information) 28, 33, 34, 37, 46, 69, 82, 101, 113, 116, 136, 143, 148, 161, 171, 199, 212, 258, 233, 261, 270
Inter-clause 25

Interactions 265
– Linguistic — 223
– Oral — 234
– Social — 211, 214, 220, 223
– Verbal — 253
Integration (Dual —) 77
Interdiscourse/Interdiscursivity 85, 250, 269, 275
Interpretation/Interpretative 58, 59, 72–74, 100–105, 137–141, 145–149, 212–220, 275
– Intertextual/Intertextuality 35, 144, 145, 146, 226, 269
Isotopy 28, 32, 95, 133, 136, 138, 139, 140, 157

Language vs. speech 14, 231
– Level(s) (Textual —) 92
– Macro-textual —, Meso-textual —, Micro-textual — 21–28, 41–45
Linguistic consciousness 169
Linguistics of enunciation 253
Local (namely in text linguistics) 30, 31, 47–49, 133, 136, 140, 142, 148, 149, 156–158, 166, 190
Localization(s), 63 ff., 136 ff.
Locutor 35, 97, 108–120, 212, 218

Macro-textual level, *see* Level
Markers 26–31, 47, 105, 110, 116, 119, 171, 174, 176, 193, 208, 232
– Aesthetic — 269
– Discourse — 57–74
– Intentional — 269
– Meso-textual level, *see* Level
Mental:
– spaces (according to Fauconnier) 77, 79, 86, 87, 94
– model 185, 188, 193
Metaphor, *see* Conceptual —
Micro-textual level, *see* Level
Middle Ages 172, 173
Modality 35, 38, 110, 115, 116
Model, *see* Mental —
Mode of genericity, *see* Genericity

Narrative texts 40, 65
"Note on discourse" (Saussure) 2, 3

Observables 6, 154, 158, 275
Old French 174–180
Oral (or written) 136, 215, 239
– "Text as — or written message" (according to Hjelmslev) 5

Paragraphs 21–55, 59–74, 134, 149, 190
Paratopic discourse 239
Participants 104, 105, 202, 222, 237, 258
Pathos 227, 228, 253, 262, 264
Period/Periodic grammar/units 21–55, 71, 72, 137, 138, 141, 144, 146, 148
Perspective:
– Cognitive — 198
– Dynamic — of reading 191
– Procedural/Structural — 185–196
Persuasion 227, 246–249, 267
Petition 261, 263
Plans (Text —) 21, 43, 48
Point of view 40, 89, 107, 117, 139, 233
– see also Vision
Polemics 260, 265
– Political poster 38–46
Positioning 107–125
– Social — 210
Posture of enunciator 107
Power relations 220, 245, 251, 252
Pragmatics 10, 80, 81, 85, 95, 134, 187, 209, 234, 248, 253, 271
Pragma-dialectics 247
Prague (— linguistics, — Linguistic Circle, — school, — text linguistics) 8, 22, 54, 77–87, 90, 92, 203
Pre-Classical French 174
Principle of access 87
Procedural perspective, see Perspective
Progression, see Thematic —
Propositional attitude, see Attitude
Prosody/Prosodic 22, 26, 27, 95, 96, 102, 134, 140, 146

Reasonable 257 (according to Perelman)
Recipient (Recipient-interpretant) 218
Recognition 34, 49, 139, 149, 169, 173, 194, 226

Referential:
– continuity 174
– disconnections 178
– expressions 173, 177, 179
Regime (Instituted —) 237
Register 68, 223, 236
Relationships (Rhetorical —) 197, 200
Responsibility (Assuming —) 107–124
Renaissance 172
Reticular 47, 243
Rheme, see Theme/—
Rhetorical relationships 197, 200

Scene 223 (according to Van Dijk)
– Enclosing —/Enunciation —/Generic — 221–223 (according to Maingueneau) 236–240
Scenography 223, 231, 237–240, 272
– Scenography (Digital —) 240
Scientific texts 204
Sequence(s) 65, 71, 84, 217, 247, 254
– According to Adam 21–23, 26, 39–49
– Narrative — 176
– of discourse 157
– Oral — 102, 103
– Textual — (according to Rastier) 178–182
Self-constituting discourse 244
Sentence, see "Beyond the —"
Semantic
– cohesion 30
– forms 133–146
Semiosis 133, 136, 149
Sign theory 133
Signification 58, 82, 88, 144, 154–166, 246, 274
Situation, see Global/specific communication —
Slogan 49, 224, 241, 260
Spaces, see Mental —
Specific communication situation, see Global/specific communication
Speech act(s 111, 112, 188, 207–227, 251
Strategies (Discursive —) 207, 227
Structural (perspective), see Perspective
Stylistics (Linguistic —, Literary —, textual —) 52, 95, 234, 269–274
Subject (of communication) 209

Syntactic (constructions) 110, 171
Syntax (Methods in —) 8, 16

Temporal frame(s) 68
Text(s):
– see Academic —
– see Descriptive —
– see Narrative —
– see Scientific —
– see "THE TEXT as abstract/empirical object" (Adam)
Text grammar 7, 39, 95, 173
Text linguistics:
– see Contrastive —
– see Diachronic —
– see Prague —
Text plans 21, 43, 48
Textual:
– analysis of discourse (according to Adam) 21
– cohesion markers 31
– competence 13, 169, 172, 182
– complexity 12, 21, 149, 160
– Icono— components 240
– typology 173, 179
Textualizing enunciations 241
TGG (transformational and generative grammar) 7
"THE TEXT as abstract/empirical object" (according to Adam) 84
– Thematic:
– coherence 189
– progression 28, 176
Theme/rheme 179 (see also Topic)
Topic (Discourse —) 63
Translation, 21 ff., 143 ff., 199
Transformations 140, 146
Transformational & generative grammar (TGG) 7
Typology (Textual —) 173, 179

Utterance (Detached —) 241

Vision (World —, according to Sweestser/Fauconnier) 87

Weltanschauung (according to Humboldt) 87
Written, see Oral (Text as oral or — message)
Works:
– Literary — 145, 269
– (Transformation between passages and —, according to Rastier) 147
– "Works" (according to Maingueneau) 242, 243
World vision (according to Sweestser/Fauconnier) 87

www.ingramcontent.com/pod-product-compliance
Lightning Source LLC
Chambersburg PA
CBHW020223170426
43201CB00007B/298